The INNER LIFE of EMPIRES

The INNER LIFE *of* EMPIRES

AN EIGHTEENTH-CENTURY HISTORY

EMMA ROTHSCHILD

PRINCETON UNIVERSITY PRESS

PRINCETON AND OXFORD

Published by Princeton University Press, 41 William Street,
Princeton, New Jersey 08540

In the United Kingdom: Princeton University Press, 6 Oxford Street,
Woodstock, Oxfordshire OX20 1TW
press.princeton.edu

Jacket art: Sir Henry Raeburn, *John Johnstone, Betty Johnstone, and
Miss Wedderburn*. Ca.1790/1795, oil on canvas. Gift of
Mrs. Robert Schuette. Image courtesy of
National Gallery of Art, Washington, DC.

Library of Congress Cataloging-in-Publication Data

Rothschild, Emma, 1948–
The inner life of empires : an eighteenth-century history / Emma
Rothschild.
p.   cm.
ISBN 978-0-691-14895-3 (hardback)
1. Great Britain—Colonies.   2. Johnston family.   3. Scotland—
Biography.   I. Title.
JV1027.R68 2011
929′.209171241—dc22
2010054189

British Library Cataloging-in-Publication Data is available

This book has been composed in Sabon and
Copperplate Gothic Light Display

Printed on acid-free paper. ∞

Printed in the United States of America

3   5   7   9   10   8   6   4   2

To Victoria

CONTENTS

The INNER LIFE of
EMPIRES

IDEAS AND SENTIMENTS

The age of revolutions of the eighteenth century was a time of transformation in political and economic relationships, and in ways of thinking about the world. This book is about some of the changes of the times, from the point of view of a large, odd, and enterprising family, the Johnstones, and of their households, friends, servants, and slaves.

The four Johnstone sisters and seven Johnstone brothers grew up in Scotland in the 1720s and 1730s and made their way, in imagination or in reality, to the extremities of the British, French, Spanish, and Mughal empires. Two of the brothers became rich, in many scenes and over many setbacks. The family lived at the edges of the enlightenment, and they were friends, at least from time to time, of David Hume, Adam Smith, and the poet James "Ossian" Macpherson. They were unusually intemperate, unusually literary, and there were unusually many of them.

All I knew about the Johnstones, when I came across the oldest brother's letter book in a library in Edinburgh, was that another brother, John, had been a candidate in a contested parliamentary election in 1774, in Adam Smith's home town of Kirkaldy.[1] They were not a celebrated family, even at the moments of their greatest successes. But they lived amidst new empires, and they were confronted throughout their lives with large and abstract questions about commerce and the state, laws and regulations, and slavery and servitude. They were expressive observers of the "Anguish Vexation & Anxiety" of modern life, in the oldest brother's words, and of the changing scenes that Elizabeth Carolina Keene, who married John Johnstone in Calcutta in 1765, described as the "troublesome, fluctuating state of human affairs," in the "constitution of states and empire."[2]

The history of the Johnstones is a story of the multiple or multiplier effects of empire, in which individuals at home were connected, by information and expectations, to events in the East and West Indies. It is a family history, in the sense that the sisters and sisters-in-law in the Johnstones' story, including the sisters who stayed at home in Scotland, were at the center of the exchanges of economic, political, and personal information in which the family prospered. It is also a history of other people in the family's lives, and in particular of two individuals—a young woman known as "Bell or Belinda," who described herself as a native of Bengal, the "slave or servant" of John Johnstone, and Joseph Knight, the African slave whose lawsuit against Margaret Johnstone's son-in-law ended slavery in Scotland—who are the most important figures in the story, in the retrospect of two centuries of public life.[3]

The economic and the political were intertwined in the Johnstones' lives, and so were the public and the private, commerce and law and conscience. Their history is a vista of the new ideas and sentiments of the times and of the eighteenth-century enlightenment. The political thought of the philosophers of enlightenment was concerned in multiple respects with the dilemmas of overseas commerce and conquest.[4] The relationships of the Scottish enlightenment to the Johnstones suggest a more intimate proximity, to the domesticity of empire.

The Johnstones were not themselves economists or ge-
ologists or historians. But they were involved throughout their lives with the philosophes of eighteenth-century
Edinburgh, and with the milieux of the enlightenment,
in the sense of the booksellers, proof-correctors, lawyers, and clerks by whom the "lights of science" or the
"atmosphere of society," in the description of their friend
the philosopher Adam Ferguson, were "communicable
to others by mere information."[5]

The Johnstones' history is a story of how individuals
made money in the eighteenth-century empires, and especially of making money by the use of information. It is
also a history of the institution of slavery, from the East
to the West Indies. At least six of the seven brothers became owners of slaves. Two of them were public opponents of slavery, and one was a prominent defender of
the slave trade. The Johnstones flourished in the half
century that has been identified, since the imperial histories of the nineteenth century, with the political institutions of modern times: a new British empire in India, a
new land empire in North America, and a new and more
enlightened (or less benighted) Atlantic economy in the
West Indies and Spanish America.[6] It was a founding
period of modern ideas in a vaster sense: of the competitive economy, of individual rights and the government of law, and of industrial or industrious transformation.[7] It was a time when laissez-faire was new and
when even the idea of the economy or of economic life—
of a distinctive space or territory of economic exchanges
—was unusual and insecure.[8] But the Johnstones' empire, or the empire of economic opportunity to which
they looked forward, was not the empire that was eventually founded. Their history is in this respect a story of

possible futures that did not come to be, and of life in uncertainty, including uncertainty about the frontiers of economic life and the frontiers of the law.

The sisters and brothers lived at a time in which even the distinctions that were most self-evident a generation later—between law and political power, or private and public life, or the economic and the political—were the subject of endless, anxious inquiry: over "what was, and what was not law," in the oldest brother's words, or "what [was] the state," or who was a servant and who was a slave.[9] The idea of empire was itself, in the Johnstones' and their friends' understanding, an idea about interior as well as exterior influence, "empire" in the sense of dominion or information or the power of words. Their story is a portrait of the outer lives of the sisters and brothers and of their households—of their voyages and marriages and debts, their petitions and packages and lawsuits. But it is also a history of their inner lives and of what the new ideas of the time, and the new connections of empire, meant to this eighteenth-century family. It is about large and abstract ideas in the lives of individuals who were not themselves philosophers or theorists of enlightenment. The frontiers between philosophical and political and popular ideas were indistinct, like so many other frontiers, in these new and modern times: a world of "internal and external sentiment," in David Hume's description of the "fluctuating situations" of moral evaluation.[10]

The Johnstones were no more than minor figures in the public events of the times, and they had an unusual capacity in their political ventures for being on the wrong side of history, or the losing side. But they left behind them an amazing amount of evidence or traces of their lives: lists of things to do, wills, codicils, mortgages, diaries about carrots, inventories, complaints about torture to the Privy Council, evidence in favor of Armenian plaintiffs, letters about bundles of muslin, lists of the names of their slaves, decrees of alimony, annuities to their servants, descriptions of the different kinds of paper used in Persian correspondence, marriage settlements, mausolea, lawyers' invoices, love letters from their lawyers, legal documents in successive lawsuits against each other and against others. They were interested in family history and in the techniques of searches in libraries; they wrote letters about sorting letters; and they were complicit, or so it seems, in the falsification of the records of their own dates of birth. There are traces of all the sisters and brothers, the most successful and the most obscure, and of many of their servants and slaves.

The history of the Johnstones and of their extended households is a story of women and men who were involved in one way or another in each other's lives, and in the vast changes of the times. But the evidence of the lives of the different individuals is extraordinarily diverse and disproportionate. It is as though there are some who can be seen in intimate detail, and from multiple points of view, and others who are a blur, or figures in a distant landscape. There are some, like Bell or Belinda, who have no names (or only the most implausible of names), no dates of birth or dates of death, and whose words are no more than the words of the clerks of courts. Joseph Knight, who was brought from Africa to Jamaica when he was "very young," remembered only that he could not remember: "he does not know anything of his being sold."[11]

The family's story is a microhistory, or a prosopography, a history of persons (of the face or the person in front of one's eye.) It is inspired in this respect by the prosopographies or family histories of the Roman empire, and the Johnstones were in a sense a very Roman family: "new men," or men who wanted not to be new, in a new empire.[12] It is inspired, too, by the microhistories of early modern Europe and the "prosopography of the lower orders," in which the poor as well as the rich can be the subject of a qualitative history.[13] It is a case study of the Johnstones and their extended connections.[14] But the history of the Johnstones is also a new kind of microhistory, in several different respects. It is a large history in relation to space, in the sense that the brothers, two of the women with whom they lived, and at least four of their slaves moved over very great distances, and in the sense that the story of the Johnstone sisters is a history, in part, of the consequences at home in Scotland of distant events.[15] It is a history of individuals of diverse legal conditions and social classes: a story that includes mistresses and servants and slaves in the same history. It extends across the frontiers between different kinds of historical inquiry, in that it is a history of economic life, of political ideas, of slavery, and of family relationships. Economic evidence, in the family's history, has been a source for political history, political evidence has been a source for the history of sentiments, the history of the law has been a source for family history, and family relationships have been a source for the history of enlightenment.[16]

The Johnstones' history is a new kind of microhistory, too, because it is an exploration of new ways of connecting the microhistories of individuals and families to the larger scenes of which they were a part: to important or "macrohistorical" inquiries. One connection is that the individuals are themselves important (as Joseph Knight was important). Another is of illustration, as the history of the Johnstones is an illustration, or a case study, of the larger history of their times. Yet another is of representativeness, or of the absence of representativeness. The new possibility, in late-modern microhistories, is of connecting micro- and macrohistories by the history of the individuals' own connections.[17] It is this possibility that I have tried to explore in the Johnstones' story: to proceed, encounter by encounter, from the history of a family to the history of a larger society of empire or enlightenment or ideas. But the Johnstones' history is also the story of disconnections or discontinuities: of departures and loss, and of individuals (like Bell or Belinda) who vanish without trace, or out of history. This, too, was the experience of eighteenth-century commerce and eighteenth-century empires.

The prospect in these new kinds of microhistory is of a new way of thinking about one of the oldest historical inquiries, or the history of the inner life. This is a history, in Adam Smith's description, that recounts the unfolding of public events by leading the reader "into the sentiments and mind of the actors."[18] It is an eighteenth-century sort of history, in the sense of a history of the ideas and sentiments of large numbers of people and how these ideas change over time.[19] The distinction between the inner and the outer life, or between an interior, private existence of the mind and an exterior universe of events and circumstances, is very difficult to identify in the lives of the Johnstones (as it is in our own lives). So too is the distinction between the intimate and the official, the universe of sentiment and the universe of reason. Adam Smith used eleven different words to describe the inner experience in the first few lines of *The Theory of Moral Sentiments.*[20] These elusive, fluctuating conditions are alluded to amazingly often, as will be seen, in the evidence of the Johnstones' lives and of the other people in their households.

The Johnstones' history begins, in what follows, with the narrative of their lives: setting out from their home in the west of Scotland, establishing themselves in Calcutta, Grenada, and Pensacola, coming home from the empire, and recollecting their earlier existence, as elderly men and women. I will use their own words, to a great extent, and the words of contemporary records; I have made no changes to the spelling of eighteenth-century letters and other writings. Their history in the first three chapters of the book is more like a novel than like an epic or epopeia, in Sir Walter Scott's distinction: "rather a history of the miscellaneous adventures which befall an individual [or a number of individuals] in the course of life, than the plot of a regular and connected epopeia, where every step brings us a point nearer to the final catastrophe."[21] But it is not a novel, or a historical novel. It is an eighteenth-century history, and one which has conveyed in a very exigent respect the limits of historical inquiry. The limits have their own story, and this is the subject, or one of the subjects, of the endnotes that are a substantial part of the book.

I then turn in the next three chapters to larger historical questions about the commercial empires and the enlightenment of the eighteenth century: about the new
economic theories and sentiments of the times; about
the Johnstones' own experiences of empire, in relation
to the institution of slavery, to the new exchanges of information, to family relationships, and to the intimacy
of empire; and about the enlightenment of the times,
also from the point of view of the Johnstones' lives and
connections. I return, in conclusion, to the history of the
inner life, in the sense of the interior of the household or
the home, and the interior of the mind, or the intentions,
character, and conscience of individuals that were discussed so endlessly in the Johnstones' own lives—and in
the sense, too, of the ideas and sentiments that are the
subject, or one of the subjects, of historical understanding. I return, too, to Bell or Belinda's story and to her
importance in history.

This is a family portrait, and the relationships between the Johnstones and the other individuals in their
extended households are at the heart of the story. But
the view from the family is also a vista of larger circumstances that are themselves, in part, the circumstances
of the interior as well as the exterior world. At least
some of the women and men with whom the story will
be concerned were continually evaluating their own
and other people's inner sentiments in the light of their
outer circumstances; others were the subject of the
evaluations of other people, in courtrooms, market-
places, prisons, and parish churches. Events, for them,
were the source of information about intentions and
values. This was the unending, reflexive observation

that Smith described in *The Theory of Moral Senti-ments*: of seeing one's own sentiments "with the eyes of other people, or as other people are likely to view them."[22] It is this eighteenth-century world of the mind that I have tried to describe.

CHAPTER ONE

SETTING OUT

The Johnstone sisters and brothers were born in Scotland in the 1720s and 1730s and grew up in Dumfriesshire, in the Scottish-English borders. Over their long lifetimes, from Barbara's birth in 1723 to the death of Betty, the last surviving child, in 1813, they were participants in a vast transformation of the conditions of existence. They lived in a time of economic and commercial revolution; of expansion in long-distance commerce and empire; of political revolution in India, North America, France, and Saint-Domingue; and of the changes in ways of thinking about individual lives, political rights, freedom of commerce, and European dominion overseas that have been associated, since the Johnstones' own times, with the birth of the modern world.[1]

The valley of the Esk, where the Johnstones' family home of Westerhall is hidden among bare, rounded hills, was at the edge of this new world of enlightenment. It was a place of sheepgrazing, smuggling, and disputes over inheritance.[2] "It's but a coarse moorish Country," in the description of a travel guide of 1729, and Daniel Defoe, in his *Journey through Scotland*, found only one impressive sight in the entire vicinity, "standing in a wild and mountainous Country, where nothing but what was desolate and dismal could be expected."[3] Scotland, with its own legal system and established religion, had been united with England under a single parliament by the Act of Union of 1707.[4] But it was still, for several generations, a "small and poor country."[5] The west of

Scotland, in particular, was in the early part of the eighteenth century a "country without Trade, without Cultivation, or money," in the description of a contemporary of the Johnstones, Elizabeth Mure, in which "some part of the old feudle system still remained."[6] Scotland was also traversed, in the Johnstones' childhood, by conflicts over religion and by the struggles over political succession—the Jacobite rebellions, and eventually the conflict of 1745–46—which were at one and the same time wars within families and scenes in the long, intermittent, and occasionally global competition between England and France.[7]

The economic and commercial expansion of the eighteenth century—an "economic revolution," especially in Holland, England and France, an increase in long-distance commerce in the Atlantic and the Indian oceans, and an "industrious revolution" in the consumption of textiles and household goods—came relatively late to the west of Scotland.[8] But in the 1740s, in Elizabeth Mure's account, almost everything began to change: "About the 40 riches began to incress considerably. Many returnd from the East and West Indias with good fortune who had gone abroad after the Union." The ideas of individuals changed, too. "It was then that the slavery of the mind began to be spocken off; freedom was in every bodys mouth." Even children were to be freed from superstition; "for their Girls the outmost care was taken that fear of no kind should inslave the mind; nurses was turned off who would tell the young of Witches and Ghosts."[9]

The expansion of long-distance commerce—or the early globalization of the eighteenth century—was most spectacular, in the Johnstones' lifetimes, with respect to the Atlantic commerce with North and South America, the Caribbean, and the West African slaving ports, and the Indian Ocean commerce with eastern and southern India.[10] The ocean had become "the great high road of communication to the different nations of the earth," as Adam Smith wrote in 1759, and the "industry of mankind" had "entirely changed the whole face of the globe."[11] The Atlantic slave trade, in which the British acquired the right to supply slaves to the "South Seas," or the Spanish colonies in America, became a flourishing commerce, connected in turn to the markets for Indian textiles in coastal and interior Africa. The European empires transported some forty-one thousand slaves per year from Africa to the Americas in the 1700s, and eighty-seven thousand per year in the 1790s; British traders accounted for almost half the expansion. By the 1790s some thirty-two thousand slaves were exported each year to the British West Indies alone.[12]

The European commerce with India was transformed over the same period by the successes of the French and English East India companies. The East India companies, private associations of merchants with trading privileges granted by Indian and European sovereigns, were the intermediaries in the expansion in sales of Indian manufactured goods, textiles, and spices, and of Chinese tea, to European, African, and American markets.[13] They were also in a position to extend their privileges, in the interstices of continuing conflicts between the Mughal empire and its Indian enemies, into territorial dominion.[14] The "great *monied* companies," in Edmund Burke's description of 1769, constituted "a new world of commerce," a system that was "wholly new in the world."[15]

The eighteenth-century epoch of globalization was a period of almost uninterrupted war, over very large distances. The half century from the outbreak of the War of the Austrian Succession in 1740 to the end of the War of American Independence in 1783—the Johnstones' own age of empire—was thought of at the time as a single conflict, with its interwar periods and its postwar periods and its periods of false or imagined or expected war.[16] The French and British navies fought over prizes and islands from Madras to northern Canada, and from the Cape of Good Hope to the Antilles; the Jacobite armies fought with French support in Scotland, and the armies of the British and French East India Companies fought in changing alliances with the princes of the Mughal and Maratha empires. It was a time, as David Hume wrote to a French friend in 1767, in which the "most frivolous Causes" were liable to "spread the Flame from one End of the Globe to the other."[17]

The age of revolutions, from the overthrow of Mughal power in Bengal in 1757–65 and the American Revolution of 1776 to the French Revolution of 1789 and the revolution of 1793 in Saint-Domingue, the modern Haiti, was the last scene of the Johnstones' lives, and of the lives of their extended households.[18] Five of the brothers lived for a time in the British colonies in North America, or were landowners in the territories that became the new United States. Bell or Belinda, who had been the "slave or servant" of John Johnstone, arrived in Virginia in 1772, as the revolutionary crisis began to unfold. William Johnstone's daughter was involved, as will be seen, in the family disputes of the French Revolution and the Napoleonic empire. Betty Johnstone was involved, with two of her nieces, in the politics of inheritance in the new American republic.[19] This was the Johnstones' own new world.

The Four Sisters and Seven Brothers

The Johnstones were the children of a young couple from the unprosperous professional classes of lowlands Scotland: Barbara Murray and James Johnstone. The young couple made a "clandestine & unorderly" (or unannounced) marriage in 1719, in the judgement of the Edinburgh justices of the peace.[20] The older James Johnstone, the children's father, was a law student, whom an acquaintance urged, some years later, to "try to disencumber yourself of that intolerable shyness which plagues you."[21] He was from a family of provincial lawyers and factors—or commissioners for the estates of rich landowners—who was the heir to the newly acquired title of baronet of Nova Scotia and to the heavily indebted family home of Westerhall.[22] Barbara Murray, the children's mother, was from a legal and professional family of the uneminent nobility, the granddaughter of an Edinburgh surgeon and great-granddaughter of an archbishop of Glasgow.[23] She was described, in a sermon preached after her death, as endowed with an "admirable power of elocution," although "her temper was ardent, & consequently liable to excess"; "she did not abound for instance in the virtue of Prudence . . . nor had any talent at making a secret of every thing."[24]

The families were diverse, like so many others in eighteenth-century Scotland, with respect to religion and

politics. The Johnstones of Westerhall were members of
the Church of Scotland and supporters of the union with
England; the Murrays of Elibank were for the most part,
in this period of fluctuating religious associations, members of the Church of England or of the Episcopal
Church in Scotland. One of Barbara Johnstone's brothers, the children's "Uncle Sandy," was a prominent Jacobite, and another was a British army chaplain and preb-
endary in the Church of England.

Barbara and James Johnstone had fourteen children
over the nineteen-year period from 1720 to 1739, of
whom eleven survived infancy.[25] This is a large population of relations to keep in mind, and it is quite difficult,
in a world of much smaller families, to imagine what it
would be like to have intimate, or potentially intimate
relationships with one's ten brothers and sisters (and ten
or more sisters-in-law, or brothers-in-law, or other companions). There were misunderstandings from time to
time, even within the family; James had to assure William at one point in 1757 that "the Ungrateful & Extravagant Brother G. mentions is Gidion."[26] I have provided in an appendix some straightforward, or fairly
straightforward biographical information about the
brothers' and sisters' baptisms, marriages, and deaths.
These are their stories, in brief.

Barbara (Johnstone) Kinnaird (1723–65), the oldest
of the surviving children, lived in Scotland throughout
her life. She married a man from a Perthshire family,
Charles Kinnaird, who inherited the title and estate of
his cousin under the complicated circumstances that
were so familiar in eighteenth-century inheritance disputes (his cousin's wife had been accused of attempting
to fabricate a pregnancy, and the birth of two male heirs,

by walking around with pillows under her dress).[27]
Charles Kinnaird came from a Jacobite family and was
arrested in 1745, with a servant of Sir James Johnstone
called Walter Scot, for "treasonable correspondence"; he
was later described in family stories as "eating his commission in prison."[28] Barbara had five children and a
shortlived period of prosperity, during which she was
able to buy "Tea-cups & Saucers" and even a carriage
with her husband's "name Copper'd and a Coronet."[29]
But she and her husband separated soon afterwards.[30]
She then lived on her own in Edinburgh and died at the
age of forty-one.[31]

Margaret (Johnstone) Ogilvy (1724–57), the second
child, was the first of the Johnstones to become well
known, or notorious, in public life. She was a Jacobite, a
supporter of the "pretender" to the thrones of England
and Scotland, and she and her husband, David Ogilvy,
spent much of 1745–46 traversing Scotland with the
rebel armies of "Bonnie Prince Charlie."[32] She was of
enthusiastic "political notions," in the contemporary description of a pamphlet, *The Female Rebels*, "with black
Eyes and black Hair, and her Person well sized, and an
easy though not very slender Shape."[33] When the rebellion was defeated and her husband escaped to France,
she was arrested and brought as a prisoner to Edinburgh
Castle. She escaped from the castle in disguise, in November 1746, with the help of one of her sisters, one of
her brothers, and an elaborate conspiracy involving a
tea kettle and "a little girl," to convince the guards that
she was ill in bed.[34] She later lived in exile in France and
died of consumption at the age of thirty-two.[35] Her
daughter, Margaret, married a man from another Jacobite family in Jamaica, John Wedderburn, who was the

owner of Joseph Knight, the slave who sued for his freedom in Perth in 1774.

James Johnstone (1726–94), the oldest surviving son, was sent to study in Leiden on the recommendation of James Boswell's father (and "after many doubts difficulties objections Answers etc. etc. and etc.").[36] He was a student there during the war of 1745, where he was described as "slow of apprehension and unsuspicious," but "the best-natured man in the world."[37] He later became a soldier in the British army against which his sister had rallied. His mother described him as "poor unlucky Jamie."[38] He was a vast figure, in the description of an English acquaintance, cast "in a Herculean mould, of an uncouth aspect, rude address, and almost gigantic proportions," which concealed "great integrity directed by strong sense."[39] He married a widow called Louisa Meyrick, moved to Norfolk, inherited the family home in Scotland, which he described as a "Crazy Rocking house," and died without legitimate children at the age of sixty-eight.[40] He was a member of parliament in the last years of his life and an opponent of slavery.

Alexander Johnstone (1727–83) also became a soldier on the government side and was sent to North America. He served in Canada and later in northern New York, where a friend of the family reported that he was "very shy, & more discontented than I ever saw any body." "He had always an oddity about him, but I was willing to impute it to his cross fortune," one of his maternal aunts wrote to his uncle in Canada.[41] He eventually became a colonel in charge of fortifications on the West Indian island of Grenada and purchased a large sugar plantation on the island, together with 178 "Negroes and Mullatoe slaves."[42] He was a member of the

Assembly of the island of Grenada, and in a case before the Privy Council in London, he accused the governor of Grenada of the torture of slaves. He died unmarried at the age of fifty-five, also without legitimate children, leaving his slaves, mills, and boiling houses to his brother James.

Betty Johnstone (1728–1813) lived with her parents until their death, except for a difficult period during the Seven Years' War when she quarrelled with her mother about a parcel of Indian textiles. She was the family's continuing source of information, about everything from tenancy contracts to the news from Jamaica, and from opinions about her sister Barbara's separation to the arrangements for her brother George's election campaign in Carlisle. She is the most obscure of the brothers and sisters, in the sense that she never entered into the public record of events between her birth and her death, or into the record of public life. After her parents' death she rented an apartment of her own in Edinburgh—"my own opinion Ever was that a person comed to my time of Life should have a place of there own that they may Retire to," she wrote to one of her brothers—and she died unmarried at the age of eighty-five, in 1813.[43]

William (Johnstone) Pulteney (1729–1805) studied in Edinburgh with Adam Smith, with whom he lived "intimately [for] four years," in Smith's own description.[44] He was described by one of his uncles as a "dealer in mystery," and he was a grave figure even in his youth; Smith wrote that "he had, when I first knew him, a good deal of vivacity and humour, but he has studied them away."[45] He was educated for the law, and he was the most respectable of the brothers and sisters. He was also the most successful. "Our friend, Johnstone, has wrote the most-super-excellent-est Paper in the World," David Hume wrote of his memorandum in a celebrated lawsuit of 1763 (over another feigned pregnancy).[46] William married an English heiress, Frances Pulteney, changed his name to Pulteney, and was a member of parliament for thirty-six years.[47] He owned property in Dominica, Grenada, Tobago, Florida, and New York and was a prominent parliamentary supporter of the slave trade.[48] He died intestate in 1805, one of the richest men in England.[49]

George Johnstone (1730–87) went to sea at the age of thirteen, where he served variously as a midshipman, captain, and eventually commodore.[50] He was a naval officer in the West Indies, Lisbon, the Cape Verde Islands, and the Cape of Good Hope, and was governor of the new British colony of West Florida in 1764–66. He was a member of parliament, and closely involved in the parliamentary politics of the East India Company and of the American Revolution, initially as a supporter of the American revolutionaries, until he was sent to the new United States as part of the peace commission of 1778, and later as a vehement defender of the British government. He died at the age of fifty-six, recognizing one child with his wife, Charlotte Dee, and four surviving children with his companion, Martha Ford, the daughter of an auctioneer in the Haymarket in London, with whom he had lived in the 1760s and 1770s in West Florida and Kensington Gore.[51]

Charlotte (Johnstone) Balmain (1732–73), the youngest of the sisters, was described as her mother's "favourite daughter," and she lived at home until she was thirty.[52] During the quarrel over the Indian textiles, she took on some of her sister Betty's responsibilities for writing letters of family information ("tho greatly her inferiore in expressing or in any way acknowledging the favours I owe you," as she wrote to their brother William).[53] She then made what her parents considered to be a catastrophically unsuitable marriage to a family friend, James Balmain, the son of the minister of a nearby church, who had become an officer of the excise, or "gauger," a collector of the duties on wines, spirits, and imported goods.[54] Charlotte and her husband had five children, of whom two survived into adulthood.[55] They lived in Scotland, where James Balmain was deeply involved in helping his brothers-in-law with searches in Edinburgh libraries into the history of their distant ancestors. Charlotte was forgiven by her father on his deathbed, and she died at the age of forty-one.[56]

John Johnstone (1734–95) joined the service of the East India Company at the age of sixteen, became a tax collector and merchant in Calcutta, Dhaka, and the inland province of Burdwan, and for a time was in charge of the Company's Persian correspondence. He was the other successful brother. He lived in India for fifteen years and was considered to be fluent in both the "Moor's language" (Persian) and the "country language" (Bengali). He was the only one of the brothers who made a large fortune overseas, and he was the source of financial support for at least five of his brothers and sisters. In Calcutta he married Elizabeth Carolina Keene, who had published translations of the love poetry of Ovid and Horace when she was a "very ingenious young Lady of fourteen," and who travelled to India with her sister in 1761.[57] He and Elizabeth Carolina returned to Scotland with several Indian servants, including "Bell or Belinda," and with a large, if fluctuating fortune, which he invested in landed estates, houses, and his own and his brothers' political careers. He was a member of parliament, for a short time, and an opponent of slavery; he died in Scotland at the age of sixty-two.[58]

Patrick Johnstone (1737–56), the next son, also joined the East India Company at the age of sixteen. His father had a "Serious Conversation" with him when he was fourteen about the "Choice of some Business for Life."[59] In his petition to join the Company, he stated that he had been "educated in writing and Accompts," and presented a certificate of having gone "thro' a complete course of Mathematick and Book keeping" with a teacher in Edinburgh; he "promise[d] to behave himself with the utmost Diligence and Fidelity."[60] In India, Patrick worked as an accountant and set up in trade with his brother John. He died in Calcutta shortly before his nineteenth birthday, in 1756.

Gideon Johnstone (1739–88), the youngest of the brothers and sisters, was the most unsettled of all of them. He joined the navy and served in the West Indies together with his older brother George. He then went to join his brother John in the East Indies as a free merchant, became an official of the East India Company, and enlisted in the Company's army. He was heard of in Basra, Mauritius, and the Cape of Good Hope. In the East Indies he was reported to have set up in business, selling the water of the Ganges to Indian pilgrims. He then returned to America, and during the Revolutionary War he became a naval officer, again in the West Indies. He also served in New York, off Plymouth Sound, and off the island of Nantucket.[61] In 1780, he married Fanny Colquitt, from a family of Liverpool lawyers and slave-ship owners, and he died in Scotland at the age of forty-nine.[62]

DIFFICULT CIRCUMSTANCES

The Johnstones were not rich by the standards of their own milieu of small landowners. The Westerhall estate was in the Johnstones' lifetimes endlessly in debt.[63] Their father was preoccupied throughout his life with the hope of finding evidence, somewhere in the archives of Scotland, that he was the rightful heir to the estates and titles of a very much richer distant cousin, the Marquis of Annandale. It was through these connections that he became an intimate associate of David Hume, who had spent a cold and melancholy winter, in 1745–46, as the "friend and comrade," or paid companion, "like a servant," to the rich cousin.[64] But the efforts were unsuccessful, and the older James Johnstone borrowed continually against his land from friends, neighbors, and the relatives of his wife (whose own father had invested heavily and disastrously in "South Sea" shares, in the company supplying slaves to the Spanish South Atlantic).[65]

By 1758, all the "Baronies Messuages Lands Tenements and Hereditaments" of the estate in the valley of the Esk were estimated, in the marriage settlement of the younger James, to amount to a "Clear yearly value of £220 or thereabouts."[66] This was an unimposing sum for a landowning family with eleven children, a little less than half, for example, of the stipend of a commissioner of the Scottish Excise, or the position to which Charlotte's tax collector husband was eventually appointed.[67]

When William moved to London, he was described by the politician Horace Walpole as the "third son of a poor Scot."[68] When the younger James died in 1794, he was "indebted to several other persons in Scotland by Bond and simple contract—to a much larger Amount than his personal Estate in Scotland," and the family estate in Westerhall was "advertised for sale."[69]

All the Johnstone children were educated, at home or in the homes of tutors.[70] They were literate, and even literary, although the girls spelled far more erratically than the boys, and their mother most erratically of all. There were books at Westerhall, many of them borrowed, and a succession of itinerant secretaries or tutors. "Pat reads now every day some piece of Virgil," one of the tutors wrote to William in 1751, and "Gideon reads as formerly only that for some time he has had Ovid's Metamorphosis in place of Caesar—I'm to begin Arithmetick with him next Week."[71] The Johnstones were connected to the expanding industry of carriers and libraries, and packmen "who ramble from town to town selling books."[72] When their mother asked George to buy her some refined sugar, it was to be sent by sea to Newcastle, directed "to Laidlaw at the Circulating Library."[73] In the inventory of the Westerhall estate, drawn up by a bookseller from Carlisle after the deaths of James and his widow Louisa, there were 785 volumes in the house and 112 magazines and pamphlets.[74]

But the Johnstones' life was almost always insecure. A tradesman in a nearby town wrote repeatedly in 1749 to ask for payment of a debt of twenty-eight shillings; "perhaps you think it is but a small item," but "I desire to be thankfull yt. there is law for poor and small people als well as for great folks."[75] "Cause send me out a pair of shoos for I am bair foot," their mother wrote to William in 1750, with her usual ardency (or overstatement).[76] There was a sense of extreme care with respect to expenditure, including in exchanges within the family. Shoes were a continuing preoccupation, and the children's tutor complained in 1751 that "the shoes sent for Pat by the Carrier are quite too little for him & too large for Gideon."[77] When Charlotte, the youngest daughter, was ill and asked her older brother William to send her sixpence worth of "Elixir of Vitriol," she assured him that "the sixpence shall be returned the first I am master of."[78] When William wanted to invite Adam Smith and one of Smith's other students, his friend Alexander Wedderburn, to visit, also in 1751—their intention, following the summer ritual of the times, was to restore themselves with goat whey—his father explained that William and his friend would have to share a room and that Smith would have to stay "above Stairs," because "the Room off the drawing Room" was already occupied.[79] There was even a dispute over some rabbit skins, which their father had promised to his two younger daughters, as Betty wrote to William, but which "my mother is to sell and keep the money to herself."[80]

It was the outside world, in these difficult circumstances, that provided the possibility of improvement. There were three main opportunities for advancement, or for the "management" of their lives: by military service, by overseas commerce, and by marriage. The children and the Johnstones' extended family of friends and relations were involved in an elaborate process of concertation or coordination: "I could have wished Sir James had gone to Edin. for Pat's sake whose future Management should now begin to be concerted," the family's tutor wrote to William, soon after Patrick's fourteenth birthday.[81] Alexander was sent to London, with a "memorand" of the letters of recommendation he was to request.[82] By the age of twenty-three, William was experienced in the procedures of recommending himself to persons of influence. "I intend to get myself recommended to the Dutchess [of Queensberry]," he wrote to his father. "I think I could do a vast deal in the way of recommending myself to people. . . . I intend to recommend myself as much as I can."[83]

Of the eleven children, seven were involved directly in the military conflicts of the times: in the British army and navy, in the Jacobite army, and in the East India Company's armed forces. Margaret was reported to have ridden into battle in 1746, with "a led horse for her husband"; "she really is much of a heroine, and might make a very fine figure in romance," an acquaintance wrote, and "she seems to feel only for the loss of the battle and the ruin of their cause."[84] James and Alexander were in the British army, George and Gideon were in the navy, and John and Gideon were for a time in the East India Company's army; when Margaret was in prison, one of the Johnstones' father's many anxieties was to "prevent any slurr upon your other children actually in the service on her account."[85] James, who was stationed in Scotland and the north of England, sought without success to become governor of a fort in Jamaica; he was promoted, late in life, to the rank of major.[86] The brothers' unending quest, in the economical armed forces of the times, was for letters of recommendation, and for borrowed money with which to buy commissions or advancement. Alexander's instructions from their father, when he went to London to look for opportunities in

the British empire in North America, were to ask for letters of recommendation from three lords and to "wait
on" three colonels.[87]

The second route of management or advancement,
through overseas commerce, was opened to the Johnstones by enlistment in the service of the East India
Company. The English East India Company, which had
been founded in 1600 as a company of merchants, was
at the outset of its period of greatest prosperity in the
1740s. Young men from Scotland, in the expansion following the political union, were conspicuous in its enterprises. John was the first of the brothers to set off,
being admitted as a writer, or junior official, in 1750, at
the age of sixteen, on the security of two of his maternal
uncles. He was "on leaving me (in my oppinion) capable of discharging the Duty of Clerk in any office with
credit," his teacher in Edinburgh certified to the East
India Company.[88] John arrived in Bengal in 1751, and
his younger brother Patrick soon followed, on the security of two London merchants.[89] Patrick arrived in 1754
and took up employment as an assistant in the Accountant's office in Calcutta. "My very worthy Brother
Johny & I are trying to establish & carry on a Good
Trade Tho We want Money to make it an extensive
one," Patrick wrote to William from Calcutta in September 1755: "I shall write you very fully of my situation & opinion of the People here by next Ship." Gideon,
the youngest brother, followed later, arriving in India as
a "free merchant" in 1762 and entering the Company's
service in 1764.[90]

The third route of advancement, through marriage,
was of mixed success for the Johnstones. Barbara's
marriage ended in a legal separation, and Charlotte's

marriage was considered to have been a family disaster. James became engaged in 1757 to a wealthy heiress, a "Miss Mendez," who, as he wrote to William, "has £12,000 E.I.S.," or East India shares. But at the very last moment he withdrew from the engagement. "Nothing ever was brought so farr the marage cloaths bought the Diner rady the company invited the poor sweat creature doatingly fond of him," their mother wrote to George of the elaborate preparations for the marriage, suggesting that he consider taking James's place; "well did I love her for she had a fine charackter and seemd a senceable wise woman. . . . would god you could love her and she you I think she would find her loss of him more than made up."[91] In the following year, James married Louisa Meyrick, the heavily indebted widow of a clergyman, heiress to a disputed estate in Norfolk and to the involuted matrilineal relationships, over three generations, of her mother, grandmother, great-grandmother, aunts, and great-aunts.[92] Louisa's estranged husband died suddenly in February 1758; she and James married later that year, to the astonishment of James's family ("who is this James is maryd to," their mother asked William).[93] William's old friend from the goat-whey summer, the lawyer Alexander Wedderburn, was more encouraging: "Jamie is perhaps not so much to blame as you suppose, I fancy Miss Mendez is but a Bitch & I hear his marriage is not a very bad one. I shall write you more when I'm better informed."[94]

The only one of the children whose economic circumstances were entirely transformed by marriage was William himself, the "dealer in mystery."[95] William was instructed by his mother and father in the language of compliments, and he outlined his own plan, as a law student, in the way of recommending himself to people.[96] In 1760 he married Frances Pulteney, in 1767 he changed his name to Pulteney, and later in the same year he inherited the vast fortune of one of his wife's cousins, an event that was greeted by his father with "gratitude to God" for his "manifold blessings" and by Adam Ferguson and Adam Smith with "joy" and high "spirits" that lasted late into the night.[97] It was Frances Pulteney's fortune, together with the fortune that John made in the service of the East India Company, that was the basis of the family's subsequent wealth.

TRAGIC NEWS FROM THE INDIAS

The war years of 1756 to 1763 were a period of extreme difficulty for the Johnstones.[98] Margaret, after her escape from prison, made her way to France, where her husband served in the army of Louis XV. The army officer who had been on duty when she fled was court-martialled in Edinburgh, but pardoned by George II.[99] In France, as Margaret wrote to her mother, she became the "ambasadredo" of the Scots officers to the French Conseil d'État, where she "waited of all the Ministers, presented my Memoirs, & told my Story."[100] Her daughter was born in France and by 1749 had "4 teeth begins to Speak and is the admiration of all the Luxumburgh."[101] Margaret later made an arduous journey to Scotland when she was pregnant in 1751, observed by officials of British intelligence, and returned to France, where she died in 1757.[102] Her death was not known to her family in Scotland until several months later: Barbara's husband wrote to William, in April 1757, that "I hope the report of Lady Oglives Death will prove false there is no

accounts comed to the family of Early [Margaret's in-
laws] I beg to know what you have heard."[103]

George returned from Jamaica in 1758, "in a very ill
stait of health," as Gideon wrote to Charlotte, and was
greeted at Plymouth by their mother's lamentations over
James's broken engagement, or "the augly beheaviour of
poor unlucky Jamie to poor Mrs Mendez."[104] "I came
home from the Wt Indias," George wrote to one of his
uncles in 1759, "with Pretensions, wch. a Clear Conscience & Ignorance of the World made me believe were
Unsurmountable." But he was unsuccessful in a dispute
concerning the division of naval prizes, or the system,
so extensive in the eighteenth-century navy, by which
the value of captured vessels was allocated among com-
manders, officers, and crews.[105] He was unsuccessful,
too, in the metropolitan milieu of what he described as
"various applications & wrigling Connections"; "I soon
found . . . that I might as well whistle to ye wind."[106] He
was eventually sent to Lisbon, and to a sequence of
minor naval postings, in pursuit of "small Privateers"
and illicit fishing vessels. "I am just going to sea, I presume you have feeling sufficient to judge of my distress
without discribing it," he wrote to William late in
1759.[107]

Barbara's marriage came to an end, also in 1759.
"Your sister and I" are on the point of "parting for ever,"
her husband wrote to William, and went on to inquire
about the premiums for "Lint & Lint Mills."[108] Betty
was sent by their father to bring Barbara home, without
her children; when her husband was asked "for what
Crime he said for non but illnature." In the arbitration
that followed Barbara was awarded £130 per year, with
£100 for household furniture.[109] She then lived in Edin-

burgh, in a "very Distresst Condition," in Betty's description. "Every body here thinks she Behaves just as she ought to Do," Betty wrote to William, and she had "never been out Except twice at Church."[110]

By the late 1750s the Johnstones' father was heavily in debt, including to his wife's brother, and so was James. James's schemes of advancement—to buy a lieutenancy in the Guards, to go to Jamaica, to become a member of parliament, to discover a lead mine on the estate at Westerhall—came to nothing, and he and Louisa were very close, in the first period of their marriage, to being imprisoned for debt.[111] They determined to sell everything they could, except her old home in Norfolk, where they settled: "we shall be free of Debt and from what I know of us both will never contract more," he wrote to Louisa in July 1759.[112] He and William were involved in a bitter quarrel that turned, in part, on James's willingness to dispose of the remaining family estates in Scotland, and on his interpretation of what he described, with heavy irony, as "True Scotian Pride," or "Noble Hereditary Clannish Enthusiasm." He had no power, James wrote to William, to sell his wife's land, and he could not in any case advise her "to part with the Sweetest most improveable Spott perhaps in the Universe for barren Hills and horrid Mountains." Sell the hills, he recommended to William, renouncing the "family spirit," the sanitation, and even the rooks' nests of his ancestors' "Crazzy Rocking house."[113]

There was terrible news, meanwhile, from India. Six of the seven Johnstone brothers were involved in the war of 1756–63, and the two who had joined the East India Company were even closer to the hostilities than James and Alexander in the army, or George and Gideon in the navy. John was in Dhaka in East Bengal when the fighting began in 1756, and Patrick was in Calcutta. Both were captured. John was released into the custody of the French; Patrick died on the night of June 20–21, 1756, in the prison of the Nawab Siraj-ud-daulah that was later known as the "black hole of Calcutta."[114] The news of Patrick's death was confirmed the following year. "I am exceedingly sorry to acquaint you that my Dear Brother Pattys Death is but too certain I cannot think of acquainting my Poor Father and Mother of it," James wrote to William in June 1757. "Good God what Distresses are accumulated on their heads."[115]

At home in Westerhall, the older Johnstones waited anxiously for news of events that had unfolded in the East and the West Indies months or years earlier. "We are in great fear for Both Sandy & Jock," Betty, who had become the family's center of information, wrote in September 1759. "Im vastly anxious to hear about Jock Sandy & George," she wrote in October, and later in October, "Im in great anxiety about Poor Sandy." In May 1760 she wrote, "There is a report here that there has been an ingagement in the East Indias God preserve Jock. . . . is there any accounts of Gidion George or Sandy?"[116] Their uncle Walter, too, who was the younger half-brother of the Johnstones' father by their grandfather's relationship with a woman named Julian Meikle, was a source of anxiety; "Uncle Watty had the Lap of his Coat Shot of by a Cannan Bulet when they came to Jameca," Betty wrote to William in 1758.[117] I have been "very uneasy," Gideon wrote to William from Jamaica in 1761, "haveing never Received but one letter from my friends for these sixteen month past."[118]

The brothers who were overseas sent presents, from time to time. Gideon, when he returned from Jamaica, brought "a present of four small Images & Seven Baskets for having frute," as Betty wrote to William. "Poor man if he had been possessed of more money he would have Bought Somthing Better for Willy he says."[119] Their uncle by marriage, who was an Edinburgh lawyer, provided advances of money: Gideon "got five pound from Mr Ferguson for which he was to send you a Bill," Betty wrote to William during the crisis over Barbara's separation; "I have likwise got forty shillings from him."[120] George sent money for Charlotte and Betty, which they used to buy "cardanells," or red cloaks.[121] There were more imposing bundles from John in India: "2 pieces dacca doreas" (or fine Indian cloth) which came over land; two pieces of "Flowred dorea" and "Busseda flowred Doorea" for Charlotte and Betty, which were sent by a Portugese ship; and "13 shirts 1 piece of fine Dacca Tanjibs & 2 pieces of Damity" for James.[122]

But these bundles precipitated one of the worst crises in the family, in the form of a catastrophic row between the Johnstones' mother and Betty. The distribution of the Indian textiles among Betty, Charlotte, and their mother was apparently not made clear in John's letter, and Betty and her mother both believed that a particular piece of muslin was intended for her. By the early spring of 1760, Betty had left home: their father "is so much Distress, its not in his power" even to answer her letters, Charlotte wrote in March 1760. "What shall I do about going to Westerhall," Uncle Walter asked William. "It is my duty but so disagreeable that I shudder at it."[123]

"It grieves me to the heart to be now obliged to tell you," their father wrote to Betty more than a year later, in October 1761, "that the many repeated Efforts I have made to bring your mother to be reconciled to you have hitherto prov'd unsuccessful"; "[she] declares she will Leave here if you come here." Charlotte reported that their mother "is as bad as ever the opening the Bundle and the muslin that was lost is now her theam." "Im Extremely sensible that nothing on Earth can be a greater misfortune to me than not having a home to go to," Betty wrote to William. She stayed with a variety of friends and neighbors, and her possessions were stored in a trunk; she wrote to William that she was thinking of becoming a "Boarder." But in May 1762, after an exile of two years, she was finally back at home. In June 1762 there was a new letter from John in India, and Betty conceded that the entire crisis had been a misunderstanding: "Youll see be it non of the Musslin was intended for me."[124]

THE FRONTIERS OF EMPIRE IN THE WEST

Within a few months of Betty's return, the end of the Seven Years' War brought a substantial improvement in the Johnstones' fortunes. The Treaty of Paris of 1763—in which Canada was ceded by the French to the British, Louisiana was ceded by the French to the Spanish, Guadeloupe and Martinique were ceded by the British to the French, the West Indian islands of Grenada, Dominica, and Tobago were ceded by the French to the British, and Florida was ceded by the Spanish to the British—opened new and confusing opportunities for British officials.[125] Alexander, whose service in New York and Canada had

been a sequence of reverses—"a million of other ob-
structions," as he wrote to his commanding officer—
was sent to the island of Grenada as a major.[126] George,
in an even more surprising transformation, was appointed in 1763 as the first British governor of the new
colony of West Florida. His wartime service, too, had
been a sequence of misfortunes, and he was at one point
despatched by the Admiralty to Lisbon, as he complained to William, with a sealed packet containing the
order that he was to be detained there: "like a Slave of
the Indies made the Porter of a Paper-Speak for my own
Punishment."[127] But by 1763 he had returned to London and to the political circles of the new king, George
III.[128] His nomination in West Florida was one of a series of appointments of Scots officers in the newly acquired colonies, or in the words of the radical *North
Briton*, "the greatest satire on the Scotch administration."[129] "It is suggested that the Ministry sent him to
Mobile to get rid of him, given that he was one of the
most ardent in the Opposition party," the French governor of Louisiana commented when George eventually
arrived in Florida.[130]

The new British colonies in the Americas were identified as the foundation of a modern British empire, to
extend from the West Indian islands towards the south
and west, into the Gulf of Mexico and to the Mexican
mainland. The sugar islands, and the Atlantic slave trade
to supply the West Indian plantations, were the most
lucrative part of this new world of American commerce.[131] The islands were expected to be the point of
entry, in turn, to a larger seaborne empire, in which the
British navy would dominate the Gulf of Mexico as far
as Honduras and the Spanish settlements that the British

called the "Musquito Coast."[132] This was to be an empire of commerce, extending to the Spanish provinces
that were still, in the 1760s, considered to be the richest
parts of the American continent. It would be a resource,
in the "next war," for an eventual British conquest of the
French part-island of Saint-Domingue, the most prosperous of the sugar colonies, and of Mexico itself.

These were also the Johnstones' own expectations.
The island of Grenada, on which Alexander was stationed with his regiment, was a prosperous slave society,
of which the population was estimated, by the new British government, at 646 "Families (Whites)," 10,531
"Blacks (Slaves)," and 3,315 "young Negroes."[133] In the
description of a British pamphlet of 1770, it was "civilized and well-cultivated"; "the most valuable acquisition made by us at the late peace," in which "the planters
[were] more civilized than the *Coureurs de Bois* of the
Continent."[134] In the exodus of French proprietors, Alexander was able to acquire a large estate, the Baccaye
plantation; he was the first of the brothers to become
involved, directly and on a large scale, in the Atlantic
slave economy. The transactions were, as so often, complicated: the plantation was sold by its French owners in
April 1763 and resold four days later; Alexander bought
the plantation and its slaves, with the financial support
of his brother William, from the widow of the new proprietor in December 1764. He was the owner, now, of
"67 men," "50 women," "29 boys," and "32 girls," "Negroes and Mullatoe slaves"; their names, listed in the
contract of sale, included "Fashonable," "Rogue," "John
Baptist," and "Johnston."[135]

But Grenada was also a scene of political, religious,
and military conflict. It was in a condition of continuing

revolution, with a substantial population of runaway slaves: "sheltered in the woody Mountains" and "more than ordinarly audacious," in the description of the new British governor, "after such a change of Properties, and from such a jarring mixture of Slaves."[136] "The whole island was in the utmost state of violence & distraction," Alexander wrote later of Grenada in the early period of British government.[137] The island had been endowed, in the new dispensation, with an impressive array of constitutional innovations: a "House of Representatives," in this island of a few hundred "Families (Whites)," together with a "Council" (or senate), provision for the political rights of Catholics, a government printing office, bilingual in French and English, and an inquiry into "the Deficiency of the Publick Records," "destroyed by Vermin, Time, Accident . . . Corruption or Negligence."[138] But within a few months, there was conflict between the governor and the military authorities, between French and British proprietors, and between more or less anti-Catholic British Protestants. There were disputes over the British and French laws of slavery, the "Government of Slaves," and the use of torture in the war against the rebels in the interior of the island.[139] In the later description of Alexander and his friends, it was "the most tyrannical, confused, and illegal series of proceedings, that ever were transacted by any men, taking upon them the management of a British Colony."[140]

Alexander was elected to the new House of Representatives of the island; he was in conflict both with the governor and with his own military command.[141] There was a dispute, in particular, over the relationship between civil and martial law, with respect to a woman who had joined the army in Cork as a "leagerlady," "one of those females who are allowed to follow the camp in order to wash the mans cloaths."[142] Alexander was eventually convicted of mutiny and dismissed from his command; "a Gentleman of his Acquaintance told me that he was more disordered in Mind than in Body," James wrote to their father.[143] But in these difficult times he had been able to make a success of his newly purchased estate. The property was valued in 1770 at £95,017, including 266 "Slaves of Particular Inventory." When the French returned in 1779, Alexander was listed as the owner of 351 slaves.[144] Far from home, he had renamed the estate "Westerhall," after the family home in the valley of the Esk; this is still its name.

The colony of West Florida, which was George's new frontier of empire, was an even more disorderly scene. It was a land of swamps in the former Spanish province of Florida and the former French province of Louisiana, which extended across the western part of the modern state of Florida, as well as much of Alabama and parts of Mississippi and Louisiana. It was insignificant in commercial terms, even in comparison with the island of Grenada; its non-native population was estimated, in 1763, at about a thousand people, most of them enslaved Africans.[145] It was also very little known; a correspondent wrote to the *Gentleman's Magazine* to request "any curious gentleman, who lives in Florida, or any of the adjacent parts, to acquaint you, whether there are any lions in the forests of those places."[146] "It is situated at the Boundary of the British Empire," George wrote of Pensacola, the capital of the province, and the "boundary with the Creeks," or the Creek tribe, was "the little Brook which surrounds this Town." The town itself was "never more than an Assemblage of miserable Bark Huts."[147]

"Mobile is terribly unhealthy," in the description of the British officers, and "near rotten Swampy Ground"; "the Bread is excessive bad; No Bread in the World deserves condemnation more justly."[148]

George set off for Florida in 1764 in imposing style. He brought with him a former whaling ship, the *Grampus*, containing "presents" for the "Indians," and he was accompanied by James Macpherson, the translator of the "Ossian" poems, as the secretary of the province; "I would advise him to travel among the Chickisaws or Cherokees, in order to tame him and civilize him," David Hume commented, with heavy irony.[149] George's companion, Martha Ford, who was pregnant at the time, came too, or so it seems. One of their children was baptised in Pensacola on December 10, 1764, according to a certification that George provided to the East India Company some years later.[150] Martha was registered as the owner of two plots of land in the province: a "garden lot in Pensacola" and five hundred acres of wilderness, together with all "mines of Gold and Silver" to be found there in the future.[151] George and she appear to have lived together in the "Governor's House," which he constructed in Pensacola in the course of 1765 (with "Paper Hangings Boards Shingles etc.").[152] A visiting clergyman from South Carolina wrote disobligingly, after a tour of the province, that "the Governour is a Single Person, keeps a Concubine, has a Child by her and the Infection rages and is copied."[153] James "Ossian" Macpherson, in a kindlier spirit, wrote from Pensacola to George, who was absent in Mobile, that "your people are well."[154]

George and "Ossian" Macpherson's grandest project, in the early months of the new government, was a political settlement with the Creek and Choctaw nations who surrounded the province. "Go, go, go away & tell thy Chief that all the Red Men desire that the English may not come here," the chiefs of the Ozages and Missouri were reported as telling a British officer, in April 1765; "we know you not, nor have we ever seen you."[155] George arrived in West Florida, in a different and more optimistic spirit, with an elaborate theory of the American political system. The "nature of the Indian Government, which is, so many united Republics, leaves a vast Competition for Power amongst them," he wrote to London.[156] He and Macpherson were the impresarios— together with an assortment of visiting British officers, including an admiral from Jamaica and a colonel from Scotland—of a series of imposing peace congresses with the Choctaw in Mobile and the Creeks in Pensacola.[157] "The two Congresses which we have held are the largest that ever met on the Continent," George informed the ministry in London.[158] He was given the Choctaw name Ungulasha Mattaha (or "Support of the Imoklashas"), and he tried to outline for his American interlocutors the multiple identities of the new empire, English, French, and Spanish.[159]

There is a "Jealousy which is Spread abroad, that we wish to possess all the Lands of the Indians. Nothing is so untrue," George declared in the congress with the Creeks. His intention was rather, he said, to "shew we are all one people." He also, "now that all other white Nations are gone," undertook to provide "a plentyfull Trade from all parts of the world" and to regulate the price of "Dutch pretties," "nonsopretties," and "Large Silk Bengall." To the Choctaws he undertook to ensure

"that every darkned Spot is enlightned" and to defend
them against the traders who supplied the "Poisonous
Liquor called Rum" ("he who is destroyed by Drunkenness shall be forgott like the Hog who has perished in
the Swamp"). To the ministry in London, he reported
that the Americans had agreed to "admit a free Trade."[160]
The "Talks are now all made White & Good, between
us & the White people," the Mortar chief responded,
and the warrior Emisteseguo outlined his own nation's
procedures: "the Eagles Tail, which I hold in my hand, is
the Custom of my Country, & spreads like a sheet of
Paper."[161]

George's other great hope in West Florida was for a
new American empire of maritime commerce to the
south and the southwest. "No country perhaps on the
face of the earth possesses so pure, serene, and temperate a sky," he wrote to an English newspaper some days
after he arrived, describing himself as "Captain General, Governor and Commander in Chief": "West Florida bids fair to be the emporium, as well as the most
pleasant part of the new world." It was particularly well
suited, in his imagination, to be the center of a flourishing Anglo-Spanish-French commerce in the Gulf of
Mexico, with a "market-place" in Pensacola, to be or-
namented by "a capacious building upon Corinthian
columns."[162] There was a potentially unlimited commerce in "Furniture" with the Spanish empire, he wrote
to the Board of Trade in London: "it might be carried to
any Extent."[163] George wrote to the new governor of
Louisiana about the "Fineza" of Spanish diplomacy and
about the prospects for a universal prosperity "far
above the little Jealousies of Commerce."[164] He was

also involved in diplomatic relations with the outgoing
French governor, who reported to the ministry in Paris
that the exchanges were extremely exhausting:

> The correspondence I am obliged to have with the En-
> glish, who write to me from all sides, and principally
> Governor Jonsthon, who is in Mobile, gives me a great
> deal to do. He is an extraordinary man. As he knows
> that I speak English, he sometimes writes to me in verse,
> he speaks to me of François I, of Charles V, he compares
> Pontiac to Mithridates. He says that he sleeps with
> Montesquieu.[165]

In Florida the new government set to work on the
enterprise of what George described as the machinery
of office, or "settling the Civil Government of the said
Province"; this included "the Statutes at Large," "Stationary Ware for the Publick Offices," "fitting up a
General Court," and "putting on frames to their Majestys pictures."[166] The new capital in Pensacola was
laid out into rectangular plots with imposing street
names; there were grants of town land to William, to
the Johnstones' maternal uncle in Edinburgh, to Martha Ford, and to "Ossian" Macpherson (on Mansfield
Street).[167] There were new political institutions, as in
Grenada, including an Assembly of the Province, with
a Speaker who prepared an elaborate address about
the Roman conquest of Britain, to be sent to the King,
"as to another Alfred." There was a council, or senate,
to which George delivered his opinion, in May 1765,
on "the words Liberty of the Subject."[168]

But George's initial high hopes for the new colony
were soon disappointed. He and Macpherson quarrelled
with the British military officers in the province within a

few days of their arrival, over the momentous question
of the relationship between military and political power,
or in George's expression, over the principle that "Imperium in Imperio cannot exist in a Common wealth."[169]
There was much "obloquoy and scurrilous language," in
Macpherson's description; Macpherson himself fell out
with the new chief justice of the province and left for
home in 1765, by way of Charleston in South Carolina.
George described him as "a Gentleman, who has had a
very principal Part in the settling this Government" and
who was in a position to return to England "now that
the Wheels of Office are set in Motion."[170] There were
disputes over the passwords to be given to sentries
(George suggested "Bedlam, Countersign, Lunacy") and
disputes over the runaway slaves of the officers.[171] West
Florida was, in George's description in his official correspondence, a place of "Jealousies," "Disturbance," and
a "Torrent of Abuse."[172] There was "pretty authentic information," he reported from Pensacola in 1766, "that
there was going to be a great Revolution or Rebellion in
this said Town shortly."[173]

The project of a new empire of universal commerce
was similarly unsuccessful. There was no "free Egress
and Regress" for vessels in the Spanish trade, and there
were very few of the respectable individuals whom
George described as "real merchants." The Indian trade
was at risk of being abandoned to "vagabonds, worse
than the very Horses who carry their Burthens."[174]
The implementation of the navigation acts that regulated shipping in the colonies was a travesty, in George's
account, of the "proper sense of the Words Importa-
tion and Exportation."[175] Less than a year after his arrival, George wrote to London that "above one Fourth

of the Soldiers have already died, and one Fifth of the Inhabitants."[176]

George's government turned, in these circumstances, to the establishment of a slave society. West Florida was a land, like so many of the settlements around the Gulf of Mexico in the 1760s, of fugitives, emigrants, and runaway slaves, into which the government sought to introduce a slave plantation economy, similar to those of the West Indian islands. Before he left the province, George signed an Act for the "Government of Negroes and Slaves," which embodied in statute the "custom" by which "color" was a "badge of slavery" and decreed new and extraordinarily violent provisions against "fugitive or runaway" slaves; the act was superseded after his departure by an even more bloodthirsty law.[177]

Even the new hopes of enlightenment were abandoned. The expectation of the native Americans, George wrote to London soon after his arrival, had been that "the English intended, first, totally to surround them and next, to extirpate them from the face of the Earth."[178] "Nothing is so untrue," he declared to the Creeks in 1765.[179] But his own government quarrelled with the native Americans over land, slaves, the theft of clothes, and attacks on Indian traders.[180] The experiment in political coexistence had come to an end, and so had the experiment in enlightened commerce (in selling Bengal silk).[181] By 1766 George was no longer willing that the disputes should be "Huddled up by an Expensive tedious & useless Congress."[182] "The present rupture is very fortunate for us," he wrote of an impending war between the Choctaws and the Creeks, and "it was undoubtedly our Interest to foment the Disputes between those Nations." "I am of opinion, we should feed the War."[183] To the military commander in the province, he proposed a new policy of vengefulness.[184] To the government in London, he wrote that "the Creeks must be chastised," and asked for a military force of 850 men, to "march forthwith against the Lower Creek Towns destroying Men, Women, and Children."[185] By the autumn of 1766, he had arrived at his own politics of desolation: "There certainly never was a time when the proper Chastisement even if thought necessary to extend to Extirpation could be so Easily inflicted."[186]

George was granted permission by the king, late in 1766, "to return to England, on your Private affairs for Six Months." In February 1767 he received a new letter, in which he was dismissed from his position, on the grounds that the king "disapproves entirely" of his "rashly rekindling the war between the Indians and his subjects in North America," and of "the Spirit of Disunion which has weakened and distracted the colony of Pensacola."[187] But George, by then, was no longer there. In January 1767, having sold to his secretary, Primrose Thomson, for one guinea, "a negro wench named Phillis," he left for home.[188]

SMALL CONGRATULATORY ELEPHANTS

John and Gideon were participants, at the other extremity of the British empire, in a different and more opulent scene. Bengal in the first half of the eighteenth century was a "paradise of the earth," in the description of Lord Clive, the official of the English East India Company who was celebrated in so many subsequent histories as the founder of "British India."[189] It was a land of "thousands and thousands of merchants," Clive said in the House of Commons in 1772, into which "the silver of the west and the gold of the east have for many years been pouring," and whose "superfluity" of "very curious and valuable manufactures" was "sufficient for the use of the whole globe."[190] It was also a land of settled government, under the rule of the Nawab of Bengal and the sovereignty of the Mughal Emperor: "within the jurisdiction of some known and acknowledged state," in the account of a pamphlet of 1773, and in contrast to the lands of no "fixed occupancy" or "vacant possession," in much of North America.[191] The English East India Company, like the French, Dutch, and Danish companies, and the Persian, Armenian, and Turkish merchant communities, was an association of traders at the periphery of this vast commercial and agrarian society. The companies were established in coastal and riverine ports and subject to elaborate permissions from the Indian governments; their business, in Adam Smith's description, was no more than "a drop of water in the immense ocean of Indian commerce."[192]

John arrived in India in 1751 at a time when "our Domain was limited within a Ditch & Rampart," in his own later description. By 1761, as he wrote in a New Year's letter to his childhood friend and future brother-in-law, James Balmain, the East India Company was "in the highest pitch of glory, Possessors & Lords of almost half Hindostan, & give Law everywhere."[193] He was an observer, and at times a leading figure in the Company's rise. "Since my arrival till now I have been very unsettled continually shifting from one busy scene to another," he wrote to James Balmain, and he was successively a merchant in bales of cloth, an officer in the Company's army,

a political or intelligence officer, a specialist in the procurement of bullocks, a civil servant, a merchant in the
inland trade in salt (eventually in partnership with his
brother Gideon), a tax farmer or subcontracted revenue
collector (in partnership with a Mughal official called
Motiram), and a high administrator of the land revenues
of the Mughal empire.[194] He was also, by the end of his
period in India, the most prominent opponent of Lord
Clive's government, and a demonic figure, for Clive, of
"Corruption, Avarice, Rapacity."[195]

The rise of the English East India Company in the
1750s and 1760s was an outcome of the political, economic, and military troubles of the Mughal empire. The
eighteenth-century revolutions began, in the Persian-
Bihari historian Ghulam Husain's description, with the
wars of the Maratha rulers of western India against
the Mughal emperor: a time of "independence and revolt," in which "the materials of a revolution becoming
daily more abundant, seemed now to be assembled in
heaps."[196] In the interstices of these conflicts, the British
East India Company arrived at a new dominance over
its European competitors and eventually over the government and commerce of Bengal.

The East India Company's servants, who had arrived
in India as merchants, were transformed into sovereigns; in the description of a German-Dutch-Portugese
factor called William Bolts, who was John's partner in
the salt trade, and who later became a highly influential
political writer in London, the Company had created a
"monstrous government" of the "Merchant-sovereign
and the Sovereign-merchant."[197] The wars between Indian sovereigns were adjusted to the almost global conflict between the English and the French, and to the

mercenary armies that were supplied to the Indian princes, respectively, by the East India Company and the French Compagnie des Indes.[198] The capture of the East India Company's domain in Calcutta by the Nawab Siraj-ud-Daula in 1756, in which Patrick Johnstone died, was an episode in the long wars. So was the victory of the East India Company's army, commanded by Clive at the battle of Palashi, or Plassey, in 1757, in which John was an artillery officer.

The war years of 1756–63 were a period of a "vast flow of money thro' so many hands," in John's description.[199] There was the Company's old-established commerce in textiles and manufactures. There was the inland commerce in commodities for domestic consumption, which the English called the "country trade," and for military procurement. There was the administration of tax revenues. There was the economy of "presents," or "acknowledgements" of services rendered, given by the Indian sovereigns, officials, and bankers to the British officials. Clive returned to England in 1760 with an immense fortune—including a *jagir*, or an entitlement to the land revenues of a large territory in Bengal, provided by the Nawab—and an imposing title, "Flower of the Empire" of Alamgir.[200] In this universe of opportunity, John was an expert in the trade of the "black merchants" and the "banyans or black agents," and in the economy of presents.[201]

John's most settled identity, in the shifting scenes of his Indian existence, was as an intermediary or translator between the Company and the "country government." In Edinburgh, he had studied bookkeeping and merchants' accounts and was "bred up in the mercantile way."[202] In India, he was in the "Office of *Persian* translator, and was employed in writing and translating the public Letters"; he was adept in Bengali. Even his enemies in the Company referred gloomily to the "deep Fund of critical Learning which Mr Johnstone displays in the Country Language." [203] He had a Persian title, *Iftikhar-ud-daulah*, or the "Distinguished of the State." [204] When the East India Company for the first time took on the administration of the interior of India, he was appointed, on the basis of his knowledge of "the Moor's language," to become chief of what he described as the "frontier country" of Midnapore and later of the opulent inland province of Burdwan.

"I . . . was sent alone to negotiate," he wrote later: "I was shut up in a ruinous house" with only "one officer;" "I was . . . assisted only with a writer;" "I continued in the management for almost two years alone." He was alone, and he was at the same time surrounded, in a vast and strange world. Burdwan, he wrote in one of his official reports, "contains near 8000 villages and near two millions of inhabitants." In his survey of land revenues in the province, he employed "from sixty to seventy writers every day for near eight months" and attracted the "resentment and ill will" of "many thousands." [205]

John was deeply involved, meanwhile, in the elaborate politics of the East India Company in India. By 1761 he had become a public figure, as a member of the Company's Council in Calcutta, or the group of officials who served as the "government" of the East India Company's settlements, factories (or trading posts), and enclaves in Bengal. He had risen in the Company's own well-defined hierarchy: in "1751 I was the 80th in the list of Compy. servants from the Governour, and there are not now above six or seven betwixt

me & the president." He described his new life in gran-
diose terms in the letter to James Balmain: "Cicero
never quitted the Senate with more joy than I have felt
today in opposing an Incroachment aimed by the
Presidt. against the publick libertys of the servants."
But he was conscious of conflicting desires with respect
to his political life, and of the extent to which it inter-
fered with his opportunities for business advancement:
"I'd be glad if I were some removes from it were my
own Intrest alone to Guide my Decision."[206]

John was involved, too, in the even more involuted
politics of the East India Company in England, through
an extended correspondence with his friends and brothers.[207] The East India Company's Court of Directors in
London was "a fluctuating, Democratic community of
traders," in William Bolts's description.[208] It exercised, or
tried to exercise, virtually unlimited power over its Council in Calcutta. The British in India, in consequence, spent
very little time talking to Indians, as Ghulam Husain observed, and a great deal of time "answering very long
letters from Europe."[209] The instructions in letters from
what Lord Clive described as the "fluctuating and unsettled" government of the Company in London were
sometimes countermanded in new letters in the next
ships to arrive.[210] It was occasionally the case, in John's
description, that the Company's servants in India would
be sent covenants to sign, renouncing "any presents from
the Indian princes and powers" and meanwhile "received
advice by the same ships which brought the covenants"
that the orders were repealed. He was himself dismissed
from the Company in 1764 and reinstated within a few
months.[211] One of his associates complained, in Calcutta,
that "the Orders from the Court of Directors have been

so fluctuating, that it has really been difficult to collect the Sentiments that were to guide our Conduct Abroad."[212] The directors in London described themselves as equally uninformed, "destitute as we are of the Informations and Lights necessary to guide us."[213]

By 1765 John was well established in the government and commerce of Bengal. He lived in the interior of the country, in the rich provincial city of Burdwan. He was diligent in the affairs of the province: "even when by fatigue and attention my health was hurt, I attended to the public business, though unable to rise from my bed," he wrote after his return to England.[214] An officer in the East India Company's army recalled John's "indefatigable Exertion" in military procurement: "he not only supplied them with Bullocks, but with Money likewise."[215] His youngest brother, Gideon, after the end of the naval war in Jamaica, had joined him in Bengal as a "free merchant," or trader who was not a servant of the East India Company. John, Gideon, and William Bolts had a successful partnership as salt merchants and tax "farmers" or subcontracted revenue officials. John was able to send money to his family in England, through the official channels of the East India Company and the unofficial channels of agents in France.[216] Their father wrote to William in 1762 about "Johns Money" for Sandy, Gideon, George, and "the Rest."[217]

John was well established, too, in the Anglo-Indian society of the times. He bought twenty-three volumes of sermons and a silver saucepan when one of the chaplains of the East India Company died in Calcutta in 1761; in the same sale, "Ramkissen Metre" bought an "Astrological Instrument," "Collychurn Pollit" bought three wigs, and the Company surgeon Tysoe Saul Hancock (who

was Jane Austen's uncle) bought "15 Sheep and a goat."[218]
John was fluent in the almost incomprehensible Anglo-
Indo-Persian of the early administration: "the Mutchulca
of the Vacqueal of *Sabut Jung* expresses fully the Terms
on which this Assignation on the Athats of *Calcutta*,
&c."[219] He had become an extreme instance of what
Lord Clive and the directors of the East India Company
described as the "moderate state": "all barriers being
thus broken down between the English and the country
government."[220]

But John's Indian existence came to an abrupt end in
1765. The crisis began, as so often in the early period of
the British in India, with a dynastic succession in the
family of the nawabs of Bengal, and with the economy
of presents or acknowledgments.[221] John was the leader
of the Company's deputation to the court of the new
nawab in Murshidabad. He was the recipient, there,
of the ritual presents from the "country" government
to the Company's officials, described by Lord Clive
as "small congratulatory Nazurs [or gifts], Elephants,
Horses &c. which I have been under a Necessity of receiving." John, too, was given the "usual" presents (a
"*sarpech* [turban ornament] set with jewels," "a sword,
a male elephant and a title"). He was also given money,
including a present that arrived in a cart, or "hackaree,"
of silver coins in small denominations; there were additional presents for himself, the other members of the
deputation, and his brother Gideon, including from the
"Seats [Seths], the great bankers of India": a total of
some six hundred thousand rupees in presents over a
few days, or about seventy thousand pounds for John
and Gideon.[222]

It was these presents that precipitated or were the pretext for the crisis of 1765. Lord Clive had recently returned from England to Bengal (via Brazil) with a mission, in his own expression, to save India by cleansing the "Augean Stable" of the Company servants' luxury: "What do we hear of, what do we see, but Anarchy, Confusion, and, what is worse, an almost general Corruption," he wrote in a letter to the East India Company in London in May 1765.[223] John was instructed to return from his position in Burdwan to Calcutta, to what he described as a "scene of terror, discontent, dissention, and anxiety," in which "spies, informers, and parasites were every where encouraged."[224] He and his partner, an official called Motiram, were called before a newly established secret committee in Calcutta, to which the new nawab complained that John had failed to offer him "Compliments of Condolance and comfort me," "I was Day and Night in a Flame." There was a dramatic confrontation between Clive and John, in which either Clive (according to Ghulam Husain) or John (according to Lord Macaulay's later account) was reduced to silence; John, accused of extortion, resigned from the Company.[225]

The secret committee, John said in two extended statements in his own defense, had assumed the unconstitutional powers of an "Office of Inquisitors," a tribunal "whose Laws and Rights we know not the Bounds of." "I see Force and Violence take the place of Law and Liberty"; "What Man would admit himself to be judged by Narratives obtained under such Circumstances?" The proceedings, he wrote, were a "Violation of that Liberty & Freedom, that as a *Briton* I had a Right to," the most unprecedented in "any *English* Colony." They were a violation, too, of the rights of his partners, including Motiram, "ignorant of our Laws and Rights," who had been arrested "with all the Terrors attending a Man already convicted and condemned of capital Offences," and Motiram's diwan, or financial officer, seized "under this Terror and Confusion." Motiram, who lived in the Company's enclave, "ought to have had his Indictment, and been allowed Counsel"; he should have been tried "under the *English* flag and by *Englishmen*."[226] Even the raja of Burdwan and the principal adviser of the new nawab had been intimidated, in John's later account: "I received letters from them both, which are in my possession, expressing the utmost dread and apprehension."[227]

The presents he and Gideon had received, John said, were consistent with longstanding custom and with Lord Clive's own earlier practices. The crisis had turned, as so often, on a mistranslation of an expression in the "country language": "Cooch booligani" [*Kuch bolega nahi*] or "[he] will say nothing," which might or might not have constituted a threat to ruin the Seats' or Seths' business, if they had not been willing to "acknowledge" his services.[228] Clive's new secret committee, in John's description, constituted a profound change in the rules of British power in India. The relationships of formal subordination to the Mughal princes, in which the British officials were rewarded with "presents" for their services to Indian rulers, and under which Clive had acquired his own fortune, were now deemed to be illegal and unseemly. The involvement of East India Company officials in the detailed administration of the Indian

princes' land revenue, in which John was so expert—
"ransacking the Accounts of the Country Govert.," in
the expression of one of his friends—was considered to
be unsuited to the dignity of the British.[229] So too were
the elaborate partnerships that John and others had established with Indian merchants, bankers, and revenue
officials. The rhetoric of rights, within the British settlements, was to be restricted in future to British or European subjects.

Lord Clive himself identified his return to Bengal, in
1765, with the end of the old compromises in India—
"Alas! how is the English name sunk! . . . I am come out
with a mind superior to all corruption"—and the disen-
tangling of economic and political power. The destiny of
the East India Company, in these circumstances, was to
become the state: "We must indeed become Nabobs ourselves in Fact, if not in Name, perhaps totally so without
Disguise."[230] It was time "to throw off the Mask" and to
set up as sovereigns of India.[231] In August 1765 Clive
travelled to Murshidabad and Benares and concluded
the treaty with the Mughal emperor that endowed the
East India Company with the *diwani* or revenue administration of Bengal, Bihar, and Orissa—the moment of
destiny that was identified by Clive's biographer, Sir
John Malcolm (whose father was an agent of the Johnstones in the valley of the Esk), as the origin of British
political and economic power, "fixing firm the foundation of the British empire in India."[232]

Over the summer of 1765, John tried to collect as
many of his debts as he could, and the debts of his brothers. His activities in India had become a family enterprise, in his early partnership with Patrick and his later

partnership with Gideon. William and Betty, too, had investments in Calcutta, which John left in the hands of a local lawyer; John made a settlement of 17,141 rupees and 14 annas on Betty.[233] He sold 98,942 rupees' worth of salt to a merchant called Gocul Chund Gosaul, "on account" for the British official who was his successor in Burdwan; he and the official disputed the currency in which the transaction was to be completed, the commission on the exchange rate (the "Batta"), the weight of the salt ("factory weight" or "Bazar weight"), and the translation into English of the contract that John had drawn up in Bengali.[234]

In September 1765 John married Elizabeth Carolina Keene. She was then in her early twenties, and she was by far the most literary of the Johnstones' extended family, in the sense that she had three years earlier published a volume of poetry about, among other things, square roots, boundless space, tears, fears, the rage-fraught ocean, and daring to know (a translation of Horace).[235] She had also, at the age of fourteen or fifteen, published a translation of Ovid in which Dido "talk[ed] like a debauchee," in the view of the poet Oliver Goldsmith.[236] Elizabeth Carolina and her sister had travelled to India in very obscure circumstances in 1761, having received permission from the East India Company to proceed to "their friends" in Madras.[237] They were passengers on an East India Company troop ship called the *Earl of Holdernesse*, which left Portsmouth in convoy, amidst the naval conflicts of the Seven Years' War, and arrived in Mozambique in July 1761. One of the soldiers died of small-pox; the ship lost sight of the convoy. They then proceeded to Madras. But their friends were not there, or were not their friends, and the sisters continued to Calcutta, arriving in the Hooghly River in December 1761.[238] They lived at first "in the Europe Captain's house that brought them to Calcutta" and then in the "gardenhouse" of an East India Company official, an acquaintance of an elderly soldier to whom they had a "letter of particular recommendation."[239]

In the spring of 1762, Elizabeth Carolina and her sister continued to Islamabad, or Chittagong in East Bengal, where they settled in the bungalow of the old soldier.[240] It was a year of epidemic disease and earthquakes: "several shocks of earthquakes . . . so violent as to rend and shatter the only strong brick building we had."[241] But they became involved, in Chittagong, in an awkward dispute with an East India Company official, their landlord in the "gardenhouse," over money that might or might not have been advanced to them by John's partner, William Bolts. In the winter of the same year, they decided to return to Calcutta; the "two Ladies have been determining and undetermining for so long that they have no determination left at last, if ever they had any," their landlord wrote of their impending departure for Lakshmipur, in the delta of the Brahmaputra.[242]

John's and Elizabeth Carolina's marriage, four years after she arrived in India, was considered to be obscure or "clandestine," in the terms of the East India Company's enclave. It led to the suspension of the Company's chaplain for having conducted a marriage ceremony, in this empire within an empire, without the permisssion of the Council.[243] On September 25 John requested a "passage to Europe" for "Mrs Johnstone with her Servants & necessaries," and on October 5 he and Elizabeth Carolina boarded a Bengal-constructed ship, the *Admiral*

Stevens, for the long journey home. This was the end of the early period of the Johnstones' story; in the words of the ship's log and the idiom of the merchant-sovereigns, "came on board Mr Johnstone saluted him with 11 guns."[244]

CHAPTER TWO

COMING HOME

The next period of the Johnstones' lives was the time of their greatest prosperity. John, Elizabeth Carolina, and their servants arrived in England in the spring of 1766, after a more than usually eventful journey, in a vessel later described by the Company as a "crazy" ship. The *Admiral Stevens* made a slow progress through the Indian Ocean ("baffling winds and rain with large confused swell"), stopped for New Year's Eve at the Cape of Good Hope, where an Indian sailor, "Canro Mahomet Lascar," died, another sailor, "Miralabdi Lascar," ran away, and one of the passengers, an aspiring merchant, bought seaweed, birds, and rhinoceros horn. They also stopped at St. Helena, where some stowaways from the garrison "swam off in the dusk of the Evening," and at Ascension Island, where the ship's crew caught a turtle that was said to have contained two thousand eggs. They were carrying a tiny horse and mare for the Prince of Wales ("no more than thirty Inches high"), and the mare was discovered to be "very big with foal." They encountered a ship going from Cadiz to New England, another ship going from Bristol to Barbados, and a Dutch East Indiaman. The *Admiral Stevens* spent a month in Lisbon, after its bow opened off the coast of North Africa. On May 9, 1766, it anchored in the Downs.[1] John had been away from home for sixteen years.

THE FINANCES OF THE FAMILY

The dispute with the East India Company continued in John's new life. He was prosecuted for restitution of the presents he had been given in India, or of everything received "from any of the Indian Princes, Sovereigns, Subahs or Nabobs . . . under the Denomination of Gifts, Rewards, Gratuities, Allowances, Donations or Compensations"; the case in the chancery courts extended to "Money Effects Jewels or otherwise."[2] John asserted his innocence in a letter to the Company, and anticipated the eventual "Approbation . . . of every Honest Man." In a pamphlet published shortly after his return, with an afterword by George, he compared the economy of presents, in which officials in the service of the East India Company received allowances from Indian princes, and the economy of prizes, in which officers in the service of the Royal Navy received a share in the value of the enemy vessels they captured. There was an "injustice," he observed, in changing the regulations of what "should be thought improper" without "a very considerable indulgence" to "those who had engaged in the service upon the faith" of the earlier regulations.[3]

The various lawsuits were eventually dropped, as the outcome of a political compromise within the different factions in the East India Company in London, and John was able to devote himself to the elaborate work of repatriating (or expatriating) his wealth. For the Johnstones, as for so many of the East India Company's servants, the process of bringing back Indian commodities (which were subject to customs regulations) and Indian gold (which was subject to the Company's own regulations) was long and complicated.[4] There were newspaper reports about hidden opulence and a consignment of jewels on the *Admiral Stevens*.[5] Even the ill-destined package of textiles for Betty and Charlotte came in part in a "Chest over Land," in part with a major who never answered George's letters, and in part via Lisbon through the hands of an acquaintance's uncle.[6] With the larger sums John brought back later, the procedures were even more arduous. His letters are full of guilders and rupees and French ships and "correspondence with the gentry in Lisbon and Holland."[7] William and Betty were among the recipients of remittances; William, who had by then changed his name to Pulteney, and had even changed the name of the estate he had acquired, sought the help of David Hume, at the time the under-secretary of state for the Northern Department of the British ministry, in convincing a French bank that a bond on the French East India Company, made out by John's attorneys in Calcutta to "William Johnstone of Auchenbedrigg," should be paid to "William Pulteney" of "Solwaybank."[8]

"I have been repeatedly bubbled & bit," John lamented to William. He and Elizabeth Carolina, who by now had a young son, were obliged to live in London, in connection with his multiple legal cases. The longer he remained in "this City of Sharpers & Pickpockets," he wrote, "the more heartily sick am I of the Law in all its branches."[9] He was preoccupied with the dilemmas of East Indian finance: "I wd. be very glad to borrow money to purchase stock in Britain but will not have any share or connection in anything done in holland," he wrote to William.[10] Even his successes were uneasy. To his brother-in-law, Elizabeth Carolina's brother Talbot Keene, a Church of England clergyman who was involved in his early negotiations over the Indian funds, he wrote that "it is most becoming in us to use our victory with moderation & gentleness . . . I dont wish to do harsh things to others though I should be vexed again to be made the dupe for my lenity & good faith."[11] But by 1770 John had returned to Scotland as a wealthy man, and the prospective owner of vast estates. He considered properties in all parts of the country, offering forty-six thousand pounds for one estate, after "very carefully walking thro every field," inquiring into a second which "is reported as very beautiful & Improveable," and buying a third property, near the Ettrick Forest, which James described as "the Elisium of the Hanginshaw, a Paradise." He was a romantic in his purchases, in William's description, or in "a sort of love fit."[12] John eventually settled with his family and servants in a rented mansion near the ancient castle of Balgonie in Fife.[13]

George, too, returned from West Florida a few months after John arrived from India in early 1767; Alexander returned from Grenada early in 1768.[14] George and Martha Ford lived in Kensington and had four more children: George Lindsay, Sophia, James Primrose, and Alexander Patrick, who were baptised in London.[15] Margaret (Johnstone) Ogilvie's daughter—the little girl who had played in the Jardins du Luxembourg—was also part of the exiles' return of the 1760s.[16] In 1769, the younger Margaret married another Jacobite exile of the second generation, John Wedderburn, who had gone to Jamaica after his father was executed for treason in 1746, and returned with "1000 a year in Jamaica and 5000 well secured at London." It was a marriage of love, and the Wedderburns settled in Perthshire, where Margaret (who had been born in France) commenced legal proceedings to become a naturalized British subject, with the help of her uncles and great-uncles. "I am really ashamed to put you upon so troublesome a piece of business as this probably will be," her husband wrote to William, "but my Wife has no body to apply to but her Mothers Brothers, & lucky she is in having such to apply to, In the ancient Fuedal notions that reign in her fathers Family, Women are only looked on as burdens & not worth taking care of."[17]

Even Gideon, the youngest and most feckless of the brothers, returned home as a fairly rich man, and by 1768 was in search of an estate in the west of Scotland.[18] He had made his way from one extremity of the British imperial world to the other: to Jamaica with George in 1757; in Jamaica again from 1759 to 1761; to Bengal in 1762 to join John. In 1764 James applied on his behalf, with a falsified attestation of his age, for an official position in the East India Company.[19] His whereabouts were frequently a mystery to his family: William was informed by an acquaintance at the Admiralty, in 1773, that "there have within these four days, been several persons to enquire about him at the office, some saying they heard he was dead, others that they had heard he was dying, and past all hopes of recovery."[20] But Gideon was in several respects one of the most enterprising of all the Johnstones. George's old Florida secretary, James "Ossian" Macpherson, even heard from his cousin in Madras in 1774 that "Governor Johnstone['s]. . . brother Gideon has made a fortune selling the water of the Ganges to pilgrims who cannot get to Benares. His price: one Rupee per bottle."[21]

Of the Johnstones who stayed at home, it was William Pulteney, with the resources of his wife Frances, who came to assume the position of the family banker, or the financier of distant opportunities. He lent money to Alexander for his plantation in Grenada in 1764; he participated in John's enterprises in Calcutta in 1765; in 1766 he bought land in West Florida. Alexander also borrowed money from John to finance the Grenada plantation and the purchase of additional slaves: "Sandy . . . has drawn another Bill at 12m sight for £370 on you & me for 12 Negroes which, very much against my Inclination I have accepted," John wrote to William in 1767.[22] William bought his own slave plantation in Grenada and estates in the West Indian islands of Dominica and Tobago, where one of the Johnstones' nephews was later governor.[23] He was involved in investments in the French-Scottish tobacco trade with Virginia, and in what he described as the "exchange & change" of buying Portugese funds with "Dutch or fflemish money," to be loaned to the West Indies on the security of estates in Jamaica.[24] He was at the same time an increasingly English figure, engaged in the development of the resorts of the English south coast and in the beautification of the fashionable town of Bath, owned in part by his wife's family and a favorite spa of the newly rich.[25] William, too, like Alexander in Grenada, constructed a virtual image of their family home: there is a Westerhall Street, still, in the English coastal resort of Weymouth.

Charlotte, the youngest sister, left home in 1763 with the childhood friend of the family, James Balmain, who had become an officer of the excise, in an elopement that was a matter of deep distress to her parents: "Charlote has just now run of with the ministers Son, its an unlucky fancy for women to get it into their head that they must have a Husband," her aunt wrote in January 1763.[26] Barbara, the oldest sister, lived in retirement in Edinburgh after her separation from her husband, Charles Kinnaird. She was occupied with the legal disputes of her estranged husband and with the prospects, in "the East or West Indies," of the family's distant connections; she provided advice about positions in West Florida and "a very kind letter" of introduction to her brother James for the poet William Julius Mickle, who was a cousin of their uncle Walter.[27] Barbara's own daughter made an unsuitable marriage in the summer of 1765, at the age of fifteen or sixteen, to a medical student from Cambridge, Massachusetts, Edmund Dana. To his American family, Dana wrote reassuringly that his wife's uncles included "the Govrs. Johnstone of W. Florida and one of the East India Provinces."[28] Barbara Kinnaird died in Edinburgh later in the same year, in October 1765.[29]

Betty continued to live at Westerhall and took over the management of the estate, having been reunited with her mother. She was at the center, still, of the brothers' and sisters' elaborate exchange of information with respect to marriages, separations, and distant encounters in the East Indias. She was also, by the time the brothers returned, an intermediary in the family's economic relationships. A very long letter of December 1764, from their father to William, about leases, litigation with tenants, the politics of the East India Company, John's position in Burdwan, and the price of claret in Bengal, was in Betty's hand. She was engaged, as the owner of obligations in Calcutta (John's settlement of 17,141 rupees), in the negotiations to remit the rupees to Scotland via the French or the Dutch, and in the intricacies of the distinction between English and Scottish law, with respect to deeds of settlement. She paid James's bills and negotiated on John's behalf about the "right of Ultimus" and bills at forty-five days' sight; she was solicited to provide instructions about George's political interests in a nearby English constituency, and when James was in trouble in Norfolk, he asked her to send, by ship, "four Masons and Two Labourers." She was the source, above all, of details of fact: "Betty knows how much the Quit Rent is," James wrote to John in 1770.[30]

Of the brothers, only James was still in difficult material circumstances by the late 1760s. He and Louisa had moved to Norfolk, near the property of her maternal relations, which he had described, in his quarrel with William, as the sweetest spot in the universe. They lived in a rented house and were still in debt; in 1772 they moved into a single room, "thro Frost & Snow," to save the next quarter's rent. He felt that he was by now, in his mid-forties, an old man. His great object was to build a house, as he wrote to John: as the "Acidity of Life aproaches Mirth Chearfulness & Gayity fly before Silence Wrinkles and Grey hairs." He was frequently ill: "I have been almost dead and what is worse rotten before I was dead," he wrote to Charlotte's husband, James Balmain.[31]

James borrowed money from everyone he could, including Betty, Charlotte, John, Alexander, James Balmain, and his lawyer, against the diminishing security of the Westerhall estates. Louisa also borrowed money from their lawyer—"could Paper blush, the Colour of this would be much changed uppon your Perusal," she wrote—in order to buy a lottery ticket. "Tis not for my self I am so Sanguine for Money would be no additional

Happiness to me, but could I be Instrumental to Procure an Addition, to my Dearest Johnstone," she explained, and concluded with detailed instructions: "If I should be so Fortunate to have a Prize the sooner I hear the Better . . . But if the Contrary I would not Hear till the Lottery is over I will have Expectation at Least."[32]

James was a "strange odd man," in the description of their uncle Walter.[33] His illnesses were redoubtable: "I was siezed all at once with that species of a Putrid Fever called Mille Harpies," he wrote to John in 1771; "In Two Days my whole Body was covered with Pustles as large as nuts and my Skin was Hot as if I had been roasted alive."[34] "The Qualifications of the Head have been dealt me with a Scanty Hand," he wrote to an old acquaintance from the valley of the Esk, Gilbert Petrie; "those of the Heart you may depend on." He was also, in the letters that he wrote from Norfolk and that he and Louisa copied into his agricultural journal, a continuing source of information about the interior lives of the family, and of consolation in difficult times. He was lavish with family counsel, in relation to the mind and the body. "Grieved am I every Time I think of my Dear John," he wrote to Betty: "Seventeen broiling years in Bengal is but Part of his Disorder" and "Tranquillity of mind is more necessary for the Radical Cure of His Disease than keeping his feet constantly dry." To Alexander he wrote, "Leave Law Sugar Bills & Acceptancys for Air Exercise Health & Friendship." To John he wrote about Betty, "Sister Betty is a Martyr to the delicate sensibility of Her Heart," and about George: "Geo. Body suffers for the Labor of his mind. Disease pursues Genius, as Night the Day. He must cease to think to be well."[35]

In the months before their father died in 1772, James had "not Credit for a shilling." "Every Creditor I owe has insisted in a way to plain to be misunderstood that they must have their money," he wrote to John, and "my Mind is in such Perturbation that I cannot write my Dear Father."[36] But the Johnstones were in a collective sense an extremely wealthy family. John and William had bought landed property in the vicinity of the family estates and across Scotland. Even the itinerant Uncle Walter had come home to one of William's properties near Westerhall: "I am wearied of wandering to & fro upon the face of the Earth," he wrote to William, and "in my dreams I am flaying burning Limeing Sowing Hedging Planting Shooting and fishing."[37] John devoted himself to the improvement of his father's estate: "go on with it my Dr Betty & get so many Good Ash Trees as you can get," he wrote in 1767. "I wd have Oak, Ash, Fir, Beech, Elm, Plantree, Chesnut & Walnut." He wanted gooseberries and "Alpine Strawberries as I hope to help to gather some of them this year."[38] The sons were richer by far than their parents. "My surprise is not that the debts are so great, but how he managed upon so trifling a Reversion for so long a period," John wrote to William when he and James went through their father's papers after his death in 1772. "I cannot help blushing when I compare the moderation of my fathers Expences with my own disbursements."[39]

THE POLITICS OF THE EAST AND WEST INDIES

The Johnstones were involved, within a short time of their return, in a family business of politics. John, George, and Alexander had all been prominent in the miniscule political institutions of the British empire: the East India Company's Council and the Mayor's Court in Calcutta, the General Assembly of the province of West Florida, the bicameral and bilingual legislature of the island of Grenada.[40] At home, five of the brothers aspired to become members of the House of Commons. Elections, in this high period of the unreformed parliament, were a contest of fortunes, and John and William's new riches were invested in political influence.[41] George, even in Florida, had been eager for a parliamentary career, and his prospects were transformed by John's return. "Considering my brothers Johnston in point of fortune," William wrote to a political friend in 1766, "I was not myself so much perswaded of the propriety of placing him immediately in that house. But the arrival of my brother John from India has removed that objection. His generosity is without any Limits."[42] "Our friend George Johnston is coming home; his brother, the Indian, desires to bring George and himself into Parliament, at any rate George," David Hume's cousin wrote to the same political friend in 1767.[43]

Four of the Johnstone brothers, James, William, George, and John, were eventually elected to the House of Commons, and from 1768 to 1805, there was always at least one of them in parliament, and sometimes as many as three.[44] The general election of 1768 was a family enterprise, with five of the brothers involved in an arc of constituencies from St. Ives in Cornwall to Cromartyshire in the Highlands of Scotland. Only William was initially successful (in one of the three constituencies in which he was a candidate). James was defeated in St. Ives and John in Haslemere in Surrey, in a contest that involved the friends of Lord Clive, his old opponent in

Calcutta.[45] Alexander, too, was unsuccessful, in Wootton Bassett in Wiltshire.[46] George was defeated in Carlisle, where Betty came to help with the organization of the election: he "stood on the *hustings* for eight days during the election, bowing to every voter who was so obliging as to poll for [him]."[47] John reported gloomily to William, in the summer of 1768, that "James was gone down to St. Ives to prepare Matters for the feigned trial," or the aftermath of a more than usually elaborate election, and "George is expected down at the Carlisle assises where some actions are to be tried against one Sturdy, an agent, for bribery."[48] George was later selected for the spectacularly corrupt constituency of Cockermouth in Cumberland and in 1774 moved on to Appleby in Westmorland, of which a contemporary political history related that "Hog-sties have been deemed freeholds here, and purchased . . . at a price exceeding all belief."[49] John was eventually elected in 1774, in a brutal contest for the Dysart Burghs in Fife, Adam Smith's home constituency.[50] James was elected in 1784 for the Dumfries Burghs.

The Johnstones were in parliament during a period of intense political drama over the two great questions of the American Revolution and the reform of the East India Company, and they were closely involved in both. The disputes over American taxation, from the Stamp Act to the American Declaration of Independence and the American wars, were juxtaposed, in the House of Commons, to the initially even more acrimonious debates over the "revolution" of 1765 in India, the overthrow of Mughal power, and the revenues provided by the East India Company to the British state.[51] The Johnstones' private interests were intertwined at every point with these public dramas, in the course of which George said of the British parliament that "the eye of the world is upon her."[52] George and William were members of the Select Committee of the House of Commons which was charged in 1772 with investigating the recent history of the East India Company, including the history of John and Gideon's presents and elephants.[53] They were relentless in their pursuit of Lord Clive, John's enemy in Calcutta, who had in turn pursued John for so long in India and in the English courts. "He & all his Brothers are my most inveterate Enemies," Clive wrote of William to a political friend. "You must know his former name was Johnston."[54] "You and George have done for poor Clive," one of their friends wrote to William, after Clive died by his own hand in 1775, in the aftermath of the investigation of his own presents; "He treated himself as he did the India Company, made it great and cut its throat."[55]

William, in what he described as "these golden times," became an expert on public finance, sinking funds, and the jurisprudence of mortgages.[56] He was a specialist, in particular, on the legislation and litigation relating to mortgages on slaves, including in the island of Grenada; the rights of foreign creditors who were the holders of mortgages on British sugar plantations; and the rights of British creditors who held mortgages on slaves on formerly French plantations.[57] He was interested in parliamentary procedure and in what he described, in a contentious debate over the civil law of property in Quebec, as "reciprocal decorum."[58] "Had we all the money in Europe at a reasonable interest, and could we actually employ it in trade, so much the better," he declared in support of the West Indian loans; "We should thus be the bankers of Europe."[59]

But the Johnstones were involved, too, in the highest and most abstract rhetoric of resistance to oppression. George's first major speech in parliament, in 1770, was an elegy to "the liberal genius of our civil policy," and a denunciation of the despotism of military government in British North America, which he compared to the depredations of Roman proconsuls in Africa, as depicted by Tacitus: "military establishments were instituted to defend our civil rights, not to destroy them."[60] He was a much admired orator in the early years of the American revolution. He fought a duel with another member over the "honour of the nation," while ill ("he had at that time an open wound in his arm, and his legs very much swelled").[61] As the American crisis deepened, George was a continuing critic of the ministry's "cruelty and oppression," and an apparently enthusiastic friend of the colonists, "unanimous against our power from Nova Scotia to Georgia." He commended the "people of New England" for their "wisdom, courage, temperance, fortitude" and anticipated that the slaves of the Americans would rally to their masters' cause—"in general, I must also observe, that masters are kind to their slaves"—and concluded in 1776 that "the war was diabolical."[62] A young Edinburgh mathematician, Walter Minto, who was the tutor of George and Martha Ford's older sons, described him in 1777 as "a man who opens the ground in which Ed. Burke Charles Fox & Col. Barré tread after him in the Parliament of G. Britain the most august assembly in the world."[63]

John was most notable, in parliament, as an opponent of the act to suspend habeas corpus, proposed by the British government with respect to prisoners seized overseas, which he described as an "arbitrary, cruel and diabolical" assault on "the grand palladium of the British constitution, the freedom of men's persons." "The confinements, commitments, massacres, and the whole train of consequences that would arise from such a system of punishment, revenge, and retaliation, probably on both sides of the Atlantic, filled his mind with horror and anxiety," he declared in 1777.[64] He, too, was in favor of the American colonists and against "those romantic dreams of American conquest, and unconditional legislative supremacy."[65] He was preoccupied, in particular, with the freedom of movement and of emigration. In a parliamentary debate of 1776 on emigration, he objected to an evocation of the "principles of liberty" in Scotland: "he could not agree in that description of a Country which . . . had stopt the Free subjects of Britain from going to any part of his Majesty's Dominions they thought proper."[66] As a justice of the peace in the county of Stirling, he defended the rights of poor Scots against the efforts of government to prevent emigration to North America: "Johnstone was compleatly absurd he spoke most violently against the Justices of Peace interfering said such a Stop woud be illegal that we had no Power, he said he wished there were more of the Common People there that he might inform them that they were their own Masters, & might emigrate if they chose it, in short it is impossible to tell you the whole of his absurdities," the local member of parliament complained, on a rainy October night in 1775.[67]

In the conflict over the reform of the East India Company, the Johnstones were similarly prominent. George described the Company, in the spirit of John's partner from Bengal, William Bolts, who had himself arrived in London, as a "monstrous heap of partial, arbitrary, political inconsistencies," sovereign-merchants and merchant-sovereigns.[68] The Johnstones even associated the two dramas of empire explicitly, in the West and the East. "The distribution of justice should flow from the throne," George said in a parliamentary debate in 1772: the king should assert his own sovereignty over Bengal, and should then "grant the lands to the East India Company, as was done in the cases of New England and several other of our chartered colonies"; the situation of Philadelphia "fully illustrates and vindicates my idea."[69]

George connected the politics of the East India Company and the American Revolution even more immediately, a few months later, when he moved a resolution in the General Court of the East India Company to obtain an act of parliament that would enable the Company "to export their surplus Teas to foreign Markets, clear of all Drawbacks and Duties, as well as to take off the three percent Duty in America."[70] It was the legislation that followed this resolution, later known as the Tea Act, that was the immediate cause of the "Boston Tea Party" in December 1773, in which American protesters, dressed as "Indians," threw consignments of tea into Boston harbor.[71] The "detestable tea, sent out by the East India Company" was evidence, for the Americans, of a "political plan" on behalf of a company that had obtained its "exclusive privilege of trade" by "bribery and corruption"; the watchmen on their rounds should be instructed to "call out every night, *past Twelve o'Clock, beware of the East-India Company*."[72] George himself lamented, in March 1774, that "the poor India Company, Sir, is the butt between America and England. I much advised the directors to desist from exporting tea to America. I foresaw it was a measure that would produce no good effect."[73]

The Johnstones presented themselves, in the debates over the East India Company, as the defenders of the oppressed people of India. In the years following John's departure from Calcutta in 1765, the East India Company had consolidated its control of the inland or "country" commerce of Bengal, including the collection of land taxes and the sale of commodities for inland consumption (salt, betel-nut, and tobacco). The British officials increased their own tax revenues and disrupted the long-established arrangements for security of provisions. In 1769–71 the country was desolated by a terrible famine, in which some two million people died, many of them in John's old district of Burdwan.[74] George spoke eloquently in parliament on behalf of "those men, wearing few clothes," who were "squeezed in [Lord Clive's] engines of oppression" in Bengal.[75] He looked forward to a new spirit of revolution in India; in the expression of the chairman of the Select Committee, of which he and William were members, "Good God! what a call—the native of Indostan, born a slave . . . a patient, submissive, willing subject to eastern despotism, first begins to feel, first shakes his chains, for the first time complains under the preeminence of British tyranny."[76]

John himself was sufficiently restored, by February 1771, that he wrote from Scotland to the East India Company with an offer to return to India as governor of Bengal, a position in the bequest of the Company's directors, and to express his conviction, "from a conscious Integrity," that there was no one who had "served the Company with more Zeal" or who had administered the revenues of Bengal "with less Oppression to the Natives."[77]

But his offer was refused, and the Company appointed Warren Hastings instead. James, in a letter of commiseration to John, expressed his condolences, too, for the people of India: "to me who think that Benevolence Justice & Humanity ought by no means to be restricted to Collour": "I am sorry so worthless a Villain as a Friend of Clives must be, has got the government of such a number of the Human Species committed to Him."[78]

THE ARTS AND SCIENCES
OF ENLIGHTENMENT

The Johnstones were politically established in this high summer of their lives, and they were established, too, in the culture of the enlightenment. They returned, after their overseas ventures, to the periphery of the high philosophical world of the English and Scottish enlightenments. David Hume described George as a "very gallant, sensible young Fellow," whom "I have seen pretty often," and he even expressed his opinion about the complicated relationships between the brothers and sisters, or about what George described as "the simple engaging & domestick Situations of Mankind." "I may fairly say my Ideas concerning my Sisters Conduct were in every thing correspondent with the Letter you sent me," George wrote to Hume before he left for Florida.[79] "Pulteney's Behaviour . . . is noble," Hume wrote of William in 1769 and sent the proofs of his *History of England* to him for franking (to save the cost of postage, since William, as a member of parliament, had the privilege of free letters).[80] John was "on intimate terms with Dugald Stewart, Playfair, Robertson & all the Literary people of Scotland."[81] There were portraits of the Johnstones by the most eminent painters of the times. William was painted by Thomas Gainsborough in the early 1770s—an odd portrait, in which he stands between his two lives and his two identities, an English springtime scene to his left, and to his right a dark and frightening forest, like the first scene of *Macbeth*.[82] His daughter Henrietta Laura Pulteney was painted by Angelica Kauffmann, dancing in a glade in a white muslin dress.[83] There is a painting by George Romney of "Mrs Johnstone," which is almost certainly of Martha Ford, with one of their younger children.[84] John and Betty were painted by Henry Raeburn, in conversation with their grandniece Margaret, the daughter of Margaret Wedderburn, with Betty in a fine white bonnet and a pale blue ribbon.

The richest of the Johnstones, William and John, became patrons of architectural projects. Robert and James Adam, the Scottish architects, built the Pulteney Bridge in Bath for William, with "Tuscan porches" and Venetian windows, and they prepared plans for the redecoration of Shrewsbury Castle with "rich gothic details" (which were never carried out). John commissioned two mausolea, one at the estate where he eventually settled—at Alva in the Ochil Hills of Clackmannanshire—and one in the Westerkirk church near the family home of Westerhall, with "a fluted frieze with occasional ox-skulls." He also commissioned the most extraordinary project of classical estate buildings for Alva, which were again never built: "a circular court 100 feet across. In the centre is a round dung hill. . . . Over the dung hill there is a round pigeon-house that supports a short octagonal turret with a pyramidal roof. The court is surrounded by eight 2-storey blocks with pyramidal roofs," and eight one-story blocks, including "a brewhouse, a poultry house, a dairy, a wash house, a laundry, a slaughter room, coach houses, a cart shed, stables, a cow house, a carpenter's shop and a smith's shop."[85]

George, of all the brothers, had a predilection for the company of poets and philosophers. After "Ossian" Macpherson, in West Florida, he took with him as secretary on one of his naval postings to Lisbon their cousin William Julius Mickle, the translator of the *Lusiad* by Luis de Camöens, the "Epic Poem of Commerce" and of the Portugese empire.[86] James, too, was "enchanted" with the *Lusiad*, and liked to declaim "his most admired parts."[87] On a later political mission to Philadelphia and New York, George's secretary was the philosopher Adam Ferguson. He even thereby caused great offense to the young Jeremy Bentham, to whom he had almost promised Ferguson's position, and whom he regaled with complaints about his brother William; he was said to be "very fond" of Bentham's *Fragment on Government* and "used to carry it about with him in his pocket."[88]

George was an observer of the science of enlightenment and of the connections of global commerce. The transport of goods "thro' the trackless Waves, by the Power of the Clouds" was the most surprising "of all the Wonders which the white Men perform," one of his Choctaw interlocutors was reported as having observed in West Florida in 1765, and George returned many years later to the idyll of communication. "After the Changeable incredible Account I have given you of our Politicks," he wrote to Ossian Macpherson's cousin in India, "I have nothing to add but an Account of a new discovery they have made in France of transporting themselves from Place to Place in the Air by means of what is called Air Balloons." "What an Animal it is!" he exclaimed of Montgolfier's invention, in the language of the Choctaw colloquy:

> The Pen Ink Paper & Marks arresting my thoughts & sending them in a Ship to my Friend at the extremity of the Globe Passing through the trackless Waves born long by the Power of the Clouds directed by the invisible Power of the Loadstone & bringing back the Treasures of the East is sufficiently surprizing but all our Inventions seem lost in this. Who shall say that all this Merchandize may not pass through the Air.[89]

The Johnstones were interested, too, in the study of history. Their enduring objective, since well before David Hume's miserable winter with their rich cousin, had been to find evidence, somewhere in the manuscript rooms and libraries of Scotland, of the family's noble descent. They were preoccupied, in particular, with their ancestor, or purported ancestor, Matthew de Johnstone and his involvement in the battles of the 1450s. Charlotte's husband, James Balmain, was occupied in the quest, together with an undiligent research assistant in the Advocates' Library in Edinburgh, known as "Mr. B—," or "Bruce." "I observe," James wrote to his brother-in-law, that Mr. B— "has consulted only Printed Books These have been Thumbed over & over again to no Purpose."[90] Even Alexander, returned from Grenada, corresponded with their cousin William Julius Mickle, in Oxford, about the "extract from Bishops Kennedys history in the Bodleian library, relative to the particulars of the Battle of Arkinholme" (of 1455) and the "opportunity of employing any person (who I mean to pay for their trouble) to take the copy."[91]

The brothers' and sisters' own children were educated in the enlightened spirit of the times. Barbara's daughter was sent to a boarding school, and her son, as her husband Charles Kinnaird reported to William, was "very fond of Vergil & talks very freely with Ovid."[92] George's cosmopolitan principle, in the "system of education" he designed for two of his and Martha Ford's sons, when they set off for Pisa with their tutor Walter Minto in the summer of 1776, was that the experience of "different Climates & different Governments gives a more liberal Turn of Thought & prevents Illiberal Prejudices while it enables us at the same time to determine truly between the Good & the Bad." The children were to read Plutarch, Ossian, and "the Beautiful Parts of Scripture . . . but without ever engaging them in any Controversy on Religion—only as a history of what is passed & what is now contended for on different sides." The "national character" of the people they were among was to be "learned from the Sober Frugal Middling Ranks." But life in Italy was not only an education in the "various Revolutions of different Communities": "Let them go to Opera or Comedy every Saturday," and "Grapes in particular they may eat of for ever."[93] To his own brother in Scotland, Minto wrote of the two children, whom he described as "my Boys," that George was "a father who loves them to distraction."[94]

THE RUINS OF THE INDIES

This, then, was the existence of the Johnstones in their happiest period: making speeches about the Roman empire, negotiating mortgages from Amsterdam bankers, reading aloud their favorite verses of Portugese epics, reflecting on the future of flight, and gathering alpine strawberries in the valley of the Esk. But their idyll was not uninterrupted, and they had not left the Indies entirely behind them. Adam Smith wrote of the servant of the East India Company in Bengal that he "wishes to get out of the country . . . as soon as he can," and "the day after he has left it and carried his whole fortune with him, it is perfectly indifferent though the whole country was swallowed up by an earthquake."[95] This is close to the judgement of Ghulam Husain, the Persian historian: "intent on his own views, he little cares about what ruins shall remain after him."[96] But the Johnstones carried the ruins of the East and West Indies with them, or the memories of the ruins, into English politics and into the Scottish hills.

Alexander was thus selected, by a group of French and English proprietors in Grenada, to protest against the "illegal, grievous, cruel, oppressive and unjust acts" of the island's governor, to the highest political instance in the empire, the Privy Council of the king's closest advisers in London.[97] He was occupied, for the first years of his return to England, with the preparation of the petition, its eight articles of charge against the governor, and the pamphlets published in support of the proprietors' case. The new British empire in the West Indies, in his and his friends' description, was a scene of private and public desolation. Alexander's own grievance, that he had been convicted of mutiny at the instigation of the governor, was intertwined with high constitutional theory, with descriptions of religious conflict between the French and the English planters, and with the evocation of an island society obsessed with the revolution of the "maroon" or runaway slaves.

The Grenada crisis was the outcome of the disregard by the government in London of "the general rights of mankind," Alexander and his friends wrote in one of their pamphlets, *A Narrative of the Proceedings upon the Complaint against Governor Melvill*, and of "a total indifference in all matters that do not immediately concern our own particular interest."[98] There was religious oppression, of a most "illiberal" sort, against the king's new Catholic subjects; there was a confusion of laws and constitutions; there were individuals who had acted indiscriminately in a legislative or judicial capacity; there were public documents that had been suppressed and secreted; there were rights under "the rule of Civil Law" and rights under the "Code Noir," or the French regulations for the government of slaves. One of Alexander's associates had been imprisoned, "in the same gaol with the run-away negroes and malefactors of every class," for the crime of reading in French "in a tumultuous manner."[99]

There were also peculiarly Atlantic oppressions, in an island of which some ninety percent of the population were enslaved Africans and that was traversed, like so many American colonies in the 1760s and 1770s, by the substantial revolution of escaped slaves in the interior of the country.[100] The process before the Privy Council on Alexander's case provided a glimpse of distant horrors for the lords of council. The "severest & most cruel tortures" had been used to extort a confession of murder from five slaves, according to Alexander's complaint. The governor, Alexander's opponent, justified the use of torture, in response, "in cases of alarm or danger": "consider to what imminent destruction the few white inhabitants . . . would be exposed, were slaves (since slavery *is* permitted) liable to no other methods of examination, trial or punishment, than free persons." There was an account of an extraordinary political crisis over a slave named Augustine, a fugitive who had gone over to the side of government and who had enticed several of the other maroons to surrender. Augustine, who was himself accused of rape and murder, was then freed, as described in Alexander's complaint, by "the passing of a Bill in *two hours* thro' both houses, entituled, 'A Bill to free Augustine.' "[101]

The personal, judicial, and political crises in Grenada were intertwined, in what Alexander and his friends described as a "multiplicity of honours."[102] There were justices of the peace who were judges in military cases, and justices of the peace who tortured slaves.[103] Alexander's own cause was a family enterprise in which George went to the Privy Council office "in the name of my brother, who is now ill and confined to his bed." William was one of the signatories of the "Memorial of the Proprietors of Lands in the Island of Grenada."[104] But the Privy Council was ill informed, in the account of Alexander and his friends, even with respect to the circumstance that "slaves are freehold, and considered as landed property in all the West india islands." Of the ten lords of council, three failed to attend on the second day of the hearings, according to the *Narrative of the Proceedings*; one said in the course of the proceedings that torture "was always used against slaves"; and one chose "to write letters of business in the middle of the most interesting point."[105] The Privy Council rejected Alexander's petition.

In John's case it was his partner in the salt trade, William Bolts, who followed him to England, and with whom John, William, George, Betty, and Elizabeth Carolina were closely involved.[106] In a three-volume book published in England in 1772, Bolts presented a frightening and Ovidian depiction of his and John's opponents in Calcutta, including Lord Clive and Harry Verelst, the East India Company official who had been so discontented with Elizabeth Carolina and her sister. It was the "multiform characters" of English oppression that were so insidious for Bolts in India, as they were for Alexander in the West Indies. The East India Company's Council were justices of the peace, judges of appeal, tax collectors, "Merchants, or Sovereigns," "all of which different characters they can and do assume, as occasion requires. . . . [It would] be difficult to trace those gentlemen through their various metamorphoses."

There were awful tales of debt and oppression, of the imprisonment of John's partner Motiram, and of "Radhoo Tagoor, a black merchant of Calcutta," who tried to collect a small debt from a member of the council on behalf of a sail-maker and "was immediately seized by his peons."[107] Bolts's book was a defense of the dissident East India Company officials, of other European and Asian residents of India, and of Indians living under British rule, whom Bolts described as new British subjects. "In speaking of British subjects, we would be understood to mean his Majesty's newly-acquired Asiatic subjects, as well as the British emigrants residing and established in India," Bolts wrote: "many millions of civilized, inoffensive and industrious inhabitants," valiant in war and tolerant in religion, who had been the denizens, under the "*black Nabobs*," of an opulent commercial and manufacturing economy, but were oppressed, under British rule, by "unbounded despotism."[108]

The years following John's return to England were a period of intense political interest in events in India. There was news from India, and there were also individuals, merchants and translators and experts on Persian seals, who made the long journey by land or sea.[109] The parliamentary debates over the East India Company, in which the Johnstones were so involved, were reported in intricate detail. "One and forty times did the House sit upon this business," Edmund Burke said in the House of Commons of the East India debates, with their books upon books, and papers upon papers.[110] The famine of 1770–71 in Bengal was described as having been caused by taxation, or monopoly, or both, as the Company's servants protected their permits and orders, even at the worst of the crisis. A correspondent of the *Gentleman's Magazine* depicted a "famished multitude," with the dead "mangled by dogs, jackals, and vultures." A later account, in 1772, wrote of the "monstrous and unconstitutional powers, with which our nabobs in that country have been permitted to invest themselves," such that they acquired "a monopoly of the necessaries of life," and of Lord Clive, that "he signed the death warrant for two millions of his fellow creatures."[111] The East India Company was charged, in George's summary, with imposing a system of arbitrary taxation and "regulations, contrary to the law of nature," that "produces famine and all other evil consequences that have followed in Bengal."[112]

William Bolts was followed to England, in the midst of these evocations of distant horrors, by two more of John's acquaintances from Bengal, Armenian-Persian merchants from Calcutta and Benares. They had been "seized in the most sudden, cruel, and inhuman Manner" on the order of East India Company officials, in the course of a dispute over commercial permits; these were the same officials who had been John and Elizabeth Carolina's opponents in Calcutta. The Armenians had travelled to England, they said, to seek justice against their oppressors, which they pursued over a period of eight years in a sequence of legal instances ending in the House of Lords. Their petition was read to the House of Commons through the good offices of the Johnstones; George declared that he was happy to defend a "poor oppressed Armenian merchant," who was a Christian, as it happened, but who could "equally" have been "Mussulman and Gentoo [Hindu]": "it was not because he was a Christian that I presented his petition, but because he was a human being and fellow-creature, and because his case brought the situation of all the inhabitants of Bengal fairly before the House."[113]

In the merchants' civil case, John appeared as a witness, together with Bolts and an Armenian merchant from Cronstadt, a native of Ispahan, now living in Amsterdam, speaking through a translator. The plaintiff charged that he had been imprisoned on the covert orders of the English officials, who had conveyed their intentions in a "rukah," or an instruction included within an instruction. John's evidence turned, as so often, on his identity as an interpreter who "had the charge of the Persian correspondence for a considerable time," and who could inform the court about letters within letters and "his idea of a Rukah," on which "anything strong & pointed" is conveyed in the East: "it is a slip of paper generally conveyed in the body of the ltre [letter]."[114]

INTRAN BELL ALIAS BELINDA

The universe of India came home, even to John's new estates in Scotland. 1771 was a year much like any other in this period of the Johnstones' lives. John was at home in his rented house in Balgonie in Fife, working on the journal entries for his and William's partnerships in India and in the Grenada plantation: an "infinite labour," he wrote to William, but "I know of nothing to interrupt me." He heard from Gideon in Basra and from George, who was ill with sciatica.[115] Charlotte and her husband came to stay with him in the spring. He and Elizabeth Carolina went to Westerhall over the summer to visit his mother, who was seriously ill; his mother came to stay in September. James, in Norfolk, was corresponding with James Balmain about the unending search for their ancestors' titles, and with Uncle Walter about decoy ducks and the London poulterers: "Life is a Continued Dream; Happyest is He, not perhaps the Richest, who has the manyest of them, so much for Philosophy; now for the Decoy."[116]

But a very different drama had unfolded in the summer and autumn of 1771, in the sheriff's court of the town of Cupar in Fife, and in the circuit court of Perth. In the last days of June 1771, the body of a baby boy, wrapped in a linen cloth and "having the marks of violence" upon him, was found in the river Leven, not far from John and Elizabeth Carolina's home. The mother could be identified, and she was taken to Cupar, where she was indicted for the crime of child murder. She was described in the indictment as "Bell alias Belinda a black Girl or woman from Bengal in the East Indies, the slave or servant of John Johnstone." In the record of her interrogation on July 4, 1771, she was described, or described herself, as a "Black Girl who calls herself Bell or Belinda." She said that she had come from Bengal with the Johnstones, that she had stayed with them for four years in London, and that she had then come with them to Scotland. On the previous Sunday, she said, she had "brought forth a child which she says was dead born That she bore the child in her Ladys Bedroom and no Body was present with her at the time nor did she ever tell any Body that she was with Child and that the Child was a Boy and she keeped it two days after it was born and then carried it away in a Cloth . . . and threw the Child and Cloth into the water." "Mr Johnston and his Lady were from home sometime before the Child was Born and were not come back when she was brought here."[117]

Eighteen witnesses were identified, six of them from the household of a neighboring tenant and four from the Johnstones' household, including "Molly a black girl, the slave or servant of John Johnstone." Bell or Belinda, it was said, had left the "bed and room" where she usually slept with the other servants, and had gone to the bedroom of Mrs Johnstone. In the words of the indictment, "[you said] that you was too hot or that you had catched cold by bathing in the River," and "you did continue altogether or for the most part in said bed room or dressing room 'till you was delivered . . . and you did remain mostly by yourself in said appartments for sometime after your said Delivery." There was no evidence of what had really happened; the indictment said that Bell or Belinda murdered her child "by strangling him, or knocking him on the head," or "by some other violent means." But under the "act anent murdering of children" that was then in force, even to have concealed a pregnancy, or to have given birth alone, was evidence of murder, and Bell or Belinda was committed for trial, at the Northern Circuit Court in Perth.[118] A servant called Mary Burgess, who had been convicted of child murder ten years earlier by the same court, had been hanged in Perth in 1762, and "publickly dissected and anatomized."[119]

On the morning set for the trial, in September 1771, an officer of the court called John Swinton, the sheriff depute of the county of Perth, asked the court for a continuance of one day on the grounds that Bell or Belinda did not "understand either the Language or Laws" of the country, and having been brought to Perth only two days earlier, "had no opportunity of applying for assistance with her Tryal sooner." The continuance was granted, and the trial opened the following morning. The defendant was described as "Bell alias Belinda a black Girl or woman from Bengall in the East Indies the Slave or Servant of John Johnston." There were two circuit judges who came from Edinburgh, of whom one was the Johnstones' maternal uncle (the uncle who had given Betty forty shillings). Bell or Belinda was present in court: "Intran Bell alias Belinda," in the legal Latin of the Scottish bar.[120] When she was asked to plead, she presented a new petition, signed by two notaries public on behalf of the petitioner, "who declares she cannot write, and who touched the pen." "She is a Native of the Kingdome of Bengall, lately come to this Country, understanding little or nothing of the Language of it, and altogether ignorant of the Laws thereof," she said in the petition: "In the event of the Tryall, she is certain she will be found altogether Innocent of the actuall murder."

But there was a new character in the story: "John Taitt a witness who she is advised is necessary for her exculpation upon the Crime," and who was for the moment "absent in London." She therefore petitioned the court, "so far as she has an interest in the Disposall of her person," to be sent away. "May it therefore Please your Lordships to Banish me to one or other of His Majestys Plantations or settlements in the East or West Indies or in America."[121]

The judges accepted the petition, and there was no trial. They sentenced Bell or Belinda to be banished to "one or other of his Majestys plantations in America or the West Indies during all the days of her Life." She was "made over" or committed to a merchant in Glasgow, Patrick Colquhoun, who was contracted to find a "proper opportunity for her Transportation": "the said Lords Transfer Convey and Make over the said Bell alias Belinda to the said Patrick Colquhoun or his assigns to be sold as a Slave for Life . . . being always accomptable to the said John Johnston Esq. and to make payment to him of the price she shall yield at a sale after deducting the Expence of her Transportation." If by some eventuality Bell or Belinda should ever return to Scotland, the judges added, in the provision that was usual in cases of transportation, she should be brought back to Perth, whipped, retransported, and "as oft apprehended transmitted Imprisoned whypt and again Transported." John was present in court during these proceedings, or at least participated in the judicial process; he signed the circuit minute book, together with the prosecuting advocate, to indicate his consent to the outcome.[122]

Bell or Belinda was sent, in the end, to North America. The North Circuit judges sentenced four people to be transported, in the space of a few days in September 1771, and all four of them—a man who had tried to bring about an abortion, a woman who had stolen some blue and white checked linen, a man who had obtained money under false pretences, by posing as a friend of the long-lost brothers of several Perthshire farmers, and Bell or Belinda—were transported to Virginia.[123] They arrived in America on a ship called the *Betsey*, of which the captain was James Ramsay, that had left Glasgow on January 12, 1772, and arrived in Virginia on March 31, 1772. The receipt for their transportation was signed in Williamsburg on April 29, 1772, by the naval officer of the Upper James River, and remitted in due order to the court in Scotland.[124]

JOSEPH KNIGHT

In Perth, in the same year, a different trans-Atlantic drama of the law had begun to unfold, which also involved the Johnstones' extended family, their slaves in Scotland, and the memory of distant oppression. The other legal cause was far more celebrated than the case of Bell or Belinda, and it had a very different outcome. It developed over the period from 1772 to 1778, and it concerned Margaret (Johnstone) Ogilvy's daughter, who had played as a little girl in Paris and had settled in Perthshire with her husband, John Wedderburn, another returned Jacobite and the young son-in-law who had written to William to seek the assistance of his wife's uncles in her application for naturalization and to lament the ancient feudal notions in which "women are only looked on as burdens & not worth taking care of."[125]

When he returned to Scotland from Jamaica, John Wedderburn brought with him a slave called Joseph, whom he had bought as a child from a Captain Knight; the slave's name was Joseph Knight. John and Margaret Wedderburn had four little children at their estate of Balindean in Perthshire. Joseph Knight also had a child, who died young, with a local woman, a servant at the estate, whom he later married; John Wedderburn gave him money to "defray the expences of the sickness and funeral of the child." But in 1772 and 1773 the relations between John Wedderburn and Joseph Knight began to worsen. In the summer of 1772, in Joseph's own account, he had "observed in the news-papers, an article which mentioned the noted decision of the Court of King's Bench, in favour of Somerset, a negro; and this naturally led him to think, that he also was intitled to be free." This was the celebrated case of James Somerset, who ran away from his owner in London, was recaptured and placed in irons on a ship bound for Jamaica, and released on a writ of habeas corpus; the case was decided in June 1772 by Lord Mansfield. The owner of James Somerset, Charles Steuart, was, like the Johnstones, an established figure in the Scottish-Atlantic colonial administration, paymaster-general of the customs office in Boston, and a friend of Benjamin Franklin's son and of the Johnstones' uncle James, the governor of Quebec.[126]

In the course of 1773, Joseph Knight decided to leave the Wedderburns' household; in John Wedderburn's description, he "became discontented and sullen, and packed up his cloaths." In November 1773 John Wedderburn requested the local justices of the peace—they met in his own house—to determine that Joseph was indeed bound to him for life, which they did. Joseph, again in John Wedderburn's description, "was much dissatisfied with this judgement: Told the Justices, that he would apply to the Sheriff, who was a better Judge than they; and had given a contrary decision in a late question."[127]

In December 1773 Joseph presented a petition to the sheriff depute of Perthshire—he had "saved his pocket-money for that purpose," John Wedderburn said—in which he stated, "The petitioner does not admit that he is a slave." The sheriff's substitute dismissed the petition. Joseph then presented a further petition in the county jurisdiction; in John Wedderburn's description, "he liked the Law of the Sheriff Depute of Perthshire better." In May 1774 the sheriff depute judged in Joseph's favor: "Finds that the state of slavery is not recognized by the laws of this kingdom, and is inconsistent with the principles thereof; And finds the regulations in Jamaica concerning slaves do not extend to this kingdom; and repells the defender's [John Wedderburn's] claims to perpetual service." It was this judgement that John Wedderburn appealed, in turn—he described it as an "extraordinary piece of usurpation of the Shiriff in point of Jurisdiction"—in a case that was heard by the highest courts in Scotland, over the period from March 1775 to January 1778: the "Joseph Knight case."[128]

The events of the Joseph Knight litigation were intertwined in the most intricate way with the lives of the Johnstones. The sheriff who decided in Joseph's favor in 1774 was John Swinton, who three years before had presented the petition of Bell or Belinda. One of Swinton's brothers, Samuel, had been a friend of George's in the navy, and another of his brothers, Archibald, was a friend of John's in India—"worthy Swinton," in John's description, than whom "none stands higher in the lists of fame or in the good opinion and regard of all."[129] John Wedderburn's initial counsel was James Ferguson, the Johnstones' first cousin and the son of their maternal uncle, who had himself been one of the two judges in Bell or Belinda's case. John Wedderburn later added another counsel, Robert Cullen, who had been, like William, Adam Smith's student. John and Margaret Wedderburn had a daughter in the summer of 1772, the summer in which Joseph Knight lost his own child; the daughter was the young girl who was later painted by Raeburn in conversation with her great-uncle and great-aunt, John and Betty Johnstone. By the winter of 1775, during the denouement of Joseph's case, Margaret Wedderburn was again pregnant, and gravely ill: "reduced to a skeleton, a constant Hectick, and so weak," her husband wrote to William in January 1775. Betty was staying in Perthshire with the Wedderburn family both in the spring and in the summer of 1775; in March, a few days after the Joseph Knight papers were filed in Edinburgh, she wrote to William that Margaret had died: "I feel her loss in the strongest degree as she was to me as my own Child."[130]

The eventual case in the court of session unfolded in the same milieu of the Scottish legal profession as the case of Bell or Belinda. John Wedderburn's lawyers presented one of the most sustained justifications of slavery in any of the polemics of the times. They invoked the book of Exodus with respect to the relations between masters and servants ("for he is his money"); the "feelings of humanity" of Plato, Aristotle, and Cicero; and the many acts of the British legislature, as recently as

1765, that "authorised and countenanced the negro-trade." Robert Cullen described the economic importance of the "negro trade" to Britain (195 ships employed in England, more than thirteen thousand seamen, two million pounds brought home each year), and the consequences among American slaves of a victory for Joseph Knight: "the profligate, lazy and discontented amongst them, will miss no opportunity of stealing across the Atlantic." James Ferguson, in this respect in advance of his time, warned of "a very shocking calamity, *viz.*, the debasing of our own race."[131]

"It is perhaps right to preserve our ideas of liberty as pure as possible, that there should be no examples of slavery before our eyes in this country," Ferguson said, in a striking juxtaposition of enlightened sensibility and prudence; but "we have chosen to be the first commercial nation in the world, and have interwoven our interests so with that of our settlements in other climates, that we cannot now exist without them."[132] "This sort of *local* emancipation seems rather whimsical," Cullen said of the origins of the case in the Perth sheriff's court. The Knight case was rather to be understood, in their view, within the circumstances of a modern world in which slavery was almost universally accepted. Laws were at first, in Cullen's description, "strictly *territorial*." But "it soon came to be thought illiberal to limit all ideas of justice to the regulations of their own particular society," and in order to "correct their local prejudices," a "regard became due to the laws of other countries." Joseph Knight's lawyers had invoked precedents of the emancipation of slaves in the French (admiralty) courts; Cullen dismissed these precedents as dating to a period "when the great commercial connections of different nations, had not yet brought Courts of Common Law to enlarge their views, and to pay just regard to the laws of other countries."[133]

The enlarged or modern or liberal position, on this view, or the unprejudiced position, was to be concerned with the ideas and the laws of the rest of the world: in the expression of the American declaration of independence, at almost exactly the same time, to "pay due attention to the opinions of mankind." It was liberal, thereby, to give judgement in the Joseph Knight case in favor of the master. But the court decided otherwise, and by a vote of seven to five, in January 1778, they affirmed the judgement of the lower court, or the local emancipation in Perthshire: "affirmed the Judgement of the Sheriff in favour of the Negro."[134] Joseph Knight had first read about the Somerset case in the *Edinburgh Advertiser* in July 1772; the outcome of his own case, another Scottish newspaper wrote in January 1778, was that "the freedom of negroes has received its first *general determination* in the Supreme Civil Court of Scotland."[135] The case of Bell or Belinda, only a few months before, had been the very last occasion, as it turned out, when the state of slavery was determined in a British court: "the said Lords Transfer Convey and Make over the said Bell alias Belinda . . . to be sold as a Slave for Life."[136]

CHAPTER THREE

ENDING AND LOSS

The legal cases of Joseph Knight and Bell or Belinda mark the beginning of the end of the Johnstones' story. It is a story that ends, like so many true stories, in sorrow and loss. "Old age makes wid strids with me now," the Johnstones' mother wrote to John, a few months before he left India, and "your poor father does not seem to have so easie a decay, he lives in a constant dread of blindness . . . all his ails was ever atended with great loness of spirits."[1] When she died in 1773, two of her daughters, Margaret and Barbara, were already dead, and Charlotte died two weeks later; Charlotte's death, like that of Margaret's daughter, was described as an aftereffect of childbirth.[2] Betty, who never married, was frequently unwell. "Poor Betty had been taken ill of the particulars attending a Cholera Morbis," their father wrote to William in April 1772, and her case was "extremely doubtfull"; she was also rheumatic and on occasion scarcely able to "walk about without Pain."[3]

The letters between the brothers and sisters were filled, like so many eighteenth-century letters, with descriptions of illness. The brothers who had returned from overseas were constantly concerned with the ailments they had brought with them: the illnesses of empire. There was James's fever "called Mille Harpies," George's flatus, Alexander's legs, and John's continuing chills: "seventeen broiling years in Bengal is but Part of his Disorder." Their feet were almost always cold. They also wrote to each other about the most repulsive sequence of remedies: "my father . . . was bled blistered vomited & had three doses of rubarb," Charlotte reported to William. There was elixir of vitriol (for which she borrowed sixpence), "decoction of the bark," magnesia, asses' milk, antimonial mercury, saline draughts, and "the extraordinary effect of semiruta in Putrid Fevers."[4]

The Johnstones were preoccupied, too, with the illnesses of the spirit. "I know by Experience how much the Mind preys on the Body," James wrote to John in November 1771. "Depression of Mind is the most disagreeable attendant of advanced Life," he lamented a few months later, before he set out to visit their elderly parents in Westerhall. All is "Care Anxiety Vexation Dissapointment," he wrote to his lawyer; "the Present, Painfull, Grievous, Unsupportable were not our Soulls to dart forward to the smilling Regions of Futurity," that "Time far from realizing follows only to deface." "I have been much out of order In my Inward man," John wrote at the time of his wife, Elizabeth Carolina's, last illness, when he was in "constant pain" in his stomach and bowels.[5] The Johnstones' Uncle Walter, their father's half-brother, was invoked, as so often in times of crisis, as when Margaret's son was reported to be in trouble in Scarborough: "Low Spirited people are not only very suspicious, but exceedingly quick sighted."[6] But he, too, was plagued by gout, as he wrote to James Balmain on a stormy day in Dumfries, "all wrapt up in blankets like a poor bastard child lying near the fire upon a low Stool."[7]

Betty, after their parents' deaths in 1772 and 1773, stayed at first with a succession of friends and relations. "I have been going from place to place without a settled

Residance," she wrote to William in October 1773, "and I own my Mind has not been quite at Ease." John had "Insisted in the strongest terms that I should stay with Mrs Johnstone and him." But "my own settled Resolution Ever was that when ever the Mournfull Event of my Father and Mothers Death happened I would have a House of my Own." John had "at last given me his consent," and she had found a "new well aird House" in Edinburgh, "consisting of four Rooms and a Kitchen." She needed therefore to draw on her own capital of one hundred pounds, which was in William's hands, and which "I alwise Intended for furnishing my House." "I have Bought my Furneter but am not to Receive them till I pay the money," she wrote to William, who had apparently responded that he was surprised by the news, and that it would not be convenient for him to provide the capital. As Betty wrote, "My own opinion Ever was that a person comed to my time of Life should have a place of there own that they may Retire to."[8]

THE DETRITUS OF EMPIRE

Of all the brothers, only John settled at home in Scotland. Alexander, George, and Gideon were no more than occasional visitors. Alexander's sugar plantation in Grenada, "Westerhall," became the subject of litigation among three of the brothers, Alexander, William, and John ("Pulteney Esqr. and others . . . agt. Johnstone Esqr."), described by James as an "UnBrotherly and unnatural Law Suit." The "Reckonings Quarrels Controversies Claims and Demands" were eventually resolved with James's arbitration and in response to the deathbed wish of their father.[9] Alexander died unmarried and without legitimate children, leaving his Grenada estate, together with his "Negroes and other Slaves Mills & Boyling Houses," in trust for James, James's "heirs male," and an arcane array of other possible heirs; William's first son "by any wife other than his present wife"; George and Martha's "eldest son" George, "in case he is now or hereafter shall become the legitimate son of my said Brother . . . within and according to the law of Scotland"; and John, Gideon, and their future sons.[10] More than fifty years later, Alexander's granddaughter Ann, "daughter of Jane Castino Johnstone a mulato daughter of Col. Alexander Johnstone," called upon John's grandson and was given "one pound sterling." She was in service with a grocer in the Canongate in Edinburgh; her husband, who was a cattle drover, had "got [his] Leg broken and otherwise Dreadfully crushed on the body."[11]

Gideon, who tended to appear in Edinburgh with news of distant friends and then to leave again, also died without legitimate children. In 1780, after rejoining the navy, he was stationed in Liverpool, where he married Fanny Colquitt, from a family of Liverpool lawyers, merchants, slave-ship owners, and port officials. Her father, who was "deputy searcher of the port of Liverpool," appeared to have been very dubious about Gideon at first and took elaborate care in his will to ensure that his daughter's income should be "wholly exempt from the Receipt power or controul of her present or any future husband"; in a codicil a year later, he described Gideon as someone "who I much respect" and included him as a beneficiary of the family estate.[12] Gideon's ship was sent to America soon after his marriage, where he served off Plymouth Sound, Nantucket, and New York.[13] On his return to Britain, he and Fanny lived in London, in a house that John had leased near Grosvenor Square, and in one of John's new estates in Scotland.[14] Gideon died in 1788, leaving legacies to Charlotte's children and his estate to "my very dearly beloved brother John," to whom he considered himself bound in "gratitude as well as Affection" for "every far-thing I may be possessed of."[15]

George, too, was restless until the very end of his life. He returned, in the interstices of his political interests in the East India Company and the American Revolution, to his earlier prospect of a new empire of commerce in the Gulf of Mexico, from Honduras to Jamaica and the Atlantic markets. His great parliamentary cause of 1777 was the "Musquito Coast," or the Mosquitia re-gion of the Gulf coast of Central America (in modern Honduras and Nicaragua), where two Scottish entre-preneurs, together with Gustavus Vassa, the emanci-pated slave later known as Olaudah Equiano, had set out to establish an export business in "expressing veg-etable oils" for use in wool production, to be followed by "the culture of cotton."[16]

In 1778 George was selected as one of the commis-sioners in the unsuccessful mission of reconciliation with the North American colonies, or the new United States—the Carlisle Commission, chaired by a young poet and court official, Earl Carlisle.[17] It was this com-mission of which the philosopher Adam Ferguson was the secretary. George was convinced, apparently, that the military victory of the Americans and the French was inevitable; his and the commission's objective, as he wrote in the letters he sent to American acquaintances, was to negotiate "a beneficial union of interests," or "the most liberal, and therefore the most lasting terms of union," which would "once more unite our interests." But George's three letters became a scandal, the more so when he was accused of offering one of his correspondents a bribe of ten thousand guineas.[18] "It is incompatible with the Honour of Congress to hold any Correspondence or Intercourse with the said George Johnstone Esq; especially to negotiate with him upon Affairs, in which the cause of Liberty and Virtue is interested," the Congress declared in the late summer of 1778. George returned immediately to London.[19]

Martha Ford, in London, and their sons, who were in Pisa with their tutor, waited for news; "you will easyly see their situation by the map of New York," Martha wrote to the children, and "your sure I must have had many anxious hours my dear boys for the welfare of your noble father. . . . In the midst of all his difficulties he mentions you all in the Tenderest manner."[20] On his return from America, George quarrelled bitterly by letter with Walter Minto, the tutor of the children.[21] He insisted that the boys, aged eleven and thirteen, be sent home immediately on a merchant ship from the port of Livorno. They were then captured, together with their tutor and "a black boy from Bengal," by a French war ship, "taken Prisoners & carryd into Malaga." In the chaotic ports of the wartime Mediterranean—"36 fish ships waiting [in Gibraltar] for convoy, their cargo's spoiling"—their destiny was the subject of intermittent diplomatic negotiation and a "very unreasonable Demand made by the French Captain for their Release." They were eventually released in Cadiz, to await "a convenient opportunity to return to England."[22]

George and Martha separated some time between 1778 and 1781. George sought another chance in the great lottery of naval captures, or the economy of prizes, and commanded a convoy to protect thirty-seven ships carrying wine for the merchants of Oporto. He was eventually in command of one of the oddest expeditions of the entire Revolutionary War, in 1781: in appearance a convoy of East India ships bound for Madras, and in prospect a plan to capture the Cape of Good Hope, proceed to the East Indies, seize the islands of Ceylon and Celebes, incorporate the private army of the East India Company, including two thousand "sepoys" or Indian troops, and return to capture the Spanish settlements in Rio Plata, in modern Argentina.[23] He was married for the first time in 1782, in Lisbon, to Charlotte Dee, with whom he had his only legitimate child, a son.[24]

George's armada was engaged in battle in the Cape Verde islands off the coast of west Africa, after the project was uncovered by a French intelligence officer in London (who was later the last person to be hanged, drawn, and quartered for espionage). The French navy reached the Cape of Good Hope before him, and his most spectacular exploit, as a portly and infirm commander, was to capture four Dutch East Indiamen ships in Saldanha Bay near the Cape, "running in under the shore in the night."[25] A part of the expedition continued eastwards to India, two ships went westwards to South America, and George himself returned to Lisbon; "so many schemes enter his head that they confound and confuse him, and leave him perfectly undetermined on any point," his closest friend among the naval captains commented, before setting sail for "the famous River

Plate, which Vomits forth half the Riches of the World."[26] The expedition ended, like so many of George's plans, in quarrels over the naval encounter in the Cape Verde islands, a court martial, and litigation that made its way eventually to the House of Lords.[27]

Over the last months of his life, in 1786 and 1787, very weak but in "a perfect disposing mind & memory," George recalled the detritus of a life of empire, in a sequence of codicils to his will: to his wife Charlotte, his pillowcases and "all pieces of silk or printed cotton that are in my possession"; all his "old China and Japan of every kind whole or Rivitted" to be sent to the estate of Alva, where John now lived, and "constantly used on Mirthful Days under the care of Sister Betty"; to his niece, William and Frances Pulteney's only child, Henrietta Laura, in remembrance of her kindness, "my Crimson Shawl"; to William his "two Busts of the Roman Emperors"; to Betty, his silver teapot and silver milk pot, "after Japan models"; to "the family at Westerhall," "my best Glasgow Edition of Milton"; to his and Martha's son James "my steel sword"; and to their son Alexander, or Sandy, "my other sword." It was as though he were disposing of all his memories and all his things; even the codicils become odder and more minimal over time, conditional upon "gaining sufficient insight into my affairs wch depending on so many contingent events." George wanted to return, in the end, to the valley of the Esk: "I desire that my Body may be carried to the Grave by Six of the poor persons who reside in the parish of Westerkirk who will receive a suit of coarse grey Cloth and two Guineas each I beg that ten Guineas worth of drink may be given to the Populace at the funeral."[28]

THE JAMES JOHNSTONES

Of all the brothers, James was the one whose existence became more comfortable towards the end of his life. On his father's death in 1772, he inherited the family estate at Westerhall, but very little money. "The Reversion to James is scarce worth mentioning," John wrote to William, in the letter about how he could not help blushing when he understood how impoverished their father had been.[29] But a few years later, after Alexander's death, James inherited the other Westerhall in the West Indies, the sugar plantation. He was at least from time to time a wealthy man. He lived in Alexander's house in London with a housekeeper, a cook, a housemaid, a coachman, and two footmen.[30] He and Louisa were still endlessly in debt: when Charlotte's widower, James Balmain, died in 1792, a friend in the Scottish excise found in his pocket book the note of a bill he had paid for James in 1772, as well as notes of a debt owed by James to Charlotte from 1760, a bond of £433 owed to James Balmain from 1786, a bill for a "Cask of Acquavita," and another bill of fifteen shillings for "Russia toweling sent to Lady Johnstone."[31] James and Louisa had no children.[32] But James had a daughter, Ann, who was married to a shopkeeper in Carlisle and whose own children Louisa helped to educate. He also had a son, called James Murray Johnstone, whose moral upbringing he entrusted to his and Louisa's housekeeper and to the housekeeper's brother, a captain on the Grenada ships.[33]

From 1784 to 1790, and again from 1791 to 1794, James was a member of parliament. His interventions had the same exuberant tone as his letters from poverty

in Norfolk. He defended hawkers and peddlers (he would
not "be willing to extract a groan or a tear from any one
individual hawker or pedlar in the kingdom"), and opposed the immunity of the navy (an "exclusive privilege
to plunder the natives of India"), the tax on maidservants ("it tended to oppress an order of individuals who
were entitled to the most humane usage"), and the duty
on pawnbrokers (it "would ultimately grind the faces of
the poor"). "If the House were to pronounce what was,
and what was not law," he said in a debate on election
procedures, "there was an end of . . . the liberties of Great
Britain." He was described as speaking "with a sort of
Lacedemonian eloquence." Even his apology for having
been obstreperous in a parliamentary debate, in 1788—
"he acknowledged he had been drunk, and hoped that
would excuse him"—left the House of Commons "in
perfect good humour." "He would suspect the Speaker,"
he was reported to have announced in a debate on the
post office, "he would suspect my lords the bishops; he
would suspect every man in that House; he was sent
there to suspect them all."[34]

After Alexander's death in 1783, James was himself
the owner of slaves, in the other, distant Westerhall in
Grenada. But he appears to have retained his earlier
opinion, expressed in his letter to John about the East
India Company's government of Bengal, that benevolence, justice, and humanity ought by no means to be
"restricted to Collour," and to have arrived at some sort
of accommodation of humanity and interest. An antislavery pamphlet of 1789 was dedicated to him as "a
humane, disinterested Planter," and he declared in 1792
that "he has bought no slaves for these last three years;
those, whom he now has, he says, shall live well and die

peaceably upon his estate; but though another pound of sugar should not be produced upon it, he will deal no more in *human flesh*!"[35] He believed, like Adam Smith, that sugar cane could be cultivated with ploughs and without the "hand labour" of African slaves.[36] In the parliamentary debate over the "gradual abolition of the slave trade" in 1792, he was reported as saying that

> he was convinced that the slave trade should be abolished immediately. He stated, that in a plantation of his own in the West Indies, he had introduced the plough, and he had found his grounds produced more sugar than when cultivated by negroes. He concluded with declaring his opinion, that if it were to be immediately abolished, it would be as much to the advantage of the planter, as for the honour of Great Britain.[37]

James corresponded with the overseers of the Westerhall plantation about the condition of the slaves; he sent "a skilful labouring husbandman" from the estate of Westerhall in Scotland, "with the common plough of that country." "I found that Sir James had even sent them out shoes," an abolitionist acquaintance wrote; the slaves were "well supplied with food and clothing."[38] His manager wrote to him in 1793, amidst the anxieties over the revolution in Saint-Domingue, that "we are still going on making Sugar. The Negroes are all in good health & spirits."[39] When James died in London in 1794, he left one hundred pounds to the manager of the Westerhall plantation "for his upright conduct," fifty pounds to "my Overseer for his humanity towards my Negroes," and twenty-five pounds to "my Ploughman in Grenada for the care he has taken in instructing my Negroes in the proper use of the Plough."[40]

At Westerhall in the valley of the Esk, too, James devoted himself to the improvement of the estate. He sunk a mine in the northern hills, where the metal antimony, much used at the time in printers' types, medicine, and military ordnance, had at last been found, and called it the Louisa Mine.[41] He had a black servant who lived with him, also, confusingly, called James Johnstone; the parish records of Westerkirk for 1778 describe the interrogation of a servant on the estate, Henrietta Allen, who had "brought forth a Child in uncleanness" and who, being "exhorted to ingenuity," named as the father "James Johnstone Negroe Servant to Sir James Johnstone of Westerhall." The parish register also records, three years later, the interrogation of (the black) James Johnstone, who "acknowledged that he had been guilty of uncleanness with her but was persuaded that he was not the Father of her Child because it had no natural resemblance to him being white."[42] When James died, he left his estate in Grenada to his wife, and an annuity of twenty pounds a year "to James Johnstone my black servant who discovered a mine of Antimony at my estate at Westerhall."[43]

There was a lending library for the mine workers, established in 1793 with a gift from the Westerhall Mining Company, of seventeen "Books for our mental Improvement," including William Robertson's *History of Scotland*, Seneca's *Morals*, "Ferguisons Lectures," and "Lavoisers Cahomestry." James's butler presented the library with a devotional work called *Human Nature in its four-fold state*, and his secretary gave the *Constitution of America*. In August 1793 the miners ordered from an Edinburgh bookseller Hume's *History of England*, *Sir Charles Grandison*, *Roderick Random*, Henry

Mackenzie's *Man of Feeling* and *Burn's Poems*. In October 1793 the minute book of the new library recorded that "the Miners this night having met & Exchanged Books thought it fit to form them selves into a Society" with a president, a clerk, a treasurer, and two inspectors. A James Johnstone or Johnston, the same James Johnstone, perhaps, who discovered the mine, was an inspector of books and a member of the society's committee; he was fined a penny in 1793 for "not Return of Books" and another penny in 1794 for "blots in books." In July 1795, "the Society thinking it very Necessary that they should have their foundamental Articles written on Vellum and have ordered it to be got"; in January 1797 "there was a Code of Laws presented to the members," and an "abridgement of the Laws"; in April 1797 they ordered Smith's *Wealth of Nations* and Robertson's *India*.[44] The landscape that James had described in 1759 as a place of "barren hills and horrid mountains" had been transformed in the space of a generation, like so much of southern Scotland, into the very microcosm of an enlightened industrial society.

INDIAN YELLOW SATIN

John Johnstone died in 1795 at his estate of Alva, in the Ochil hills of Clackmannanshire. He and Elizabeth Carolina had left their rented house in Balgonie the year after Bell or Belinda was sent to America; they returned only "to pack up our Baggage, & bid adieu to the old Castle," he wrote to William in 1773.[45] One of the other young men and women who had been part of John's Anglo-Indian household left too. A James Johnstone who was baptised in April 1773 in the church of

Kirkandrews upon Esk, a few miles to the south of Westerhall and across the frontier into England, was described in the parish register as "a Mollato aged about nineteen years, who was brought from the East Indies by Mr. John Johnston of Westherhall in Scotland": he was the same James Johnstone, perhaps, who was or was not the father of Henrietta Allen's son, or who discovered the Louisa mine, or who was the inspector of books in the miners' library.[46]

John's troubles with the East India Company had diminished after the company abandoned its prosecution, and after he was passed over, in 1771, for the government of Bengal. His partner William Bolts left the country—"Poor Bolts is gone youll see; a heavy stroke upon my Dear Sister as well as Mrs. J & myself," John wrote to William—and was heard of in Lisbon, loading Brazilian snuff for a voyage to the East Indies, in a vessel with a mutinous crew, under the colors of the Empress of Austria.[47] Even the sequence of John's lawsuits, over his Indian presents and over the Grenada investments, had dwindled away: the East India Company against Johnstone; Johnstone and Bolts against Fatio (of the East Indies and the mortgages on the slaves in Grenada); Johnstone, Pulteney, and others against Bolts (on behalf of Mrs. and Miss Johnstone, or Betty and Elizabeth Carolina); Johnstone against Johnstone (the unbrotherly law suit among William, John, and Alexander).[48]

In his semiretirement John devoted himself to family responsibilities. His household in Balgonie consisted of one male servant and three women servants, in addition to Bell or Belinda: these at least were the individuals who were listed to be called as witnesses in her trial.[49] In

Alva, the estate for which the round pigeonhouse with the octagonal turret was designed, he lived in grander style: in the returns for taxes on male and female servants, he declared four female servants and six male servants, including a butler, a valet, and a coachman.[50] "All the old drawing room furniture [was] thick Indian yellow satin covered with velvet Gods or Goddesses," his and Elizabeth Carolina's granddaughter recalled many years later, with "magnificent India China" and a "rare library" with "Indian correspondence upon vellum powdered with gold & silver."[51]

Elizabeth Carolina died at Alva in 1778, leaving a young son and daughter. John's happiness, he wrote to James Balmain, was placed "more on the Social pleasures under my Own Roof than in Any I have yet found to depend on Externals."[52] He cared for George in his last illness; the "only thing [that] gives him ease . . . seems to be Chafing his head with our hands & the Opium," he wrote to William. He wept over a funeral eulogy to George by William Julius Mickle.[53] He was the trustee of Barbara's children, a "second father" to George's youngest son, and solicitous, after George's death, of both Martha Ford and George's widow. James wrote of "my dear Johns Goodness," and Uncle Walter described him as "Dutiful noble spirited John."[54] There is a mausoleum to Elizabeth Carolina by Robert Adam in the churchyard at Alva, and a mausoleum to the Johnstones' parents, also by Adam, in the Westerkirk churchyard, near the family home of Westerhall.[55] John was a subscriber, together with his young son James Raymond Johnstone and his brother-in-law James Balmain, to the Society for the Abolition of the African Slave Trade, founded in Edinburgh in 1788, which petitioned parliament and reprinted William Cowper's "The Negro's Complaint":

> Men from England bought and sold me,
> Paid my price in paltry gold;
> But tho' their's they have inroll'd me,
> Minds are never to be sold.[56]

John was Gideon's and George's executor, and he sorted his father's and George's papers; his own extremely respectable children and grandchildren were sought out, well into the nineteenth century, with the woes of distant relations, the descendants of the nephews and nieces of John and Elizabeth Carolina.[57] But John's earlier life was never entirely distant. He referred in his will to the reversion of the settlement of 17,141 rupees and 14 annas "on Miss Betty Johnstone my well beloved Sister," the settlement he had made in the last anxious days before he left Calcutta in October 1765.[58] John was described as having reflected, in the last days of his life, on the brothers he had lost, and on the persistence of family relationships in the world to come. "I am *fully* persuaded we *shall meet thereafter*," the philosopher Adam Ferguson, who had become an intimate friend, wrote to him shortly before his death: "that you will know your *Brother*, & that I shall know you both."[59]

THE TREASURER

The Johnstones' family home of Westerhall was put up for sale after James's death. William inherited the title of baronet and was by James's will the residual heir. He declined to take over the estate in Scotland, because

"he would have become responsible for the Debts";
Louisa, too, "declined proving the will in Scotland seeing the personal estate there to be insolvent."[60] Louisa
and William quarrelled bitterly over the other estate, in
Grenada; "that scoundrel Sir William Pulteney has
played us a Trick which I really had not given him credit
for baseness enough to have done," Louisa's lawyer
wrote in 1796.[61] In her own will Louisa left everything
to her maternal family in Norfolk, with a bequest for the
"education of all or any of the children" of James's
daughter.[62] "I certainly Exist, but can hardly be said to
Live," she wrote to her cousin and heir shortly before
her death in 1797, in her old sprightly literary language;
she was oppressed by gout, the news from Grenada, and
the "Unfortunate, irreparable, ever to be Lamented Loss
Death of my adored, beloved Husband, Sir James Johnstone with whom my All my Every Happiness in this
World was with him Burried in his Grave, lost & gone
for ever Never Never, more to return."[63]

William, the most circumspect of the brothers and the
brother who never went to the Indies, was the longest
lived. His wife, Frances Pulteney, died in 1782.[64] Their
daughter, Henrietta Laura, was sent to a convent school
in Paris and returned to England in 1784, described in
the *Whitehall Evening Post* as "the greatest heiress ever
remembered in this country."[65] She had been educated,
in William's view, with "too much indulgence," and he
made an attempt, with a new governess or chaperone, at
what he described as "a plan of coertion."[66] He also devoted sustained effort to the negotiation of a suitable
marriage, first with the Prime Minister, William Pitt, and
then with a succession of English lords. "Miss Pulteney
was certainly offered to Mr Pitt by her father," a New

York newspaper reported in 1789, "provided he was created Earl of Bath."[67] Henrietta Laura was married in 1794 to the son of her great-aunt.[68]

In a cartoon of 1798, William was depicted as "Le Trésorier," the treasurer, crouched over chests of bills and bonds.[69] He was a treasurer, too, of parliamentary constituencies, or of "borough jobbing," in the description of his nephew, Barbara Kinnaird's American son-in-law; "he is as anxious abt. buying & selling seats as any boroughmonger in England."[70] The *Gentleman's Magazine* reported in 1805 that "he was supposed to be the richest Commoner in the kingdom. His funded property amounted to near two millions sterling; and he was the greatest American stockholder ever known."[71] After James's death William was involved in the detailed management of the Grenada plantation. He negotiated the rental of slaves from his own estate of Port Royal in Grenada to the Westerhall estate; their names included "Calcutta" and "Dumfries."[72] He was also involved, in the most abstract detail of uses and prices, in the exchange of a slave called Pierre, who had been carried or "carréd," in the French-English idiom of the island, from Grenada to England and in whom James's old Westerhall manager also took an interest. As William wrote to the lawyers for Louisa's estate:

> It does not occur to me that there can be any objection, to the Exchange which Mr Keith [the manager] proposes of another seasoned negro for Pierre, but he does not say, what negro he proposes, nor who shall judge, whether the negro he may offer, be equal to Pierre . . . as Mr Keith has had the use of Pierre ever since he left the Island.[73]

William's land interests extended, by now, far into the North American continent. An informant had written to him enthusiastically in 1780 about the prospects for improvement in New Orleans and the Mississippi delta: "the soil is the same with that of Lower Eygpt, & formed in the same way by the slime of the River."[74] In 1791 he initiated the largest of all his investments, with the intervention of Benjamin Franklin's grandson. In partnership with Patrick Colquhoun, the young Glasgow merchant who had been charged in 1771 by the Perth Circuit Court with selling Bell or Belinda in America, and who soon after became a pillar of the enlightened establishment, William bought the vast expanse of New York State known as the Genesee Tract; some 1,300,000 acres.[75] In 1804 he married for the second time, to Margaret Stuart, the widow of one of his and Adam Smith's old Edinburgh friends.[76]

At the very end of his life, early in 1805, William played a critical role in the complicated parliamentary procedure whereby William Wilberforce's bill for the abolition of the slave trade was defeated by the House of Commons.[77] An amendment that was supported by William and his friends had the effect of delaying the eventual abolition by more than a year, and was prepared by "a canvass, more importunate" than on any previous occasion "by those interested in the continuance of the trade."[78] The delay affected the lives of more than a hundred thousand people: one hundred two thousand people were embarked as slaves in the Atlantic trade in 1806, of whom fifty-nine thousand were sent under British and United States flags.[79] William, in his last important parliamentary intervention, declared in opposition to the bill that "this bill was built on theory, and he was not fond of theories"; "the same principles would lead as far as entire emancipation."[80] He died intestate in the same year; his widow died more than forty-four years later, in 1849.[81]

DISTANT DESTINIES

The infatuation with empire continued even into the next generation. Three of George's sons with Martha Ford joined the service of the East India Company; his son James died in India at the age of twenty-two, and his son Alexander died there at the age of twenty-five, leaving three small children.[82] Barbara's son Patrick Kinnaird went to India, where he died in 1771.[83] Charlotte's son George Balmain also went to India.[84] John's oldest granddaughter, who was named Elizabeth Caroline, became a historian of Etruria and of a lost world of commerce, "long before the people of the ancient world were bound together under the leaden yoke of universal empire."[85] Barbara's son-in-law, the medical student from Cambridge, Massachusetts, became a clergyman in the Church of England. His own daughter, Barbara's granddaughter, was married in Boston to an official of the East India Company—"his person and manners were disgusting to me," her American uncle wrote—and settled in Calcutta; one of Barbara's grandsons was despatched to the family tracts in upper New York, and another was in "the Egyptian expedition" of 1802.[86]

Margaret (Johnstone) Ogilvy's granddaughter, Margaret Wedderburn, the little girl who was born during the summer when Joseph Knight first read about slaves being entitled to be free, and who was painted by Raeburn in conversation with her great-uncle John and her great-aunt Betty, settled with her sister in Prince of Wales Island, which is now Penang in Malaysia. Her husband was the East India Company's first British governor, Philip Dundas, and her sister also married an East India Company official in Penang. Margaret died, like her mother and grandmother, in the aftermath of childbirth, in Calcutta in 1806.[87] Her husband died soon afterwards, and so did her sister's husband; in a codicil to his will, her husband noted that their two little boys were in the care of "a female slave," "whose name I cannot set forth."[88]

The disputes over the American properties continued in the generation of the Johnstones' children. George's youngest son quarreled with his cousin by marriage, Henrietta Laura's husband, over the vast family lands in upstate New York: a dispute that ended, as so often, in a complicated lawsuit, in this case in Geneva, New York, and turned on the rights of aliens to own land in New York; the original agreement between William and Patrick Colquhoun; and the prenuptial agreements between William, his daughter, and their spouses.[89] The former American vice president Aaron Burr, when he visited Edinburgh, was enlisted by John and Elizabeth Carolina's daughter, Anne Elizabeth, and Charlotte and James Balmain's daughter, Elizabeth Caroline, in the affair of the American lands.[90] Henrietta Laura "declared to my son," George's widow wrote in 1805, "that she did not Consider Him as a Relation, and that Mr Willm. Pulteney from the time he changed his name did not consider himself as having any thing to do with the Johnstone family."[91]

Laura Pulteney was the only one of all the Johnstones' children who tried to find her way out of the circle of imperial and family relationships. The history of the Johnstones has been a Balzacian story: of the endless, recursive connections of individuals and marriages, like the "strange, boundless, immeasurable mass of interweaving destinies and lonely souls which is the unique feature of Balzac's novels," in Georg Lukács's description.[92] Laura's story was Balzacian, too, in the sense that these recursive relationships were connected, in the end, to the politics of the French revolutionary empire. Laura reserved the right, when she married her cousin, of making a will and disposing of her estates "as if she were a feme sole"—in her own words, "as I should see fit and as if I was sole and unmarried." She chose to leave bequests to two female friends: the wife of a clergyman in Nottingham, free of the control of "her present or any future husband" or "her present or any future coverture"; and a young girl in a convent in France, the daughter of another childhood friend. But the clergyman's wife turned out to be the defendant in an extremely intricate divorce case involving climbing in and out of rectory windows, and Laura's estate became the subject of litigation on behalf of her friend's ten children by her first husband and four children by her second husband, the co-defendant or co-respondent.[93] The destiny of Laura's old friend's daughter in France was even more spectacular. She became an imperial princess, the adopted daughter of Napoleon, and a rueful observer of the "gothic ideas" of customary law in post-Napoleonic Germany.[94]

Martha Ford lived for more than forty years after George's death. She survived all four of her sons; her son

George Lindsay Johnstone, who returned from India, left her a large annuity of £1,500 per year, or more than five times the value of the old Johnstone estate in Dumfriesshire.[95] Her daughter, Sophia Johnstone, married a Sicilian duke.[96] Martha Ford died in London in 1830, at the age of eighty-six; her house eventually became the home of the Royal Society of Medicine.[97] In her own will, she left her fortune to her grandchildren and to Sophia, "for her own sole separate use and benefit and my will is that her present husband or any future husband shall not intermeddle therewith."[98]

Betty was the last of the Johnstone brothers and sisters, and she has been at the very center of this story, with her bundle of textiles and her rupees and her chronicles of family news. She lived in Edinburgh in the four-room apartment, the "House of my Own," with two "Old Women" overhead who "neither Spin nor make any noise whatever"; this estate agent's description is due to the philosopher Adam Ferguson.[99] She later lived in a villa that John and Gideon had owned in the Edinburgh suburb of Hawkhill, where her nieces brought Aaron Burr to visit her, to whom she served Madeira wine: "Asked into Mrs J's room. Pretty place; view of the Forth . . . Repast; *delic. Vin Mad.*"[100] To her niece Anne Elizabeth, or Betty, she wrote, when she was eighty, with encouraging words—"go on and prosper"—and with news of her health: "I find nothing does me so much good as exercise."[101] Betty died in 1813, and her will, like George's, is a reminiscence of the residues of empire. Her niece, the younger Betty, is directed to divide up her clothes, including her new black silk gown; the picture of her brother George is to be given to his son John (the litigant in upstate New York); there is a locket for poor Margaret Dundas, in Penang; the "silver teapot I got from brother George" is to go to Charlotte's daughter; and "poor Sandy Johnstones sword to be sent to Mrs Johnstone for her son" in India; John's daughter Betty is "to keep the piece of spoiled India silk." Her estate was worth £740.[102]

CHAPTER FOUR

ECONOMIC LIVES

The history of the Johnstones is an eventful story, full of lawsuits and loss and distraction. The John-stones were unusually enterprising, and there were un-usually many of them. But they lived in interesting times, and their history can provide a vista—the view of a particular extended family—of large and important historical changes. They were surrounded by the insti-tution of slavery and by individual slaves; their suc-cesses were the outcome of economic information, which was also information about private relationships; their empire was a family enterprise, of which the con-sequences or multiplier effects extended far into the in-terior of Scotland; and it was an empire of intimate ex-changes. Their history is a view of future possibilities that were lost, in the founding epoch of modern em-pires, and in particular of the unlikely possibility of an empire of individual (or family) enterprise: of laissez-faire when it was new.

The Johnstones and their slaves and servants lived in the origins and end of empires, and in the ruins of other possible outcomes. To be observers of the beginning of new times was to observe the old times that were com-ing to an end, and the other futures, likely or unlikely, that were anticipated in hope or fear. It is difficult, now, to forget the asymmetry of historical knowledge with respect to time: that historians know, as the individuals in the past into whose lives they seek to enter, did not know, how events turned out, or how the story ended. It is difficult, too, to forget this asymmetrical knowledge with respect to space or information: to try to imagine what it was like to have only a very indistinct idea of the difference between the East and West Indies, or America. It is difficult, most of all, to imagine all the other future lives, or ways of living and ways of thinking, to which individuals in the past looked forward. But these expectations were themselves part of the Johnstones' experience of empire.[1]

The world in which the Johnstones flourished, and in which three of them (Alexander, William, and John) made their large and insecure fortunes, was a time of new empires, in the description of individuals at the time, and of subsequent historians. The Johnstones lived at the edge of three sets of events that have been identified, in nineteenth- and twentieth-century histories of empire, as the founding moments of the modern Anglo-American world. There was the East India Company's acquisition of power over the financial administration of Bengal, Bihar, and Orissa, in the disputes of 1765 in which John was so prominent: the point when the British officials decided "to become Nabobs ourselves," in Lord Clive's expression; or to become virtuous, in Lord Macaulay's later description, in an instance of moral destiny from which "dates the purity of the administration of our Eastern empire."[2] There was the American Revolution, or the "flattering object" that William described with laborious irony in 1778 as "the idea of establishing a new and magnificent empire upon the pillars of freedom."[3] There was the construction, over the period from the decision in James Somerset's case in 1772 to the abolition of the slave trade in British ships in 1806, of a new and less impure British empire in the

West Indies and the South Atlantic, the "palliation" of the Atlantic slave economy, in J. R. Seeley's late Victorian description, in which "we published our own guilt, repented of it, and did at last renounce it."[4]

The Johnstones's world of opportunity was a time of innovation, too, in the vaster sense of a revolution in the mind, or in ways of thinking about economic and political life. They lived amidst what was described at the time, and in later histories, as the period of foundation of the science of political economy, of the politics of individual rights, and of the idea of a distinctive space, or territory, of economic relationships. It was at "the moment when *Smith* wrote," according to the French economist Jean-Baptiste Say's early nineteenth-century history, that political economy was distinguished for the first time from the science of politics.[5] The definition of a science of political economy was only possible, in turn, in John Stuart Mill's later account, because the "facts" of the production and distribution of wealth had become "associated in the mind." The exchanges that constituted the object of political economy were for Mill like a new territory that had been cultivated by settlers and had not yet been enclosed within a city wall: "without any intentional classification, the facts classed themselves."[6] The most enduring discovery of the founders of the science of political economy was in this view the discovery of economic life itself, or of a set of relationships of economic exchange.

This was the drama of transformation in which the Johnstones lived. But they were on the losing side in all these innovations, in the sense that they were continually in opposition, to an almost eerie extent, to "the relatedness of the whole flow of events from the past

into the present," or to the "victory of what, in the retrospect of later history, became the forces of progress"
(as in Bernard Bailyn's description of the losers in the
American Revolution), or of the forces of empire.[7]
They were opposed to Clive's Indian settlement of
1765. They were enemies, eventually, of the American
Revolution. They were involved from the 1760s to the
1800s, or some of them were involved, in the sustained
expansion of slavery in the British empire. They were
on the wrong side in the political revolutions of the
times, and on the wrong side in their conceptions of
economic opportunity.

The Johnstones used the new language of political
economy to a striking extent in their public and political
speech. They were among the early administrative figures to invoke the freedom of commerce, "free Trade,"
and the "security of possession," well before the publication of *The Wealth of Nations* in 1776.[8] John's public
statements in Bengal in 1761–65 were full of references
to free competition, freedom to trade, freedom of self-
improvement, and the prospect of gain. So were George's
statements, in West Florida in 1764–67: freedom of
commerce, free egress and regress, free importations and
exportations, free trade, "exact Justice" in the Indian
trade, plentiful trade "from all parts of the world."[9] But
the Johnstones' empire of individual initiative was only
in the most indistinct sense a purely economic enterprise. The prospect of exchange on which David Hume
and Adam Smith's systems of economic freedom were
founded—the "ordinary course of business" or the
"common course of business and commerce," in the expressions that are repeated so frequently in *The Wealth
of Nations* and in Hume's *Essays*—was for the John-

stones a sequence of personal and political crises.[10] They were the projectors of a new world that was not to be.

POSSIBLE EMPIRES

One of the Johnstones' distinctive idioms, over most of a century, was their enduring preoccupation with insecurity. "The wretched, lost ELIZA dies," Elizabeth Carolina wrote in the book of translations from Horace that she published after she left England for India in 1761, lamenting the troublesome, fluctuating condition of states and empire.[11] Betty wrote to William about being vastly anxious for news of John, and in great fear for Alexander. James wrote to John about "Anguish Vexation & Anxiety." "It has given me a world of uneasiness," John wrote to William, in a letter about dividends and lawyers' fees.[12] James wrote to Betty about his grief over the insecurity of John's property, "connected with men who exist only by the Circulation of Paper."[13] John's and George's political speech was a series of iterations of abstract nouns of an ever more lurid sort: "punishment, revenge, and retaliation," "miseries, mischiefs and oppressions," and "jealousy, distraction, and distrust."[14] The new frontiers of the British empire were scenes of desolation, in the brothers' public descriptions: "terror, discontent, dissention, and anxiety," as John wrote of Calcutta, or "violence & distraction," in the depiction of Grenada by Alexander and his friends, an "incongruous and unsettled mixture of privileges and jurisdictions."[15]

The future of the British empire, in the descriptions of the Johnstones and their friends, was itself a fluctuating and unsettled prospect. Even the largest choices, between different sorts of empire, were identified as unresolved.[16] The Johnstones were self-conscious, in an ironical sort of way, about the experience of living in the founding moment of a new epoch. "If we live in the advanced period of Empire & reap the advantages of a great society, we must put up with the inconveniences without repining," George wrote in an elaborate letter of solicitation, shortly before he left for West Florida.[17] The different destinies of empire were jumbled together in their projects. George was preoccupied in West Florida with the rise of the Roman republic, and the routes to becoming "Masters of the World," and a few years later, in England, with the decline of the Roman and Spanish empires.[18] The Portugese empire, which was the "first commercial empire of the modern world," was a different dispiriting precedent: "this held up as a mirror to England," as their cousin William Julius Mickle wrote to George.[19] The Dutch empire was more encouraging, at least for William, who looked forward in his project of colonial mortgages to a kind of Dutch destiny for Britain, as the "bankers of Europe" or as a "storehouse or magazine for the goods of all nations," like the North Sea island of Texel, where the great trading ships unloaded their commodities for the Amsterdam markets: "how else have the Dutch flourished? Is not their whole country a kind of Texel?"[20]

In an interesting family rhetoric of the anxieties of empire, the brothers were elaborately uneasy about the prospects of lasting dominion.[21] It was "a golden dream," George said in parliament in 1774, of the government's ideas of "the riches to be drawn from the East Indies."[22] The hopes of American conquest were "romantic dreams," John said in 1777.[23] The idea of a new and independent American empire was flattering, William wrote in 1778, but the "defects" were "too apparent to escape observation"; "are there no rocks or quicksands to be dreaded?"[24] "Their Golden Dreams (as they termed them) were indeed at an end," one of George's friends wrote of the projected expedition to Celebes, Ceylon, and the South Seas in 1781, and described himself, a few weeks later, as "bidding adieu to the *Imaginary* Golden Views off of Rio La Plata."[25] The British empire in India, George and Martha's son George Lindsay Johnstone said in parliament in 1801, was "an empire of opinion," founded on the disinclination of "the natives to reflect upon their own strength"; "he would not say how long we could expect to retain our dominions in India; but he was a sanguine man, indeed, who could expect our empire there to continue for 200 years."[26]

Even the largest reorganization of political space was insecure in the Johnstones' new world of commerce. The Johnstones and their households were the embodiment of the indistinctiveness of the eastern (or Asiatic) and western (or Atlantic) empires, and of north American (or virtuous) and south American (or slave) societies.[27] The many founding moments of the 1770s and 1780s—of the British empire in India, the American Revolution, and the humanitarian movements in opposition to Atlantic slavery—have been seen, in retrospect, as a reordering of economic and political geography. There was a crowded and impoverished eastern empire in India and a new territorial republic in North America, expanding to the west across an empty continent.[28] There was a virtuous republic in the American north, with slave societies in the tropical empires of the Caribbean, and slave-owning societies in South America. But this was not the Johnstones' geography of empire. It was Bengal, in John and his associates' descriptions of the 1760s, that was the richest and most industrious of all modern societies, a "paradise of the earth." George's prospect in West Florida was of a new seaborne empire of commerce, from the West Indies southwards and westwards towards the Bay of Honduras and the Spanish Main, and of a slave plantation economy in the Gulf of Mexico and Mosquitia, as in Jamaica or Saint-Domingue.[29] His sense of the new American republic, in 1779, was coastal or riverine: "the situation of their country, full of creeks and bays, and intersected with rivers, made the watery element almost natural to them."[30] It was an empire of shipping more than an empire of settlement.

The words of Bell or Belinda's petition in September 1771—"to Banish me to one or other of His Majestys Plantations or settlements in the East or West Indies or in America"—were the expression of this indistinction, or of the continuity of the eastern and western and southern empires.[31] So was her life, with her terrible traverse of enslavement in the age of the American Revolution, from Calcutta to London, and London to Fife, and Fife to Virginia. But the Johnstones, too, were indistinctly Indian, American, and West Indian. Gideon lived successively in or around Jamaica, Murshidabad, Benares, Basra, Mauritius, the Cape of Good Hope, Nantucket, New York, and again in Jamaica. John, who was described by David Hume's cousin as "the Indian," owned property in West Florida and Grenada. William's investments extended from Calcutta to Barbados, Grenada, Tobago, Dominica, New York, Virginia, and Florida.[32]

The minor figures in the Johnstones' history, or the friends who came and went in their ventures, lived in the same unsettled world of possible empires. The Johnstones were unusual in the capaciousness of their ambitions. But their acquaintances also moved restlessly among different scenes of commerce and conquest, in the East and the West Indies. There are other family histories that the Johnstones encountered, and that are also stories of multiple empires. Even John Swinton, the sheriff depute of Perthshire who intervened so momentously in the lives of Bell or Belinda and of Joseph Knight, was connected to the opportunities of the distant Indies.[33] His brother Samuel was a naval officer in the West Indies, who later settled in London as a publisher of French newspapers, and became a wine merchant, specializing in the supply of claret to officials of the East India Company in Calcutta.[34] Another brother, Archibald, who went to India as a surgeon and became a Persian translator in Bengal, was an expert on the authenticity of Persian seals and signatures; he returned to Scotland in 1767 with an emissary of the Mughal emperor, a Bengali scholar of Persian and the author of the earliest travel accounts of Europe written (in Persian) by a Bengali.[35]

The family of Alexander Wedderburn, the old friend of the Johnstones and Adam Smith from the goat-whey summer of 1751, was similarly restless. Wedderburn became Lord Clive's lawyer in his disputes over the East India Company, and the owner of a tract of twenty thousand acres of land in East Florida.[36] His brother, David Wedderburn, who participated in the congress of Creek warriors in Pensacola when George was governor, had arrived in Florida undecided between going "upon the

Conquest of Mexico, or Peru" or "making rich" in the upper Mississippi.[37] He then became a general in the service of the East India Company in Bombay. "I have two houses, two carriages, six horses, and fifty three servants at this moment," he wrote to his sister in 1771: "the climate here is delightful, the atmosphere is clear," and "I believe I shall return to Europe with fear and trembling." He died two years later, in an assault on the fortress of Baruch, in northwest India.[38]

The two London merchants who provided Patrick's security when he joined the East India Company in 1753 were respectively a treasury clerk, lottery projector (of a fraudulent lottery to raise money for the purchase of Sir Hans Soane's museum), and agent for Barbados and Virginia; and an East India Company proprietor, former doctor in Jamaica, and part-owner of Bance Island in modern Sierra Leone.[39] James "Ossian" Macpherson, after his employment with George in West Florida and his journey to South Carolina, became an agent in London of the Nawab of Arcot and a historian of the East India Company.[40] The Johnstones' friends the Petries, to whom James wrote about the qualifications of the head and the heart, were the children of a clergyman in the Valley of the Esk. One was an East India Company Army officer in Bengal, where he was John's attorney and took refuge in Gideon's house in Calcutta; he was later a sugar merchant in London and the proprietor of estates in Tobago. A second brother was an East India Company official in Madras, who later became a banker in London and died as governor of Prince of Wales Island, the modern Penang. A third brother was governor of the Cape Coast Castle in modern Ghana and later secretary of the Assembly of Tobago.[41]

George's secretary in West Florida, Primrose Thomson, to whom he sold the "negro wench named Phillis," remained in America after George's departure.[42] He became an expert on the wheels of office in the British empire, including the preparation of expense accounts; he instructed George's successor in "the methods, which I have hitherto pursued, not knowing till then, that it was absolutely necessary to take Vouchers for *every trifling* disbursement."[43] Primrose Thomson then made his way to India, where he became "Quarter Master General of the Vizier's Army in Bengal" and died in office. His own brother, who had also served in West Florida during George's government, became a lieutenant in the expedition, in the convoy under George's command, to the Cape of Good Hope, and either Madras or the Rio Plata; in his will, he acknowledged debts to both John and George, to be repaid out of the "sixteen thousand rupees" that he had been left by his brother Primrose in Bengal.[44]

WHAT IS THE STATE?

The Johnstones' frontiers of empire were insecure, in a more insidious sense, because they were frontiers in the mind, or frontiers of the public and the private, of commerce and power and law. Like the legal world of the eighteenth-century American colonies, in Hendrik Hartog's description, the Johnstones' economic world was a "strange and unfamiliar place." It was strange to them, as well as in the retrospect of historical understanding. "The very possibility of thinking of law as a separated, bounded, distinctive sphere of activity and thought" was an innovation of the late eighteenth and early nineteenth centuries in North America, in Hartog's account; and so too, in America and elsewhere, was the idea of the economy or of a distinctive sphere of economic or commercial or business life.[45] An economic empire, in which "commerce is extended all over the globe" (as in David Hume's prospect of peaceful exchange), was a world in which buying and selling, killing and conquering, ruling and governing, were interwoven, or interconnected.[46]

The exchanges of commerce, in the new theories with which the Johnstones were so familiar, were made possible by political institutions, and in particular by the security of persons and property, and the impartial administration of justice.[47] They were made possible, too, by the new sentiments of the times, or by the mildness and moderation—the disposition to obey the laws and to resolve disputes without intimidation or violence—that were so admired by the Edinburgh philosophers. Economic exchanges were both distinct from and contingent upon political (or legal) and social (or psychological) institutions. But the ordinary course of events, or "buying and selling, the more common and ordinary transactions of human life," in Smith's description, was at the same time continually at risk from bad political institutions and bad dispositions. It was most immediately at risk, in Smith's theory, in long-distance commerce, or from the "regulations of the mercantile system," of which "those which concern the trade to America and the East Indies derange it perhaps more than any other."[48]

The relationships among economic, political, and military exchanges were the object of abstract reflection in the Johnstones' lifetimes, even to merchants and soldiers. "A trading and a fighting company, is a two headed monster in nature that cannot exist long," one of John's acquaintances in Calcutta wrote in 1765, "and thus we shall go on, grasping and expending, until we cram our hands so full that they become cramped and numbed."[49] "We are at once Tradesmen & Soldiers to America," Adam Ferguson lamented in 1772, to Ossian Macpherson's cousin, "and the Question has now become complicated in the highest degree."[50] "What is the state?" Alexander Wedderburn asked in a parliamentary debate on East Indian affairs in 1773, and what "if you say the Company is the state?"[51] Even William returned at the end of his life to earlier disputes: "the character of traders and sovereigns was inconsistent, and their union had never failed to prove ruinous to the mercantile concerns of these counting-house kings."[52]

The relationships of commerce and power were at the same time connected to the most immediate choices of the Johnstones' lives. It is extremely difficult, now, to imagine oneself into the eighteenth-century world of the mind, in which there was only a very vague sense of the economy, or economic life, as a distinct and well-defined subset of human existence, and even more difficult to imagine oneself in a world in which these distinctions and definitions were themselves the object of anxious reflection.[53] But these were the circumstances of the Johnstones' empire. The brothers were confronted, as John was in Bengal in the 1760s, with a multiplicity of interests: his own private interest, which could be pursued in the public economy of presents or the private economy of the country commerce; his public interest in the commerce of the Company, which was itself private; his private interest in his position in the

Company's public council; and his public interest, within the council, in defending the "liberties of the servants." The Johnstones became rich in the course of activities that were not in subsequent terms, and not even in the terms of *The Wealth of Nations*, commercial: marriage, friendship, office, the semi-economic, semi-military economy of prizes, and the semi-economic, semi-political economy of presents. When John was accused of having become angry, in 1765, when his present from the banker Jagat Seth was sent in public and not "privately," he responded that it was not the publicness but the conveyance of the present that he objected to, being sent in a cart, or "hackaree."[54]

All the Johnstone brothers except William, and one of the sisters, Margaret, were involved, at one time or another, in military life. But military relationships were themselves substantially financial, or commercial. Patrick, who was in the service of the East India Company as an accountant, was the only one of the brothers and sisters to die violently in wartime. John, who entered the Company's service as a writer, came into and out of military occupations in the Company's own army, as a paymaster, an artillery officer, a "commissary," and a purveyor of bullocks: "I'm I believe at Last quite of the Army," he wrote to James Balmain from Calcutta in 1761.[55] Gideon, who served in the Royal Navy in the West Indies and went to India as a free merchant, also joined the East India Company's army in Patna.[56] The Company's army was a private military enterprise that offered "larger pay, the hopes of wealth, the spirit of adventure and enterprise, but, above all, the not being inlisted for life," in David Wedderburn's summary of

1772.[57] But the king's army, too, was an economy of fluctuating prices, as in the tariffs for lieutenancies and majorities that were such a feature of Louisa, Charlotte, and Betty's correspondence.[58] When John and William were poring over the history of their transactions with Alexander over the Grenada plantation, one of the items was the interest on a loan of one thousand pounds: "it is certain you Paid that Money for his Commission."[59]

The economy of naval prizes in which George and Gideon were involved was similarly intricate. George's letters from his wartime posting in Lisbon were full of cruises and pursuits: "I forgot to tell you I took two small Privateers . . . [and] a Snow with Fish for all which I shall touch about 200£," he wrote to William in 1761.[60] The possibility of advancement was the outcome of changes in naval intelligence, in the value of cargoes, in admiralty regulations, and in the decisions of prize courts. It was dependent on personal relationships, which were also economic relationships.[61] Even the Johnstones' elaborate investments in estates in the Scottish borders were inspired by the prospect of naval fortune. When Gideon was thinking of returning to Scotland, John advised him to purchase no more than a modest estate, sufficient "to make a good Vote at least" (or a vote in a parliamentary election) and "easiest to be attended to by a factor," "till you Catch a Spanish Register Ship & be able to take In the half of the County."[62] An Edinburgh accountant who was still struggling with the residue of George's estate, more than twenty years after his death, wrote in 1809 that "there are many transactions, obscure and unfinished," in part having to do with prize agents and navy agents: "the Accountant has some doubt of being able to institute a proper account."[63]

The economy of presents imposed an even more changeable mixture of political and commercial advantage. There was no senior officer or East India Company official, Lord Clive said in the House of Commons, "not a governor, not a member of council . . . who has not received presents. With regard to Bengal, there they flow in abundance indeed."[64] One of the Johnstones' political friends was reported to have "with great humour, entered into the history of presents": "when taken, he said, without consent, they were plunder; when taken with consent they were gifts, and when taken by connivance, they became inland trade."[65] But for John, the legal and moral circumstances of his Indian presents were a question of the utmost seriousness. He had received presents of the sort that were given, like Lord Clive's *jaghire*, from a superior to an inferior, and presents, like the "acknowledgements" he was given by the Seat (or Seth) bankers, of the sort that were given by an inferior to a superior.[66] They had been given to him as a political figure in the Company's government, and as a merchant who was no longer in the Company's service. They were "fair and avowed presents," in his own description, "agreeable to the universal practice of the country" in all ages; "no presents were ever received in India upon a more honourable footing." It was the practice of the Company, rather, that was unsettled, changing with "a critical exactness of weeks, days, or hours," and with the voyages of ships that arrived in India bearing the orders that specified a new regulation, and the "advice" that the order was already repealed.[67]

WHAT WAS, AND WHAT WAS NOT LAW

The law itself was for the Johnstones a changing and unreliable condition. The sisters and brothers were involved in an dizzying array of legal causes and legal instances: infanticide, treason, naturalization, the law of slavery (in Perthshire) and the law of slavery (in Grenada), inheritance, illegitimacy, salvage, debt, restitution, elections, bankruptcy, courts martial, entail, torture, alimony, the law of separation in England (Louisa's) and the law of separation in Scotland (Barbara's). "Heartily sick am I of the Law in all its branches," John wrote to William, amidst the legal disputes with the East India Company over his presents and jewels. James, with his dire experience of litigation over Louisa's inheritance, described lawyers to Alexander as "the most worthless and abandoned of Mankind."[68]

The frontiers of economic life were indistinct in the new world of commercial exchange, and so were the frontiers of the law. But the Johnstones also had an imposing conception, like so many others at the time—the miners of Westerhall, with their "foundamental Articles written on Vellum" and their "Code of Laws," or Laura Pulteney's heiress in France, the German princess, who believed that "it is easier to restore customary law than gothic ideas"—of the law as an abstract ideal. It was an ideal, in turn, that they described as being in danger from one extremity of the British empire to the other. In Burdwan John had sought to point out to the "Country People" "how they may have Justice" "publicly tried, entered, and registered in Books for that Purpose."[69] The East India Company "give Law every where," he wrote from Calcutta in 1761, and then, in 1765, that its secret committee had constituted itself as a court "whose Laws and Rights we know not the Bounds of." The attempts of the local magistrates to prevent emigration were "illegal," he exclaimed years later in Stirling.[70] Alexander described the torture of the slaves in Grenada as "illegal & unnatural proceedings," his own prosecution as "illegal and malevolent," and the acts of the government of Grenada as "Illegal, Grievous, Cruel, oppressive and unjust."[71]

"I . . . observe the Word Illegal is somewhat frequent in your Correspondence, and I was also favored with a Sight of the Word Anté constitutional," George wrote from West Florida to the British commander in chief, in 1765.[72] His letters to the Board of Trade were a cascade of commentaries on "Language without a Meaning" and the "abundance of Words, without any precise Idea": "tho I do acknowledge, the Word Civil as sometimes opposed to Military Affairs, and sometimes opposed to Criminal Affairs, and as sometimes opposed to Canon Law, and as sometimes opposed to Common Law, and as sometimes opposed to Statute Law, with many other Interpretations, are sufficient to bewilder Brains more distinct than those of West Florida."[73] George's letters were also commentaries on the practice of the law, and on the details of "settling" the civil government: "the Registers of the Country threatened to be thrown into the Streets," just as the minutes of the council of Grenada, in the case of Augustine, the fugitive former slave, were "omitted, lost, or supprest," "so many public documents being wanting."[74] "It is virtually understood that the power that makes the laws will not infringe them," Ossian Macpherson wrote in Florida, and one of George's last official acts in the province was to sign a law "appointing where the laws of this province shall be lodged."[75]

The confusion of laws was particularly intricate when it involved the legal systems of different societies and religions and institutions: the bilingual law of Grenada, or the quadrilingual law of West Florida, or the law of the "Mayor's Court" of Calcutta.[76] George was concerned in the case of an escaped slave and an indentured "mulatto," who survived a shipwreck in the Gulf of Mexico, in a jurisdiction that was either French or Spanish or maritime.[77] West Florida was a land of many identities and many islands, as George sought to explain in his Creek and Choctaw congresses, and in his correspondence with his French and Spanish interlocutors: the English and the French "Red Men," on the two sides of the Mississippi, the French in New Orleans as Spaniards, the French in Florida as English, and so forth.[78] Alexander's dispute with the governor of Grenada involved the relationship between civil and martial law, in the case of the "leagerlady" who had joined the army in Cork.[79] John was deeply involved in a dispute in Bengal over whether the English officials' "gomastahs," or commercial agents, should be subject only to English courts, a policy of which John's ally of the time, Warren Hastings, wrote that "this is not only to deprive [the inhabitants of India] of their own Laws, but to deny them even the Benefit of any."[80]

The law of slavery was both a domestic or household law and a regime of multiple jurisdictions. Joseph Knight's legal victory in Scotland in 1778 turned on the relationship between the "municipal laws of Jamaica" and the "Law of Scotland [which] acknowledges the Law of Nature as its rule"; on the just regard that was due, in a time of "great commercial connections," to "the laws of other countries"; and on the presence or absence of a "written contract in the *Whidah* or *Anamaboe* language."[81] There were individuals whose lives were at the intersection of these connections: Joseph Knight himself, or the Armenian merchants who came to seek justice at the King's Bench in London; or John's partner Motiram in Calcutta in 1765, of whom John said that, although he lived in the East India Company's enclave, he was "ignorant of our Laws and Rights."[82]

Bell or Belinda, in her petition in Perth in 1771, described herself as a native of the kingdom of Bengal, lately come to Scotland, and, in the same expression that John used of Motiram, "altogether ignorant of the Laws thereof." She had been the subject, successively, of the jurisdictions in India that the English described as the "country" courts (either "Gentoo," or Hindu, or "Cadi" or Muslim): of the East India Company's own jurisdiction; of admiralty law at sea, of Dutch colonial law in the Cape and Portugese law in Lisbon; of English law, Scots law, and again of admiralty law. She invoked her understanding of the awfulness of infanticide in her petition ("a Crime against the Laws of God and nature in every kingdome, and which she abhors"), and she also invoked her condition as a thing, or an object of property rights (the rights of her owner), "so far as she has an interest, in the Disposall of her Person." She was described as a "Slave or Servant" in the court papers in Scotland and as one of four "convicts" in the papers sent to Scotland from Virginia. When she landed in Virginia, she became the subject of yet another jurisdiction, in which "all negroes, Moors, and mulattoes, except Turks and Moors in amity with Great Britain, brought into this country by sea, or by land, were slaves."[83]

The legal roles of individuals changed over time, in the frightening oscillations of commerce, sovereignty, and jurisdiction that William Bolts described in India— the metamorphoses of judges and justices—and that John anticipated, in one of his speeches about the suspension of habeas corpus in North America, as a sequence of "confinements, commitments, massacres, and the whole train of consequences."[84] The laws also changed, and so, most insidiously, did the distinction between laws, rules, regulations, instructions, and values. "Judicial, administrative, and legislative powers were blurred and diffuse," as in Hartog's description of eighteenth-century North America, and so were personal rights and property rights, judgements of law and judgements of fact, and the rhetoric of "legal, moral and political arguments." The possibility of thinking of the law as an autonomous sphere was an innovation in North America, and it was an innovation too, or a distant prospect, in the Johnstones' own scenes of administrative power. The frontiers or boundaries of economic, political, and military existence were indistinct in the Johnstones' experience, and so were the boundaries of the law: in James's words of 1785, "what was, and what was not law."[85]

A SOCIETY OF PERSONS

The Johnstones' failures of imagination—or their tendency to be on the losing side of the history of the British empire, as they made and risked so many fortunes—

were the outcome of these conflicting and changing objectives, and of the tension between commerce and political power. All the brothers and sisters, at home and overseas, were economic individuals, who used and thought about money in Adam Smith's sense: "every man thus lives by exchanging, or becomes in some measure a merchant, and the society itself grows to be what is properly a commercial society."[86] They were enterprising in their ventures, and in the invention of their own lives: new names, new identities, new furniture, new houses. George's first political oration in North America, to the Choctaws in March 1765, was in part an incantation of prices: "I should inform you that this Liquor is bought for almost Nothing and that you get it at a great Price . . . The Handkerchief which I now hold in my hand Cost in those Miserable times, the Sum of thirty Dollars, and the Like Can now be had for at most half a Dollar."[87]

But the Johnstones were at the same time participants in the "mercantile system," or the highly regulated commerce between Europe and the two new worlds of Asia and America, that was Smith's principal object of criticism in *The Wealth of Nations*.[88] John and Gideon were for short periods "voluntary, unconnected settlers" or free merchants in India. They were individuals making their own fortunes, as in Smith's theory of free trade to India, in the description of the Johnstones' cousin William Julius Mickle: a "Chaos of Confusion" or the "plan, that Government should leave every subject to the course of his own industry."[89] The brothers were at other times the servants of established institutions: the East India Company, the Royal Navy, or the Board of

Trade. They were sometimes unconnected, and sometimes lived by the connections of office, family, and political influence.

The Johnstones flourished in the changing and contested space between the political and the economic: economic exchanges, economic dispositions, and economic regulations, including the regulations that were the foundation of all private exchanges and the regulations that were no more than the protection of particular private interests. In the unending enterprise that John described as "the Scramble for Power & Perquisites," they competed on the basis of economic information, including information about reputation, influence, and interests.[90] But it was this promiscuity of interests, in turn, or this extensive prospect of economic exchange, that was the explanation for the Johnstones' most obvious failures of political insight or political foresight.

In the disputes over the American Revolution, the Johnstones were on the wrong side in the obvious sense that their expectation, like the expectations of almost everyone else in British public life, was that the independence of the new United States would be ephemeral, in economic if not in political terms. They were on the losing side, more idiosyncratically, in that they were so consistent in seeing the conflicts in America as a question of interest and compromise. William's pamphlet of 1778 on American affairs was addressed to men of moderation, "sufficiently divested of passion and prejudice, to be able to discern the true interest of America."[91] George's ill-timed letters, as a member of the commission of conciliation with the American colonists, were an evocation of "the real interest of your country," as he

wrote to the brother of Barbara's son-in-law, "a beneficial union of interests."[92]

The Johnstones' prospect of economic empire, in the
Americas, was of multiple, innocuous investment opportunities. The establishment of "a more regular form
of government" was essential to the security of property, as George and John declared in the dispute over
the venture of the Scottish entrepreneurs in Mosquitia
in the Bay of Honduras. But the specific institutions for
the protection of commerce were multiple and fluctuating. The idea of a colonial government, or of an outpost
of empire, was elusive even to the British administration. The British settlement in Mosquitia was purely
private, as the ministry said in response to George's
complaint: "it had never been considered in the light of
a colony, but rather a society of persons."[93] When William resumed his own North American investments in
the 1790s—his project of land acquisitions in the new
American republic—it was in association with an imposing array of political friends: Patrick Colquhoun,
the Glasgow merchant to whom Bell or Belinda was
consigned in 1771, Aaron Burr, John Adams's son-in-
law, Benjamin Franklin's grandson, Alexander Hamilton, and Barbara's American grandson.

Even the Johnstones' most unlikely expectation—their
prospect of a new Atlantic empire in Central and South
America—was the outcome of these ideas of a moderate
or interested state. In the Johnstones' geography of empire, the opportunities for future prosperity in the Americas lay to the south and the southwest, and in the coastal
and riverine commerce that George described as "watery." They and their friends were preoccupied, in par-

ticular, with access to the Pacific or the South Seas, "by way of the Lake of Nicaragua" (in the Mosquitia venture), or via Cartagena (as in their uncle's earlier expedition), or via the Rio Plata in modern Argentina (in the unsuccessful project of capturing Ceylon and Celebes).[94] They were preoccupied, too, with islands, trading ports, and waterborne commerce. The island of Grenada was "civilized and well-cultivated," a "most valuable acquisition," for Alexander's friends in the 1760s; Pensacola was to be the emporium of the new world; Mosquitia was for George's friends in 1777 "a delightful and most valuable country"; Trinidad was for Patrick Colquhoun a "fine island [that] only requires an extensive and industrious white population to render it among the richest and most productive countries in the world."[95]

The new empire to the south was a society of persons, or merchants, in these visions of future investment, more than an empire of land and settlement. It was an empire without a state, with the protection of naval rather than military power. It was also an empire of slavery, as will be seen, or of the new plantation economy in which the individuals who were the instruments of production were themselves objects of exchange.[96] It was a society of endless interest and endless prudence. "He was not to be dazzled by splendid theory," William said of the perfect statesman, in his speech against Wilberforce's bill for the abolition of the slave trade; "he was much more—he was a man of prudence."[97] The investor, too, was a man of prudence, weighing all the circumstances of a case. As William observed in the same speech, "If it were merely to talk of humanity and justice, and those popular topics, the task would be easy; but in the present instance the considerations were more important, as involving the great interests of the country."[98]

A MODERATE EMPIRE

The Johnstones' ventures in India, too, were a shifting mixture of commerce and empire. John was the only one of the brothers who was an important figure, in an indirect sort of way, in the nineteenth- and twentieth-century epics of progress and empire.[99] He was the emblem, in particular, of the early East India Company system of "corruption," which Lord Clive was described as having vanquished in the moment of destiny of 1765. John was, in Lord Macaulay's description, "one of the boldest and worst men" in the Company's government.[100] His fall from power in the East India Company's council in Bengal, in the aftermath of the presents that he, Gideon, and their friends had received from the Nawab of Bengal and the Seth bankers, was the outcome of a ritual of purification, in Macaulay's historical story: the moment in which "English power came among them," no longer "unaccompanied by English morality."[101] It was the repudiation, at last, of the moderate state, in which "corruption and frequent revolutions must in the end overset us."[102]

But the moderate empire was identified at the time as a dominion of free economic exchange. The dispute between John and Lord Clive, in Calcutta in the summer of 1765, was over the relationship between the East India Company and the Indian sovereigns, and the regulation of the British officials' involvement in Indian commerce, at least as much as it was over the much-despised presents (of which Clive had earlier been an even more opulent recipient, as the Johnstones pointed out on many occasions).[103] John's criticism of Clive was to a striking extent a defense of freedom and competition. He described the proposed reform of the inland commerce in salt as a "Monopoly," in contrast to the earlier scene, where there were "Competitors," a "Power of bettering ourselves by selling to others," and "every Merchant has been . . . at Liberty to trade" with "the Zemindars [or landlords] under the Nabob's jurisdiction."[104] His own evocation of economic exchanges in the interior of Bengal, in 1761, had been a scene of universal industry for Europeans and Indians. There was even the possibility of buying and selling landed estates, "the property in the Lands also being alienable and saleable, much in the same manner as with us": "from the prospect of Gain, and security of possession, industry and agriculture will thereby be promoted."[105]

The opposing side in India, or Lord Clive's side, were, by contrast, the proponents of a strong and regulating state. Clive identified himself explicitly with the security of government (or corporate) regulation, as against the free trade in which "every Servant and Free Merchant corresponded with whom they pleased."[106] The conflict in which he and John were leading figures was a dispute over independence, in the sense of the freedom of individuals from the restrictions of established institutions. It was the "forward Spirit of Independency," in Clive's expression of 1765, that was at the heart of the crisis: an "independent Way of thinking and acting," or an "independent and licentious Spirit." On his return to India, Clive recounted, he had discovered among the British officials a scene in which "all Distinction ceased, and every Rank became, in a Manner, upon an Equality." This "too little Inequality of Rank" was tending even to "democratic Anarchy."[107]

The crisis in India in 1765 was a conflict, at the same time, over the relationship between British officials as subjects and Indian princes as sovereigns. The moderate state was so abhorrent for Clive because it was a political system in which East India Company officials relied, as they had relied for more than a century, on the protection of Indian princes and Indian laws. The English were merchants, not sovereigns. They had by settling in India become almost Indians themselves, all the barriers being "broken down between the English and the country government."[108] They were emigrants, in the expression of John's partner William Bolts: "the British emigrants residing and established in India."[109] John, with his hackarees and Athats and his Persian prepositions, lived close to the Indian land that he could not own and that he could "farm" only with respect to salt, or tax revenues.[110] He was the emblem of a different destiny, and even of the Persian historian Ghulam Husain's unlikely prospect of invaders who, "although they keep up a strangeness of ideas and practices," "fix the foot of residence and permanency in these countries."[111] As Clive complained during his conflict with John in the summer of 1765, "There seems to me to have been a combination between the blacks and whites, to divide all the revenues of the Company between them."[112]

ECONOMIC THEORIES

The Johnstones lived in a new world of laissez-faire, in all these respects, and at the same time they lived in an old world of compromise and political interest.[113] They were the embodiment of "the true spirit of commerce," in William's expression of 1788, and of its conflicts.[114] They sought to compete by all respectable means, or by all means that were decorous or honorable. But the frontiers of the decorous were in continuing flux, in their lifetimes, and with their own changing circumstances. Their individual choices were almost exactly the choices with which the theorists of political economy were so preoccupied: about how to compete, and whether to seek advancement by influence, or information about prices, or political office, or the opportunity of regulation.

The generation following the publication of *The Wealth of Nations* has been seen, since the early nineteenth-century histories of economic thought, as the founding epoch of a new system of political economy, in the high or scientific theory of economists, and in the "'middle' principles" or "intermediate maxims" of public life (in the expression of the economic writer Walter Bagehot).[115] It was the moment of origin of the ideas and systems that were eventually triumphant, in the genealogy of nineteenth- and twentieth-century thought. But the system of freedom of commerce was also the object of serious and sustained critiques, in which several of the Johnstones' friends were involved and in which they were themselves, as in so many other instances, on almost all sides, and on different sides at different times.

In a first critique, the new system of political economy was described as unrealistic, in that it disregarded the extent to which commerce required the protection of well-enforced laws and of military force, especially in relation to overseas ventures. This was William Julius Mickle's criticism of Adam Smith's theory of Asian commerce—in a long introduction of 1778 to his translation of the *Lusiad*—or of a "free trade with India." Smith's prospect of voluntary or independent or purely economic settlers included "not one idea of Indian jealousy and hatred of Europeans," Mickle wrote: "It is, according to the Doctor, as safe to settle in, and trade with India, as to take a counting-house near London-bridge, or to buy a peck of peas at Covent-Garden."[116]

Long-distance commerce, in the early criticism of Smith by Mickle and others, required at least one of several possible types of political order. There was the order provided by the sovereigns of the countries in which the commerce took place; the order provided by the mercantile corporations themselves, including the East India Company and the other merchant-sovereigns; the order provided by the sovereigns of the merchants' own countries, which was the recourse of empire, in a military and political sense; and the order provided by as yet uninvented institutions that would transcend the frontiers of existing political societies. The theorists of free trade were opposed to both corporate and imperial power, as their critics observed. They were thereby in the position of abandoning European settlers to the protection of jealous local sovereigns, or of visionary political projects.[117] These were disputes over the theory of political economy and over the politics of race. But they were also the debates in which John and Clive were involved as protagonists in Calcutta in 1765: over independency and free trade and the possibility of "a combination between the blacks and whites."[118]

A second critique of the new theory of free trade was that it was unrealistic in that it was founded on an excessive confidence in the wisdom of individuals. It was oddly ingenuous, in the view of its critics, in its presumption that individuals pursue their own interests by economic competition and not by competition for political positions or restrictions. "Mr Smith . . . thinks that trade should be left to itself, because individuals understand best their own interests," the Edinburgh publicist William Playfair, an associate of William and of Patrick Colquhoun, wrote in his own, augmented edition of *The Wealth of Nations*; he commented that Smith at the same time complained "in unusually bitter terms of that desire of monopoly which is, and which must be, the concomitant of a desire to accumulate and become rich."[119]

In the real world of commerce, that is to say, and especially in the real world of empire, individuals were not always wise or foresighted. They pursued their own interests most efficiently by understanding the rules of political influence: of recommendations, parliamentary boroughs, indirect taxes (as in George's project of the East India Company's exporting tea to America, and again in his project of vegetable oil plantations in Honduras), the changing regulations governing gratuities from Indian princes, and the jurisprudence of mortgages on slaves. William was "totally absorbed in the accumulation of wealth," the Johnstones' American nephew wrote at the very end of his life: "his character is distant & reserved and the principal occupation of his mind at present is, borough jobbing. If this is respectability of character I am at a loss to define the word."[120]

The new system of political economy was considered to be both unrealistic and dangerous, thirdly, in that it disregarded the extent to which commerce required civility and virtue, and it thereby contributed, in turn, to the subversion of virtue itself. Its tendency, in the view of its early critics, was to undermine the social foundations of order. This was the criticism made by William Julius Mickle and others (including James's old school friend Alexander Carlyle), of the infidelity of David Hume and Adam Smith: "introducing that unrestrained and universal commerce, which propagates opinions as well as commodities."[121] The criticism was elaborated later, in the period following the French Revolution, into a large theory of social destruction. For the poet Robert Southey, Smith was a Diogenes of the modern subject, poised to "pluck the wings of his intellect, strip him of the down and plumage of his virtues."[122] The effect of materialist doctrines was to transform society into an anarchy of interests and desires, in which individuals would be more terrifying to each other than the "cayman of the Ganges and the tiger of Zara."[123]

All these early criticisms of laissez-faire political economy were familiar, in one form or another, to the Johnstones and their friends. James, who had been "enchanted with the first edition" of William Julius Mickle's translation of the *Lusiad*, immediately borrowed a copy of the new edition, with its vehement criticism of Adam Smith. "When he has seen that part where you cut off the heads of those Gigantick Errors you have found in Dr Smiths book I doubt not of his being highly pleased & making known his opinion to every body," the Johnstones' Uncle Walter wrote to Mickle.[124] But the dismal choices that the critics described—to live under the protection of Indian princes or to become sovereigns oneself, to choose between one's immediate and enduring interests, to choose what sort of person one wants to be, or seem to be—were also the choices of the Johnstones' own lives. They were enchanted with works of economic theory and economic criticism, and they lived amidst personal choices that were also choices of economic systems or worlds of thought.

The early criticisms of political economy were addressed, implicitly or explicitly, in the nineteenth-century epics of the history of economic thought, which were also delineations of the territory of economic life. They were implicit, too, in the other nineteenth-century epic of virtuous empire. Even in the most civilized societies, in these historical stories, there were imperfections to be reformed (as in the semi-economic semi-political institutions of the army, the navy, the parliamentary boroughs, and the East India Company). In uncivilized societies, or the societies that John Stuart Mill described as existing in a condition of infancy, or "nonage," there were by contrast no conditions for economic freedom; there was only empire, or the far-off prospect of improvement. Political economy was itself a source of virtue in civilized or commercial societies. It was a Christian way of thinking and the foundation of consistent customs, or norms, of civilized competition and enlightened self-interest.[125] This was the intellectual world of the Johnstones' respectable grandchildren in nineteenth-century Scotland and the nineteenth-century British empire. But it was not their own world of opportunity.

Chapter Five

Experiences of Empire

The Johnstones' experience of empire was indistinctly public and private, economic and political, reckless and prudent. It was disorderly in multiple respects, with regard to the forces of progress, or the forces of empire. But the family's history and the history of their extended households provide a circumstantial view of eighteenth-century economic life. Their stories show the multiplicity of connections between the slave economies of the times and the enlightened officials of East Indian and Atlantic commerce. The history of the Johnstones' fortunes—of how these brothers and sisters, who grew up with the prospect of penury and loss, were able to make money out of information, and out of the returns on their initial, unlikely prizes (William's wife's inheritance and John's presents from the Indian princes)—is an unusual story of economic improvement. The story of the Johnstones' family exchanges is the vista of a multiplier effect by which distant events were of consequence in the interior of Scotland, and by which the empire at home became an information order of sisters and nieces. It is a vista, too, of intimate exchange.

Slavery in the British Empire

The Johnstones were minor participants in the political history of British slavery over more than forty years. They were on different sides at different times and in different circumstances: Alexander, as an opponent of the torture of slaves, in 1770; George, as a defender of the kindness of American slave-owners, in 1775; John, together with his son and his brother-in-law, Charlotte's widower, as subscribers to the Society for the Abolition of the Slave Trade, in 1788; James as a supporter of the immediate abolition of the slave trade, in 1792, and of the gradual abolition of slavery; and William, as a prominent defender of the slave trade and slavery in 1805.[1] Margaret's son-in-law, John Wedderburn, was the owner and the loser in the case that ended the law of slavery in Scotland; the Johnstones' nephew was his legal counsel. The Johnstones' two slaves, Bell or Belinda and Joseph Knight, were figures of world-historical importance in these dramas of progress. Bell or Belinda was the last person who was determined to have been a slave by a court in the British Isles, and Joseph Knight's law suit against John Wedderburn ended the legal recognition of slavery in Britain.

Of the seven Johnstone brothers who set out from the valley of the Esk in the 1730s and 1740s, at least six became the owners of other people. James inherited Alexander's slaves in Grenada. Alexander bought the Baccaye plantation and its slaves with money borrowed from William and John. William owned slaves in Grenada, Dominica, and Tobago. George owned the slave called Phillis, in West Florida. John owned Bell or Belinda, and "Molly," and some share in Alexander's slaves in Grenada. Gideon married into the Liverpool business of the Atlantic slave trade, and his father-in-law, Scrope Colquitt, was a Liverpool lawyer, a parliamentary lobbyist for the "Free and open Trade to Africa," and the part owner in the 1740s and 1750s of three slave ships trading between the Gold Coast and Jamaica, Antigua, and Tortola.[2] Elizabeth Caroline Johnstone, the historian of Etruria, remembered a nursery maid who "was a half Negro—Her father a fine & noble looking man was the liberated slave of my G. Uncle Gideon Johnstone who bought Hawk Hill & left it & his slaves to my Grandfather."[3] Only Patrick, who died at the age of eighteen, was uninvolved in the slave economy of the times, or involved only to the extent of the fortunes of the two merchants, one a political agent of Virginia and Barbados, and the other a proprietor of the slave-trading island of Bance in Sierra Leone, who provided the security in 1753 for his passage to India.

For the Johnstone sisters and sisters-in-law, the experience of setting out for the empire was from the outset an encounter with slavery and with slaves. When the *Earl of Holdernesse*, in which Elizabeth Carolina Keene, later Johnstone, and her sister travelled to India in 1761, was close to Madagascar, "two canues with two men in each came on board"; "they spoke a little Broken English and . . . they would fane have had us go in, telling us there was plenty of Bullocks and Slaves to be had."[4] Martha Ford lived in a slave society in Pensacola. Margaret Wedderburn lived in Perthshire with a slave, Joseph Knight. John, Elizabeth Carolina, and their son lived in Fife with Bell or Belinda; Betty, Charlotte, and Charlotte's husband, James Balmain, were frequent visitors. When Margaret Wedderburn's daughter and son-in-law died in Calcutta and at sea, their sons were left in Penang in the care of a European servant and a "female slave."[5]

The Johnstones and their children—or all of them except Alexander and his "mulato daughter"—lived at a distance from the exchanges of the slave economy.[6]

James, who was identified in his will as "Sir James Johnstone of Grenada," never visited the plantation he inherited, although his manager wrote to him from time to time about the transactions of the estate: "the Mulatto carpenter purchased in October last, as formerly advised," who "is really a valuable acquisition," or "Ten fine Stout young Men & Women at £56 p head."[7] John reported to William that Alexander had drawn on their credit "for 12 Negroes," very much against his inclination.[8] Even in Jamaica, John Wedderburn lived high above the exchanges of the slave market, in a literal sense, or "up" from the port in which the slaving vessels were unloaded, in Joseph Knight's description. "He was sent up from the Ship to the Petitioners house in Jamaica," Joseph Knight recalled of his arrival in the Americas, in the statement of his own history that he presented to the magistrates in Perthshire, at the outset of his law suit.[9] When a namesake of Patrick Colquhoun, William Colhoon or Colqhoun, the son of a lesser Glasgow merchant, became chief mate of a "very fine vessel" bound from Senegal to Virginia in 1770 with a hundred and fifty slaves, he wrote to his sister in Glasgow that "it is a very precarious cargoe as for me it is the first time we always have plenty of noise and stink in proportion."[10] There was no first time, for the Johnstones, in the immediate experience of the Atlantic slave trade: no noise and stink.

But the institution of slavery was at the horizon of the Johnstones' expectations of empire, from the East Indies to the Gulf of Mexico. They planned their involvement in the sugar industry, or "branch." "Among my Papers I observe a Plan No. 1 'To Settle a Plantation.' This was one you gave me 1766, when our engaging in this branch was first thought of in Consequence of [Alexander's] Letters," John wrote to William, in one of their continuing exchanges over the partnership in Grenada.[11] Alexander named five of his brothers and three of his nephews in his will as potential future owners of his slaves and boiling houses.[12] Louisa, as James's widow, inherited the Grenada plantation and was its owner at the time of the Grenada slave revolution of 1795; "tranquillity is completely established," her friends were informed in 1796, which "holds out the prospect of Lady J's enjoying before long a handsome revenue from the Estate."[13] William's daughter Henrietta Laura became the owner of the Grenada estates that were the subject of litigation between her heirs and George's grandchildren. Louisa's mother, many years earlier, had been left an interest in estates in Ireland, England, Wales, and Barbados, as had her grandmother, the beneficiary of estates in Ireland, England, and Barbados.[14]

These expectations were not even unusual in the Johnstones' milieu of the Scottish law and in their circles of friends and associates. To move outwards from the Johnstones' experience is to find the same normality of empire in the lives of their friends. Alexander Wedderburn, who spoke so eloquently of the East India Company ("what is the state?"), was in correspondence with the governor of East Florida in 1775 about "the expense of settling a Plantation," and even about settling in America himself, or "commencing an East Floridan": "Estimate of the purchase of 30 Negroes and other Necessaries for the Settlement of an Indigo Plantation."[15] His brother, George's friend David Wedderburn, travelled to West Florida via the slave societies of St. Christopher, Antigua, and Jamaica. A few weeks after his arrival in Mobile in

1765, he wrote home about "a Negro Servant of mine [who] was shot t'other day in the Shoulder by accident" and the promise he had been given by one of his new friends: "if I believed my Slave had been Shot designedly by an Indian he would bring me the Indians head that shot him before the Sun went down."[16] Once he was settled in India in 1771, David Wedderburn wrote to his sister with details of the society of the English settlement, a narrative of the politics of the East India Company, and "a pretty exact account of my revenue, my expences": "the first year, I was at a considerably larger expence, for many obvious reasons, than I shall any succeeding one furniture, linnen, China, Horses, Carriages, Slaves, House &c. &c. were all to be purchased."[17] When he died in Baruch in 1773, the inventory of his estate, sent back to his sister and brother in England, included "5 Goats & 6 Kids Slaves 4 Coffrey Boys 4 Malabar do. 1 Box China Fireworks."[18]

The minor figures in the Johnstones' story had much the same experience of overseas enterprise, in which slavery and and the enslaved, or the once enslaved, came and went, on the horizon of empire. Samuel Swinton, the wine merchant and newspaper publisher, and John Swinton's brother, lived in London with a black servant whom he had "brought . . . from the West Indies" and later with a servant described in a court case of 1771 as "a little tawney boy belonging to Mr. Swinton."[19] A spectacular legal case of the period, in which John Swinton was one of the advocates, involved another close acquaintance and neighbor of the Johnstones, Sir William Maxwell, who was later both Alexander's and James's trustee; the case turned on Maxwell's wife's inheritance, his brother-in-law's divorce, the

alleged adultery of the brother-in-law's wife with Maxwell's former footman, and the inadmissibility of the
evidence of Maxwell's slave, Latchemo, on the grounds
that he was first, a slave, and second, not a Christian.[20]
A lady called Miss Isabella Hall, in the east of Scotland,
received the sad news in 1765, from a wartime colleague of John's in Calcutta, that her brother had died
in Sumatra, leaving her as his heiress and also as the
guardian of his little daughter of five, "Miss Peggy,"
who had been born in Sumatra and who was sent to
Scotland with "one pair of Gold Sleeve Buttons" and
"One Slave Woman named Betty": "the Nurse is a slave
& must return to India."[21]

For some of the Johnstones' acquaintances, including
their long-standing friends the Petries, the slave economy was far more immediately present in Africa, as well
as in the East and West Indies. Gilbert Petrie, to whom
James wrote in 1771 about the qualifications of the head
and the heart, had recently returned from his position as
governor of the slave-trading and mercantile fort, the
Cape Coast Castle in modern Ghana. He sent James the
present of an "Animal," in remembrance of earlier services; it was to Petrie's credit, James responded, that
"sixteen broiling years on Sultry Sands cannot Efface
the Slightest Obligation." Petrie and his younger brother
John, who had been John and Gideon's friend in Calcutta, visited James in Norfolk, where they discussed the
effect of "Semiruta in Putrid Fevers."[22] Gilbert Petrie
later moved with his slaves to Tobago, and John Petrie
became the most extravagant of all the defenders of
slavery in the House of Commons. "The abolition of the
slave trade would be the scourge of Africa; as a planter,
he wished it to take place; but as a cosmopolite, he de-

sired its continuance out of humanity to the inhabitants of the coast of Africa," he declared in opposition to Wilberforce's abolition bill in 1799; in a later orator's summary of his speech, "'the heart shudders to conceive what must be the state of Africa without the Slave trade.' "[23]

In North America, too, the Johnstones and their acquaintances lived amidst the relationships of a slave-owning society. Barbara Johnstone Kinnaird's grandson had very little prospect of "bettering his condition" in his property within William's New York estates, his Massachusetts uncle wrote in 1804; "he has no slaves to cultivate it."[24] In 1776, when James Ramsay, the captain of the *Betsey*, on which Bell or Belinda had been transported to Virginia in 1772, was en route from Barbados to Glasgow, the *Betsey* was captured by American privateers. The prisoners, who included Captain Ramsay, two "gentlemen passengers," and "a Negroe Boy belonging to the said James Ramsay," were taken to Rhode Island and thence to Cork in Ireland.[25] At the end of George's unsuccessful mission of American conciliation, the chairman of the commission, Lord Carlisle, wrote to his wife from New York to inform her that George would be bringing letters home, and to report on the acquisitions of his American household:

> I bid Frederick purchase a black slave for me if he could find one about 12 or 13 years of age. . . . Today after dinner he told me he had one to show me, but believed it was rather too young. I desired to see it, and he produced one of not quite four years old, which he would fain add to the company of the raccoon, grey squirrel, fish-hawk, and other beasts which his love of natural history has filled my house with.[26]

The history of the Johnstones' and their friends' encounters with slavery is the story of individuals who became rich in the later eighteenth century, and whose encounters in the British empire were ventures into the
economy (and the society) of enslavement. But it is also
part of a larger story of change over time that is very
different from the narrative of humanitarian or legal or
political progress, in which at least two of the brothers
were also participants (the drama of "palliation," in J. R.
Seeley's description).[27] The forty years in which the
Johnstones were active in public life, from the new settlements of 1763 to the abolition of the slave trade (in
British ships) in 1806, were a time of humanitarian sentiment, as in the abolitionist associations in which James
and John were involved, and at the same time, of con-
solidation and expansion in the Atlantic slave economy.[28] This was a matter of the numbers of slaves transported across the Atlantic: the peak of the French slave
trade came in 1790, the British slave trade in 1799, the
slave trade in U.S. ships in 1807, the Portugese slave
trade in 1829, and the Spanish slave trade in 1835.[29] It
was a matter, too, of the politics of race, of the administration of slave societies, of anxiety about slave revolutions, and of reflection on the future of slavery.[30]

The idea of race was indistinct in the Johnstones'
postwar world of the 1760s and 1770s, like the ideas of
empire, or law, or economic life. Bell or Belinda was described variously in the court papers of 1771 as a "black
girl," a "native of Bengal in the East Indies," and a "Negroe Girl." Adam Smith used the word "race" in *The
Wealth of Nations* in a variety of senses: the "race of
animals," the "race of the kings of France," the "race of
labourers," the "race of mendicant friars," the "unpros-

perous race of men commonly called men of letters."[31] But the scientific racism of the nineteenth-century epics of the history of empire, of master castes and stronger races, was already in view, as in the Johnstones' cousin James Ferguson's reference, in Joseph Knight's case, to "a very shocking calamity, *viz.*, the debasing of our own race."[32] The "general's people are Samboes," a Jamaican historian wrote in the report on Mosquitia that George submitted to parliament in 1777, and they had "inherited some of the worst characteristicks of the worst African mind."[33] William, in his speech against the abolition of the slave trade, in 1805, presented the choice before parliament as a question of species: "the real fact was agreed upon by all parties to be this: the West Indies cannot be cultivated by Europeans, whose constitutions will not bear fatigue in that climate. It is therefore necessary, if they are to be cultivated at all, that it must be by some other class of the human species."[34]

The Johnstones were at the margin, once again, of these scenes of change. Even John, in India, was a transitional figure in the new politics of race. He was a conspirator, in Clive's foreboding view, in a combination of blacks (or Indians) and whites. His references to differences of race, in his self-defense before and after leaving India, veer wildly between sympathy for "the Sufferings of *Mootyram*" (a man with "a House and Family" who had been confined with "all the Terrors attending a man already convicted and condemned of capital Offences") and for his Persian correspondents ("I received letters from them both . . . expressing the utmost dread and apprehension"); dismay, that even the merchants in the Calcutta market now refuse his goods ("How ready the Black Fellows are to curry Favour"); and large questions about race and power: "Has . . . any Black Man in the Country, now either Resolution or Power" to question the Company?[35]

In West Florida, George's government was a forced march through the slow transformation of the racial politics of empire.[36] The new government in Florida was occupied from the outset with the establishment of a slave society, and with the legal position of fugitive, captured, restituted, salvaged, and "lost" slaves. Even George's expense account included reimbursement to a visiting naval officer of "the Value of his Negro lost in a Boat."[37] There was a "most ticklish" case of the trial "of a White Man for the Murder of an Indian," which involved "the Question of Infidel Evidence," the "Distinction between Murder and Manslaughter," and the treaty obligations entered into with the native Americans. There was also the case of a black slave who escaped from Florida to New Orleans, where he was "received on board a Spanish Frigate," and four slaves who escaped, together with the indentured "Mulatto Man," but were shipwrecked on the Chandelier Islands—from which the two survivors, one of the slaves and the mulatto, were rescued by "a Frenchman" and taken to New Orleans, where they were held for "Charges (including Salvage)." It was a case, George wrote to the outgoing French governor, that raised not only the "maritime laws of Oleron" and the principle of "mutual Restitution" of runaway slaves, but also the "established Humanity of the French Nation": "I must declare it is the first time I have ever heard of a mere Layman asking Salvage for a Living Soul."[38]

The act for the regulation of negroes and slaves that George signed before he left the province was the codification of a new society, in which "it will be necessary to employ a great many Negroes" and "where custom has prevailed to distinguish their color for the badge of slavery." All negroes, Indians, "mulattoes," and "mustees," with the exception of those who were free, were declared to be "chattels personal in the hands of their owners"; there was a schedule of punishments "if any Negro or slave shall offer violence or strike any white person," "(not extending to life or limb)." In the new and more bloodthirsty act passed after George's departure, the schedule was increased to "death or any other punishment," and to the crimes of the mind: "if any slave or slaves shall compass or imagine the death of any white person . . . such slave or slaves shall suffer death."[39]

In Grenada, too, the Johnstones were caught up in the changing politics of race, and in the regulation of a society at war with its slaves. Grenada, like West Florida, was a society obsessed with the slaves' own revolutions. The "disquiets and animosities" in which Alexander was involved in Grenada were disputes, as in Pensacola and Calcutta, between British settlers or British officials. But they were also disputes over the law and the social relationships of slavery. Alexander's complaint to the Privy Council turned on the events of the slave revolution in the interior of the island, on the use of torture against slaves, and on the transition from the "Code Noir" of the French colonies to the British "Government of Slaves." The "Act to free Augustine" to which Alexander so objected was the consequence, as recounted in one of the pamphlets by the Johnstones' friends, of the distinctive social circumstances of the island: the "very complicated degree of relation" between Alexander's opponent (the island's governor); his "intimate friend" Augustine; the friend's companion, "a black wench, a near relation to the famous Augustin"; and the friend's "incestuous family, particularly with his mistress, daughter, and granddaughter, all which dear and endearing appellations are applicable to one and the same person only."[40]

The Westerhall plantation in Grenada was a part of the Johnstones' lives over three generations, and its descent by inheritance was a journey through the early history of empire. Alexander was the most prosperous of all the absentee proprietors in Grenada when the French recaptured the island in 1779, or at least the owner of the largest number of slaves—the slaves whom he had bought with credit from his brothers.[41] The Westerhall plantation later became a celebrated example of enlightened production, in the years when it was owned by James: of cultivation with the plough, by slaves in shoes. It was virtually untouched, according to the abolitionists' histories, by the epidemic illnesses that afflicted the island, and by the political sequence of slave revolutions, including Fédon's Revolution of 1795–96.[42] When William inherited the plantation, in the description of his new manager, "the plough was abandoned, because, on that Estate, it was found to accomplish no saving of expense, no acceleration of labour, and because it added nothing to the crop." The manager, in turn, became one of the most prominent theorists of slavery of the nineteenth century: "I know Westerhall Estate, Grenada, well—every cane hole in it," he wrote of the "rage for everything that was black," and "the ignorant population of Africa, can only be raised to the blessings and advantages of freedom through personal Slavery."[43]

The future of slavery was a matter of legal and administrative reorganization, in these scenes, more than of political or parliamentary reform. It was also a matter of expectations about the political lives of the enslaved.[44] The Johnstones and their friends were surrounded by the anticipation and the anxious observation of slave revolt. Grenada, when Alexander arrived, was an island of revolt, with its "jarring" mixture of slaves, "sheltered in the woody Mountains." The crisis over the fugitive Augustine was an episode in a century-long war in Grenada between the European colonists and the maroons of the interior, former slaves and descendants of slaves. The Grenada "Act for the better Government of *Slaves*" spoke of "Great Terror and Manifest Hazard" and the legislation in West Florida referred to "fugitive or runaway" slaves.[45] William's proposed reforms of mortgages on West Indian estates in the early 1770s, and his associates' litigation with respect to the English and French law of mortgages on slaves, came at a time of "true panic" in the French colonial administration, over slave revolts in Surinam, Guyana, Berbice, and Saint-Domingue.[46] His last parliamentary strategy on mortgages was a private bill regarding the Westerhall plantation in Grenada, passed in 1796, to "raise Money by Mortgage for repairing the Damage done thereto in the late Insurrections."[47] "Before there was a white American revolution, there were already black and brown ones sweeping through South America and the Caribbean," as Simon Schama has written, and before the political conflicts over the slave trade, there were military conflicts, which were also political.[48] This too was the Johnstones' narrative of slavery and empire.

"The storm is fast gathering; every instant it becomes blacker and blacker," William Wilberforce said in his peroration at the end of the parliamentary debate of 1805, in which William Pulteney played such a prominent role in delaying the abolition of the slave trade—a defeat of which Wilberforce wrote that "I never felt so much on a parliamentary occasion. I could not sleep after first waking at night. The poor blacks rushed into my mind."[49] The debate turned, as on previous occasions, on the "great interests of the country." But it was also concerned to a novel extent with events in Saint-Domingue, now the independent state of Haiti, and with "the minds of the negroes."[50] "They were capable of reflecting on their physical powers," Wilberforce was reported to have said of the slaves in the West Indies (in an interesting echo of George's son's comment, four years earlier, on the transient disinclination of the natives of India "to reflect upon their own strength").[51] "That they had feelings, and could think and act like men was, he supposed, hardly disputed," Wilberforce also said; "an instance had been lately shewn that black men could feel, could conceive, and could execute what they planned as well as we could."[52]

The condition of slavery was widely diverse across the vast distances that the Johnstones and their friends traversed. The East India Company in Calcutta and London was actively involved in the slave trade from Madagascar, Angola, and Guinea to St. Helena and the West Coast of Sumatra; even the letter that Lord Clive sent to London on the *Admiral Stevens* in 1765, with John and Elizabeth Carolina, reported on the successful conclusion of a slaving voyage from Madagascar to Sumatra.[53] The "domestic slavery" of the interior of India was different from the "chattel slavery" of the West Indies and North America.[54] George, in his elegy to the Mosquito shore, was shocked by the "shameful traffic" of the British merchants, seizing "the surrounding tribes of Indians" to be "conveyed as articles of commerce to the English and French settlements in the West-Indies."[55] The slave laws of the French, English, Spanish, Dutch, and Portugese empires were disparate, and they changed over time. So too did the slave laws of the North American colonies. The legal regimes of individual estates changed as islands and colonies were ceded from one European empire to the next. The descriptions of individuals were elided: Bell or Belinda, who was a "slave or servant," or "Molly a black girl, the slave or servant of John Johnstone," or David Wedderburn's "Negro Servant of mine" in Florida in 1765, who was also, for his native American friends, "my slave."

But for the enslaved, including the individuals who were slaves in the Johnstones' households, the diversity of slave regimes was itself a continuing constituent of the experience of slavery. Almost all the individual slaves in the Johnstones' history had information about different kinds of slavery and different slave societies; almost all also lived in a world of "choicelessness."[56] To be without choice was to be subject to sudden, tragic transition from one regime or condition to another. It was to be carriable, in particular, from the domestic slavery of Europe or Asia to the plantation slavery of the Americas.

James Somerset, who had been brought by his owner from the North American colonies to England, escaped from enslavement in London and was recaptured; when he was freed by court order, he was in irons on a ship bound for Jamaica. Joseph Knight was bought in the Cape Coast of modern Ghana, brought to Jamaica, and then carried onward by his owner, John Wedderburn, to Scotland. The immediate claim, in his case before the Perth Court in 1774, was to "inhibite and discharge Sir John Wedderburn from the sending the Petitioner abroad . . . either by carrying furth of this Country or in other ways"; John Wedderburn's counter-claim was "he ought to be allowed to carry the pursuer back with him to the West indies, if he should chuse, altho' he does not insist on this in point of fact, as he has no such intention."[57] Bell or Belinda lived in the "domestic slavery" of the East Indies and in the domestic servitude of Scotland; it was a court in Scotland that determined that she was not a "slave or servant" but a "Slave for Life," and sent her to the slavery of Virginia.

"THIS AGE OF INFORMATION"

The Johnstones' rise to fortune, in so many scenes and over so many setbacks, was an enigma to their contemporaries, and it is enigmatic still. The family's efforts to find evidence of their descent from Matthew de Johnstone—described by James as the "Great Desiderata of my father"—ended only in 1881.[58] The claims of the Johnstones of Westerhall were then repudiated with derision. The Johnstones were only tenuously related to the nobility, the genealogists of the successful heirs claimed. They had been a family of local lawyers and commissioners, or agents working on commission, "successively employed as factors or otherwise on the affairs of the Earls and Marquises." They had the "freest access" to the muniments or archives of their distant relations; both the Johnstones' father and their grandfather, according to the successful claimants, had used their legal position to obfuscate the historical record.[59] The Johnstones, as so often, had invented themselves.

The possibility of economic decline was as likely, in the Johnstone brothers' and sisters' early years, as the possibility of fortune or economic advancement. The family was not poor in the terms of their neighbors in the Valley of the Esk (although William, even in 1767, was identified in London as the "third son of a poor Scot").[60] But they lived with the prospect of falling from indebtedness into landlessness, and into social ignominy. "I wish the Poor Girls were Safe," George wrote to William at the family's low ebb of fortune in 1759.[61]

The successes of the Johnstones were the consequence of opportunity, resolution, and the efficient use of information of the most diverse sort. The brothers were not war contractors or slave traders or bankers or the conquerors of provinces (like Lord Clive); they were not even merchants in Adam Smith's sense of the man of speculation who "is a corn merchant this year, and a wine merchant the next, and a sugar, tobacco, or tea merchant the year after."[62] Only John, in India, and Patrick and Gideon, over a shorter period, made money out of buying and selling commodities—bales of cloth, salt, and the services of bullocks. The Johnstones lived in the early period of the industrial-scientific revolution in Scotland, and the sites of industrial transformation were at the edge of their fields of vision, or of what could be heard. "The distant din of war reaches us but seldom but from the Carron the farce I suppose must now be at an end," John wrote to James Balmain during the American revolutionary war, in reference to the Carron Iron

Works, a few miles from his home in Alva. The letters of James, John, and Betty are full of references to looking for coal in the hills of Scottish estates.[63] But the Johnstones' own ventures in industry were almost always transient—experiments with canals and sulphur and antimony. They made money out of money, and out of information.

There were two initial sources of the family's newfound prosperity. The first was the money that John, the ninth of the eleven children, was able to send or bring from India—his presents from Indian princes and bankers, and the profits of his commerce in muslins and salt. The second was the inheritance of William's wife, Frances Pulteney, anticipated from 1760 and confirmed, to the jubilation of William's Edinburgh friends, in 1767. John and William were rich men by the late 1760s, and they invested their money in property, bonds, and political opportunities. They provided loans and stipends to their brothers and sisters, to their nephews and nieces, and to Uncle Walter. Their older brother Alexander, or "poor Sandy J.," with his "oddity" and his "cross fortune," was the third of the brothers to become rich, as the owner of the Westerhall plantation in Grenada, bought with money borrowed from William.[64] The family was itself an investment opportunity and a society of information.

In the new world of information of the late eighteenth century, the Johnstones were able to turn these initial endowments (or prizes) into enduring fortunes. The sisters and brothers were conscious of living in the inquisitive times that their contemporary, Vicesimus Knox, described as "this age of information."[65] They were interested by "disposition"—like Fanny Price in *Mans-*

field Park, the most Indian of Jane Austen's novels—in "information for information's sake."[66] Their understanding of commerce, like that of Adam Smith, was founded on a sense of the importance of information; the "unavoidable ignorance of administration" with respect to the relative importance of different political figures in the distant colonies; the "uneasiness" of the merchant with respect to the "character and situation of the persons whom he trusts"; and the "intelligence requisite" for distant speculations.[67] So was their understanding of politics. They were like North Americans, as described by another colonial official of the time, with East Indian and Atlantic connections (the brother of the official with whom George corresponded in West Florida): "the acquirement of information . . . forms a *character peculiar to these people*," a "turn of character which, in the ordinary occurrences of life, is called *inquisitiveness*."[68]

The Johnstones described themselves as well informed, and they were described by others as persons of information. "He seems a man of much information & strong feelings, his manner awkward but expressive," a British diplomat wrote of George in 1779, during the negotiations over the captivity of Martha and George's two young sons.[69] The letters of the family and their friends were concerned, to a striking extent, with exchanges of information. Patrick promised William, in the letter that arrived after his death in Calcutta, that "I shall write you very fully of my situation & opinion of the People here by next Ship."[70] Margaret wrote to their mother from Paris about her daughter's teething, her grandmother's illness ("I fear I fear she's dead"), and her success in presenting the Scottish regiment's requests to the French court.[71] "As you ask a perticular account I shall inform you of every thing I know," Betty wrote to William, after Barbara's separation.[72] "Write me minutely about Your Children and about every thing else that you know I am anxious about," David Wedderburn wrote to his sister from Bombay. To his brother, en route from Antigua to Jamaica, he wrote of his plans "to get (if I can) some information about Johnson's [Johnstone's] warlike preparations," and of "the Ideas I have formed for myself upon my present information which, is very imperfect."[73]

William, whose collection of letters is the largest single repository of the family's surviving correspondence, was an economist, in the eighteenth-century sense, of bills and bonds. He was also an economist of useful information, about everything from the Nile-like soil of the Mississippi delta (as described by his informant in New Orleans) to the reputation of his sister Barbara (she had never been out except to church, Betty wrote after the Kinnairds' separation).[74] He identified himself in the House of Commons as the recipient and purveyor of authentic information. "I have my information from a person who has universally acknowledged abilities [and] has had opportunities of enquiry," he said in a debate about fraud in naval procurement. In the debate over Wilberforce's abolition bill, he said that "he could assert, from his own knowledge and means of information, that [slaves] were universally much better treated now."[75]

There were multiple respects in which the Johnstones' late eighteenth-century empire was an "information society," in the classification of modern historians of information.[76] It was a time of exuberant expansion in the public media of newspapers, pamphlets, and books, especially in Britain and France, but increasingly in the rest of Europe, in the Americas, and in the East Indies.[77] The modern industry of public opinion was an innovation of the Johnstones' own lifetimes. "One and forty times did the House sit upon this business," Edmund Burke said in a parliamentary debate of 1772 over the East India Company: "books upon books, and papers upon papers were brought up and piled upon your table."[78] "The eyes of the world have been blinded by publications," Clive said of the descriptions in England of the consumption of salt in Calcutta.[79] John Swinton's brother Samuel became the publisher of two French newspapers, *Le Courier de Londres* and *Le Courier de l'Europe*, which he offered to enlist, in 1794, in the circulation of news in Ostend, Martinique, and in northern France. He was a virtuoso, in prospect, of overseas public opinion, and of the new media of bellicose information, to be distributed

> by means of light paper Balloons painted black sent up by means of spirit of wine from different parts of the border of France when the wind blows fair, *also* by means of messengers sent in the night time to leave them on different parts of the high Road near the large Towns, *also* by means of Dogs set on shore on different parts of the Sea Coast of France with Packets in bladders tied to their necks.[80]

The Johnstones' world of empire was a time, too, when the old media of unwritten and whispered exchanges coexisted with the new world of print. The news of distant exchanges was a juxtaposition of information in the most diverse public and private media, written and spoken and brought by ship's captains, or intercalated in family or commercial correspondence. Two of James's friends, when they were students in Leiden during the war of 1745, travelled to Rotterdam "to learn if they had heard anything by fishing-boats"; "having gone so far and brought back no news," they decided they would "frame a gazette," in the form of a "banker's private letter he had got by a fishing-boat."[81]

In Calcutta, after John's departure, his friend William Bolts produced a gazette in manuscript, "having in manuscript many things to communicate, which most intimately concern every individual," which could be copied at his home between the hours of ten and twelve in the morning.[82] There were American newspapers in Chittagong in 1762.[83] But there was also news from passing ships, as when the captain of the ship in which Elizabeth Carolina and her sister arrived in Madras caught sight of a "country boat," or an Indian boat, from the Maldive Islands, who "informs us . . . that Pondicherry has been in our hands this four months."[84] There was false news: "I hear the Armenians in Calcutta have received accounts, that Russian's have taken Constantinople," one of Samuel Swinton's correspondents was informed. There was news, even, of the marriage of Marie Antoinette to the future Louis XVI, in a letter from Dunkirk to Calcutta in 1770: "He is a poor Weakly Lad both in mind & body & she a fine bouncing German Lass so they are very unequally matched, but it is thought it will be a means to preserve peace in Europe for a long time."[85]

The Johnstones' world of private information, like the information society of mid-eighteenth-century Paris, in

Robert Darnton's description, was a "communication network made up of media and genres that have been forgotten."[86] The sisters and brothers were preoccupied with letters, of instruction or credit or solicitation, and also with the mechanisms by which the letters were identified with signifiers of time and place (sent by particular ships, or forgotten by Gideon, or returned, in the case of a letter from John to William, from the Belgian town of Spa). The only transient glimpse of emotion that William showed in his thirty-seven years as a member of the House of Commons, as related in the parliamentary reports, was on the unlikely subject of franking, or free postage privileges for members of parliament: "Franks, he observed, often produced gain to the post-office revenue, by calling forth answers to letters . . . He argued also on the cruelty of diminishing the comfort and satisfaction enjoyed by persons at a considerable distance from each other, who conversed familiarly by letter while their letters could pass free."[87] One of George's last projects was for the "opening of the Communication by Suez to the E. Indies" by a British consul in Cairo, with the "hospitality incident to the country" to be financed by a "small charge upon private letters."[88]

The family were preoccupied, too, with the complicated conversations, written and spoken, by which the information in letters was evaluated. In the elaborate communications of the Johnstones and their friends, the exchange of information was to a great extent a question of letters about letters, or news about news. "You seem uneasy that all my letters have been open'd, and so am I too," David Hume wrote to their father: "I think I have in all of them us'd the precaution to name no-body, and to date from no place."[89] There were letters to India

that were partially in Gaelic and letters that were spirited away, like their maternal uncle's letters to his son,
which "may have been secreted . . . from my connection
with the Johnstones." There were letters of William Bolts
in cipher, in which "Port-au-Prince" denoted "Sind,"
"Baltimore" was "Bengal," and "American Congress"
was "Tipu Sultan."[90] John was involved in intricate detail with the exchange of letters within letters: letters
written on Rukahs, like the information he explicated in
the Armenians' case in London, or the "packet of Letters
intercepted by one of his Chokies" (or custom house officials), which he sent from Jellasore to Calcutta in 1761,
and which may or may not have been forgeries, "sealed
with a Seal which any Engraver can counterfeit."[91]

The Johnstones' late eighteenth-century empire was a
society in which the establishment of an information
order was at the heart of imperial power, as C. A. Bayly
has shown of rural North India in the early British period—a "talkative, knowing society, highly competitive
about the use and diffusion of information."[92] For the
Johnstones and their friends, the information of empire
was in particular a matter of the knowledge of languages. John's identity in India was as an interpreter of
Persian correspondence and the "Moor's language," or
as an intermediary between empires and idioms. The crises of his Indian existence turned on translations and
mistranslations—the expression "Cooch booligani"
("he will say nothing"), or whether the "words of friendship" in a Persian letter of 1765 were "ironical," with an
expression meaning "nevertheless" mistranslated as
"moreover."[93] Archibald Swinton, when he was asked to
interpret the signatures on Persian letters that had been
sent to George in England, described them as being

"marked Vussalaam, which means 'Farewell,' "or perhaps "*ne plus ultra*."[94] George included six different Indian interpreters in his expense account for his period
in West Florida, and Martha Ford's concession was
bounded to the north by the Indian interpreter's camp.[95]
David Wedderburn was the interpreter for the French
officials in the Choctaw and Chickasee congresses of
1765, and he anticipated that he would learn Choctaw
("which does not seem difficult as it does not consist of
many words").[96] On his way to India in 1770, he came
upon the survivors of a Dutch East India ship that had
been cast away in the Cape Verde islands, including
"about twenty German soldiers," to whom he spoke
German and whom he took with him to the East India
Company's army in Bombay.[97]

The Johnstones and their friends lived in India during
the period of transition that the historian Ghulam Husain described as "these times of half-knowledge," or
half-conversation, in which the English were interested
only in information that they could write down, and not
in "inquiring into the characters and tempers of men."[98]
But in John's early imperial world of almost-assimilated
and almost-Indian merchants—the world that Clive repudiated—the character of both Indian and European
officials was the object of endless observation. John's
self-defense in 1765 was a description of his relationships to his partners (Motiram), his partners' subordi-
nates, his bankers (the Seths), the princes by whom he
was employed (the raja of Burdwan), and the princes
whom he distrusted (the nawab of Bengal). His correspondence with his English friends in India was concerned with the evaluation of the "country" officials
upon whom they were so dependent: the character of a

Bihar Maharaja ("he is deserving my utmost confidence") and of the financial officer of an English general ("whatever his father-in-law may be, I will be bound for his never being never concerned in a plot").[99] Clive's objective, John wrote in his letter of resignation from the Company in 1765, was to diminish his "Rank of Credit" to a condition "now become of so little Consequence in the Eyes and Opinion of every Body": "to render me cheap and of no consequence in the Eyes of the very Country People."[100]

The Johnstones' understanding of empire was founded on a self-conscious sense of the power of words: the words of friendship in a Persian letter, or words that were like bullets, in Mobile, or the eagle's tail, in Pensacola, that "spreads like a sheet of Paper."[101] They were conscious of themselves, too, as observers of their own information society. They were critics of words: "justice, prudence, moderation, &c. &c. . . . such a commonplace jingle of words," as George said of Lord Clive's speech about the eyes of the world.[102] John expressed his suspicion of what he described as the "narratives" of the East India Company in Calcutta in 1765: "Narratives extorted by Hope of Favour, or Fear of Disgrace," the contradiction between Motiram and Jagat Seth's "Narrative," and the contradiction between Reza Khan's first and second narratives: "what Man would admit himself to be judged by Narratives obtained under such Circumstances?"[103] They were interested in the destiny of public records, thrown into the street in West Florida or eaten by vermin in Grenada. They were efficient, or so it seems, in the obfuscation of public or parochial records, as with Gideon's birth certification in Westerkirk or George Lindsay Johnstone's in Pensacola.

These were all opportunities or sources of economic information. The Johnstones lived in a new information society in the sense of the sustained expansion in commercial and financial information, both in the public media of business newspapers and in the "correspondence of the moneyed and the mercantile world," in Edmund Burke's description of 1796, a "kind of electric communication everywhere."[104] But the information that the Johnstones amassed was difficult to classify as political or financial. The different kinds of knowledge were intermingled in their ventures: the public and the private, the personal and the financial and the political. They were interested in information about opportunities for bettering themselves by inheritance, military promotion, public office, the sale of East India Company stock, chancery litigation, naval intelligence, and insurance against changes in the price of sugar. The family was its own society of economic advancement.

The Johnstones were specialists in the exchanges that historians have described as "affective information," or the information that is exchanged within families and within intimate relationships.[105] But these exchanges were concerned with prices and military promotions, as well as with illness and childhood. It was the Johnstone sisters, and Betty in particular, who were the essential figures in the family's organization of information, including information about events in India and the West Indies. A very long letter from the Johnstones' father to William—about East India Company politics, the price of claret in Calcutta, a lawsuit in Edinburgh, John's position in Burdwan, and his own apprehensions ("when three parts of four of one is already in the grave and the grasshopper is become a Burden")—was in Betty's hand.[106] Louisa copied James's letters to John about heritable bonds and the acidity of life, to Betty about the "appearances of Coal," and to Gilbert Petrie about scorching sands.[107]

John's letters to his brothers are filled with descriptions of papers: a letter from William that Gideon forgot to deliver, a letter to Alexander asking for "some large trunks to Inclose to you Giddes papers," and the "infinite labour" of working on the journal entries for the Westerhall plantation, in the winter when Bell or Belinda was pregnant.[108] "Frightful all searches amongst musty papers are now to me," their father wrote to David Hume.[109] John was asked by their father "to go thro his Papers with my Brother, & look into the state of his Affairs"; he later inherited Gideon's and George's papers. "I hope it will cast up," he wrote to William Julius Mickle, of a letter that Mickle wanted him to find in the "multitude of Papers" that he had inherited from George. After Louisa's death her heirs were informed that William was "entitled to have the writings of the Estate of Westerhall," together with other papers and letters, but that if one of their friends "would take the Trouble of looking them over and destroying all that contain nothing about the payment of Debts I should suppose it would answer."[110]

John and Gideon's partner William Bolts was even more elaborately self-referential, or self-conscious of himself as an individual who lived by information. In his will, written in Lisbon in 1805, he identified his assets as his volumes of books and a share in a "patent or privilege for the manufacturing within the dominions of Portugal of Crystalized Lemon juice." It was his papers that were at the center of his existence, or his imagined end.

"All my manuscripts & books of accounts and papers epistolary Commercial historical political Biographical philosophical polemical," he instructed his executors, were to "be all burnt in a Bonfire to be made in the largo do Quintella at a convenient distance under my windows the said being previously tied up into bundles and thrown over the balcony progressively."[111]

Information was a source of political influence, in the Johnstones' world of opportunity, and it was also a source of profit. It was economic information in a capacious sense, including information about the character of business correspondents and public officials. The brothers invested in stocks and shares and in relationships. There was news about positions and news about prices. "I think we may tomorrow try if we can sell 1000 at 273 or higher . . . & watch the market for another 1000," John wrote to William of their East India Company stock.[112] There was news, too, about time and place, as in a lawsuit that William brought in 1800 against the brokers to whom the sugar from the Westerhall estate in Grenada had been consigned and who had (in his view) sold it prematurely: "Sir William [had] strictly prohibited them, as he expected the market to rise."[113]

But the Johnstones' information was also about economic sentiments, or rules about rules. There was a "species of injustice," as John wrote on his return from India, in the fluctuating understanding of economic regulations and of what "should be thought improper" in public or private life. The rules of economic exchange changed continuously, in the unrestrained and universal commerce that was, in the view of the early critics of laissez-faire, so destructive of the foundations of economic order.[114] John's commerce in salt in partner-ship with the "black merchants" was unseemly, on the principles that Lord Clive introduced in the British set-tlements in India in 1765. His presents were against the (new) regulations of the East India Company, which was itself a regulated private enterprise, and against the new norms of race and virtue. The British were now considered to be conquerors and not men of commerce. "I have no Concern in Salt, or any other Trade whatso-ever," Clive wrote to John, as John and his household were preparing to leave India.[115]

Clive's own financial transactions—or his insider trading, in modern terms—were considered to be un-seemly, in turn, in the disputes over the regulation of the East India Company in which George and William were later so involved. In 1773 the committee of which they were members published Clive's private letters from the summer of his return to India. "See what an Augean Sta-ble is to be cleansed," Clive had written to the East India Company from Madras, on his way to Calcutta; and to his attorney, on the same day, he wrote with instructions to his stockbrokers, in a letter in cipher to be sent by a French ship from Pondicherry: "Whatever Money I have in the Public Funds, or anywhere else, and as much as can be borrowed in my Name, I desire may be, without Loss of a Minute, invested in *East India* Stock."[116]

The Johnstones' information, which was the enduring source of their success, was a compendium of public, private, political, economic, and philosophical (or senti-mental) intelligence. It included news about laws, regu-lations, expectation of changes in regulations, norms of reciprocal decorum, and expectation of changes in norms. The brothers and sisters lived in a new world of

economic possibility, and of transformation in economic
sentiments. These were the changes in sentiments that
were so insidious for the critics of political economy:
with respect to the political conditions for long-distance
commerce; or the interconnectedness between economic
and political choices (as in Adam Smith's own critique
of merchants who sought to pursue their interests by
political influence); or the consequences of economic
opportunities for virtue, honour, and respectability of
character (in the expression of the Johnstones' American
nephew, writing of William in 1805). The family's information, in this fluctuating scene, was about economic
choices, and about the choice of which choices were economic, or licit.

FAMILY HISTORIES

The empire was a family enterprise for the Johnstones,
and for the sisters as well as the brothers. It was family
relationships that constituted the connection between
the future and the past, and between the Indies and
home: the multiple or multiplier effect of empire. "In
what Part of the Kingdom has not some Parent lost his
son, or some Son your Parent, in your Service?" George
asked in a speech to the East India Company's General
Court, and the suggestion was, as so often, over-
wrought.[117] There were no more than a few hundred
British subjects in the employment of the Company in
India in the 1760s, and perhaps two thousand more in
London, or at sea: an infinitesimal proportion of the
population of India and a tiny proportion of the population of Britain.[118] Even if the thousands of British subjects who went to the West Indies were included—the

soldiers or colonial officials or enterprising individuals, like James's ploughman who was sent to Grenada to instruct the slaves on the Westerhall estate and who stayed on, "making money, by instructing the slaves of other proprietors"—the overall number of individuals involved in colonial commerce and empire was small.[119] The "frenzy of migrating" to North America, with which John had such sympathy as a magistrate, was itself a matter of no more, in the 1760s and 1770s, than some one to two percent of the British population.[120]

But in this early modern world of large, well-informed families, the statistics of employment or emigration provide only a partial indication of the different respects in which the exterior world of the Indies extended into the interior of the British empire, and into the interior experience, or the inner lives, of the women and men upon whom it impinged. It is as though there were an extended effect of information and expectations, in which each individual who went to sea, or went to the Indies, was connected to sisters and brothers who were vastly anxious for news, or who were the heirs of their brothers. The distant and the lost—described by George in the same speech to the East India Company as the "pale figures of my departed friends"—were connected to events at home by exchanges of information, inheritance, commodities, and coerced or uncoerced journeys.[121]

The multiplier effect of empire, in the economic sense of the expenditure that was the outcome of projects connected to the East and West Indies, was evident in the Johnstones' lives.[122] The classical estate buildings designed for John in his new house at Alva in Stirling, with the round dung hill and the octagonal turret, would have been the source of employment and income for ma-

sons, carpenters, and pigeon-keepers. The family's litigation over the Westerhall estate in Grenada, with its
"reckonings quarrels controversies claims and demands,"
was the source of employment and income for lawyers,
accountants, and lawyers' clerks. But there was a more
extensive multiplier effect of information and expectations, in which the masons and pigeon-sellers in Stirling
had ideas about the Indies, and about the Johnstones, as
well as income from the Johnstones' "disbursements."[123]
So did the lawyers' clerks in Edinburgh and Lincoln's
Inn. All individuals were curious, in Adam Smith's description, and interested in the characters of other people; all also had expectations about their own future
lives.[124] This more extensive multiplicity of empire—this
empire of indistinct ideas—extended into the deep interior of the English and Scottish countryside, and into the
interior of family life.

The Johnstones lived in an imagined and remembered
web of family relationships. They and their friends referred endlessly to the family, or to families: the family
at Westerhall, to whom George left his edition of Milton; the feudal notions in Margaret's husband's family;
the conflict between proper family spirit and clannish
enthusiasm of which James wrote to William in their
quarrel of 1759; or in the East Indies, the suffering of
Motiram, a man with "a House and Family."[125] The
words that described family connections were in flux in
the Johnstones' lifetimes. There was the household family, of individuals living in the same house or household
(even when the household was itself on the move); the
lineage family, constituted by birth or blood or ancestry;
and the kinship family of smaller or larger relationships.[126] John referred to Elizabeth Carolina as his

"family" after their father's death: "I intended to have returned sooner to my family, who most deeply feels this great loss of one whose kindness exceeded that of her own father to her."[127] But all these families were changed by the outcomes of empire.

The experience of empire was for the Johnstones, and especially for the slaves in their households, a sequence of departures into unknown and frightening seas. Joseph Knight was "very young" when he was taken by Captain Knight from the Cape Coast Castle in West Africa to Jamaica. Bell or Belinda went from India to England with Elizabeth Carolina in 1765–66. In the summer of 1771, she was taken from the house in which she lived, and in which her son had died, to a prison in the town of Cupar; she was then taken to a different prison in the town of Perth; from the prison in Perth, she was taken to "the next adjacent shore," according to the order of the court, and "so from shore to shore till she is brought to the Port of transportation there to be imprisoned." She was in Glasgow in the depths of the winter of 1771–72; her last journey, or the last journey of which there is a record in the labyrinth of the law of Scotland, was the Atlantic crossing to Virginia in January–March 1772, in the *Betsey*.[128]

Even for the individuals in the Johnstones' story who were not enslaved, setting out for the empire was a frightening venture. George was thirteen when he went to sea, and John was sixteen when he left for India in the service of the East India Company. Patrick was sixteen when he joined the East India Company and eighteen when he died in Calcutta. Elizabeth Carolina was eighteen when she and her sister sailed from England in the spring of 1761, "proceeding to their friends at Madrass," and to the "bungalow" of the old soldier in Chittagong to whom they had a "letter of particular recommendation."[129] Martha Ford was twenty, and eight months pregnant (on the evidence of the East India Company record of her son's christening), when she arrived in West Florida, after a journey of which George wrote, from the island of St. Christopher, that "every thing fortunate hath as yet attended."[130] George and Martha's son George was eleven when he and his brother were taken prisoner by privateers and "carryd into Malaga."[131] "I own I can scarce keep up my spirites," Barbara's son Patrick wrote to his brother when he was waiting to sail for India: "the leaving ones country and parting with our relations is a dreadfull thought."[132]

But family relationships, including the relationships of virtual families and households, were the setting within which all these histories unfolded. Even Joseph Knight's case turned on the relationships of property within a household that extended over vast distances of space, time, and law. His first petition, in the long sequence of requests that led to his freedom in 1778, was in part an account of a conversation with his owner: "Sir John at that time said he would not give him his ffreedom here because he would starve as nobody would imploy him but that he would give him his freedom in Jam.a [Jamaica] and a house and some Ground where he might live Comfortably all the days of his life. . . . It is not 12 mos. Since this Conversation happened."[133] John Wedderburn, in turn, in his "Complaint" against Joseph Knight, recounted his own conversations and his observations about Joseph Knight's wife, who was also a servant in the family. He placed himself in the position of the father of the family, or the head of the household, in an economic and a moral sense: "the Child having died the Complainer would have inclined the Connection to have broke off as he had no good opinion of any of that Ladies Virtues. But he [Joseph] insisted . . . in marrying her."[134]

For the Johnstones' immediate relations, the family constituted a virtual economic enterprise that extended from the East and West Indies to the Scottish countryside. The letters of credit within the family, or letters of lamentation about credit, were themselves a medium of information. The brothers and sisters had elaborate relationships of quantified obligation, from the time when Charlotte promised, in 1751, to repay the sixpence borrowed from William for elixir of vitriol. When Barbara's marriage ended, she stayed in Edinburgh with Betty "at her own Expence," as "Rooms taken was not proper in her situation."[135] Betty wrote to William, when she had quarreled with their mother, about a transaction involving herself, William, their father, and their uncle: "I think it will be proper for you eather to Burn or Return me that Receipt which I gave you."[136] Their father wrote to William, while John was still in India in 1762, about "keeping Johns Money designed for Sandy & Gidion in Scotland," paying "Georges Sum" to him in London, and getting receipts for "what is intended for the Rest."[137] Alexander, five years later, had "drawn" the bill on John and William for the twelve slaves in Grenada. James, in Norfolk, "drew on" John, Alexander, Betty, Gideon, and Charlotte. Betty drew on William for her furniture and discharged "your Bill to me": "am very sorry it should be in the smalest Degree inconvenient for You to answere my Demand."[138] "If there is an error of £2..12 I am satisfied that you will give me Credit for it," James wrote to John from Norfolk. "I have not calculated the Interest as I have no Interest Book."[139]

The transactions within the family veered wildly between small and large amounts. "I will pay you Honestly and Thankfully (if not all at once at different Times)," Louisa wrote to James's lawyer in 1771, when she borrowed money from him for a lottery ticket.[140] On other occasions the sums involved were imposing: "My brother cou'd be in cash," John wrote of Alexander to one of the family's business associates earlier in the same year, and he proposed to "send over my servant with Ten Bills for Ten Thousand pounds at three days sight."[141] "I am sorry from the Circumstances of my own Affairs, I shall not been able to assist you with the Sum you have occasion for," John wrote to William in 1769, with respect to a large and unspecified purchase, and then in 1773, with respect to one of his own purchases, "I know so little of your Ability to assist me that I dare only mention my Want without saying anything more."[142]

The economy of assistance extended to the older and younger generations. Alexander included George and Martha's son George in his list of virtual heirs, and Gideon left annuities to Charlotte and James Balmain's children. John and William took responsibility for Edmund Dana, the American husband of Barbara's daughter.[143] The Johnstones' Uncle Walter was a part of these extended exchanges as he came and went in the family's lives ("all wrapt up in blankets like a poor bastard child," as he wrote of himself, at the age of sixty-two).[144] "I knew from John the first day that you and he gave jointly £10 a month," he wrote to William, of his subvention from his nephews, in the course of a dispute over a rumor that he had complained of William's lack of generosity: "who or What your informer can be I cannot tell. . . . it has almost madden'd me."[145]

The Johnstones' family transactions varied between exchanges of sentiments and exchanges of pensions. "I could wish you to consider Georges Situation & of settling some plan for making his Circumstances Easy," John wrote to William, in a letter about the Grenada estate, and then, "I wish I could accomodate George with Land instead of Houses. . . . I am sure George will not be averse to accept our assistance while we act consistently & united on the same plan."[146] James was anxious when John failed to answer his letters, and he asked Betty whether John had been saying anything disagreeable about him.[147] Charlotte wrote to William of her "fear of being thought ungratefull."[148] Betty found it impossible, during the crisis over the family presents, to discover the extent of George and John's "generosity" to her and Charlotte, because "my Father will show me non of the Letters" and "my mother would not alow him to show us the Letter."[149] Uncle Walter reminded William of their long-ago friendship in a letter about his longing to retire to one of William's estates, where "the proprietor can . . . settle his Uncle"; "now Willy be you the same honest Doctor I used to carry on my back through the Esk."[150] James reassured Charlotte's husband, in the midst of the unsuccessful search for the family's noble descent, that "I do know you," and "the real sentiments of your soul not of yesterday, but long before we took our solitary walk from Shiells to Westerhall."[151]

It was the Johnstone sisters and aunts, once again, who were at the center of this family history of empire. The world of the colonial and East India Company administration was elaborately masculine, even though the Johnstones were involved with two of the unusual women who made their own routes to the "Indies": Elizabeth Carolina, who published her poems about wretchedness and loss before setting out with her sister, amidst the naval battles of the Seven Years' War, for the delta of the Brahmaputra; and Martha Ford, who set out for West Florida by way of Jamaica, and who ended up owning her own land by the Indian interpreter's camp.[152] But the women who stayed at home were also part of the exchange of information about distant opportunities.

The economy of recommendations, even in the colonial and East India Company administration, was in substantial part a matter of exchanges with sisters at home. Barbara wrote to James about a position for William Julius Mickle in the West Indies. Their aunt wrote to their uncle in Canada about her "recommendations" of two officials, an additional recommendation for a third official, on the basis of the "charecter I get of him from his companions," and the unsuccessful efforts of their older brother with respect to another of her sons ("his interest has failed & all expectations over"). She also described the "minds & capacities," marriages, and marriage prospects of her daughters and nieces: "as you desire a touch of Domestick History."[153] David Wedderburn wrote to his sister from Bombay about "your Captain" ("a very good sort of man"), "your Miss Baillies," another official "that you wrote about," and the officials recommended by another friend—"I will shew every civility . . . to every Person she may be pleased to consign to me."[154] He also wrote to his sister (in French) about East India Company politics and East India Company prices: "I have just learnt that you have been at the office of the East India Company giving your opinion in opposition to some of my friends: but for my own part, I very strongly approve of the directors you have chosen. When the shares rise to 260, which will probably happen within a few days, my view would be that you should sell your shares."[155]

The lives of the women who stayed at home were influenced in innumerable respects by exciting and awful anticipation. "Dont keep me on the rack," the Johnstones' mother wrote to George in 1759, about the transposition of her "propos'd felicity in your coming home & being made captain" into dread, having heard "that you was arrived at plimoth in a very ill state of health."[156] "My mind is on the Rack imagining that if you had good newes to send me this neglect would not have happened on your part," their father wrote to William in 1764, in a letter in Betty's hand, asking "what passed at the Generall Court" (of the East India Company, concerned at the time with John's position in Bengal).[157] Barbara's husband in Perthshire did not believe the reports of Margaret's death because Margaret's husband's family in Angus had heard nothing; James believed that the reports of Patrick's death were "but too certain"; William, in London, had reason not to believe the reports of Gideon's death because it "would certainly have been mentioned in the dispatches."[158] To John, in India, their mother wrote that "the world does you perfect justice, no body has any unfriendly thing to say of you."[159]

These were not even the idiosyncratic misfortunes of the gentry. The Johnstones' impoverished factor in Dumfries, George Malcolm, wrote to William in 1771 that "the bad news from Bengal has filled us all with the outmost Uneasyness. May I ask the Favour, that if you have heard any Accounts about our Lads, that you will be pleased to communicate them."[160] Patrick Colquhoun's namesake, William Colhoon, wrote to his sister, also in 1771, when he was about to leave for Africa, that he "had the pleasure to receive your letter this day about Seven o clock at Night but found it not your own writing which I was a little surpris'd at."[161] "Dear Brother This comes with my Love to you," one of the men who was transported to Virginia with Bell or Belinda in 1772 wrote in a "forged and fabricated" letter he delivered to a farmer in Perthshire, and defrauded thereby him of 30 shillings; to another family he wrote in the assumed person of "your dear and loving brother till death."[162]

The insecurity of the Johnstones and their friends took the form of what can described as an instability with respect to time or tense. They lived in the future, that is to say, or in a condition of expectation (about future happiness, future profits, presents that were soon to arrive, coming home) and anxiety (about future distress or future changes in the rules of empire). They also lived in the past: in long-remembered childhood walks, and in the virtual Westerhall in which John "hope[d] to help to gather" alpine strawberries, or that William and Alexander imagined in the Westerhall in Dorset and the Westerhall in Grenada, with their slaves named "Johnston," "Calcutta," and "Dumfries."[163]

"They treated it rather as a South Sea bubble, than as any thing solid and substantial: they thought of nothing but the present time, regardless of the future," Lord

Clive said in one of his speeches in the House of Commons, about the East India Company proprietors' attitude to their new Indian empire. But the servants of the empire who were in India, or en route to India, were almost the opposite, in the experience of the Johnstones and their friends. They thought endlessly of the future and of a distant past of dales and hills; it was the present that was airy and insubstantial. They were like the young men that Clive described "at their very setting out," who "inflame one another's expectations to such a degree, in the course of the voyage," and the same young men, arrived in India, "in anxious suspence to learn whether they were punishable or not for misconduct," as the regulations of office changed with the "direction" of the Company at home, "fluctuating and unsettled."[164]

"Grieved am I every Time I think of my Dear John," James wrote to Betty in 1772; "His Property I am afraid is connected with men who exist only by the Circulation of Paper and whom a Blast on Credit must annihilate."[165] The Johnstones were conscious of living in what William described as "these golden times," and they were also conscious that their hopes with respect to the East Indies were no more, in George's expression, than a "golden dream."[166] Even at home in Scotland, John was endlessly on the move, from his rented house in Balgonie to the family home at Westerhall, the estates he inspected or planned to inspect in Orkney and Berwickshire, the estates he bought in Hangingshaw near Ettrick and in Denovan near the Carron, and the estate where he eventually settled, at Alva in the Ochil Hills. "I own it is my wish to fix my wandering feet on some speck of Earth I could call my own," he wrote to James in 1769; his wish, in 1771, was to return to India.[167]

CONNECTIONS OF THINGS

Family relationships constituted the connection between home and the empire: connections of information,
obligation, and commodities. The Johnstones' letters,
like so many family letters, were about things. William,
when he was a law student with Adam Smith, was asked
to send shoes for Patrick and Gideon; Betty sent spades
to William; there were letters about rabbit skins and po-
tatoes. But the flow of commodities, by the end of the
1750s, was more modern and more foreign. Barbara
wrote to William about "tea-cups & Saucers" that were
"extremely pretty"; their mother asked George, in the
letter about James's broken engagement, to send her
"coffee cups out of the indea ships," blue and white
bowls, and refined sugar, to be sent via the circulating library; Betty corresponded with William about the price
of "Green tea."[168] Alexander Wedderburn wrote to his
brother in Bombay, in a letter that arrived after his death,
about the "false Ideas" in William Bolts's book, his own
"anxiety about Money," his expectation that his "regrets
will increase," and his wife's new interests: "Mrs. W. has
taken a fancy to make a collection of natural history, several people have sent her shells & a great deal of dirty
stuff besides. She will be much obliged to you for any
sort of trash that your world affords."[169]

The Johnstones and their friends even tried to send
things to the Indies. A long letter of 1764 from their father to William, in Betty's hand, recounted John's discontent over "the Badness of the Claret that was sent
out in the Beginning of 1763."[170] Samuel Swinton supplied "Chateau Margaux," "Lafitte," and "red Cham-
paigne" to officials of the East India Company in Cal-

cutta.[171] James Balmain sent John a "3 part song," which did not arrive, and a violin. "I'm sorry you parted with so valuable an acquisition as the true Cremona, to so bad a hand as mine," John wrote from Calcutta; "The damps of the Rainy season brought it all to pieces before I arrived & the *Company* I would say Clumsy hands we have here to put it together I'm afraid will hurt it greatly."[172] David Wedderburn asked his sister to pack up and send to George in West Florida "a repeating watch in a small box & a muff in a case forgot in the parlour."[173]

There were new households overseas, filled with the flora and fauna of home. The *Earl of Holdernesse*, on which Elizabeth Carolina and her sister travelled to Calcutta, was carrying "cuttings of Sallow, willow & alder," which "all died in the Passage," as John and the other members of the East India Company's Council in Calcutta wrote to London in 1762; "the Seeds had been set in many different Soils but none of them had come up."[174] The Chittagong official in whose house Elizabeth Carolina and her sister lived ordered pears, quinces, and plums trees from Mocha and wrote of "planting fruit trees all over my hill."[175] David Wedderburn, in Bombay, asked his sister to send him "sixteen or twenty pounds of the best sort of Barley."[176] George's friends' expedition to settle Fort Johnstone, on an uninhabited island in the South Atlantic, carried "All kinds of Trees to Plant and Grasses of every kind—Seeds both Cape and European without number and without name."[177] Even Samuel Swinton, in Sloane Street in London, established himself as a merchant in fine foreign trees: peaches, nectarines, plum trees, almond trees, fig trees, and red and white mulberries from China.[178]

In Bombay, David Wedderburn established a "family," in the military sense of a society of soldiers, and a new imaginative family. "I love my horses, my dogs, my cats, my chickens, my soldiers, my servants; why then should I not love my wife if I had one," he wrote to his sister (about an unexciting romance on one of his visits to England). Once he had arrived in India, he wrote to her in greater detail: "believe me, you have no chance of having an Indian sister," although "you may, perchance, have an Indian Nephew, or a Niece."[179] After his death one of his friends in India—who had earlier been with him in West Florida, when George was governor—wrote to David Wedderburn's brother that "there is a Mogull Woman who lived with the Genl. For 12 or 14 Months, he had a very particular regard for her."[180] The inventory of his household in Bombay, sent to his sister when he died, was a compendium of his new and old lives: 8 China Images, 2 Clarinets, 1 Box Persian Sweetmeats, 1 Box for Smoking Stockings, 1 Printing Press, 1 Cask Mango Pickles, 1 Rabbit House, 68 Ducks, 1 Abissinia Sheep; and the 8 slaves.[181]

The family exchanges were a matter, above all, of pieces of cloth. "The history of textiles is fundamentally a story about international commerce in goods and ideas," Laurel Thatcher Ulrich has written, and for the Johnstones and their households the experience of international or long-distance connections was a story about linens and muslins and shawls.[182] George's peace congress with the Creeks turned on the exchange rate for "Dutch pretties" and "Large Silk Bengall."[183] The commerce in fine textiles was the foundation of John and William Bolts's early ventures in India, and of the exchanges of commodities with home: flowered dorea, fine

Dacca tanjibs, and damity, in George's listing of 1758, or the "Tanjibs flower'd" and "Mulmules" that John sent to James, for Louisa, on Christmas Eve of 1761.[184] William Bolts's denunciation of the oppression of the East India Company was the evocation of a lost society of industriousness and exquisite muslins, in which "by the Gentoo-accounts, the former manufactures in Bengal were incomparably finer than any thing now produced."[185] The Cape Coast Castle in West Africa, at the time when Captain Knight was there on his way to Jamaica—the Captain Knight by whom Joseph Knight was bought and sold—was an emporium of "Patna Chints," "Cherriderries," "White Linnen," "Bejutapauts," and "Mohair Buttons."[186]

For the non-Indian brothers, too, the exchange of linens and cloth was a continuing preoccupation in the enclosed masculine world of the army and the navy. I am "in a very bad situation having lost all my Light clothes and but very little linning," Gideon wrote to George in 1759, and two days later to William, I have "had the misfortune to loose all my Westindia cloths and Linnings."[187] In a codicil to his will, George left "all my wearing apparel" to his servant, who had behaved with "Assiduity Affection & Attention to me during my long illness."[188] Even in India, the East India Company officials yearned for cloth from home. Samuel Swinton, the entrepreneur of French newspapers and red champagne, was a purveyor of "Scarlets & other Cloths, Gold & Silver Lace, Shoes, Hatts, Silk Stockings, Books, Pamphlets &c," to the British in Calcutta.[189] Elizabeth Carolina's landlord in the garden house in Calcutta ordered "good Broad Cloth, of either Pepper and Salt, Chocolate, or Purple Colors, for the lining a Chaise," in Chittagong, and from another official in Dhaka, to whom he had sent a "supply of pickled Oysters," "a sett of crimson Tassells for my Palanquin."[190]

The lives of the Johnstone sisters and sisters-in-law, at home, were changed by the new empire of things. There is a sense in the family letters of a transformation in the color and texture of daily life—of a spade-colored or shoe-colored world that was suddenly bright. The textiles that were sent from the Indies, or that Betty and Charlotte bought with the money from their brothers (the "cardinals," or red cloaks) were novelties in the interior of the Scottish countryside.[191] The muslins in Betty's parcel were valuable objects of exchange, and they were also objects that were unlike the other clothes and cloths in the family's Westerhall home.[192] George evoked the old world of the Scottish-English borders in his imaginary mise-en-scène of his own funeral, with the poor of the parish clothed in "coarse grey Cloth." To his wife he left his pillow cases and his pieces of silk or printed cotton; to his niece he left his crimson shawl. One of Louisa's innumerable debts was for "Russia toweling," and one of her cousins in 1766 left to her younger son "my Crimson Mohair Bed and Bedding with the Taffitee Window Curtains."[193] Betty, in the family portrait by Raeburn, is dressed in black, like an elderly Scottish lady: a fine deep black, with wide sleeves of black velvet and a facing of black ribbons, a gauzy white neckerchief, and a white bonnet with a pale blue silk bow.

The color and the softness of life were of consequence for the Johnstones' extended households as well. Joseph Knight, when he was examined by the justices of the peace in Perthshire, said that "he has been entertained and clothed as well as the Rest of Sir John's servants but that his stockings were generally Coarse except four pair."[194] Janet Abernethy, the woman who was transported to America with Bell or Belinda, had been convicted of stealing "a piece of blue and white Linen Cheque" from one merchant in Aberdeen, and a "piece of spotted Camblet or cloth" from another merchant.[195] Even Bell or Belinda's own tragedy turned on a piece of cloth. "You did murder said child," the indictment against her stated, "and more particularly having wrapt said child in a Linin Cloth, you did throw him into the water or river of Leven." The linen cloth was lodged in evidence, and sent with her from judicial instance to judicial instance. "She the declarant brought forth a child which she says was dead born," she said in her first, coerced examination in Cupar; and "she keeped it two days after it was born and then carried it away in a Cloth which is just now showen to her to the Water of Leven and threw the Child and Cloth into the water," and "declares that the Cloth abovementioned is the same cloth in which she carried the Child to the water."[196]

INTIMATE LIVES

The consequences of empire were connections, in these circumstances, of intimate relationships. For the Johnstones, like so many of their friends in the East and West Indies, did not return home alone. There are six individuals, in the records of the Johnstones' lives, who can be identified as having been "brought" or "carried" or "carréd" from India or America. There is Bell or Belinda, who said of herself in Cupar in 1771 that "she came from Bengall in the East Indies with Mr Johnston and his Lady and has staid with them four years in London and afterwards has staid with them in Scotland ever since."[197] There is Molly, who was listed as a witness against Bell or Belinda, and who was described only as "a black girl, the slave or servant of John Johnstone." There is Joseph Knight, who told the justices of the peace in Perthshire in 1773 that he "was brought from the Coast of Guinea by one Capt. Knight when he was very young and carried to Jamaica," and that John Wedderburn "brought him w. him from Ja. To Britain about 4 years ago."[198]

There is Pierre, who was "carréd" from Grenada to England, and exchanged by William in 1797 for another "seasoned negro" of equal value. There is "Jane Castino Johnstone (Granado)," the "mulato daughter" of Alexander, in Bexley Heath. There is James Johnstone, the "Mollato" who was "brought from the East Indies by Mr. John Johnston," and baptized in Kirkandrews upon Esk in April 1773, the year after Bell or Belinda was sent to be sold in America and after Joseph Knight had read in an Edinburgh newspaper about the law of slavery in England. The "molatto" James Johnstone may or may not have been the same person, in turn, as the James Johnstone, "Negroe Servant to Sir James Johnstone," by whom Henrietta Allen said she became pregnant in 1778, or the "James Johnstone my black servant" to whom James left an annuity in his will, or the James Johnstone who was an inspector of books in the Westerhall Miners' Library.[199]

It is disquieting that there is so little to be discovered, in all the bundles and writings and registers of the times, about the lives of these children, or these women and men. I have referred to "Bell *or* Belinda" in this way

because that is how she was said to have described herself in the prison in Cupar: "4th July 1771 Compeared
the above mentioned Black Girl who calls herself Bell or
Belinda."[200] But there is a very remarkable proliferation
of "ors" in the successive courts' descriptions of her: a
distancing of the law from her history or her life. She
was "a black Girl *or* woman," "the slave *or* servant" of
John Johnstone; she understood "little *or* nothing of the
Language"; she was described as having left her room
on a "Friday *or* Saturday night" and as having told the
other servants that "you was too hot *or* that you had
catched cold"; she was "altogether *or* for the most part"
alone in Elizabeth Carolina's "bed room *or* dressing
room," and was "delivered in one *or* other of these places
as aforesaid *or* in some other place"; she was said to
have killed her child "by strangling him, *or* knocking
him on the head"; and "said Child was found dead *or*
said Child was and still is amissing." Sometimes she was
"Bell *or* Belinda" and sometimes "Bell *alias* Belinda";
her own initial declaration was said to be "unsigned by
you (because you said you could not write)." She petitioned the court in her last declaration to be sent "to one
or other of His Majestys Plantations *or* settlements in
the East *or* West Indies *or* in America."[201]

There is very little to be discovered, or that I have
been able to discover, about where Bell or Belinda, or
Molly, or James Johnstone were born and where they
died. If Bell or Belinda "came" to England with John and
Elizabeth Carolina, and James Johnstone was "brought"
by them, then they sailed from India via the Cape of
Good Hope and Lisbon on the *Admiral Stevens*, in
1765–66; James would have been a boy of eleven. But
there is no sign of them, or of "Molly," in the ship's two

log books, with their registers of "Lascars" or Indian sailors, and their dispiriting news ("baffling winds and rain with large confused swell"). They are invisible in the diary of the merchant with the seaweed and the birds. They are invisible, too, in the petitions with respect to servants' servants (the servants of the servants of the "Honourable Company") that are so conspicuous in the East India Company's records of a later period.[202] They are to be glimpsed, if at all, in John's laconic request in Calcutta in September 1765 "to accommodate with a passage to Europe . . . Mrs Johnstone with her Servants & necessaries."[203]

Bell or Belinda was invisible once again in her Atlantic passage: the passage to the destiny ordered by the court in Perth, of being sold as a "Slave for Life," "so as the person to whom she is sold may have a property and interest in her service during all the days of her Life."[204] She arrived in Virginia with three other convicts on the ship called the *Betsey*, according to the certificate that was sent back to Scotland; the *Betsey* was itself certified as having landed with five passengers and a crew of eleven. One of the people "imported" on the ship, a boy called James Patteson, was reported in a Virginia newspaper to have run away from his master, and then to have come back on board and stolen a blue waistcoat lined with white flannel.[205]

It is evident, all the same, that Bell or Belinda, and Molly, and "James Johnstone," and Joseph Knight were in no respect invisible in the remote estates in rural Scotland to which they were brought. Joseph Knight had a romance with Ann Thomson, who was a maidservant in John and Margaret Wedderburn's house and whom he married in Edinburgh. (He was "under the dominion," in his owner's disobliging description, "of one of the Fair Sex not very famous for her virtues").[206] James Johnstone, or one of the James Johnstones, had a romance with Henrietta Allen, who was a maidservant in James and Louisa Johnstone's house, and whose son James had no natural resemblance to him, "being white."

Bell or Belinda had some sort of romance, or some sexual encounter, in or in the vicinity of John and Elizabeth Carolina's house. The tragedy of her own child's death, and her indictment, impinged upon a very wide society of the east of Scotland: a multiplier effect of interior connections, again. Of the witnesses who were to be heard in Bell or Belinda's trial, four, including Molly, were identified as servants of John Johnstone; there was also the neighboring tenant, his wife, and four of his servants; there were three midwives, a surgeon, two officers of the court, and the two "writers" in Cupar who had written down her self-inculpating and unsigned declaration. In Perth there was John Swinton and the two notaries public who signed Bell or Belinda's new declaration; there were four witnesses to the notaries' declaration; there was John Taitt, the witness who was not there.[207]

The Johnstones, who wrote to each other about so many events, about illnesses and anxieties and teacups, said nothing at all in any of their surviving letters, or in any that I have been able to find, about "Bell or Belinda," or Joseph Knight, or the James Johnstone who was baptized in 1773, or the black James Johnstone. But it is difficult to imagine, in our own worlds of the mind and our own times, that their relationships to these young women and men, who had come with them as children from the other side of the world, were not of importance in their lives: in the intimate experience of empire.

One of the most elusive conditions of eighteenth-century life, the conditions that are most difficult to think oneself into in modern opulent societies, is the physical intimacy of the household, the juxtaposition in space of mistresses and servants and slaves. Bell or Belinda came from India in the confined space of the *Admiral Stevens* with John and Elizabeth Carolina, just as Joseph Knight came from Jamaica with John Wedderburn. Even when they were rich, the Johnstones did not live the sorts of lives in which the gentry and their servants were far removed from each other in a spatial sense. There are moments in their letters when there is a vivid impression of what their houses and their rooms were like: when their father writes about William and his friend sharing a bedroom, or when John writes from Balgonie to apologize for having mislaid one of the plans of the Grenada plantation: "after a search I found the Roll of Maps I had most carefully wrapt up with my own hands & which Mrs Johnstone had as carefully laid by in her Drawers when removing my Luggage from one Room to another in my absence."[208]

The Johnstones' lives were intertwined with the lives of their servants in time as well as space. John was in Balgonie in May before Bell or Belinda's baby was born in June 1771, although he and Elizabeth Carolina had gone away by the time of the birth; it is likely that Elizabeth Carolina was herself pregnant at the same time.[209] Charlotte, her husband James Balmain, and their family were also staying at Balgonie in the April before Bell or Belinda's baby was born; Charlotte too was pregnant in the summer of 1771.[210] Betty was a constant visitor to

John's homes; she passed through Balgonie in February 1771 and was there again in March 1771. She was staying in Perthshire with the family of her niece Margaret Wedderburn in the spring and again in the summer of 1775, at the period of intense crisis in the drama of Joseph Knight and John Wedderburn. The succession of events that unfolded in the Johnstones' extended households in 1771–74—Bell was sentenced to be banished in 1771, Joseph Knight read about the Somerset case in 1772, in 1773 the "mollato" James Johnstone was baptized in England and Joseph Knight declared that he was not a slave, in 1774 Joseph Knight's case was decided by the sheriff depute of Perthshire—were events in the lives of these three young people, who had come to Scotland as children from India and from Africa, via Jamaica.[211] But they were events, too, in the lives of the "masters" and "mistresses" by whom they had been carried.

The consequences of the distant empire, for the Johnstones, extended far into the interior of Scotland in a geographical sense: into the inland valleys and hills in which they settled or to which they returned, with their teacups and damity and terrible news from the Indies. The empire extended, too, into the interior of their homes and their households: in the lives of the individuals who returned with them, and who had to make lives for themselves, in these cold, inhospitable hills. It extended, even, into the most interior or personal spaces of the Johnstones' houses, in Fife or Perth. Bell lived in a "bed and room" with the other servants, or so the court in Cupar was told in July 1771. She left the room in the last days of June, and she went into "her Ladys Bedroom and no Body was present with her at the time": "you did

continue altogether or for the most part in said bed
room or dressing room 'till you was delivered . . . and
you did remain mostly by yourself in said appartments
for sometime after your said Delivery."[212] This, too, was
the intimacy of empire.

CHAPTER SIX

WHAT IS ENLIGHTENMENT?

The Johnstones lived at the edges of empire and at the edges of the enlightenment. The brothers and sisters were not themselves philosophers or chemists or historians; only Elizabeth Carolina wrote a work of literature that was published, and only William wrote a political pamphlet of any substantial pretention (about his thoughts on the American conflict, in 1778, and on the unlikelihood that the colonists, with their "uncertain theory" of a new system of government, would be able to establish "a new and independent empire").[1] But the Johnstones were friends or acquaintances of the philosophes of eighteenth-century Edinburgh, including David Hume, Adam Smith, and Adam Ferguson. They lived in the "atmosphere of society," in Adam Ferguson's expression, in which "minds should become enlightened, in proportion as they should have occasion to receive information from the frequent discussion of subjects, which they are concerned to understand."[2]

In the Scotland to which the Johnstones returned, there were at least three different senses of enlightenment, or of "lights." There was the sect of philosophers of the science of nature and human nature.[3] There was the milieu of the enlightenment, in the sense of the assortment of booksellers, printers, proof-correctors, itinerant tutors, lawyers, advocates' clerks, translators, and editors who constituted the business of enlightenment in Scotland as in France: the individuals by whom the lights of science were communicated.[4] There was the disposition of enlightenment, or enlightenment in the principal eighteenth-century sense of a condition of mind or way of thinking: Kant's sense, in the 1784 essay "What is Enlightenment?"; or Elizabeth Mure's sense of a change in manners in the west of Scotland; or the sense of a "cultura populorum," in the translation of the word "Aufklärung" that was sent to the Royal Society of Edinburgh in 1788: the enlightenment of large numbers of people, or of the "populi."[5]

The Johnstones were figures of enlightenment in all these senses, at least from time to time, and their lives provide an odd and disturbing perspective on the transformation that Adam Ferguson described as the "progress of information," the "progress of society," or the "principles of progression in the human mind."[6] They were a connection, in the most intricate respects, between the enlightenment and the empire, at home and in the Indies. Their dramas of empire unfolded in the world of the philosophes, and the philosophes also lived in or were familiar with the Johnstones' world of empire.

THE SECT OF PHILOSOPHERS

The political thought of the eighteenth-century enlightenment was concerned to a striking extent with the dilemmas of overseas empire.[7] The promise of David Hume's *Political Discourses*, the book of which he wrote that it was "the only work of mine that was successful on the first publication," was of a commercial society that extended across the globe.[8] Ferguson's *Essay on the History of Civil Society* was a drama of mercantile virtue and the corruption of empire.[9] Approximately a third of *The Wealth of Nations* was about empire, or at least about the long-distance commerce that in Smith's description was so intricately entangled with the eighteenth-century empires. Of the last additions that Smith made to *The Wealth of Nations* in 1783, more than three-quarters were about wool, herrings, and the East India Company.[10]

The highest and most abstract questions of enlightenment philosophy were at the heart of these discussions of empire: about the universality of human nature; or the respects in which sympathy is refracted by distance; or the uncertainties of government over extended societies—the politics of distance—that were so intriguing to David Hume. The new circumstances of empire were at the heart, too, of the divisions within even the closest friendships of the Scottish enlightenment. Adam Smith denounced American slavery in *The Theory of Moral Sentiments* in "as bitter an invective as ever fell from the tongue of man," in the expression of an Edinburgh-educated Virginia lawyer; he "exalted into heroes" the African slaves and "debased into monsters" the American colonists.[11] Smith's comments on slavery were invoked by Joseph Knight's lawyer in 1775 as "the Indignation of a generous mind."[12] David Hume devoted a notorious footnote in his essay "On National Characters" to the natural inequality of different "species of men": "I am apt to suspect the negroes to be naturally inferior to the whites." Hume's footnote was itself invoked in the disputes of the 1770s on the opposite side, by the supporters of slavery, and refuted in detail by his critics in Scotland.[13] In the "Abolition Map" in Thomas Clarkson's *History of the Abolition of the Slave Trade*, with its multitude of waters flowing into an ocean of emancipation, Adam Smith and the critics of David Hume are contiguous, as rivers of virtue.[14]

The philosophers of enlightenment were widely identified as no more than theorists, in these controversies over empire and commerce. "We well know with what a sovereign brow of contempt some of our modern philosophers look down from their lofty dictatorial chairs on the nameless crowd below," William Julius Mickle wrote in his defense of the East India Company.[15] Smith's criticisms of empire, for Mickle, were "the dreams and dotage of Theory." William (Johnstone) Pulteney, in his last speech in support of the slave trade, declared that "this bill was built on theory, and he was not fond of theories"; "some say, that it is much better to employ free negroes than slaves. . . . This is, however, only a supposition, a mere theory."[16] Even for the critics of empire, the philosophers of the Scottish enlightenment had no more than a distant view of imperial oppression. As the poet Richard Clarke asked in a satire of 1773, called *The Nabob*, which was in part a denunciation of Hume's views of race and slavery:

> Concerns it you who plunders in the East,
> In blood a tyrant, and in lust a beast?
> When ills are distant, are they then your own?
> Saw'st thou their tears, or heard'st th'oppressed groan?[17]

The history of the Johnstones and the philosophes suggests a different and more disturbing possibility, that the ills of empire were not all that distant from the world of the Scottish enlightenment. In degrees of separation— did Adam Smith, for example, who wrote so eloquently against slavery, know anyone who was a slave? did he

know anyone who knew anyone who knew a slave?—
the Johnstones were themselves the connections between
a large part of the high enlightenment and the oceanic
scenes of empire.

The intimacy of the Johnstones with the philosophers
of the Scottish science of man, or the sect of the high
enlightenment, began in their childhood. Their father
was the intermediary in the affair of David Hume's unfortunate employment as companion to the Johnstones'
rich and disturbed young cousin or kinsman, who was
declared a "lunatic" in England in 1747, and in Scotland in 1757—by what was known as a "Brieve of Furiosity"—and who was the aspiring author of a novel
about blighted and eventually triumphant love.[18] Hume
wrote twenty-one letters to the older James Johnstone
over the course of a few months in 1745–46, when he
was living with the rich cousin and in a spirit of increasing despondency: "God forgive you, Dear Sir, God forgive you, for neither coming to us, nor writing to us."
They were still in correspondence many years later over
what the Johnstones' father described as the "dark remembrance" of the affair.[19] Two of the Johnstones' uncles, including the judge in Bell or Belinda's case, were
among Hume's close friends in Edinburgh; he described
them in 1764 as "those with whom I have long liv'd in
the greatest Intimacy."[20]

The younger Johnstones were themselves Hume's
friends: George, whom Hume described as a gallant,
sensible young fellow, and William, "Our friend, Johnstone." Hume even seems to have invited George, in
1763, to "interpose" with their father with respect to
their "Sisters conduct," writing to him, ingratiatingly, as

"the Son of the greatest Influence, & the Brother of the Strongest Affections."[21] Hume was solicited by William, when he was under-secretary of state in 1767, in the effort to return the family's Indian fortunes to Scotland, via the good offices of the French Compagnie des Indes. He solicited his publisher's vote, on behalf of William and his friends, in the East India Company intrigues of 1772 and 1774.[22]

The relationships between the Johnstones and Adam Smith suggest a similar scene, in which the East and West Indies were at the edge of the horizon, or the field of vision, of the Scottish philosophes. Adam Smith, like Hume, described his connection to the Johnstones, or at least to William, as close.[23] He celebrated William's wife's inheritance late into the night in 1767, with Adam Ferguson and Hugh Blair at the Edinburgh "Poker Club."[24] In 1772 William tried unsuccessfully to procure a lucrative office for Smith as a member of the East India Company's commission of inquiry into its own affairs; Smith addressed him as "my dearest Pulteney."[25] In London, where Smith lived from 1773 to 1777, and where he finished and published *The Wealth of Nations*, his acquaintances were also the acquaintances of William, George, and John, in and around the "British Coffee-House" in Charing Cross to which Smith's letters were addressed.[26] Smith was involved in the solicitation of positions for his relations and the friends of his friends: together with George, on behalf of Edmund Burke's cousin in India; and together with Burke, on behalf of one of William's old friends from New York (the friend who had described Alexander as "more discontented than I ever saw any body"). James "Ossian" Macpherson, George's former secretary in West Florida, described Smith, in a letter of solicitation to his cousin in Madras, as "Dr Adam Smith, one of my best friends."[27]

In Scotland Smith's relations with the Johnstones were more complicated. John's rented estate in Balgonie, where Bell or Belinda's baby was found in the river in 1771, was only an afternoon's walk from Smith's home in Kirkaldy, where he was living at the time. Smith and John were almost certainly acquainted, if only through the affairs of the Duke of Buccleuch, Smith's friend and former pupil, and the landowner of whom the Johnstones were tenants in Westerhall, and neighbors in the Ettrick Forest. "When you mention to Mr Smith your scheme for beautifying the Face of Byken, (which I much aprove off) I would sound him wither the D. would create new Votes in the Forrest and Join you," James wrote to John in April 1771, in an apparent reference to Smith.[28] John was also actively involved in the politics of the town of Kirkaldy. His election to parliament in October 1774 was for the boroughs that included the town, and his unsuccessful opponent was the son of Smith's oldest family friend, James Oswald, the secretary of the Leeward Islands, and a cousin of the Oswalds who had established the largest of all the Scottish merchants' slave-trading empires in Africa.[29] One of John's letters to William, in October 1767, was dated from Kirkaldy, and he wrote again, in September 1768, that "it was necessary I should go to Kirkaldy to settle the affair I spoke to you of." "I was at Kirkaldie at that time," he wrote of his travels in June 1771.[30]

The Johnstones came and went, too, in the lives of the scientific figures of the enlightenment. Betty was preoccupied, during her exile from Westerhall over the matter of the muslins, in transmitting samples of different minerals and ores to William Cullen in Edinburgh, the eminent professor of chemistry and medicine (and the father of Robert Cullen, John Wedderburn's lawyer in the case against Joseph Knight). "You have never said whither you Received the Minerall Stones yet or if Doctor Cullen has trayed what they containd we are all very anxious," she wrote to William in 1762.[31] "You will remember my Coal Sulphur &c and my Fathers Mines in your Perigrinations," James wrote to her from Norfolk in 1770, and then again in 1772, "Have you conversed your Mineral Friends?"[32] John, William, and George were involved with the two prominent medical theorists of the time, William Hunter and John Hunter, in an exchange of elections and obligations, in which the Hunters supported the Johnstones in the politics of the East India Company, and the Johnstones supported the Hunters in the politics of St. George's Hospital. William Hunter had "acted the kindest part," in John's description, and John Hunter was "a man of that Stamp as makes me think him worthy to be ranked in the number of our friends."[33] Smith and Hume's friend, the Edinburgh "philosophic chemist" Joseph Black, was engaged by William in the endorsement of a patent medicine, Dr Velnos's Vegetable Syrup.[34] The eminent geologist Etheldred Benett was Louisa's cousin (and the granddaughter of the cousin with the crimson mohair bed). Another eminent chemist, Sir James Hall, a student of Joseph Black and the geologist Joseph Hutton, was the first cousin of "Miss Peggy," who was sent from Sumatra to Scotland with the slave woman named Betty.[35]

Walter Minto, the tutor of George and Martha's older sons, lived with them in Pisa in the house of the astrophysicist Josephus Slop de Cadenberg. Minto was himself converted from the study of Italian antiquities—when Hume had offered him the position of tutor, on George's behalf, "he and a friend were about to go [to Italy] as pilgrims relying on the charity of the pious"—to the mathematics of celestial orbits.[36] When he and George quarrelled, Minto had the opportunity of going to join "an umarried uncle I have in Jamaica" on "his own estate near Montego Bay." He emigrated, instead, to Princeton, New Jersey, where he became the first professor of mathematics. He exhorted his students, in a commencement address in 1788, to "preserve this rising and extensive empire from the ill-boding spirit of conquest," and donated a portion of his salary to provide a medal for the best essays on "the unlawfulness and impolicy of capital punishment" and "the unlawfulness and impolicy of African slavery."[37]

Adam Ferguson was the closest of all the Scottish philosophers to the Johnstones, and his own changing circumstances provide a vivid illustration of the connections between the high Scottish enlightenment and the empire. Ferguson's aspiration, at the time of the publication of his *Essay on the History of Civil Society* in 1767, was to be appointed as governor of West Florida in succession to George.[38] In 1772 one of the Johnstones' Edinburgh correspondents reported to William that the studies of "our literary friends here," and especially of Ferguson, "have also taken the route of India." Ferguson hoped by then to be named, with the support of David Hume and the Johnstones, as secretary to the East India Company's supervisors in Calcutta, and was again disappointed. In 1774 he went to Geneva as the tutor to a young lord ("I may have much to Say in Europe as well as in Asia," he wrote); in 1778 he was appointed as George and Lord Carlisle's secretary in America.[39] George determined in his will that his youngest son should be sent to live in Scotland as soon as he reached the age of either four or six; the little boy, whose guardians included John, Betty, and John Wedderburn ("my beloved and respected friend"), was brought up eventually by Adam Ferguson ("most worthy of the human race").[40] George's older sons in India and their mother Martha Ford remained on friendly terms with Ferguson. Ferguson corresponded with Betty about John's illnesses and helped her to find a tenant for her apartment in Edinburgh; he and John corresponded, as John was dying, about the possibility of eternal life.[41]

David Hume, Adam Smith, Adam Ferguson, and William Cullen were all members of the discussion club called the "Select Society," which was the founding instance, as recounted in multiple histories, of the Edinburgh enlightenment. William was also a member; so were his uncles Lord Elibank and James Ferguson (later the judge in Bell or Belinda's case); so too was John Swinton (who presented Bell or Belinda's petition), William's childhood friend Alexander Wedderburn, and his brother David Wedderburn of West Florida, the Cape Verde Islands, and Bombay.[42] William and James were members of the "Poker Club," which was the continuation of the Select Society, together with Smith, Hume, Ferguson, their uncle Lord Elibank, their nephew John Wedderburn's two legal counsels in the Joseph Knight case, and another nephew, the future husband of Charlotte's daughter Caroline.[43] The Johnstones were figures in the social relationships of the Scottish enlightenment, and the philosophers of the enlightenment were figures in their own social relationships of empire.

THE MILIEUX OF ENLIGHTENMENT: BOOKS AND BOOKSELLERS

The sense of the overseas connections of empire as almost within sight, in eighteenth-century Scotland, extended well beyond the philosophers of empire. The sect of the high enlightenment, as described in a satire of 1774 called the *Scots Review,* was so exiguous that there were no more than eight copies of Hume's *Treatise of Human Nature* in the entire country; and the "exact number of all the freethinkers in Scotland" amounted to only "six hundred three score and six." But there was a more flourishing industry of enlightenment—of tutors, schoolmasters, keepers of small academies, doctors of divinity, and editors who aspired "not only to review authors, but the taste and judgments of the public itself"—and this too was among the scenes of the Johnstones' lives.[44]

The Johnstones were preoccupied, from their earliest years in Westerhall, with borrowing and buying and storing books. Their father borrowed a copy of Grotius from Adam Smith's family friend James Oswald and sent it to David Hume to be returned.[45] Patrick and Gideon's tutor borrowed *Aesop's Fables* and *Dunlop's Greek Grammar* from a neighbor, but was obliged to return it when the neighbor came home.[46] James borrowed a translation of Horace from William: "I have taken Francis Horace and no other Books Jas. Johnstone," he wrote on the reverse of the letter to William from Barbara's husband, about the report of Margaret's death in Paris.[47] There were elaborate inventories of books in the probate records of James's and Charles Kinnaird's estates in Scotland: Machiavelli and Descartes in the Kinnairds' home, and in the library at Westerhall, Plato, Voltaire, "Muncaster on the slave trade" and "Mrs McAulys History of England four volumes."[48] George left his best Glasgow Milton to the family at Westerhall and his three books of the navigation compendium *The Neptune François* to one of David Hume's young cousins.[49] Betty wrote in her will that "I promised to Mrs Playfair my maid Dr Blairs Sermons and desire they may be given her."[50] The initial list of subscribers to William Julius Mickle's translation of the *Lusiad* in 1776 included Betty, James, William, Alexander, George, John, David Hume, John Swinton, Archibald Swinton, "Primrose Thomson in India, 2 *copies*," the Johnstones' maternal uncles Elibank and Pitfour, Uncle Walter, and Charlotte's widower James Balmain.[51]

Books and booksellers were a medium of exchange between distant friends and the extremities of the empire. There was Laidlaw at the circulating library in Newcastle, to whom George was supposed to send their mother's refined sugar. The Johnstones' father made elaborate arrangements to send books to John in India.[52] When the chaplain of the East India Company died in Calcutta, John bought twenty-three volumes of sermons, and there were forty more volumes, shared among seven other officials.[53] George, when he was ordered to Lisbon in 1759, asked Samuel Swinton to take charge of his books, and he heard from Newcastle, where Swinton had been sent on the "Impress Service" (or the gang of naval officers who pressed reluctant sailors), that "wherever my Furniture goes your Books shall also go."[54] Even William Colhoon, on his way to Africa, wrote to his sister that "you may send my Brown Close and what you think convenient to serve and a few Books of different kinds."[55]

William Bolts, when he was expelled from India by the East India Company in 1768, was allowed "about two hours to put together his own and his wife's cloaths, together with some of his books and papers, into chests, to be taken with them." A captain in the Company's army then "marched him through the streets surrounded by soldiers; *leaving the doors of his house open, and his papers and effects at the mercy of the populace.*"[56] In his will Bolts left "printed Books consisting of about fourteen hundred Volumes of all Sizes," to be sent to the "Island of Guernsey" and there sold, "after the distribution of catalogues in London Amsterdam and Paris."[57]

The world of the booksellers was influenced, in turn, by the opportunities of empire. This was a matter of the books that were sold: Robertson's *History of South America,* which the Westerhall miners ordered in 1796, or "Robertson's *India,*" which they ordered in 1797.[58] "The country is over-run with a kind of literary packmen, who ramble from town to town selling books," the counsel for the London booksellers said of Scotland in 1774, in the celebrated debate over literary copyright in the House of Commons, in the course of which George defended the freedom of ideas, in opposition to Edmund Burke's defense of booksellers' property: "In every little town there is now a printing press. Coblers have thrown away their awl, weavers have dismissed their shuttle, to commence printers." The books to be sold were themselves, from time to time, adventures: Hawkesworth's *Voyages*, for example, with its East Indian encounters in the South Seas, which was the booksellers' most extravagant property and which the attorney general described in parliament as "very low indeed," a "mere composition of trash."[59]

The opportunities of empire were also a matter of the printers' and publishers' own lives. The two "Miss Baillies" who arrived in Bombay in 1772, "stupid, awkward [and] perfectly vertuous," were recommended by "your freind Donaldson the bookseller," David Wedderburn wrote to his sister.[60] Samuel Swinton, after he had established himself in London with his black servant from the West Indies, his "little tawney boy," and George's books, became the employer, in Boulogne, of the political writer Jean-Paul Brissot. He also supplied "Magazines and Pamphlets to my sundry friends and good Customers in Bengal . . . not being able to find storage for them any where else, I put them into a Trunk of Millinery Ware."[61] William Julius Mickle, whose father had been employed by the London booksellers in correcting the translation of Pierre Bayle's *Dictionary*—"the great part of the notes to which were the production of his pen"—and whose brother was a journeyman printer, was the corrector of proofs at the Clarendon Press in Oxford. He too was "on the point of setting off for Carolina" in 1765 or for "some settlement in the East or West Indies," with "letters to the West Indies" from the Johnstones' Uncle Walter.[62]

The owner of James Somerset, Charles Steuart, was the brother of an Edinburgh lawyer, James Steuart, the son-in-law of an eminent grammarian, printer of the *Caledonian Mercury*, keeper of the Advocates' Library in Edinburgh (where he was succeeded by David Hume), and author of Ruddiman's *Rudiments of the Latin Tongue*.[63] James Steuart's letters to his brother are filled with allusions to the distant vicissitudes of empire: a "servant in my house" who "on leaving it went to the East Indies to an Uncle who happen'd to die before their meeting"; a "gentleman's son" who had been a sailor in St. Petersburg and "proposes going to London soon to try his fate either for the East or West Indies"; his own son, whom he hoped to see as a "writer in the East India Company" but whom he eventually bound "as an apprentice in our printing house" ("I propose he should also set up a shop as a Bookseller"); his third son, who aspired to "going out to the East or West Indies according as recommendations may cast up."[64] James Somerset was brought to Edinburgh in 1771 on a family visit; in January 1772 James Steuart invited his brother to return for a "longer stay," "and Anne [his daughter] desires you will send Somerset before you."[65]

LEGAL INFORMATION

The milieu of the law in Scotland, the other prominent setting of enlightenment, was also connected to the opportunities of empire. The Johnstones' maternal family consisted of lawyers and soldiers of empire. Their mother's oldest brother, the advocate Lord Elibank, who provided the security for John's first position in the East India Company, had earlier served in the unsuccessful expedition against Cartagena in what is now Colombia; their maternal grandfather lost a fortune in the "South Sea bubble" of commerce in slaves and contraband to the Spanish south Atlantic, as did the father of Hume's other friend and the Johnstones' other uncle, Lord Pit-

four, the judge in Bell or Belinda's case.[66] Of Lord Pitfour's own sons, one was John Wedderburn's lawyer in
the case against Joseph Knight (the lawyer who talked
of the calamity of the debasing of race), one was "made
the Merchant" and became governor of Tobago, and
one was an army officer in North America and in Alexander's regiment in Grenada and Tobago, "where he was
of great service in quelling very formidable insurrections
of the negroes," in Adam Ferguson's account.[67]

The sense of overseas opportunity in the large legal
families of eighteenth-century Scotland extended well
beyond the Johnstones' own relations. When David
Wedderburn landed in Antigua on his way to West Florida, he found an old acquaintance of his brother Alexander "who was called to the Bar the same day with you
came up to me in the Street . . . & invited me to his house
from which I write at present."[68] Alexander Wedderburn, the author of the "manifesto of the Scottish Enlightenment" (in the description of David Hume's biographer), was in correspondence about the details of
settlements in East Florida: "N.B. In the within Calculation there is no Allowance made for the death of Negroes; Because if there are a sufficient Number of Women
the Children should nearly make up for this loss."[69] John
Swinton's son became secretary of the East India Company's council in Calcutta; it was his grandson of whom
Sir Walter Scott, whose mother was Swinton's first
cousin, told a celebrated story in 1826: "Curious expression of an Indian-born boy just come from Bengal, a son
of my cousin George Swinton. The child saw a hare run
across the fields and exclaimd 'See there is a little tiger.' "[70]
Scott, whose father was a solicitor, or writer to the signet, and who was himself an advocate, recounted his

own pedigree as a sequence of overseas connections: his brother who was a naval officer in the "haunted *keys* of the West Indies" and died in the service of the East India Company; another brother who died in Canada and left a son in the East India Company's service in Bombay; a brother who "died on his return from the West Indies"; and his wife, whose fortune consisted in an annuity from her "very affectionate brother," "Commercial Resident at Salem in India."[71]

Even in the Scottish countryside, the inland or interior consequences of the Johnstones' unsettled existence were mediated through the law. The wills that James, Alexander, George, Gideon, John, Louisa, and Betty made; the annuities the brothers left to their children and servants; the bonds in which their wealth was brought home from India; their purchases of estates; their mortgages on land and slaves; the conflicts over their inheritances and marriage settlements: all these relationships were the occupation of innumerable lawyers and clerks, in the universe of the law that Sir Walter Scott described as the "dry and barren wilderness of forms and conveyances."[72] This wasteland, which was the milieu or one of the milieux of the Scottish enlightenment, was also a scene in which the insecurities of empire were an enduring preoccupation. George's will was conditional, with its reverie of gaining sufficient insight into so many contingent events, and so was William Julius Mickle's: "as the contingencies of human life are uncertain and inscrutable."[73] John's will was an expectation of uncertainty to come, or an instruction with respect to "the Laws and practice of the respective Countries where my Estate means and effects real and personal or any part thereof may happen to be situated at the time of my death."[74] The family lawyer who bought Louisa's lottery ticket, and to whom James wrote about the smiling regions of futurity, was the executor of Martha Ford's mother's will and the trustee of her grandsons in India; he was also the part owner with Samuel Swinton of the *Courier de l'Europe*.[75]

The public procedures of the law were in turn a source of information, or misinformation, about distant events. The legal process in eighteenth-century Scotland was still a public spectacle: of magistrates and judges on circuit processing through the streets. *Songs in the Justiciary Opera*, a satire of provincial justice composed by James Boswell and other young lawyers in the 1770s, begins with a "Grand Procession," and turns on the petition for banishment of the "pannel," or accused:

> O send me oure the lang seas
> My ain kind lordie, O . . .
> O send me east, or send me wast,
> Or send me south or nordie, O.[76]

There were public punishments, like the sentence imposed on a woman called Christian Crawford on Christmas Eve of 1760, by one of the judges who later voted against Joseph Knight, that she should stand in the pillory in Edinburgh from noon to one in the afternoon on the ninth of January, "with a paper affixed on her breast, with these words written on it in large characters, *Infamous prevaricator upon oath in judgment*"; or the punishment that would have been inflicted on Bell or Belinda if she were to have returned to Scotland, "upon the first market day after her Incarseration" to be "whypt through the streets of Perth by the hands of the Common hangman receiving the ordinary number of strypes upon her naked back at the usuall places and accustomed time of day."[77]

Bell or Belinda's own case was reported in the *Scots Magazine* with a strikingly inaccurate headline on the front cover: "A criminal slave adjudged to be sold for behoof of the master." But the magazine's account provided information beyond what was recorded in the circuit court minutes: that the advocate-depute consented to the outcome "in respect of the particular situation of the pannel" (the accused, or Bell), because "it appeared from an inquiry made since taking the precognition, that there was no sufficient evidence of intentional murder."[78] A slightly different law report in the *Caledonian Mercury* added further information about Bell or Belinda's state of mind and the import of the missing witness: "though she was conscious no actual murder could be proved against her, yet, as by the absence of a person at London, to whom she had revealed her situation."[79] A report in the *Public Advertiser* referred to her as "Bell alias Belinder," sentenced to "Banishment for Life."[80] A few months later, the *Scots Magazine* reverted to Bell or Belinda's case in its account of James Somerset's lawsuit in London in June 1772, and of the scene in the court of King's Bench. "It was wished that a late trial at one of our circuit-courts," the magazine added, citing the report of Bell's case, "had been transferred to Edinburgh, in which case, the question now determined in the court of king's-bench, might perhaps have been fully debated."[81]

Joseph Knight's case, in the following year, was from the outset a case about information, including his own information about the law and the information of other slaves. It was eventually an extraordinarily public cause:

"the pleadings in this case, have been all along attended by a female audience. The galleries yesterday were quite crouded with Ladies of fashion," the *Caledonian Mercury* reported in 1776, the day after a rousing speech about "the consequences of introducing slavery here. . . . In this country, so fertile for improvements, we may soon see a *team* consisting of two horses, two oxen, and two slaves."[82] But it had begun with Joseph Knight's knowledge of James Somerset's case. "What made him resolve to go away was a paragraph that he read in Mr Donaldson's news papers published the third day of July," he declared in the magistrates' court, which was sitting in justice in his owner's house, "and from that time he has had it in his head to leave his service." Joseph Knight had later come to know of another case involving a slave in Scotland: "he afterwards liked the Law of the Sheriff Depute of Perthshire better who by a scots newspaper he found had discharged a servant formerly a Slave from all service or dutie to his master."[83] His lawyer in Edinburgh anticipated a more far-reaching discussion: "he looked forward with enthusiasm to some future day, when, in an African Code of Laws, a new species of manumission should be mentioned . . . that, if this poor negro had any friends or relations in his native country, the joyful news might reach them."[84]

In the courtrooms of the justices of the peace, the sheriff-substitute, the sheriff-depute, and the lords of session, Joseph Knight's case impinged on the lives of hundreds of writers, ushers, clerks, advocates, and legal reporters: another multiplier effect of empire. John Cairns, in his remarkable study of the Scottish law of slavery, has identified seventy-eight cases of black men and women in Scotland in the first three-quarters of the eighteenth century, almost all of whom were involved, in one way or another, with the processes of the law.[85] Bell or Belinda's case, too, impinged on the armies of the law in the east and west of Scotland, as she was taken from prison to prison, and "so from shore to shore." She passed through the worlds of the writers in Cupar, who wrote down her first declaration, the declaration "tending to show your guilt," and of the "Sheriff Officer" in Cupar who witnessed the declaration; of the officers who undertook the subsequent inquiry into her intentions; and of the "co-notarys public" in Perth who wrote down her second declaration and subscribed for her, when she "touched the pen," "by order of the said Bell or Belinda, the petitioner above named."[86]

Even the missing witness, the mysterious John Taitt who was absent in London, to whom Bell said that she had "revealed her situation" and "who she is advised is necessary for her exculpation upon the Crime," was almost certainly an officer of the law. He was the same John Taitt or Tait, perhaps, writer to the signet, who petitioned in the same Sheriff's Court in Cupar three years later with respect to the entitlement of the Countess of Rothes to the "family writings" in her brother's house, or her "right to the writings."[87] He was also, perhaps, the John Tait who appears in the correspondence of the Johnstones' Grenada estate as the person who was designated to take care of "unpleasant matters:" "you will please write to Mr Tait to look after the matter".[88] Or the John Tait who was the "doer" or agent for the Johnstones' disturbed cousin, in 1766, in the matter of the family's ancient descent.[89] Or the "Mr Tait" who visited the Johnstones' father in 1762, in connection with "Johns Money designed for Sandy & Gidion:" "it was no small Mortification that Mr Tait Behoved to leave me befor he could Draw out what Number of Acres are Contained in Glendining."[90] It is possible, even, that he was the John Tait who died intestate in 1817 and whose son, also John Tait and also a writer to the signet, recorded that he left "debts considered good" from "Sir John Johnston" of £19.15s.8d, and "debts considered desperate" from "Sir James Johnston & Reprs" of £107.1s.31/4d.[91]

CLERKS AND CLERICS

There was another important milieu of the enlightenment in Scotland, of itinerant men of letters: clerics, clerks, tutors, and secretaries. The Johnstones were a family in whose lives religion played an inconspicuous role. In all her letters and her descriptions of journeys, Betty says almost nothing about religious observance: only that her sister Barbara, in Edinburgh after her separation from her husband, was thought to have behaved "just as she ought to Do" and had "never been out Except twice at Church."[92] Louisa, at the end of her life, was interested in deism, or in the beliefs of Mexicans and Mahometans, "whom we call Idolaters, Infidells, & Heathen."[93] John, like the Johnstones' father, referred to religious belief in moments of extreme solemnity (after their father's death, in John's case, and after the news of William's inheritance, in their father's case), and at the very end of his own life, in his conversation with Adam Ferguson about the "thereafter" and the possibility of being reunited with his brothers in the world to come.[94] Elizabeth Carolina, of whom so little was known, even to her children, was perhaps the most devout. Her

daughter described her, in an inscription in the mausoleum in the Westerkirk churchyard, as having led "a life
of unaffected piety," and her poems, published when she
was in India, included a hymn for the General Fast of
1758, and a version of Psalm 139.[95] It was only the
Johnstones' mother, in all the family letters I have looked
at, who described her reflections on eternity: their disturbed mother with all her anger and all her losses, who
wrote to John in India, in a letter that was even more
than usually distraught, that "upon a frequent and
narow examination I feel no steps in my life that gives
death any additional horror and I bless God I am quit
content with the part I have acted."[96]

But the connections to the Church of Scotland and
the Church of England were abundant in the Johnstones' lives, as in the lives of so many others in the
eighteenth-century British empire. They were involved
within their extended families with the established
(Presbyterian) Church of Scotland, the Episcopal (Anglican) Church in Scotland, and the Church of England.
William was for a time the "ruling elder" (at the age of
twenty-six) of the presbytery in which Westerkirk was
included.[97] Charlotte, James, and John all married into
clerical families. Charlotte's father-in-law, who was
supposed to have signed the false attestation of Gideon's date of birth, was the minister of the Westerkirk
church. Louisa's first husband was a Church of England
vicar, and she was the great-niece of an archbishop of
Canterbury.[98] Elizabeth Carolina's brother, with whom
John corresponded about moderation and gentleness in
the affairs of the East India Company, was also a Church
of England vicar; her nephew was a curate and aspiring
naval chaplain, who tried after his father's death to sell

his copy of Hume's *History of England* to his more opulent cousins in Scotland.[99] Barbara's son-in-law from Massachusetts, Edmund Dana, the former medical student, became a Church of England clergyman and the rector of a parish in Shropshire, in the bequest of William's wife Frances's estate.[100] William Julius Mickle's father was a minister.[101] Laura Pulteney's heiress's first husband was a clergyman (the clergyman into whose house her second husband was supposed to have climbed), and her father-in-law was the archbishop of York.[102] Even John Tait, or one of the John Taits (the "doer" John Tait), was the grandfather of a nineteenth-century archbishop of Canterbury.[103]

The Johnstones were involved, too, with a larger and more indistinct world of clerks, in the sense of the clerical, or the educated. John was described by his teacher, when he left for India, as "capable of discharging the Duty of Clerk in any office with credit," and the Johnstones were themselves almost clerks: individuals who could have been clerk-like.[104] One of the many odd aspects of their story is their continuing mobility, in space, economic circumstances, and social condition. They could have been clerks in offices, if the fortunes of war had been different or if their own resolution had been less. Their prospects rose and fell and rose again. They had been "employed as factors or otherwise," in the description of the successful claimants in the eventual dénouement, in 1881, of their father's great cause of the Annandale peerage. There was even an old leather bag of documents that the Johnstones' father was supposed to have secreted at some point before 1766, and that was discovered in 1876 in the Edinburgh offices of John Tait's former law firm.[105]

The Johnstones and their friends were surrounded by a changing scene of writers and clerks. There was the tutor who lived in the family house in Westerhall, read Virgil with Patrick and taught arithmetic to Gideon, and despatched William into the world in 1751 with the parting advice "that you would retain your primitive Integrity at least till you can get handsomely off with it—And whatever your Sentiments & Practice be keep always your wonted Gravity & Circumspection."[106] There were the writers, or the semi-clerks, who wrote and copied letters. John Wedderburn lamented to William in the winter of 1775, when his wife was dying and Joseph Knight had sued for his freedom, of "having no body at hand to write for me."[107] David Wedderburn resolved, before he left for West Florida, to "read & save money," as he wrote to his sister; "I have found a very good Mathematician & a good Scholar whom I shall carry north with me instead of a Valet de Chambre."[108] There were the teachers to whom John, Patrick, and Gideon were sent and who provided the certifications that the East India Company required of its "writers."[109] George and Martha's third son attended a class in bookkeeping "and acquired a perfect knowledge of it"; he was also instructed in Edinburgh in the principles of Persian grammar, "in prose and poetry."[110]

The Johnstone sisters, and the sisters of their friends, were for the most part self-instructed, or self-improved. Their mother was highly literary in her prose and almost illiterate in her spelling. Betty's spelling was phonetic in her earliest letters and in letters dictated to her by her father; it was highly accomplished by the time she was living on her own. "You ask me if I know anyone who is more useless to society than you," David Wedderburn wrote to his sister in French in 1767. "Yes, I know thousands," he responded, recommending a course of self-instruction, to begin with Voltaire's *Histoire Universelle*.[111] The Johnstones' aunt Anne Ferguson wrote of the education of one of her own daughters that "she has cost me more trouble than all the rest, for her genious bewitched me, & some times got the better of my Reason"; there had been instruction in "Hunting, Riding, Shooting, & Latin," as well as "a little musick, Bowling & Chess which I indulge her in."[112] By the late eighteenth century, it was fairly common for the Johnstones' daughters to be educated in schools. Barbara's daughter Elizabeth was sent to school in Kent, William's daughter Henrietta Laura to school in France, and George and Martha Ford's granddaughters to schools in Hammersmith and Chelsea.[113] The early nineteenth-century notebooks of John and Elizabeth Carolina's grandaughter included observations on Salic Law, the constitution of Tyre, and Greek, French, Italian, German, and Hebrew texts.[114]

There was a wandering society of educated individuals who appeared and vanished in the Johnstones' lives. James and Louisa's man of business, during their long exile in Norfolk, was a curate called Edmund Nelson, who paid their bills for the *London Chronicle*, negotiated on their behalf with a tenant named Sanctuary and an exigent turnip farmer, and was eventually an executor and beneficiary of James's will.[115] John and James employed "Mr. B——," or John Bruce, to make "Discoverys" in the Advocates' Library in Edinburgh with respect to the "Great Desiderata" of their father, or the evidence of the family's claim to their disturbed cousin's estate. To Mr. B——, James sent instructions in the procedures of historical research: "whether he found the account he gives in more than one Author"; "what number in the Manuscripts"; "I want Mr. B likewise to send me the exact Orthography"; "if He makes any more Searches He should be instructed to look at Manuscripts or Records only." To James Balmain, who was Mr. B——'s friend, he sent advice on remuneration: "do not send away a man of that Manly Spirit he appears to be with a Frown on his Face Make him Smile tho my whole £19, should go into his Pocket."[116]

The lives of the itinerant clerks and clerics are extraordinarily elusive. It is as though the Johnstones' tutors and writers were almost literally invisible, like the "Dominie" in *Guy Mannering*, the closest of all Sir Walter Scott's novels to the Johnstones' existence, who is fitted out by a returning East Indian colonel with "two suits of clothes, one black and one raven-grey."[117] They were figures of the countryside, even within the society of enlightenment in which, in Hume's idyll, men "flock into cities; love to receive and communicate knowledge."[118] They moved between different positions and between different classes or ranks: between the "high" and the "low" scenes of the enlightenment, or between the respectability of the church or the law and the "low life" of writers and tradesmen. The Johnstones' tutor in Westerhall wrote to William that "for myself I have nothing more to hope or to fear than when you left me—I have some thoughts of making my way among the Dissenters in Engd. (when my Pupils are disposd of) if the smallest Encouragement offers for it—I add no more."[119] David Hume was a "gentleman" when he was the companion to the Johnstones' cousin, and he was also a servant. The dispute that continued into the 1760s was over the salary that had been "due for that quarter in which Mr Home leaves his service" because "a servant, who is dropt betwixt terms, is not suppos'd to find ready employment."[120]

These clerks, or these insecure men and women of letters, were the intermediaries of information in the Johnstones' households: of "light" or enlightenment, in Adam Ferguson's sense of knowledge that was communicable to others by information, or in Hume's sense of a "conversible World," in which everyone "mutually gives and receives Information."[121] Even the unrespectable Uncle Walter, who was a source of expertise in so many family crises, and who loved the rhymes of German poetry, was a tutor, or a schoolmaster, to his great-nephews and great-nieces, who were sent to live with him in Dumfries.[122] It was Uncle Walter, too, who wrote to William (in the words of *Candide*) of "wandering to & fro upon the face of the Earth & being convinced by a certain learned Christian called Voltaire that God gave man the Earth ut opereratur Cum," and of his "Hobby horsical passion for country diversions" (in the words of *Tristram Shandy*), in which he dreamed of limeing and sowing and hedging.[123] It was William Julius Mickle, in the controversy over the booksellers' property, who instructed George about the perils of restrictions on copyright in "an opulent and a reading country": "books of dirty paper & dirty crowded print, notes left out and the text mutilated at the mercy of the Lord knows who, are the certain consequences."[124]

Betty, of all the brothers and sisters, with her "Perigrinations" around the country and her "Mineral Friends," going from place to place "without a settled Residance," was the closest to being a clerical figure in this sense, a woman of letters or an intermediary of information. She and her sisters-in-law, in this extended family of literate women, wrote or copied hundreds of the family's letters.[125] Louisa copied out James's letters about being rotten before he was dead, his instructions to Mr. B, and the deeds of 1634 in the inheritance case, in an "Orthography" that followed the size of the characters (from 8 point to 24 point).[126] Betty wrote her father's letters to William about claret and East India Company politics. She was also a continuing source of legal, political, financial, and family information, as she crisscrossed Scotland. "I learn from Miss Johnstone who passed here yesterday, that the copy of the opinion . . . has never yet reached Westerhall," John wrote from Balgonie to one business associate, and to another, "I shall draw a Receipt upon you to my Sister Miss Johnstone who . . . will send it you when she arrives at Hawick." To Betty herself, he wrote "You were Impowered to conclude this matter. . . . You can get it for Bills at 45 to 59 days sight."[127] Even when she was eighty, the last of the brothers and sisters, she was a source of family news for her nieces, and of letters about letters: "both the letters were good," she wrote to John and Elizabeth Carolina's daughter in 1809, "go on and prosper."[128]

This was even the world of the minor figures in the Johnstones' history. Patrick Colquhoun, who was contracted to transport Bell or Belinda to Virginia and to sell her as a slave for life, was the son of a "local Judge and Register of the Records" in the west of Scotland.[129] He emigrated at the age of sixteen to become a clerk in Virginia, and on his return he established a commerce in convicts.[130] He then entered the linen and muslin trade. He was later involved in the "plantation busi-

ness" in the Bahamas and interested in the sale of "Got-
tenburgh Herrings at Cork for the West India Consumption" (or food for the West Indian slaves).[131] He
became Lord Mayor of Glasgow and a prolific writer
on the police, the British empire, and the definition of
poverty. He introduced himself to William in 1787 as a
writer with a shared "zeal & anxiety to do good." He
and William were partners in the purchase of land in
New York.[132] He had "been honoured by the society of
the most eminent men of the age in which he has lived,
among others Mr Burk, Dr Adam Smith, Earl Sheffield,"
he wrote in a memorandum of his own public service,
which was his self-reinvention as a figure of the enlightenment; "he is stated a *Public benefactor*."[133] Colquhoun's projects of reform, his biographer (and son-in-
law) wrote in 1818, "will be gratefully hailed by millions
yet unborn." He was identified, almost two centuries
later, as among the "leading figures of the Scottish
enlightenment."[134]

THE MILIEUX OF POLITICAL THOUGHT

The industry of politics, or of the production of political thought, was itself a milieu of enlightenment. The
Johnstone sisters and brothers were involved in political
life at a time of drastic innovation in institutions and
ideas. They had been engaged from their childhood in
the old, established world of what George described in
1759 as "various applications & wrigling Connections."[135] Alexander was instructed to "wait on" colonels, and William recommended himself to duchesses, in
a neo-Roman court politics of empire: "The Emperor's
court is like the house of Fame, / The palace full of

tongues, of eyes, and ears."[136] Margaret was involved in the court of the pretender to the British throne and in the French court, where she waited on ministers and presented her memoranda.[137] In Murshidabad John was an expert in the court politics of the Mughal empire. George even identified himself as an expert on court etiquette in the Ottoman empire (or on how to "command an influence with the Beys, and a respect from the Arabs," in the new postal service from Suez to Cairo).[138] His appointment to office, in the post-war settlement of 1763, was widely attributed to the influence on the young George III of the Earl of Bute and of his Scottish secretary.[139]

But the Johnstones and their friends were involved, too, in a new proliferation of elections and votes, from the House of Representatives in the island of Grenada to the General Assembly of the province of West Florida, and from the East India Company's court of directors in London ("a fluctuating, Democratic community of traders," in William Bolts's description) to its council in Calcutta.[140] They lived in a period of innovation in the political institutions of the European empires, or of Europeans in incipient empires: in the West Indian assemblies, the North American colonies, and in India. These were the institutions that John took so seriously when he compared himself to Cicero, in Calcutta in 1761, in his defense of the public liberties of the servants (or the Company officials).[141] "I have business enough to keep away ennui, but, not enough, to fatigue me. I have opposition enough in our little politicks here, to keep me sometimes Alert, but never enough to vex me," David Wedderburn wrote to his sister in 1771, of his new life in Bombay.[142]

The Johnstones lived in a time of innovation in the political procedures of the British parliament and in the finance of elections.[143] In the House of Commons, James, William, George, and John were the elected representatives, between them, of nine parliamentary constituencies in England and Scotland; there were at least nine other constituencies in which they, Alexander, and Gideon were "interested," as unsuccessful candidates or as proprietors. Betty was an intermediary for George in the notorious parliamentary contests of 1768 in Cumberland, in the course of which George stood on the hustings for eight days, bowing to every voter, and was visited, while "employed in canvassing the citizens," by his and William's old friends from the Select Society and the Poker Club.[144] "I earnestly wish you will write me fully," one of his political agents wrote to Betty in Carlisle, and asked for instructions "if I should Send off the Stewarts on Wednesday morning or what other day."[145]

The Johnstones were engaged, in turn, in a newer and far more abstract politics: a politics of enlightenment. They used the language of philosophical system in their family letters, their official correspondence, their pamphlets, and their speeches. They wrote and spoke about "public liberties" and "civil rights," the "distribution of justice" and the "general rights of mankind," "Benevolence Justice & Humanity." George's first reported speech in parliament, after his bowing on the hustings, began with the imposing preamble, "Sir; if we look into the antient historians, Tacitus particularly."[146] His nine speeches in support of the North American colonies, in the course of 1775, were eulogies to ancient liberties ("my system . . . is for preserving them sacred and inviolate") and elaborations of the theory of power ("I say, a free government necessarily involves many clashing jurisdictions" and "Great Britain is the only government in the world which has found out the art of carrying power to the distant parts of the empire, by satisfying the people that they are in security against oppression").[147] His published writings included an elaborate essay on the politics of "*whim*, which is essential to the happiness of mankind."[148]

The Johnstones were participants in a new politics of words in the British empire: a government of language, or of "powerfully resonant and powerfully abstract words" that served, as in Daniel Rodgers's description of the politics of the early American republic, to "unify and mobilize," to "legitimize the outward frame of politics."[149] They were extraordinarily self-conscious with respect to their roles in this new politics of what George called "sounding words and unmeaning phrases," and of the new process of production of political ideas.[150] They were conscious, too, of living in a period of continuing expansion in the meaning of political words, including the expression "Liberty of the Subject," or "Liberty in one of the seven significations of the word," about which George expatiated to the council of West Florida in 1765.[151] They used the words "freedom," "liberty," and "rights" in the old sense of corporate entitlements (the "libertys of the servants" of the East India Company), and in the new sense of the late eighteenth-century revolutions, or of the "general rights of mankind" (as in the Grenada pamphlet of 1771 by Alexander and his friends).[152]

The parliamentary world of the Johnstones was almost exactly that of Sir Lewis Namier's structure of politics, in which an earlier and illusory prospect of "faithful service to your country" had given way, by 1760, to "the service of one's friends."[153] But it was also a world in which interests were adorned with ideas, and ideas were in turn interests. The parliamentary opposition was unified by the rhetoric of resistance to oppression, as well as by the opportunity of office and the interests of merchants. The political parties were associated, in David Hume's description, with "a philosophical or speculative system of principles, annexed to its political or practical one," and "each of the factions, into which this nation is divided, has reared up a fabric of the former kind, in order to protect and cover that scheme of actions, which it pursues."[154] The fabric of philosophical principles, by the time of the Johnstones' most prominent political activity, in the disputes over habeas corpus in the American colonies, the abolition of the Atlantic slave trade, the regulation of the East India Company, and the origins of the Bengal famine, was itself a political or practical system: an industry of political enlightenment.

The Johnstones' multiple lives provide an interesting glimpse, in these circumstances, of the new milieux of late eighteenth-century politics, and of the connections between principles, ideas, and interests. There was the production of political correspondence, or the government by letter, of which the Persian historian Ghulam Husain observed that the East India Company's servants spent so much of their time "answering very long letters from Europe."[155] There was the government by description, in which the Johnstones were so experienced, in their depictions of disturbance (in Florida), distraction (in Grenada), and "discontent, dissention, and anxiety" (in Calcutta).[156] Even David Hume was a virtuoso of the official letter, in his period as secretary to the British ambassador in Paris and later as the secretary to whom official letters were sent in London from "Europe, Asia, Africa and America."[157] The Johnstones themselves had secretaries in their political lives: John, in Burdwan, with his sixty to seventy writers (or transcribers of property rights), and George, with Ossian Macpherson in Florida, William Julius Mickle in Lisbon, and Adam Ferguson in wartime New York. There was an empire of paper and of the abstraction (or subtraction) of rights. The East India Company had omitted to send a "supply of Stationary," John and his colleagues complained in a letter from Calcutta in 1762; and they had been obliged to "make use of the Country Paper."[158]

The Johnstones' political speech, too, was a collective enterprise, or a subcontracted industry of enlightenment. The great political events of the times were exercises in declamation, from John's speeches in Calcutta ("Cicero never quitted the Senate with more joy") to George's address to the Creek nation in Pensacola about "the Great God of the World" engraving the mark of Justice "on the minds of Man."[159] "I never heard a better digested, better Reasoned, or more forcible speech," John wrote to James Balmain in 1778, after listening to an oration on military contracts in the "present disgraceful, ruinous and inglorious war."[160] William, with all his circumspection, was noticed when he arrived in London as "an orator at the India House."[161] Parliamentary oratory, by the time the Johnstones were active in political life, was an elaborate mise-en-scène of the transcriptions of debates, the reproduction of speeches in monthly magazines, the preparation of reports, the compilation of evidence, and the arrival of unexpected witnesses, like the Armenian merchants from Bengal. The palace was full of eyes, and the House of Commons was in the "eye of the world."[162]

It is even possible to see, in the Johnstones' lives and speeches, the process of production of these new political spectacles, or the machinery behind the mise-en-scène. One of George's most elaborate speeches, about Massachusetts, the East India Company, and the "horrors of civil war," ends suddenly when he says, "I cannot see my other memorandums, and therefore I shall conclude."[163] An oration by William on the injustice of the "double government" of the Mayor's Court in Calcutta was compiled out of a letter from John and information from William Bolts.[164] The production of political ephemera was itself a collective enterprise. John published a pamphlet about the political economy of Indian presents, with an afterword by George; George published eight pamphlets, on India, America, and his complicated dispute over the encounter between the British and French fleets in the Cape Verde islands. George also wrote a long letter to the *Public Advertiser* in response to a pamphlet by Lord Clive and in defense of John, "a most respected Brother, who is confined to his Bed by a long and severe Sickness." William published four political pamphlets in addition to his *Thoughts on America*, one of which was a defense of George in the Cape Verde lawsuits.[165]

The Johnstones were interested in the smallest details of these ventures, from the translation into French of "two brochures on the affairs of the India Company" to the posthaste production that a friend from Scotland proposed to George: "give me your ideas which I will throw into Language for you in three days, provided my name is never to be heard of."[166] The oddest of the brothers' pamphlets was the *Narrative of the Proceedings upon the Complaint against Governor Melvill*, the very long, anonymous annex to Alexander's complaint to the Privy Council about torture and oppression in Grenada, "appealing to the world against their decision by a narrative of the facts." It begins in the first person of the anonymous author ("I desire the public will judge ... my own conduct") and continues as a third person description of the Johnstones' involvement in the case: "Mr George Johnstone, on that day, went to the Council Office, by the desire of his brother, who was sick." It is a compilation of Alexander's charges, annotated with references to official documents in the left and right margins (identified as "PROOF"), his opponent's answers, annotated with self-refuting footnotes, his own responses to his opponent's answers, and a fifty-five page appendix. It is a compendium, too, of the Johnstones' obsession with "evidence," "minutes," and "public documents," a virtuoso production of the printing of marginalia and notes, in the booksellers' genre of the early-eighteenth-century dictionaries of the French critic Pierre Bayle (and of William Julius Mickle's father).[167]

But the *Narrative* is at the same time a philosophical and even a moving work. It is a description of Alexander's elaborate complaint against the governor of Grenada, who presided over his dismissal, and an evocation of the "general rights of mankind ... such as men of moral sentiments have confessed to belong to human beings, in all ages." It is also a defense of religious freedom, and a vindication of the rights of the colonies, with their "system of distributive justice." It is a defense of the right not to be tortured: "That no one shall be tortured into confessions or discoveries of any sort."[168] It is an identification, in the midst of the intimate friends and incestuous families of Anglo-French slave societies, of the "most essential rights."[169] The complaint by Alexander and his friends was about their interests, about their sense of having been disregarded, and about the largest and most philosophical foundations of a slave society. It turned, in the version presented in the *Narrative*, on the question of whether it was permissible, in "cases of alarm or danger," as the governor argued, and "for the better prevention of such atrocious murders in future," that slaves should be "put *slightly* to the question." "This very expression carries a degree of cruelty equal to the torments which the negroes suffered," the anonymous author or authors—or Alexander and George—responded; slaves were by law liable to no "torture of any kind," and torture "is contrary to the first principles of natural justice, and always defeats the purpose for which it is intended. . . . It is from arguments such as these, that the most unfeeling tyrants vindicate their proceedings."[170]

THE ATMOSPHERE OF SOCIETY

Political enlightenment, in all these scenes, was a jumble of high or philosophical ideas and of the misrepresentations described in one of the Grenada pamphlets as "Grub-street productions."[171] The Johnstones were involved in the diverse milieux of the eighteenth-century enlightenment—in the high enlightenment of the philosophes and in the medium enlightenment of booksellers, lawyers, clerks and clerics, and the new political industry. They were the connection, or one of the connections, between these milieux and the distant opportunities of empire. Their encounters provide a glimpse of celebrated and uncelebrated individuals who were on the point of setting out for the empire, or who were waiting for news of their brothers, or who longed to set out for somewhere. Even David Hume had determined in his youth to "toss about the World, from the one Pole to the other" and settled in Bristol "with some recommendations to eminent merchants"; "his Master dealt in sugar," in a contemporary account.[172] In 1746, after the melancholy winter with the Johnstones' cousin, he too set off for the empire (or for Boston), only to be redirected, in the end, to an expedition against the French East India Company port of Lorient.[173]

The Johnstones' lives also provide a view of the connections between the different milieux of the enlightenment at home. The tripartite understanding of enlightenment in modern historiography—as a sect of philosophes (the "high" enlightenment), as a milieu of the communication of ideas, including the ideas of the philosophers (the "medium" enlightenment, or the enlightenment as medium), and as a disposition, in the principal sense of Kant and other contemporaries (the "low" enlightenment of large numbers of people, or of the "populi")—was already established, as has been seen, in the disputes over the "enlightened mind" in late eighteenth-century Scotland. It was implicit in Adam Ferguson's prospect of the lights of science, which were communicable to others by mere information and by which the human mind was itself enlightened. It was the scheme, too, that was parodied in the *Scots Review* of 1774: of a limited sect of philosophers, a flourishing industry of doctors of divinity and reviewers of the public taste, and "a dissipated, giddy, unthinking age," together with "false alarms of the growth of infidelity and scepticism."[174]

In the Johnstones' own involvement in the milieux or media of enlightenment, these distinctions were far more elusive. There was no orderly sequence in their lives in which the "high" thought of the enlightenment was diffused, in various media, to the opinion of the public or the people, and no causal sequence in which the political thought of the philosophers was the explanation for political events. There were allusions, certainly, to high philosophical thought in parliamentary and political life, or at least to the thoughts of philosophers. When William's old friend Alexander Wedderburn, by then the solicitor general, asked, "What is the state?" and talked about Molinists and Jesuits as powers within the state, he was using the words of Hume's *Essays*, and so was the Secretary of State, Lord Halifax, when he exhorted George, in West Florida, to "mildness and moderation."[175] George's own politics of whim was an allusion to Hume's essay on the progress of the arts, and his longest printed piece, his pamphlet on East Indian affairs, was an effusion of references to Homer, Helvetius, Montesquieu, Mirabeau, Harrington, Pope, Hume, and Adam Ferguson.[176] Adam Smith was invoked explicitly by Joseph Knight's lawyers, and implicitly in Alexander and George's *Narrative* of Grenada: the "general rights of mankind," as acknowledged by "men of moral sentiments" to belong "to human beings, in all ages."[177]

But the sequence of influence was also, on occasion, the opposite. The political atmosphere of the age, or the "medium" political thought of the Johnstones and others, was diffused to or expressed in the "high" thought of philosophers. Some of the subsequently celebrated expressions and explanations in Adam Smith's own political descriptions of empire—about the "golden dream" of conquest in America, or the East India Company's constitution as both a sovereign and a merchant, or the dilemmas of carrying power over great distances— were already familiar in the ephemeral and political writings and speeches of the 1760s and early 1770s.

"The extravagant ideas conceived by government, of the riches to be drawn from the East Indies, was in fact a golden dream," George said in parliament in May 1774, in the Johnstones' familiar idiom of the pessimism of empire; and again in October 1775, of the government's American policies, he said, "the purpose was clearly to amuse the people on this side the Atlantic, and to divide the people on that." "It is surely now time that our rulers should either realize this golden dream . . . or, that they should awake from it themselves," Smith wrote in 1776 in the celebrated last paragraph of *The Wealth of Nations*: "the rulers of Great Britain have, for more than a century past, amused the people with the imagination that they possessed a great empire on the west side of the Atlantic."[178] "If the trading spirit of the English East India company renders them very bad sovereigns; the spirit of sovereignty seems to have rendered them equally bad traders," Smith wrote in his similarly celebrated diatribe against the Company's policies in Bengal, echoing William Bolts's description, in which "the Company continue there the Merchant-sovereign and the Sovereign-merchant," in unending quest of the power of "erecting *imperium in imperio*."[179]

The philosophical thought of the high enlightenment and the low political thought of public and parliamentary opinion are blurred or blotted together here, as in the bestselling novel by the Johnstones' distant relation Charles Johnstone, *Chrysal: Or, the Adventures of a Guinea*, a circulation romance of the East Indies and America that was described as having been written on the paper used to wrap butter, with the consequence that it consisted of "a number of fragments," "almost the whole philosophical part having been erased."[180] It is possible that Smith, during the virtually undocumented two years that he spent in London while he was finishing *The Wealth of Nations*, was among the contributors to William and George's "memorandums," in their parliamentary speeches, or that they were given pages or fragments of his manuscripts. But Smith was also, like the Johnstones and like the Grub-Street writers, a part of the shared world of "sounding words." There was a new public philosophy of empire in the process of being invented, in these letters and pamphlets and speeches, as the political ideas of the philosophers were diffused to the milieu of administration, and the interested oratory of political administration was diffused, in turn, to the philosophers' ideas.

"Every man has a right to his ideas. Most certainly, every man who thinks has a right to his thoughts," Lord Camden said in the House of Lords proceedings on literary property, with respect to which George was harangued on the subject of dirty crowded print: "but what if he speaks, and lets them fly out in private or public discourse? Will he claim the breath, the air, the words in which his thoughts are clothed? Where does this fanciful property begin, or end, or continue?" It was this world of flying and floating ideas, the ideas of philosophers and the ideas of politicians and proof correctors, that was the milieu of political enlightenment.[181]

THE ENLIGHTENMENT OF THE JOHNSTONES

The last scene of enlightenment, in the Johnstones' lives, is the scene of their own inner lives; of the extent to which they were themselves women and men of enlightenment, in Kant's sense of a disposition of mind or a way of thinking. The eighteenth-century idea of the circumstances of the mind (a *Denkart*, a *cultura*, a *disposition des esprits*) is an oddity in modern histories of the enlightenment, as it has been since the post-enlightenment or post-philosophical historiography of the early nineteenth century.[182] It is an idea of conditions of mind that are characteristic of large numbers of individuals or of entire societies: circumstances, in the terms of Hume's or Kant's idylls of enlightenment, of openness to new ideas, inquisitiveness, interest in knowledge, the tendency to question established opinions, emancipation from superstitious fears.

The Johnstones were undoubtedly figures of enlightenment in all or most of these senses. Their restlessness in space and time—going from place to place without a settled residence, like Betty, or wandering to and fro upon the face of the earth like Uncle Walter, or longing, like John, "to fix my wandering feet on some speck of Earth I could call my own"—was also a restlessness of the mind, or the spirit. They were curious about the natural and the social world: the meaning of Persian prepositions, the political organization of the Choctaw confederacy, the minerals in the Eskdale hills, the incidence of depression, the fondnesses of birds. The diary that James began to keep when he and Louisa moved to Norfolk was a compendium of the inquisitiveness of the times: "some late Experiments" with respect to the effects of lime on the growth of oats, "the account sent me by my Brother of the making Salt Petre in the Province of Patna Bengal," the sixteen sorts of cyclises, "various Experiments I have made on Carrots," and the "Indian Method of making Stucco."[183]

Elizabeth Carolina, in the book of poems that she published after she left for India, translated the passage from Horace—*Sapere Aude*, or "Dare to be wise!"—that was the motto of "What is Enlightenment?", and the Johnstones can be thought of as a little society of enlightenment in something close to Kant's sense.[184] They were willing to question almost all kinds of established opinion; they were unfrightened of new circumstances; they were emancipated from tutelary authority; they were educated and interested in the education of their own children; they amused themselves with ideas (as in Adam Smith's wonderful evocation of the advantages of education, in the lectures he gave in Glasgow, that when a child who has been educated is grown up, he will have "ideas with which he can amuse himself").[185] Their own milieu of the extended family was for the most part uninfluenced by religious observance, as has been seen. It was free, too, of the superstitions that were such anathema to the philosophers of enlightenment. Louisa's letter about the lottery ticket is the only occasion in all the thousands of family letters and other documents I have read in which any of the Johnstones refers to destiny or fortune, and it is in a context of highly literary irony: "she is not only Hoodwinked but tottally Blind, God Grant she may stumble on me & 383."[186]

The lives of the Johnstones were a vivid illustration, in all these respects, of the change of manners described by their contemporary Elizabeth Mure, when "the slavery of the mind began to be spocken off; freedom was in every body's mouth. . . . For their Girls the outmost care was taken that fear of no kind should inslave the mind."[187] The Johnstone sisters were unintimidated in their marriages, journeys, and political involvements; so were the women with whom their brothers were involved. They were in no respect "docile creatures," in Kant's expression, not "daring to take a single step without the leading-strings to which they are tied."[188] Betty's assertion of independence to William, with its imposing sequences of "owns," was a continuing negotiation with the established institutions of women's property: "my own settled Resolution Ever was that . . . I would have a House of my Own," "my own opinion Ever was that a person comed to my time of Life should have a place of there own that they may Retire to."[189]

Margaret's daughter, the wife of John Wedderburn, was intensely engaged in the legal negotiations over her naturalization; it "was the thing on earth that vexed her the most," her first cousin, Barbara's son, wrote after her death. Her granddaughter, who died in Penang, was depicted in the Raeburn portrait, with her great-aunt Betty and her great-uncle John, as avid, learned, and unafraid: telling a story, with a paperbound volume in her hand, bent back upon itself to the page she was reading.[190] Betty encouraged her nieces to "go on and prosper." Her first cousin, the daughter of the judge in Bell or Belinda's case, was instructed in "Shooting, & Latin."[191] Even William encouraged his daughter Laura: "your last letter is a masterpiece," he wrote to her in 1791, and urged her to "take a full view of your real merit, it will not make you too vain, it will only correct your propensity to undervalue yourself."[192]

The family was in general unconvinced with respect to the rights of fathers and husbands. In their wills, they declared their opposition to the established institution of coverture—in which a married woman was "covered over by her husband," with her "very being or legal existence . . . incorporated or consolidated into that of the husband"—and to the race of husbands.[193] James left an annuity to his daughter, "so as not to be in any way subject to the debts engagements or Controul of her now present or any future husband . . . notwithstanding such her Coverture," and another annuity to the mother of his son, also "notwithstanding her Coverture." Laura made her will "as I should think fit and as if I was sole and unmarried," with a bequest to her friend, the clergyman's wife, "notwithstanding her present or any future coverture." Martha Ford's mother, the widow of the auctioneer in the Haymarket, left "to my said grandson George Lindsay Johnstone my Brilliant diamond ring which my late husband used to wear," and the dividends on her 3 percent annuities to her other daughter, subject to "writing under her own hand," "whether sole or covert." George and Martha's oldest son left money to his sister, his mother, and his two daughters, "separate and apart from any husband with whom she may hereafter intermarry" or "any present or future husbands." Martha left her estate to her daughter, "and my will is that her present husband or any future husband shall not intermeddle therewith . . . but the same and every part shall be at the disposal in every respect of the said Sophia."[194]

There were no sisters or daughters in the Johnstones' immediate family who fell out of their lives, in the sense that a young woman called Janet or Jean Kinnaird fell out of the life of Barbara's relations by marriage, the Kinnairds. "I was so happy with Jeannie Kinnaird that . . . it made me humane, polite, generous," James Boswell wrote in 1768, after an evening of celebration at the Faculty of Advocates in Edinburgh:

> I drank too much. I went to . . . seek a girl whom I had once seen in the street. I found a natural daughter of the late Lord Kinnaird, a fine lass. I stayed an hour and a half with her and drank malaga and was most amorous, being so well that no infection remained.[195]

Janet Kinnaird was in this account the daughter of Barbara's husband, Charles Kinnaird (who had died the previous year and whose separation had been arranged by Boswell's father). She was the half-sister of the Johnstones' nephews and nieces; she is otherwise invisible in the history of the family and their friends.

The Johnstones' enlightened disposition extended to prejudices of different sorts as well. James used the abstract language of enlightenment in the most matter-of-fact way in his private letters to his brothers and sisters, as when he described himself to John as someone "who think[s] that Benevolence Justice & Humanity ought by no means to be restricted to Collour," or wrote to Betty, with respect to the seeds to be used by one of their tenants, that "it would be unjust and Unreasonable for us to interfere in His Management of His Farm."[196] Margaret's son-in-law John Wedderburn, who was so shocked by the ancient "feudal" notions of women's entitlements in his father-in-law's family, was shocked, too, by the intolerance of the British government with respect to the Irish: "I allways looked upon the Irish to be oppressed," he wrote to William in 1778, and "I think the scheme you mentioned of emancipating the Roman Catholicks . . . is an excellent one."[197]

There was no "reason for inserting the word Christian that does not equally apply for putting in the words Mussulman and Gentoo," George asserted in his defense of the (Christian) Armenian merchants in the House of Commons.[198] Alexander and his friends complained in Grenada of "illiberal cries of a difference in religion," suited to "the most barbarous times of ignorance and enthusiasm."[199] John defended the rights of his partner Motiram in Calcutta, and his other partner, William Bolts, was a powerful critic of the racial prejudices of East India Company officials: "let such who place their security in the pretended degeneracy or effeminacy of the natives recollect, that they are those very natives who fight our Indian battles."[200] James congratulated the House of Commons that "religious toleration was making such rapid advances" in 1789 (in the relief of Anglicans in Scotland and the prospects for Catholic emancipation): "every man should be indulged in the exercise of his religious opinions; to exercise a tyranny over the body, was bad enough; but to exercise it over the mind, was intolerable."[201]

The Johnstones even identified themselves as the defenders of the oppressed at home, of hawkers, peddlers, maidservants, and the "common people" of Scotland. The right of habeas corpus, which John described as "the grand palladium of the British constitution, the

freedom of men's persons," was a preoccupation, successively, of at least five of the Johnstones in their public
lives: Alexander in Grenada, George in opposition to the
denial of habeas corpus in the North American colonies
in 1775, John in opposition to the "Bill to suspend Habeas Corpus" in 1777, William in opposition to the
"Habeas Corpus Suspension Indemnity Bill" at the time
of the anxieties over Ireland in 1801, and George's son
George Lindsay Johnstone, also in 1801, who moved an
amendment to the same bill, in protest against the "oppression" of the Irish and in support of "his hon. Relative."[202] John was completely absurd, his neighbor complained on the rainy night in Stirling in 1775; "he said he
wished there were more of the Common People there
that he might inform them that they were their own
Masters. . . . In short it is impossible to tell you the whole
of his absurdities."[203]

THE COEXISTENCE OF ENLIGHTENMENT
AND OPPRESSION

The Johnstones were modern figures in all these respects, and figures of enlightenment. But their enlightenment coexisted, in scene after scene of their lives, with
the terrible ills of empire and slavery. A narrative of British rule in Bengal, some years after John's return, described a land of "laughing husbandmen," where "the
manufacturer sung unmolested under every shady tree,"
transformed into a "famished multitude," with the dead
"mangled by dogs, jackals, and vultures."[204] In West
Florida the outcome that the native Americans anticipated in George's account—that the Anglo-Americans
intended "to extirpate them from the face of the Earth"—

was set in motion in George's own government and in his own instructions.[205] The outcome of the initial period of British rule in the island of Grenada, in which Alexander made the foundations of his fortune, was an "excess loss of Negroes" amounting to 86,500 individuals, or more than five times the initial population of the island, in the evaluation of French officials after the colony was reconquered in 1779.[206] There was a continuing "retrograde—a diminution," Patrick Colquhoun wrote of the "black population" of Grenada at the end of the Johnstones' lifetimes, in his new idiom of enlightened political economy: an excess of deaths over births so great that "according to this rate of diminution, the slave population would be annihilated in about forty years."[207]

The enlightenment of the Johnstones was an accompaniment to these horrors, juxtaposed in time and in space. The legal disputes over empire and slavery were concerned to a striking extent, in their liefetimes, with ways of seeing, or with the possibility of seeing oppression. This was the point of their cousin's speech against Joseph Knight—"it is perhaps right to preserve our ideas of liberty as pure as possible, that there should be no examples of slavery *before our eyes* in this country"—and it was the point of Joseph Knight's own lawyer's speech as well: "in this country . . . we may soon *see* a team consisting of two horses, two oxen, and two slaves."[208] But the Johnstones and their friends had seen the ills of empire. They were surrounded, even "in this country," or in Scotland, by the economic consequences of empire. They were surrounded, too, by other people, some of whom were themselves slaves and who had their own memories and their own images of evil: other people who could see the enlightenment.

The Johnstones could remember their earlier lives in the East or West Indies, and so could the individuals they brought with them. The most sensational case involving a slave in Scotland (the case of Sir William Maxwell's sister-in-law) was about the events that a slave, "Latchemo," had seen or might have seen. Bell or Belinda, in her petition in Perth, invoked her understanding of the dispositions of other people, of how she was seen or would be seen in the future by the people among whom she lived, "understanding the crime with which she is charged is obnoxious to every well disposed subject of this Country, and that she cannot have any happiness in it after being so charged."[209] Joseph Knight's case turned on his memory or lack of memory of events in Africa, and on the conversations he had had with his owner about different possible futures in Jamaica and in Scotland. Joseph Knight's lawyer, in his written memorial, invoked his own conversation with a different individual in Scotland who had once been a slave: "the Counsel for the Mem.ist has at present a Black servant who remembers perfectly his being taken up when playing himself put in a Bag & carried on Ship board."[210]

In the disputes over slavery of the late eighteenth century, one of the familiar comparisons was between the slave owners of modern times and the slave owners of antiquity, with their "soiled virtues" or the "excuse" of "the invincible error of universal custom."[211] The Johnstones did not have this excuse. They lived in a setting, or a series of settings, in which slavery was sometimes the condition of almost all individuals (as in the island of Grenada under French and British rule), sometimes in flux (as in England and Scotland), sometimes in expansion (as in British West Florida), and sometimes the subject of intense, wrenching dispute. The error of custom was never, in their experience, invincible.

Even within the setting of their own family, or their complicity of intimacy and exchange, the Johnstones' relationships to chattel slavery were extraordinarily disparate. James, who inherited Alexander's slaves and sent shoes and the Scottish ploughman to Grenada, argued in the House of Commons for the immediate abolition of the slave trade. Alexander, the only one of the brothers who lived in or near their West Indian plantation, argued in the Privy Council against the torture of slaves. William was one of the last and most effective of all the supporters of the slave trade in the House of Commons. George described the kindness of slave owners in the American South—"in general . . . masters are kind to their slaves"—and denounced the enslavement of Musquito Indians as a "shameful traffic."[212] John, to whom the proceeds of the sale of Bell or Belinda in Virginia were supposed to have been remitted in 1772, was a subscriber, eighteen years later, to the Society for the Abolition of the African Slave Trade. The Johnstones' relationships to their slaves changed over time, and so did their relationships to each other and to the institution of slavery. This, too, was a part of their experience of enlightenment.

There were officials in the new British empire of the 1760s who were vastly more cruel than the Johnstones. The evils for which they were so execrated were acts of insubordination, in general, or of avidity. The worst desolation in Bengal, in the famine of 1770–71, came after John's return to England, as he suggested in his own recollection of having governed "with less Oppression to the Natives." But their language of enlightenment—their discourses on rights, in the midst of conquest, and on freedom, in the midst of terror—is still extraordinarily difficult to make sense of. It is as though the words that are so inspiring, and that are so familiar, even now, the words at the heart of our own public life, fluctuate and vanish in the Johnstones' lives. "Does the Governor think that by an eternal repetition of the words, humanity, benevolence, candor, delicacy, &c. that the qualities follow like water in a pump," Alexander asked in his complaint about torture. "In my Ears it is a cant Word without any idea," John said of one of the expressions used against him by the East India Company. The language of the Johnstones, too—of rights and oppression and justice—is in our ears, at least from time to time, cant: words without ideas.[213]

CHAPTER SEVEN

HISTORIES OF SENTIMENTS

The history of the Johnstones has been a series of scenes or episodes in an unsettled world. It has been concerned with events in the early British empire, and in the eighteenth-century enlightenment. But it is also a history of the public and private lives of a number of individuals, who were connected to each other through a single extended family; of how they described the experiences of empire; and of how they were described. Even Bell or Belinda, in the courtroom in Perth, described her own state of mind: "she is certain she will be found altogether Innocent of the actuall murder," in the formal speech of the lawyers to whom she had applied for assistance with her trial; and, in the reported speech of the *Caledonian Mercury*, "she was conscious no actual murder could be proved against her."[1]

THE EYE OF THE MIND

The experience of the inner life was a continuing preoccupation, in the Johnstones' unsettled existence. Their ideas of inwardness and outwardness, like their ideas of empire, or of the economy, or of the history of the human mind, were in flux, like so much else in their lives; they were not the same over time, or the same as our ideas. "I know by Experience how much the Mind preys on the Body," James wrote to John in the winter of 1771, while Bell or Belinda was in prison in Scotland, and for the Johnstones, as for everyone else in their own times (or in our own times), the frontier between the mind and the body was itself indistinct. "I have been much out of order In my Inward man," John wrote to Charlotte's widower James Balmain, when Elizabeth Carolina was dying, and he was ill in his stomach and his mind.[2] There were *Diseases of the Body, and the Disorders of the Mind Depending on the Body*, as in the title of one of the books in the library in Westerhall.[3] The Johnstones referred frequently to oppression and anxiety, and these were conditions of the body, the mind, and the empire in India. There was the "cruelty and oppression" of the British in North America, the "anxiety" of the East India Company in Calcutta, and "Lowness, Oppression or *Anxiety*," to be relieved by "Assafoetida" or "Paeony-water."[4]

There was only an indistinct frontier, too, between the inner life of the mind and the inner life of the spirit: for the Johnstones as for everyone else. The "outward Man," in the description of the author of *Diseases of the Body*, was constituted by the material system of things, which was the union of the body and the "Rational Soul." The "inward Man" was constituted by the spirit, "which is fitted only for communicating with the Supreme Infinite."[5] The life within was thereby invisible, and it was at the same time visible to God. "Before I think, thou know'st, O Lord, / What all my thoughts will be," Elizabeth Carolina wrote in the volume of poems she published after she and her sister left for India, in verses paraphrased from Psalm 139: "Say, whither shall I screen my soul, / From that all-seeing eye?"[6] Her brother, many years later, when he was ill and blind and his nephew James Raymond Johnstone had sent him some money, responded with "a few lines": "The Mind has an

Eye, an Eye, brighter far / Than the bright sun himself, for the Mind is Gods Star."[7]

Even the frontier between the inner life, of the mind or of the spirit, and the outer events of public life was indistinct in the Johnstones' lives. The empire in India was in their description "an empire of opinion," and the empire in the Americas was an artistry of power, "satisfying the people that they are in security against oppression."[8] The enlightenment was a disposition of mind and an atmosphere of society. The Johnstones and their friends were continually evaluating their own sentiments and the sentiments of other people, in India and Scotland and the American colonies. They were interested in the character of officials in the court of the nawab of Bengal in Murshidabad, and of military contractors in Pensacola. The information with which they were so preoccupied was knowledge, in particular, about "the People here," as in Patrick's last letter from India.[9] They were surrounded by intimations of the transformation of the human mind, as in Elizabeth Mure's history of "the change of manners in my own time," or Walter Minto's history of "the customs and manners of the people" in America ("they are in a very fluctuating state").[10]

Public life was itself, in the Johnstones' theories, an exchange between internal and external circumstances. "Men, accustomed to affairs, are apt to look more to the characters and principles of those who speak, than to what they say in the moment: They are apt to look to the nature of the human mind," William declared in one of his pamphlets about the East India Company and the British constitution.[11] Like the law, with its evaluations of intention and cognition, or like commerce, with its extended observations of "character and situation," in Adam Smith's description, political life was a sequence of predictions about individuals and societies. The gravest danger of an abolition of the slave trade, William said in the peroration of his last parliamentary speech, the speech against Wilberforce's bill, was that "such a measure must give a very strong turn to the minds of the negroes now upon the islands: they might well say, if you think the situation of slaves is so dreadful, that you will not allow any more of our countrymen to be made slaves, why are we to continue slaves still?"[12]

THE HISTORY OF THE HUMAN MIND

The history of the Johnstones and their far-flung households has in these respects been a history of inner as well as outer lives, of "internal and external sentiment," as in David Hume's description of the "fluctuating situations" of moral evaluation.[13] It is thereby both an old-fashioned and a new venture. The object of historical investigation, for the historian of Rome Barthold Georg Niebuhr, the inspiration of so much nineteenth-century historiography, was the *Innere*, or the "inwardness of the ordinary life" of antiquity: an insight into how it really was, through the clouds or the mist (the *Nebel*) that separate us from the past, or a glimpse, as though in a clear light, of the individuals of those other times, "living and moving." It was an understanding of events as they were seen by individuals at the time, as Goethe wrote to Niebuhr in 1812, in which "the Past can be made present to the inward eye and imagination."[14] These are the images, still, or some of the images, of historical investigation: an inquiry into an "un-glimpsed world" that is "obscured from view by clouds," or a "verifiable world of interconnections" that is also a "depiction of interior worlds" and of their relationship to the "exterior world" of historical events.[15] They are the images, in turn, of one of the grandest and longest-lasting of historical investigations, or the history of the human mind and how it changes over time.

The possibility of an interior history is enticing, be-cause it is a history of how it really was, at some moment in the past.[16] "All history is the history of thought," for the idealist historians of the early twentieth century, and the "re-enactment of past thought in the historian's own mind."[17] Or some history, at least, is the history of thought: the history of empires in particular.[18] The his-tory of the mind is enticing, even more imposingly, be-cause it is or can be a history of change over time. This is the enlightenment historians' prospect of a universal human nature, or a universal disposition of mind, that is transformed by the historical circumstances of legal, commercial, and social institutions. It was David Hume's prospect, in particular, of a peaceful exchange of com-modities and ideas, in which "the minds of men, being once roused from their lethargy, and put into a fermen-tation, turn themselves on all sides," and "it is impossi-ble but they must feel an encrease of humanity, from the very habit of conversing together, and contributing to each other's pleasure and entertainment."[19]

The difficulties of an interior history of this sort were evident even in the eighteenth-century historians' sci-ence of human nature. There was a "scarcity of monu-ments," the philosopher Condorcet wrote in the 1790s in his own sketch of a "history of the progress of the human mind," or a lack of archives, records, and other evidence with respect to the lives of the vast majority of individuals. There was also a lack of observable relationships, even with regard to "the history of a few men," between interior consequences and exterior, "public and known" events.[20] There were very few details about the inner (or outer) lives of almost all individuals, and even with respect to the individuals for whom there were such details, there was very little evidence of sentiments, ideas, or the interior consequences of exterior events.

This is still the dilemma of histories of the inner life, which historians have sought to address in innumerable ways, through histories of mentalities, myths, and ideologies, or through the social history of ideas, or through microhistory or prosopography, the history of persons. It is even a moral dilemma. For if historians ask questions about how it really was in the past, then the answers must be concerned, in part, with the ideas, sentiments, motives, and values of past individuals. But there is very little evidence about the ideas of the vast majority of these individuals. So the dilemma is that there can be a history without ideas and sentiments, or a history without most individuals in it: a history of only the great or the important or the philosophical, the individuals who wrote about their own ideas, or who were written about in their lifetimes. There can be a history of ideas that is no more, as in Condorcet's description, than the history of a few men, or a history of the "mass," that "can only be founded on observations."[21] This is itself a very eighteenth-century dilemma, in the sense that to relinquish the possibility of a history of the interior lives of the uneminent is to relinquish the deepest presumption of the late eighteenth-century enlightenment, which is the presumption of inner equality: that all individuals without exception are discursive and inquisitive, with moral sentiments and ideas about the world.

The history of the Johnstones and their households has been a microhistory, in the terms of these old historical dilemmas. But it is a large microhistory. This is in part because the Johnstones were themselves such a large and disorderly family, and moved around over such large distances. It is in part because there are so many other individuals who were involved in their lives, including the two slaves or servants, Bell or Belinda and Joseph Knight, whose stories have turned out to be so important. It is in part, too, because the history of the Johnstones, who traversed or transgressed the distinctions between different sides of eighteenth-century life, economic, political and domestic, is a transgression, in turn, of the distinctions between different kinds of history. The colonial and East India correspondence has been a record of administrative procedure, and of "discontent, dissention, and anxiety."[22] The history of the law has been a history of legal decisions, and also of "individuals caught in the web of the law."[23] The history of economic life—of presents, prizes, and mortgages on slaves—has been a history of ideas and sentiments. The history of families has been a history of empires. There are events in the Johnstones' lives, and in the lives of the others with whom they were involved, that can be observed, to use an eighteenth-century image, from multiple points of view, as travellers see a distant town.[24]

FAMILY SECRETS

The Johnstone brothers and sisters wrote to each other, from time to time, about their own interior dispositions. "I dar say you feell for me as I do for Every thing that concerns you," Betty wrote to William, in the difficult period of their estrangement from their parents.[25] "I am just going to sea, I presume you have feeling sufficient to Judge of my distress without discribing it," George wrote, also to William, in the course of a different estrangement.[26] Martha Ford wrote to Walter Minto, the tutor of her sons, that "no one can feel more sincerely than I did, for your Situation, it must be a heavy Charge, other People's Children."[27] But the Johnstones were not the sort of people who discoursed at any length about their inner selves. James did begin to keep a diary, but he abandoned it after a few pages, reusing the blank notebook, some years later, as his "private" letter book, and it was mostly, in any case, about starches: "by various Experiments I have made on Carrots I am certain that they are one of the most fattening of all Vegetables Every Animal and all sorts of Poultry are fond of them."[28] There is an unusual intimacy in the Johnstones' letters: the intimacy, in part, of the relationships between eleven sisters and brothers who survived into adulthood, who were all literate, and who lived in different places, with different reasons to write letters to each other.[29] But the letters have the sometimes distracted quality of conversations, veering from one subject to another, or from the intimate to the agricultural and the ornamental. Barbara's husband wrote to William in 1759 about his impending separation, and inquired about the premiums for "Lint & Lint Mills." Barbara, their mother, wrote to George in the same year about her "brocken and afflicted heart," her anxieties for his health, and to ask him to buy her the coffee cups "out of the indea ships."[30] Even the brothers' official letters veer in much the same way from the intimate to the administrative. John, in his last letter to the East India Company before leaving Calcutta, described the "terrible Apprehensions" of Muhammad Reza Khan; the "Anxiety of his Mind," and the "Pains and Terrors" of Motiram; and then reverted to the "Monthly Cash Accompts."[31]

The information about the other individuals in the Johnstones' lives is different and less intimate. The Johnstones were a family with long-lasting secrets, many of them involving women, and some of them involving individuals who had no names, or no names in the acknowledgment of the law, in the sense that their first cousin, the (illegitimate) son of their uncle Patrick, wrote from India in 1785 that "I am the son of nobody."[32] Louisa was married to someone else ("your poor dear Husband," in her lawyer's expression) when she became involved with James; her mother had only an approximate name ("Elizabeth Mary Louisa commonly called Elizabeth Mary Louisa Montgomerie"); and the name that was wrongly attributed to Louisa herself in Namier and Brooke's *History of Parliament* was the name of the second husband of the widow of her mother's brother.[33] The evidence of Martha Ford's history has been no more than a succession of birth certificates, death certificates, and passing references in other people's letters, and the two letters saved by her sons' tutor. She is mentioned in only one of the many hundreds of letters of the Johnstone brothers and sisters, or at least of the letters that I have read: a solicitous reference in a letter from John to William Julius Mickle, with whom Martha was staying after George's death.[34]

The life of Elizabeth Carolina, the most pious of all the Johnstones, was a profound secret, even to her own children. She is commemorated in two monuments in white marble: a tablet in the churchyard of Westerkirk, placed by her daughter Anne Elizabeth, and a bas relief in the churchyard of Alva, the profile of a beautiful young woman with a necklace in her hair. But there is almost nothing that is known of her early life, or her parents, or of why she went to India in wartime, in the spring of 1761. John wrote in a letter to William, after their father's death, that he was very eager to return to his wife (his "family") after the "loss of one whose kindness exceeded that of her own father to her."[35] That is all there is, of the family history of Elizabeth Carolina (as she was described on the title page of her book), or Caroline (as she was described in the request to the East India Company for permission to go to India), or Elizabeth Caroline (the name on the monument in Westerkirk), or Caroline Elizabeth (the name on the monument in Alva). Her son James Raymond Johnstone wrote in a letter to his sister, in 1815, that their mother's father was "Colonel William Keene of Norfolk," and "my grandmother whom he married in Dublin was the widow of Mr Madden of that City. Her maiden name was O Carrol." But there was nothing else he knew.[36] "I wish I could give you the information you want about our beloved parents, but of our mother as she died in our infancy I know none of the particulars you require, but the day of her death at Alva," he wrote again to his sister in 1819. He concluded, as in an eighteenth-century novel, "this will be delivered to you by our housekeeper who is now waiting for it, & as she goes by the [illegible] Boat I cannot detain her."[37]

With respect to the other individuals in the Johnstones' history, there is far less evidence. The information about the Johnstone brothers and sisters has been information, for the most part, of the sort that is available about individuals with names, who write letters and own property: even unvaluable property, like "the piece of spoiled India silk" that Betty left to her niece. The information about the individuals in their extended households, or their wider connections, is far more disparate. Even the name has been a will-o'-the-wisp from time to time, including in relation to places that are relatively rich, like England and Scotland, in parish registers and family historians and digitized records.

There were 20,426 people called Johnstone or Johnston whose baptisms were entered in the old parish registers in Scotland in the lifetime of these Johnstones (from Barbara's birth in 1723 to Betty's death in 1813). There were multiple James Johnstones, even in the Johnstones' own story. There was their father. There was their brother, who married Louisa. There was "James Johnstone," "my nephew," who went to West Florida with George; James Johnstone, the "mollato," who came from India with John and who was baptised in 1773; James Johnstone, "Negroe Servant," who confessed to "uncleanness" with Henrietta Allen in 1778; James Johnstone, "my black servant," who discovered the antimony mine and to whom James left an annuity in his will; and the James Johnstone who was an inspector of books in the miners' library. There was a James Johnstone with whom Alexander's "mulato" daughter lived at Hangingshaw; and a James Johnstone—or several James Johnstones—who was the father of eight children whose births were recorded in the old parish register of Westerkirk between 1781 and 1798, with the evocative names of James, John, Louisa, Margaret, William Pultney, Barbara, George, and Wilhelmina.[38] "There were multitudes of Johnstones in Annan," one of the judges complained when the family's claim to the Annandale peerage was eventually heard in 1881: "there are so many James Johnstones."[39]

There is even less information about Bell or Belinda. She had no birth certificate, so far as I know, no property, no death certificate that I have been able to find, and no name: no family name, at least, and only the most insubstantial of first names, or conjunctions of names. She was a thing, as well as a person, and there is no record of her having been bought or sold. She was reported on three different occasions, in her interrogation in prison in Cupar, in her indictment, and in her petition in the courtroom in Perth, to have described the events of the summer of 1771, when her son was born and died in Scotland. But the events she recounted were not a description of sentiments, and the words reported were not her own words: "she the Declarant brought forth a Child," in the third person of her initial declaration in Cupar, or "you did only make answer that," in the second person of the indictment against her.[40]

Even in the Johnstones' own letters, the hundreds of letters in dozens of collections, it is the silences, as so often, that have been eloquent. The Johnstones were involved in the two dramatic legal cases involving slaves in the east of Scotland, in 1771 and 1773–78, that have been at the center of this history. But there is no mention in any of the family letters that I have seen of either Bell or Belinda, or Joseph Knight. Was this because the cases were not all that important in the busy and (in this period) afflicted lives of the family? Was it because the cases were important, and the Johnstones were careful, even in letters to their closest relations, to make no reference to them, that they had conversations about the cases but did not refer to them even indirectly in their letters? Or was it because the letters about the two cases were among the papers that John, in particular, must have destroyed, in his own version of his friend William Bolts's Lisbon conflagration (the bonfire of philosophical papers)? James wrote to John at the beginning of the summer of 1771 and received no response, which made him "very uneasy" ("pray write me if he was mentioning any thing in Relation to me that was disagreeable to him," James wrote to Betty in September); a few months later, after Bell or Belinda had been sent away to be sold in Virginia, and in response, apparently, to a letter from John that does not survive, James sought to console John for the "Lowness of Spirits [that] will chill every faculty." He concluded, a little implausibly, with Aeneas's words to Dido, about the self-consciousness of the righteous mind.[41]

Joseph Knight, unlike Bell or Belinda, is an individual about whom there is a great deal of information: who was examined often, and who sent many memorials to many different judicial instances; who signed his own declaration in the magistrates' court in Balindean in November 1773; and who described his conversations with his owner, the feeling of his stockings, the paragraph he read in a newspaper of July 3, 1772, and his own inner life of the mind, "from that time he has had it in his head to leave his Service." He remembered, even, what it was that he could not remember: "declares that he was brought from the Coast of Guinea by one Capt. Knight when he was very young and carried to Jamaica . . . that he does not know anything of his being sold"; he "was not made acquainted with that sale & knows nothing more of the matter."[42] But Joseph Knight, too, is someone of whom there is a vast amount that is not known, including when he was born, or where he lived after his world-historical victory of 1778, and when he died.

Even the history of Joseph Knight's name turns out to be a blank wall of anonymity, a collision of the individual and the statistical. Captain John Knight of Bristol made two voyages from the Cape Coast Castle in modern Ghana to Jamaica, arriving on a ship called the *Phoenix* in June 1760 and in April 1765. But if the little boy who was later Joseph Knight was on one of the voyages, he was recorded as no more than a number: one of the 292 "slaves disembarked" from the *Phoenix* in 1760, or the 290 "slaves disembarked" in 1765.[43] All the individuals in the Johnstones' story were involved with each other, intimately or at a distance; they are part of the same story. But they are the subjects, or the possible subjects, of entirely different sorts of history.[44] They seem to impose different genres: the history of a social condition ("slavery"), or the political history of public officials, or the history of marriage, or financial history. They impose, most insidiously, the inequality of individuality: of who is, and who is not, the subject of her or his own history.

THE DISCONTINUITY OF SIZE AND SCENES

The family history of the Johnstones has been a "multitude of views or glimpses," as in David Hume's description of probability, or "a bundle of little episodes," as in *The Man of Feeling*, the novel by the Edinburgh writer Henry Mackenzie that the Westerhall miners ordered in 1793.[45] But it is thereby a new as well as an old-fashioned kind of historical inquiry. It has been made possible by the spectacular increase in information about early modern individuals, which is the consequence of late modern technologies of historical investigation. The quantity of information or evidence about the Johnstones is the outcome of their own age of information, and of the choices of nineteenth- and twentieth-century keepers of public and private records, including the Johnstones' own grandchildren, with their bundles of accountants' notes and "Letters of Affection & Curiosity."[46] It is the opportunity of access to all this information that has been transformed beyond recognition in the historians' new world of the twenty-first century: by the computerization of the catalogues of public and private archives, the very large-scale digitization of newspapers, books, and other records, new technologies of reproduction, and the Web sites of public and private family historians, which are almost entirely unconnected (too unconnected, perhaps) to the scholarship of historians.

The possibilities of a microhistory of the uneminent or the unimportant have been multiplied, in the new world of historical research. In the prosopography of the lower orders that Carlo Ginzburg and Carlo Poni described in their manifesto of microhistory of 1979, the name was to be the red thread, Ariadne's thread in the labyrinth of the archive. In the period of less than a generation, the technology of looking for individuals by their names has become literally unrecognizable.[47] The new technologies offer the possibility of a new way of connecting the microhistories of individuals and families to the larger scenes of which they were a part. One connection is of illustration: as the history of the Johnstones is a case study of the larger history of their times. Another is of representativeness, or the absence of representativeness. The Johnstone brothers and sisters, like Bell or Belinda, were in no respect median or characteristic figures; and their history indeed imposes a very exigent sense of how difficult it would be, with the incomplete evidence available about early modern populations, to arrive at the sort of precise descriptions on which quantitative measures of the median can be founded.

The new possibility is of connecting micro- and macrohistories through the history of the individuals' own connections and discontinuities. These are connections in space and time: in the case of the Johnstones and Bell or Belinda, connections from India to the Americas, and over their long lifetimes. They are also connections of friendship and business, in the various milieux or media of empire and enlightenment with which this book has been concerned: medium-size histories. The increase in the quantity of information can thereby make possible a change in the quality of information, or in the resolution or the size of microhistories.[48]

This is the simile of historical insight, once more, or the figurative language of seeing: of the glimpse, or the point of view. The sources of information about the

Johnstones and their households are like a multitude of vistas, or photographic images. It is as though the different individuals can be seen at different distances and with different resolutions: portraits and horizons and landscapes. "The point is that you can't get at the thing itself, the real nature of the sitter, by stripping away the surface. The surface is all you've got. You can only get beyond the surface by working with the surface," the photographer Richard Avedon said of the "performance" of portraits.[49] The surface, in the history of the Johnstones, is sometimes at a distance and sometimes in the intimate closeness of a portrait: a multiplicity of pictures or a "multi-resolution experience."[50] The promise of the new microhistory is thus of a variability of historical size or historical resolution, in which the micro- is set in many different scenes, of different dimensions, and seen from different points of view.[51]

THE INCOMPLETENESS OF INFORMATION

The new microhistory of connected lives imposes a tolerance for the diversity of historical evidence: flimsy lists of things to do, large parchment mortgages, "private letters of no consequence," like James's letters to Louisa, or the "Porteous Roll" for the county of Fife, the bundles of papers concerning criminal cases that were carried around Scotland from court to court, and of which one of the characters in Sir Walter Scott's "The Surgeon's Daughter" says that eighteenth-century writers were such admirers, "choosing their heroes out of the Porteous Roll."[52] It also imposes a tolerance for indeterminacy, in the sense that it is a history that changes direction in unexpected ways. The history of the Johnstones, their servants, and their slaves has been a story of voyages, in space and time. But it has also itself been a voyage, in space and time and in the ever-changing metaspace of the technologies of historical research. I came across the Johnstones, as I mentioned at the outset, because of John's involvement in the parliamentary election of 1774 in Adam Smith's home town of Kirkaldy. There was in the end almost nothing to discover about the election (or that I have so far discovered). But in looking for the circumstances of the election, I found James's letter book from his exile in Norfolk—the letter book about "Anguish Vexation & Anxiety"—and a glimpse of a larger and odder family of sisters and sisters-in-law.[53]

The voyage changed direction, even more unexpectedly, because of a different chance encounter. The history of the Johnstones has been in large part about the family's relationships to Atlantic and Indian Ocean slavery, and to individual slaves. But these relationships were quite unexpected, in relation to the history of the public Johnstones, in the East India Company, or the navy, or the society of the enlightenment in Edinburgh.[54] The thread of evidence, in this case, was the relationship of property, and the will in which Alexander left his slaves, mills, and boiling houses to James. It was also a thread that began with an individual, or with the judicial description of an individual, "Bell, alias Belinda," the "slave or servant of John Johnston": a chance encounter, in the late modern way, with the outcome of an internet search for "John Johnstone."[55]

The new microhistories impose a tolerance, above all, for incompleteness. Bell or Belinda's petition is not very much more than a fragment or a residue, like the judicial declaration by a woman called Brinda, who lived in rural Bengal some three generations after Bell or Belinda's time, in Ranajit Guha's essay "Chandra's Death." It inspires the sense of conflict described by Guha, between "the phenomenon of fragmentation" and the "urge for plenitude" that "constitutes the driving force behind much of historical research," "an insatiated, indeed insatiable urge for more and more linkages."[56] But the new technologies also inspire a more insidious sense of incompleteness. This is the incompleteness of historical research, or "searches," in a universe of information that is itself changing continuously over time. It is almost a Hegelian "bad infinity," of doing the same thing again and again (looking for Bell or Belinda) and not knowing how to stop.[57] I have not found out who bought Bell or Belinda in Virginia in April 1772, or which of George and Martha Ford's children was baptised in Pensacola in 1764. But these are the sorts of things that could be known: that someone will know, eventually, or will not know.[58]

So the history of the Johnstones is both new and old-fashioned. It has come close, in a number of respects, to the historical novel.[59] It has been inspired in substantial part by inquisitiveness, or by the curiosity into "characters, designs, and actions" that Adam Smith described as the condition of "every age and country of the world."[60] It is the depiction of an eighteenth-century world in which large numbers of individuals were interested in novels: Margaret's granddaughter, in the portrait by Raeburn; or the miners of the Louisa antimony mine; or Lord Camden, who spoke in the House of Lords about rights to ideas, and who was sitting by a window seat heaped with novels when one of the Johnstones' former friends went to talk to him about the East India Company; or George himself, who wrote a novel or novella, which he sent to William in 1759: "I send you by this Coach, a little book wrapt up in Brown Paper," "some Jeux d'Esprit of mine," the stories of romantic and naval life.[61]

But the Johnstones' history is not a novel.[62] It is a history of eighteenth-century life, and one that has conveyed, in a very old-fashioned respect, the restrictiveness of the historian's investigations. I can perhaps explain what I mean in terms of the observation, made by so many novelists, that the characters in their novels have a life of their own, or run away with the story. The experience of writing a family history is almost the opposite. The novelist's observation is an expression, or so it seems, of the circumstance that the author of a novel starts by imagining a character, with certain characteristics, and that various unexpected developments then follow from these initial characteristics. The historian's circumstances are the opposite, in the sense that she starts by not knowing anything about a character, a man or a woman or a child, "James Johnstone," or Bell or Belinda, who once existed. So the inquiry, or the sequence over time (the historian's time), is a process of finding pieces of evidence with which to try to make sense of these individuals. The condition with which the novelist begins, or the character, is the condition with which the historian ends, or the very distant end, rather, at which the historian never arrives. The details that are for the novelist a way of conveying the verisimilitude of an individual who is imaginary, are for the historian a way of discovering the circumstances of an individual who was once alive: a way of convincing others, and also of convincing oneself.

The Johnstones and their friends were modern or postmodern characters: at least as cunning and as self-conscious as historians. They subverted public or semi-public records, and they were intrigued by self-subverting instructions, or letters within letters; they destroyed documents, intercepted packets of official correspondence that turned out to be forged, and composed instructions about throwing manuscripts over balconies. Their history imposes a high degree of suspicion with respect to birth certifications, and even to the most decorous of works of record (like the *Burial Registers* of Westminster Abbey); an old-fashioned critique of sources. It also imposes a high degree of indulgence for the incompleteness of historical evidence, of fragments of sources. But it has at the same time inspired a sense of awe with respect to these fragments of evidence, or to the apparently infinite possibilities of historical inquiry into the lives of individuals in the past: new sources to be discovered and new things to be done with information. This is itself a very old-fashioned history.

CHAPTER EIGHT

OTHER PEOPLE

Elizabeth Caroline Johnstone Gray, who was John and Elizabeth Carolina's granddaughter, wrote in her *Tour to the Sepulchres of Etruria, in 1839*, that the history of the Etrurians was a collection of "fragments," or "half-broken, tarnished, hideous things," "ranged along the wall in melancholy confusion and neglect, without a place in the catalogue." But it was also a history, in her description, of "ancient modes of thinking and acting" and of individuals who once were alive: "there they lay, not with a look of death, but as if they had a tale to tell, if there were anyone present willing to listen."[1]

This, too, has been a history of fragments, which is at the same time, or so I hope, a history of the sentiments and thoughts of other times. It is an eighteenth-century sort of history, in David Hume's sense of "a cautious observation of human life," as it appears "in the common course of the world, by men's behaviour in company, in affairs, and in their pleasures."[2] But it is also in the spirit of Adam Smith's description of the process by which individuals make their own moral lives, out of an endless exchange of observations of themselves and other people. It has been a view of the outer lives of individuals who were themselves observing the lives of others, and coming to conclusions about intentions and dispositions, who were evaluating the inner in relation to the outer, or the relationship between the inner and the outer: individuals for whom "the surface is all you've got."[3]

THE JOHNSTONES AND THE MIND

The brothers and sisters who have been at the center of the story are in a sense uninteresting, because they are so often unestimable. In the evaluation of character with which their friends and connections in the Scottish enlightenment were so preoccupied, they would have been considered, as indeed they were considered, to be severely remiss. They were almost entirely lacking in the easiness or milkiness that Hume described in his account of his "own character"—"of mild dispositions, of command of temper," "little susceptible of enmity, and of great moderation"—and that was the highest achievement of enlightenment virtue.[4] All of them, or at least all of them of whom it is possible to make this sort of evaluation, had very different values in different circumstances: at different times in their lives, in different places, and in the different sides of their lives, private and public. But they all quarrelled amazingly often in these different circumstances (or at least all of them except Patrick, who died so young).

There are times in their private letters when the brothers and sisters are relentlessly unsentimental. His mind was like "a gloomy mansion fared to Mammon," Barbara's son-in-law wrote of William at the end of his life, and from their earliest correspondence with their father to the exchanges of slaves, estates, and constituencies of the 1780s, the brothers were an economic enterprise: a family partnership.[5] But there are other times when their passions overflow. Even William, with all his decorum, quarrelled with their father ("what you say I cannot belive to be the Result of Calm Reason," Betty wrote to him reproachfully); with their mother ("till your mother and you have a meeting things will never make up betwixt you," their father wrote to him in 1762); with James (over the description of the family home of Westerhall as a crazy rocking-house); with Alexander (over the Grenada plantation); with George (over letters of recommendation); and with Betty (over the money for her furniture).[6] Charlotte quarrelled with their father, and Betty quarrelled with their mother. John and William quarrelled with Alexander; George quarrelled with almost everyone, including his two beloved little sons (who had "disobeyed disappointed and disobliged" him).[7]

The family were at times wildly uninhibited in their descriptions of their relationships to each other. "I will take care she be keept from anoying me wt. greater expedition than her sister did," their mother wrote to William about one of his sisters, either Betty or Charlotte: "furious fool."[8] To George, she suggested that he marry "Miss Mendes," whom James had abandoned: "I think she would find her loss of him more than made up."[9] Their father warned James not to tell his secrets to William, and he promised Betty that he would come to see her in Edinburgh, if he could "get quite" of her mother. "My mothers Spleen will distroy her," George wrote to William, "I wish the Poor Girls were Safe."[10] Even James, who was so often a conciliatory figure within the family, had an eccentric tendency to add and subtract sentiments: "I scarce knew that I loved him so well till he was in Danger," he wrote to John of George, and, of their father, "my F. loves me better than any Thing on Earth"; to Betty he wrote that "no Body loves you more than I do."[11]

But the Johnstones also lived, as everyone lives, in the midst of moral choices or moral sentiments. There were occasions when the brothers and sisters, and their children, were movingly considerate. Betty wrote to William, in 1759, to implore him to visit Barbara's daughter in her boarding school in Kent, in order to inform her of her parents' separation and to advise her about "what part she is to act": "its a melancholy and disagreeable office at the same time its an act of Charety as it might Shoock the Child Doubly hearing it from any indifferent person."[12] George was described by his sons' tutor, with whom he later quarrelled so grievously, as a father who loved them to distraction.[13] George and Martha's children and their grandmother, Martha's mother, were conspicuously solicitous of each other in the legal documents that are almost the only evidence of their domestic life. George Lindsay Johnstone, who may or may not have been born in Pensacola, wrote from Lucknow, after his father had abandoned his mother, to thank William Julius Mickle for the "attention you have shown my good Mother," the "Character you have given me of my Sister," "your kindness to my mother & Brothers," "your Conduct to my beloved Parent."[14] Alexander Patrick, his youngest brother, in a will that he made in Benares in 1799, referred to "my worthy and affectionate mother," "my dearest and incomparable sister," and to "the uncommon generosity of my dearest Georges disposition and the warm and unbounded affection which he bears for me."[15] There is a monument to George Lindsay Johnstone's memory in Westminster Abbey: "a sister prostrate in all the effusion of hopeless woe upon a brother's tomb."[16]

John, who was described by Lord Clive in the most diabolical terms of "Corruption, Avarice, Rapacity," "Extortion," and "Falshood," was within the family a figure of enduring virtue.[17] "No body has any unfriendly thing to say of you," his mother wrote to him in India, and for Uncle Walter he was "Dutiful noble spirited John."[18] This was a consequence, at least in part, of his position as the source of financial support for almost everyone in the family; in William's description, "his generosity is without any Limits."[19] But it was a consequence, too, of his generosity of mind. It was John, of all the brothers and sisters, who was kind to Martha Ford and her children, "little George" and "my Dear Miss Sophia."[20] He looked after George, during his last illness: "Chafing his head with our hands," as he wrote to William.[21] He was solicitous even of the family's business associates: "poor Scott," "poor Petrie," the "pains and Terrors" of Motiram, the "very affecting visit" he had received from the distressed daughter of an old acquaintance.[22] He and Betty, above all, were endlessly considerate of each other. John "is better," Uncle Walter wrote to William in 1773, "but he was ill during your father's last illness, & since that, while he remained at Westerhall waiting for Bettys recovery, (for Grief & fatigue had brought on her old distemper), & she for his. They went away together."[23]

The Johnstones were elaborately self-conscious, in their public lives, with respect to their own moral sentiments. It was "from a conscious Integrity," John wrote to the East India Company in 1771, that he sought to return to India as governor of Bengal; there was no one who had served with "less oppression to the Natives." Of his gratuities, he wrote that "no presents were ever received in India upon a more honourable footing."[24] "I have no personal or interested views," William wrote in a draft of a letter about an election in Shrewsbury, "&

look for no other reward but that which arises from the consciencious discharge of my duty to the Public."[25] George described himself as having come home from the West Indies with "a clear Conscience & Ignorance of the World."[26] "When you find that I vary from my Word or bear a double Tongue, I desire you will Immediately mistrust & desert me," he exhorted the Creek chiefs in Pensacola in 1765; to the Secretary of State, he wrote that "we are conscious of having acted with the utmost Integrity."[27] His subsequent defense of the North American colonists was the outcome of a "conscientious belief" in free institutions, he declared in parliament in 1775: "I here defy any man to say I was ever actuated by interested motives during the course of my life."[28]

Even in their private letters the Johnstones were self-conscious, self-interested, and interested in their own consciences, in an unsettled combination. "I should think I was a Villain if Stamps and Parchment only bound me," James wrote to Betty, with respect to the lease of one of their tenants; and then to Alexander, with respect to his quarrel with John over the Grenada plantation, he wrote, "I should think myself a Villain . . . not to use my Pygmy Influence with him to join Two Brothers." "It would be like taking an advantage of your necessities to make that the Condition of my Assistance," John wrote to James, when James had said that he would be willing to sell him the family home of Westerhall: "I never can suppose that to be voluntarily the case."[29] Betty described herself to William as a character in a play, in the episode of the muslin from India: "I trust in God no part I shall ever act shall make me suffer what I have of Late."[30] George's last days were lightened, in John's description, by "the Joy he felt on looking back &

viewing his honor safe, his fame secured": the deathbed scene depicted by William Julius Mickle in the elegy over which John wept so copiously.[31] It was the reflection of doing good, like Dido—"and may mens sibi conscia Recti digna ferant Praemia"—with which James sought to console John in the winter of 1771: the winter of Bell or Belinda's trial and of her journey to the *Betsey*.[32]

The history of empires is itself, in these circumstances, a history of the inner life. The Johnstones, their servants, and their slaves lived in multiple, shifting moral universes. They were lonely, and they lived with memories of loneliness. This is most intense in Bell or Belinda's life: "altogether or for the most part" alone, and "mostly by yourself," in the interior of John and Elizabeth Carolina's rented house. John, too, described himself as alone: "I . . . was sent alone to negotiate," "I continued . . . for almost two years alone." "Nothing on Earth can be a greater misfortune to me than not having a home to go to," Betty wrote, when she had been sent away with her trunk. Gideon was very uneasy in Jamaica, "haveing never Received but one letter from my friends for these sixteen month past."[33]

The anxiety to which the brothers and sisters referred so frequently was a condition of bad expectation. "I will have expectation at least," Louisa wrote of her lottery ticket, but there was also the anxious expectation of loss. It was a condition, from time to time, of insecurity in relation to their own identity, or to the mind and the self. When John came home after fifteen years in India, he had become an "Indian," in the expression of David Hume's cousin: "his brother, the Indian."[34] He was unsettled in Scotland, and he still expected, in 1771, to return to India. All the broiling years in India were only a part of his disorder, as James wrote to Betty, and "tranquillity of mind" was more important for the cure of his disease than "keeping his feet constantly dry." John himself seems to have described a transformation in his interior existence, in a letter to his mother that has not survived, and to which she responded in the more than usually distraught (and more than usually wildly spelled) letter about eternal life: "You had one expresion struck me, you say fiveten years in indes has made a great choing in your constitution it ought to be now in its prime all it can afoord you is not worth risquing it oh come home."[35]

INTRAN BELL ALIAS BELINDA

Even Bell or Belinda's history, which is so odd and evanescent, has been a history of moral circumstances. She has been at the center of the history of the Johnstones because her destiny provides a glimpse or an illustration—a view, as though through the clouds or the mist of distance—of a transnational life, in the eighteenth-century world of global connections. The narrative of her life, or of the fragments of a life, is itself remarkable. She was a native of Bengal; she came to London and then to Scotland; she had a son in Scotland, who died and whom she threw into the river (or whom she laid to rest in the river); she was imprisoned in two small towns in Scotland, and sentenced to be sold as a slave; she arrived in Virginia in the early years of the American Revolution. She is not a representative figure, in the sense that she can stand for one or more of the populations of individuals of which she was a part (or one or more of the territories in which she lived).[36] But she is an important and even a world-historical figure, as the last person who was deemed—"adjudged," in the words of the headline in the *Scots Magazine*—to be a slave by a court in the British Isles.

Bell or Belinda is important because of her place in the sequence over time of legal decisions involving slavery in the British empire. Her case was heard in Perth on September 13, 1771 and was reported in the *Caledonian Mercury* in the issue dated September 14, 1771. James Somerset ran away from his owner in London on October 1, 1771, and the first writ of habeas corpus was issued in his case, by Lord Mansfield, on December 3, 1771. Bell or Belinda left Glasgow for Virginia on January 12, 1772; the decision in the *Somerset* case, which had the effect of ending slavery in England, was delivered on June 22, 1772.[37] The case that ended slavery in Scotland, *Knight v. Wedderburn*, began, in turn, when Joseph Knight read an article about the Somerset case in an Edinburgh newspaper published on July 3, 1772: "and this naturally led him to think, that he also was intitled to be free." The Joseph Knight case began in a magistrates' court in Perthshire on November 15, 1773, and was decided by the highest court in Scotland on January 15, 1778.[38] There was, so far as I know, no case after Bell or Belinda's in which the state of slavery, in the British Isles, was determined by a British court.[39]

It is possible, even, that Bell or Belinda's case was known to and of importance to James Somerset and Joseph Knight. James Somerset's and Joseph Knight's legal choices were made in a knowing, well-informed world of individuals who were slaves and who had conversations, access to newspapers, opinions about officers of the law, and letters from their friends. This was also Bell or Belinda's world, in London and the east of Scotland. There is nothing in the Johnstones' letters to show that Bell or Belinda or Joseph Knight were among the servants who accompanied the Johnstones or the Wedderburns on their repeated family visits. But at least some of the servants in the Johnstones' households were continually on the move between Westerhall, Edinburgh, and the family estates in Balgonie and Balindean.

James Somerset had himself been in Edinburgh shortly before Bell or Belinda's trial and had stayed in the household of his owner's brother, the Edinburgh lawyer who was the son-in-law of the publisher of the *Caledonian Mercury*. He ran away in London two weeks after the publication, in the *Caledonian Mercury*, of the report of Bell or Belinda's being sent to the West Indies or North America. Joseph Knight read in another Edinburgh newspaper about James Somerset's case; his owner, John Wedderburn, had been on the list of assizes to be called as a jury in Perth, in the summer before Bell or Belinda's case had come to trial.[40] The county judge to whom Joseph Knight appealed in December 1773, on the grounds that he "had given a contrary decision in a late question," was John Swinton, the sheriff depute of Perthshire who had presented Bell or Belinda's request for a continuance, in order to prepare her petition. It was John Swinton's decision that the high court eventually upheld: "finds that the state of slavery is not recognized by the laws of this kingdom, and is inconsistent with the principles thereof."[41] The "mollato" James Johnstone, in turn, left John and Elizabeth Carolina's household at some point before he was baptized in England in April 1773, or in the aftermath of Bell or Belinda's going away, and in the interval between James Somerset's and Joseph Knight's cases.

Bell or Belinda is an important figure, in all these respects. But she is also an individual who lived amidst moral choices and moral sentiments. In her own petition, the petition written by the two notaries public, she describes herself to a striking extent in the language of moral responsibility, or moral self-consciousness. She is "certain" she will be found innocent, she "abhors" the crime of child murder, she has little "understanding" of the law of Scotland, she is "advised" as to the statute, she is "desirous," she has "understanding" of the obnoxiousness of the crime with which she is charged, she has an expectation as to her future "happiness." But she at the same time expresses her uncertainty as to whether she is a person or a thing: "she is willing for her part, so far as she has an interest in the Disposall of her Person."

These words are writers' words: the evocation of at least three arguments that were familiar in the Scottish courts of the time, about actual versus statutory murder, finding happiness, and witnesses who were in England; and one that was unfamiliar, about whether or not she was her own property, in relation to the rights of her owner, which were the rights that John Johnstone asserted in countersigning the court's decision. But Bell or Belinda takes possession of the words, in the most immediate sense. The earlier declaration in Cupar, in which she said that she had never told anyone that she was with child, was "unsigned by you (because you said you could not write)." The declaration in Perth was signed by two notaries public and four witnesses, "by order of the said Bell or Belinda," "who declares she cannot write and who touched the pen."[42]

There are things that can be known of Bell or Belinda with a substantial degree of probability. It is reasonable to see her as someone who was extremely resilient, in a physical sense: who survived an eight-month journey from Calcutta via the Cape of Good Hope to London, childbirth alone, six months in a succession of Scottish prisons, and a two-month journey, in mid-winter, from Glasgow to Virginia. She can be seen as resilient, or independent, in an emotional sense as well: in her choice to stay on her own in Elizabeth Carolina's bedroom, or in her description of the days after her baby's birth, "she kept it two days after it was born and then carried it away in a Cloth," or in the other servants' description of what she said when they asked, "what was the matter with you": "you did only make answer that you was too hot or that you had catched cold by bathing in the River." But here again there is no evidence, only circumstances and the reports of conversations.

The "precognition" in the summer of 1771 was a judicial inquiry into Bell or Belinda's state of mind, while she was expecting her child, and over the course of three days in June. So was the later "inquiry" ("made since taking the precognition"), with its determination "that there was no sufficient evidence of intentional murder." There are only fleeting indications of what being pregnant—or being in "expectation"—meant to Bell or Belinda, or of her loss. One is a glimpse, or an inference, of her own memories. For the sequence of events that was so shocking to the neighboring tenant farmers—"she kept it two days after it was born and then carried it away in a Cloth . . . and threw the Child and Cloth into the water"—was almost exactly the repetition of the burial rituals of the society in which Bell or

Belinda had once lived, or of her own earlier life. "They burn not . . . an infant who has not cut its teeth, but bury them, or throw them into the river," in an eighteenth-century translation of a description of Hindu burial rites. In the description of later archaeologists and anthropologists, infants "are buried and not cremated, though at some places by the river side they are wrapped in cloth and submerged in the river"; "when the deceased is a young child," the period of mourning "is generally telescoped so that it ends on *trivatri*—after 'three nights.' "[43] There is one image, or view, that was the neighbors' view, of a slave or servant throwing away her baby. There is another view, of a young woman (a young mother) with her own images or her own imagination of distant remembered scenes: an individual seeking, by the riverside in Balgonie, to do that which she had long ago seen done.

The relationship between Bell or Belinda and the Johnstones is itself no more than a sequence of glimpses or inferences. The circumstances of the events of the summer of 1771, when Bell or Belinda stayed on her own in Elizabeth Carolina's bedroom, are an indication of the intimacy of her relationship to either John or Elizabeth Carolina or both, or at least of the other servants' sense of this intimacy, and of her independence within the household. There is no suggestion, in the court records that I have seen, or in any kirk records that I have been able to find, of an inquiry into who the father of her child might have been, and this silence may itself suggest that the father was not someone whom the courts or the kirk wished to identify. I have no reason to suppose, on the basis of John's letters over this period, or indeed over the entire period of his life with Elizabeth

Carolina, that he was the father of Bell or Belinda's child. It is more likely that the "James Johnstone" who came with him from India, and who left the household after Bell or Belinda was sent away, was John's son: a half-Indian son, born soon after his arrival in the 1750s, to whom John gave his father and brother's names. This James Johnstone, who would have been sixteen or seventeen in 1770, on the basis of the parish records of Kirkandrews upon Esk, could even himself have been the father of Bell or Belinda's child: the child who died, and who would have been John's grandson.[44]

Bell or Belinda's legal defense is also obscure, with the involvement of the sheriffs of two contiguous counties, and the missing witness who was himself, or so it seems, an officer of the court, and one of the Johnstones' lawyers. It is enigmatic, too, in the sense that it was expensive. Someone, John Johnstone or John Swinton or John Taitt, the missing witness, must have paid for Bell or Belinda's food and lodging in the long months of prison in Cupar, in Perth, and in Glasgow. Someone must have paid for the "inquiry made since taking the precognition." Someone must have paid the fees of the notaries public.[45] There are at least two possible explanations for John's involvement in Bell or Belinda's case. One is that he was vindictive and wanted to assert his property rights in her as his slave (this is the explanation that is implicit in the inaccurate headline in the *Scots Magazine*, "criminal slave adjudged to be sold for behoof of the master"). The other is that he wanted to save her from being condemned to death: that he cooperated with John Swinton in a legal defense in which statements that were usual in cases of child murder in Scotland were augmented by the very unusual statement that she was not her own property, and that her owner, too, had rights with respect to her eventual punishment.[46] The second explanation seems to me to be the more likely. But this is no more than a balance of probabilities. The family connections between the Johnstones and the Swintons seem to indicate that John and John Swinton might have cooperated in Bell or Belinda's case; John Swinton's involvement, three years later, in Joseph Knight's case against John Wedderburn indicates that he was on the opposite side from at least some of the Johnstones, or their extended family.

The last intimation of Bell or Belinda's life that I have been able to find is a public record: the receipt signed in Williamsburg in April 1772 by the naval officer of the Upper James River. Her future, or the future that was before her in America, is in other respects a blank, just as her past was a blank in the courtroom in Scotland. She arrived in Virginia at a time that has been of intense interest to historians (and to family historians): the period of financial and economic crisis that immediately preceded the American Revolution. There are persons with names, or with names that are more plausible than the name ("Bell alias Belind a black girl") that she was given in Williamsburg, who were connected to her new life. There were the three men who signed the receipt in Virginia, there was the captain of the *Betsey*, there was the merchant to whom she was consigned (Patrick Colquhoun), there were the three other convicts on the ship, and there was the indentured servant who ran away and came back to the *Betsey* for the blue-and-white waistcoat. But there is nothing in these other peoples' histories that has led me, so far, to Bell or Belinda's own life. It is possible that she died a slave in America. It is also possible that she was never enslaved, or not for long. In September 1772 a man in Brunswick, Virginia, placed an advertisement in the *Virginia Gazette* to announce that a "likely Mulatto Fellow named BARNABY" had run away and that "a young Mulatto Wench, named BELINDA, went off at the same Time, who is short and very fat." It is possible that this was the same Belinda, or the Belinda from Bengal: well, fat, and free.[47]

All these possibilities are disconcerting, in a historical inquiry: the possibility that an individual, a person with a moral existence, could simply vanish in the historical record, or from the historian's sight. But there is something even more disturbing, which is the possibility that Bell or Belinda also vanished from the sight, or the memory, of the individuals with whom she had lived for so long. I have looked for her in the letters of John and his brothers and sisters, in Patrick Colquhoun's letters, and in the letters of Virginia merchants. I have tried to imagine John and Elizabeth Carolina saying good-bye to her, or instructing that she should be sold, in the way of the British officials of the time, to a "good master." I have tried to imagine what she meant to them.[48] But it is also possible, and this is what is so difficult to imagine, that she meant nothing at all: that she vanished over the horizon in January 1772 and was forgotten by all of them, as though she had never existed.

OTHER PEOPLE

The history of the Johnstones, and of Bell or Belinda, has been "fluctuating, uncertain, fleeting, successive, and compounded," as in David Hume's description of the circumstances of the human mind.[49] But it is also a history of moral sentiments. It is a history, at least, of individuals in circumstances that are moral circumstances, in our own, modern understanding, and in an eighteenth-century understanding as well: of individuals in circumstances that imposed either the exercise of moral imagination, or the refusal of moral imagination. They were circumstances in which entirely new scenes of oppression were both remote and close ("when ills are distant are they then your own?"), and in which individuals lived in contiguous and conflicting cultures, and found themselves alone in empires. They were circumstances, too, in which the language of universal and individual rights coexisted with extreme brutality; where many hundreds of thousands of women and men lived in relationships that were at one and the same time relations between individuals and relations of power, in which their own individuality, or their own humanity, ebbed and flowed. I said earlier that it is extremely difficult, now, to imagine ourselves in an eighteenth-century world in which there was only a very indistinct sense of the frontiers of empire, or race, or law, or economic life. But it was a difficult world of the mind for individuals in the eighteenth century as well.

The history of empires, or the history of enlightenment, is itself, in this sense, a history of the inner life. To describe the circumstances of individuals in the past, and to imagine how they thought about these circumstances, is to describe the history of values. The history of the Johnstones has been an effort to imagine, or to think oneself into the lives and the values of individuals in the past, on the basis of disparate kinds of evidence and information, which is also true information. This is an historical inquiry. But it is also a moral inquiry, at least in an eighteenth-century sense. Individuals made moral judgements, in Adam Smith's description, by surveying their own sentiments "with the eyes of other people, or as other people are likely to view them": by placing themselves in imagination in the situation of others. This was similar to the experience of reading history; we "transport ourselves in fancy to the scenes of those distant and forgotten adventures."[50] But it was also a description of the process by which moral values came into existence, in an endless exchange of observations or views between the interior and the exterior life, and between more or less distant individuals.

Smith was extraordinarily insistent, in *The Theory of Moral Sentiments*, on the figurative language of seeing: of eyes ("the eye of the mind") and of imagination (the "illusion of the imagination").[51] This is also the figurative language, or one of the languages, of history: Bartold Niebuhr's language, and the language of Elizabeth Caroline Johnstone Gray, the historian of the Etrurians. I have talked often about "evidence" and "information," and there is a very important sense in which historians aspire to the attributes of magistrates, with respect to intentions and truth. But historians have also aspired to the attributes of insight, of being able to see glimpses of distant and forgotten worlds, in "half-broken, tarnished, hideous things."[52] This sort of history of the inner life is Smithian, in the sense that it is an exercise in observing the moral sentiments of other people. It is Smithian, too, in that it is itself an exercise in moral observation, or in moral imagination.

ACKNOWLEDGMENTS

This book began with the Tanner Lectures on Human Values that I gave at Princeton University in April 2006, and I am grateful to Anthony Appiah, Steven Macedo, and the Tanner Committee for the invitation to give the lectures, to Jan Logan, to Dipesh Chakrabarty, Susan James, Fania Oz-Sulzberger, and Kathleen Wilson for exceptionally interesting comments, and to Jeremy Adelman, Hendrik Hartog, and Daniel Rodgers. Several friends have read the manuscript, and I am immensely grateful to Victoria Rothschild, Indrani Sen, Amartya Sen, Sunil Amrith, Shane Bobrycki, Johnny Grimond, Walter Johnson, Brigitta van Rheinberg, Charles Rosenberg, David Todd, and two reviewers for Princeton University Press for comments. I am most grateful to Sir Raymond and Lady Johnstone and to Lady Erskine-Hill for many conversations about the eighteenth-century Johnstones. I would like to thank Sunil Amrith, Caitlin Anderson, Bernard Bailyn, Chris Bayly, Sugata Bose, John Cairns, David Cannadine, Sophie Cartwright, Dipesh Chakrabarty, Linda Colley, Robert Darnton, Barun De, Philip Fisher, Durba Ghosh, Anthony Grafton, the late Simon Gray, Ranajit Guha, Hendrik Hartog, Walter Johnson, Colin Kidd, Philipp Lehmann, Susan Manning, Gabriel Paquette, Nicholas Phillipson, Bhavani Raman, Lisbet Rausing, Daniel Rodgers, Charles Rosenberg, Victoria Rothschild, Elaine Scarry, Indrani Sen, Amartya Sen, Gareth Stedman Jones, Julia Stephens, David Todd, and Robert Travers for many helpful conversations. Shane Bobrycki, Sophie Cartwright, Aditya Balasubramanian, Mary-Rose Cheadle, Rachel Coffey, Justine Crump, Leigh Denault, Geoff Grundy, Ian Kumekawa,

Philipp Lehmann, Inga Huld Markan, Giles Parkinson, Pedro Ramos-Pinto, Amy Price, Rosie Vaughan, Kirsty Walker, and others associated with the Joint Center for History and Economics have lived with the eighteenth-century Johnstones for almost a decade and have helped tremendously in the preparation of the book. I am most grateful to Crayton Scott Walker of Harvard University Library for preparing the maps. The book is an extended exploration of archives, and I am exceptionally grateful to the staff of the archives where I have worked in the course of preparing the book, and especially to the staff of the Archives Nationales in Paris, the Burdwan (Bardhaman) Old Record Office in West Bengal, the Bedfordshire and Luton Archives, the Beinecke Library of Yale University, the Bentpath Library in Dumfries and Galloway, the Bristol University Library, the British Library, the Cambridge University Library Manuscript Room, the Clackmannanshire Archives in Alloa, the Edinburgh University Library Rare Books Room, the Glasgow City Archives, the Glasgow University Library, the Houghton Library of Harvard University, the Huntington Library in San Marino, the London Metropolitan Archives, the Massachusetts Historical Society, the National Archives in Kew, the National Archives of Scotland, in Register House and in West Register House, the National Library of Scotland Manuscripts Room, the Norfolk Record Office, the Oriental and India Office Collections of the British Library, the Perth and Kinross Council Archives, the Pierpont Morgan Library in New York City, and the Wren Library in Trinity College, Cambridge. I am also grateful to the staff of the Advocates' Library in Edinburgh, the William L. Clements Library of the University of Michigan, the Cheshire Record Office, the Cumbria

Record Office, the Hertfordshire Archives, the Public Records Office of Hong Kong, the North Yorkshire County Record Office, the Royal Society of Medicine, the Signet Library in Edinburgh, the Wellcome Library, and the City of Westminster Archives for providing copies of and information about documents. Professor Robert E. Lewis of the University of Michigan was extraordinarily helpful in relation to the Minto papers in the Clements Library. Parts of the book have been presented at the American Society of Legal History, the University of Chicago, Edinburgh University, the Harvard Law School, the Humanities Center at Harvard University, New York University, the University of California at Berkeley, and the University of Cambridge, and I am most grateful for helpful comments. I thank Sir Raymond Johnstone for permission to quote from the Johnstone of Alva Papers in the Clackmannanshire Archives, the Huntington Library for permission to quote from the papers of William Pulteney, the owners of the James Townsend Oswald papers for permission to quote from the Oswald papers, the Duke of Buccleuch for permission to quote from the papers of the Montague-Douglas-Scott Family, Dukes of Buccleuch, on deposit in the National Archives of Scotland.

APPENDIX

CHILDREN OF JAMES JOHNSTONE AND BARBARA MURRAY

William, b. 1720 [d. 1720]

Elizabeth, b. 1721 [d. 1721]

Henrietta, b. 1722 [d. 1722]

Barbara, b. 1723 d. 1765 m. Charles Kinnaird
> children: George, Patrick, Elizabeth, Helen, Margaret

Margaret, b. 1724 d. 1757 m. David Ogilvie
> children: Margaret, David

James, b. 1726 d. 1794 m. Louisa Meyrick
> children: Ann Scott [with ——], James Murray Johnstone [with Jean Swanston]

Alexander, b. 1727 d. 1783
> child: Jane Castino [with ——]

Elizabeth, b. 1728 d. 1813

William, b. 1729 d. 1805 m. 1, Frances Pulteney, 2, Margaret Stuart
> child: Henrietta Laura Pulteney (with Frances Pulteney)

George, b. 1730 d. 1787 m. Charlotte Dee
> children: [John], George Lindsay, James Primrose, Sophia, Alexander Patrick (with Martha Ford); John Lowther (with Charlotte Dee)

Charlotte, b. 1732 d. 1773 m. James Balmain
> children: Caroline, [John], George

John, b. 1734 d. 1795 m. Elizabeth Carolina Keene
      children: James Raymond, Anne Elizabeth
Patrick, b. 1737 d. 1756
Gideon, b. 1739 d. 1788 m. Fanny Colquitt

Abbreviations

AN-Col.	Archives Nationales, France-Colonies
BL	British Library
BUL-W	Bristol University Library, West India Papers
EUL	Edinburgh University Library
EUL-L	Edinburgh University Library, Laing Manuscripts
FHA-NRO	Norfolk Record Office, Folkes of Hillington Mss. (Additional)
GCA	Glasgow City Archives
GUL	Glasgow University Library
GUL-PC	Glasgow University Library, Special Collections, Copy Letter Book, Patrick Colquhoun
HL-P	Huntington Library, San Marino, CA, Papers of William Pulteney
JA-CLA	Johnstone of Alva Papers, Clackmannanshire Archives, Alloa
JJLB-CLA	John Johnstone Letter Book 1767–71, Johnstone of Alva Papers, Clackmannanshire Archives
JJLB-EUL	James Johnstone Letter Book 1770–74, Edinburgh University Library
KR-PKA	Kinnaird Family, Rossie Muniments, Perth and Kinross Council Archives, Perth
MHS	Massachusetts Historical Society
NAS	National Archives of Scotland
NAS(WRH)	National Archives of Scotland, West Register House
NAS-SR	National Archives of Scotland, Papers of the Sinclair family, Earls of Rosslyn
NLS	National Library of Scotland

ODNB	*Oxford Dictionary of National Biography* (Oxford, 2004– 10), online ed., http://www.oxforddnb.com
OIOC	Oriental and India Office Collection, British Library
PH	Parliamentary History
TNA	National Archives, United Kingdom
UMWCL	William L. Clements Library, University of Michigan
UMWCL-MS	William L. Clements Library, University of Michigan, Minto-Skelton Collection
WJM-Y	Osborn Mickle Papers, Beinecke Library, Yale University
WP-BLA	Wrest Park (Lucas) Manuscripts, Bedfordshire and Luton Archives

Notes

Introduction: Ideas and Sentiments

1. James Johnstone Letter Book 1770–74, Edinburgh University Library, Gen. 1734 [JJLB-EUL].

2. Elizabeth Carolina Keene, *Miscellaneous Poems* (London, 1762), pp. 10, 105.

3. "Petition for Bell or Belinda a Black Girl," September 13, 1771, National Archives of Scotland [NAS], High Court of Judiciary Processes Main Series, 1771, JC26/193/3; John W. Cairns, "Knight, Joseph (*b. c.*1753)", *Oxford Dictionary of National Biography* (Oxford, 2004–10), online ed., http://www.oxforddnb.com [ODNB], article 93749; and see below, chapter 2.

4. On English, Scottish, and French philosophers' ideas of empire, see Emma Rothschild, "Global Commerce and the Question of Sovereignty in the Eighteenth-Century Provinces," *Modern Intellectual History* 1, no. 1 (April 2004): 3–25; and see below, chapter 6.

5. Adam Ferguson, *Principles of Moral and Political Science; Being chiefly a Retrospect of Lectures delivered in the College of Edinburgh*, 2 vols. (Edinburgh, 1792), 1:268, 281.

6. The "age of revolutions" began in the 1740s, in contemporary descriptions, and lasted until the 1790s. "We live in an age of revolutions so sudden and surprising in all parts of Europe, that I question whether the like has ever been known before," in the Irish philosopher George Berkeley's description of 1742. Letter of March 5, 1742, to Isaac Gervais, in *The Works of George Berkeley*, 2 vols. (Dublin, 1784), 1:xcii. There was a "stupendous diversity of events and revolutions," the Persian-Bihari historian Ghulam Husain Khan Tabatabai wrote of the Mughal empire in the 1740s, in which "the materials of a revolution becoming daily more abundant, seemed now to be assembled in heaps." Seid-Gholam-Hossein-Khan, *The Seir Mutaqharin; Or, View of Modern Times, Being an History of India*, trans. Nota Manus, 3 vols. (Calcutta, 1789), 1:40, 281. On Gholam-Hossein or Ghulam Husain and his translator, Haji Mustafa or "Nota Manus," see Kumkum Chatterjee, "History as Self-Representation: The Recasting of a Political Tradition in Late Eighteenth-Century Eastern India," *Modern Asian Studies* 32, no. 4 (October 1998): 913–48; and Robert Travers, *Ideology and Empire in Eighteenth-Century India: The British in Bengal* (Cambridge, 2007), pp. 141–42, 225–29. On the new empires of the times, see below, chapter 4, and C. A. Bayly, *Imperial*

Meridian: The British Empire and the World, 1780–1830 (London, 1989) and P. J. Marshall, *The Making and Unmaking of Empires: Britain, India, and America c. 1750–1783* (Oxford, 2005).

7. See E. A. Wrigley, *People, Cities and Wealth: The Transformation of Traditional Society* (Oxford, 1987) and Jan De Vries, *The Industrious Revolution: Consumer Behavior and the Household Economy, 1650 to the Present* (Cambridge, 2008).

8. See Emma Rothschild, *Economic Sentiments: Adam Smith, Condorcet and the Enlightenment* (Cambridge, MA, 2001).

9. Speech of James Johnstone of February 1, 1785, proceedings in the House of Commons relating to the Westminster Scrutiny, *The Parliamentary History of England, from the Earliest Period to the Year 1803*, 36 vols. (London, 1806–20) [PH] vol. 25, col. 124; speech of Alexander Wedderburn of May 10, 1773, debate in the House of Commons on General Burgoyne's Motions relating to the Conduct of Lord Clive in India, PH, vol. 17, col. 865; and see below, chapter 4.

10. David Hume, *Enquiries concerning the Human Understanding and concerning the Principles of Morals* (Oxford, 1962), p. 228.

11. Extract, Process Joseph Knight against Sir John Wedderburn of Ballendean Bart., 1774, NAS, CS235/K/2/2, p. 8.

12. On the new men of the Roman Empire, see Ronald Syme, *The Roman Revolution* (Oxford, 1939). On the Johnstones' and their friends' own Roman references, see below, chapter 4.

13. Carlo Ginzburg and Carlo Poni, "Il nome e il come: Scambio ineguale e mercato storiografico," *Quaderni Storici* 40 (January–April 1979): 181–90, p. 187.

14. On the case study, see Carlo Ginzburg, *Clues, Myths, and the Historical Method* (Baltimore, 1989), Jacques Revel, "L'institution et le social," in *Les formes de l'expérience: Une autre histoire sociale*, ed. Bernard Lepetit, 63–84 (Paris, 1995), and Jean-Claude Passeron and Jacques Revel, "Penser par cas: raisonner à partir de singularités," in *Penser par cas*, ed. Jean-Claude Passeron and Jacques Revel, 9–44 (Paris, 2005).

15. There have been a number of important recent works in the microhistory of long-distance connections, including Natalie Zemon Davis, *Women on the Margins: Three Seventeenth-Century Lives* (Cambridge, MA, 1995), Durba Ghosh, *Sex and the Family in Colonial India: The Making of Empire* (Cambridge, 2006), Linda Colley, *The Ordeal of Elizabeth Marsh: A Woman in World History* (London, 2007), Miles Ogborn, *Global Lives: Britain and the World, 1550–1800* (Cambridge, 2008), Rebecca J. Scott, "'She . . . Refuses to Deliver Up Herself as the Slave of Your Petitioner': Émigrés, Enslavement, and the 1808 Louisiana Digest of the Civil Laws," *Tulane European and Civil Law Forum* 24

(2009): 115–36, and Margot Finn, "Slaves out of Context: Domestic Slavery and the Anglo-Indian Family, c. 1780–1830," *Transactions of the Royal Historical Society* 19 (2009): 181–203.

16. On the history of the law as a history not only of legal doctrines but also of "habits and dispositions revealed by law" and of "individuals caught in the web of the law," see Hendrik Hartog, *Man and Wife in America: A History* (Cambridge, MA: 2000), pp. 2, 5. On the history of economic life as a history of ideas and sentiments, see Emma Rothschild, "An Alarming Commercial Crisis in 18th Century Angoulême: Sentiments in Economic History," *Economic History Review* 51, no. 2 (May 1998): 268–93.

17. The new microhistory is late-modern in the sense that it has been made possible by the diversity of information now available about the eighteenth-century worlds of empire, and by the extraordinary expansion in access to this information as a consequence of new technologies of history. The technologies of looking for individuals by their names are literally unrecognizable—in a world of searchable databases and digitized archive catalogues—in comparison to the technologies of early twentieth-century Roman history, or of the mid-twentieth-century history of British parliaments, or even of the late twentieth-century history of individuals in early modern Italy. On the prosopography of the Roman empire, see Arnaldo Momigliano, "Ronald Syme, *The Roman Revolution*," *Journal of Roman Studies* 30, pt. 1 (1940): 75–80, and Glen Bowersock, "Ronald Syme, 1903–1989," *Proceedings of the British Academy* 84 (1994): 539–63. On Sir Lewis Namier's prosopography of eighteenth-century British politics, see Linda Colley, *Namier* (London, 1989). There is more evidence, of a more diverse kind, about different kinds of individuals—slaves and mistresses and itinerant tutors—in different and distant places. The technology of looking for words or expressions makes it possible to traverse—and in a sense to flatten—the distinctions between different kinds of printed texts (political and administrative, high or philosophical, and low or popular). The new historical evidence is disorderly in all sorts of respects. But it is full of possibilities for microhistory and for a history that is variable in size or scale, micro- to medium- to macro-, as the story and the evidence or the indications unfold.

18. Adam Smith, *Lectures on Rhetoric and Belles Lettres*, ed. J. C. Bryce (Oxford, 1983), p. 113.

19. Adam Smith's own lifelong study, in the account of his first biographer, Dugald Stewart, was of "human nature in all its branches, more particularly of the political history of mankind" and of the "natural progress of the human mind." Dugald Stewart, "Account of the Life and Writings of Adam Smith, LL.D" (1793), in Adam Smith, *Essays on*

Philosophical Subjects, ed. W.P.D. Wightman and J. C. Bryce (Oxford, 1980), pp. 271, 291–92, 295–96, 305, 314–15. On the philosophical histories of David Hume and William Robertson, and the Scottish "science of man" as a historical science, see Nicholas Phillipson, *Hume* (London, 1989), pp. 137–41, J.G.A. Pocock, *Barbarism and Religion: Narratives of Civil Government* (Cambridge, 1999), pp. 199–221, Rothschild, *Economic Sentiments*, chapter 1, and Nicholas Phillipson, *Adam Smith: An Enlightened Life* (London, 2010).

20. "Emotion," "sentiment," "passions," "idea," "imagination," "conception," "sensibility," "sensations," "impressions," "sense," and "sympathy." Adam Smith, *The Theory of Moral Sentiments*, ed. D. D. Raphael and A. L. Macfie (Oxford, 1976), p. 9. The word "sentiment" was defined, in the *Universal Dictionary* published in Edinburgh in 1763, as "thought; notion; opinion. The sense considered distinctly from the language or things." The word "idea" was defined as "mental imagination; object of perception." *An Universal Dictionary of the English Language, in which the Terms made use of in Arts and Sciences are defined* (Edinburgh, 1763), entries for "sentiment" and "idea," n.p.

21. Sir Walter Scott, "Introductory Epistle," in *The Fortunes of Nigel* (1822) (Edinburgh, 1863), p. xi.

22. Smith, *Theory of Moral Sentiments*, p. 110.

CHAPTER ONE. SETTING OUT

1. See Bayly, *Birth of the Modern World*.

2. The administrations of customs and excise were distinct in England and Scotland, following the union between the two kingdoms in 1707, and the old-established patterns of smuggling (French) brandy and other regulated commodities persisted into the nineteenth century. As Sir Walter Scott wrote in his notes to *Redgauntlet*, in 1824, "The neighbourhood of two nations having different laws, though united in government, still leads to a multitude of transgressions on the Border. . . . About twenty years since, as far as my recollection serves, there was along the frontier an organized gang of coiners, forgers, smugglers, and other malefactors." Scott, *Redgauntlet* (1824) (London, 1985), pp. 411–12.

3. John Macky, *A Journey Through Scotland*, 2nd ed. (London, 1729), p. 12; Daniel Defoe, *A Tour Thro' the Whole Island of Great Britain*, 3rd ed., 4 vols. (London, 1742), 4:103.

4. On the political consequences of the Act of Union, see Colin Kidd, *Union and Unionisms: Political Thought in Scotland, 1500–2000* (Cambridge, 2008), and Susan Manning, *Fragments of Union: Making Connections in Scottish and American Writing* (New York, 2002).

5. This was Lord Cockburn's description of Scotland in the 1790s. Cockburn, *An Examination of the Trials for Sedition Which Have Hitherto Occurred in Scotland*, 2 vols. (Edinburgh, 1888), 1:76.

6. Elizabeth Mure, "Some Remarks on the Change of Manners in My Own Time, 1700–1790," National Library of Scotland [NLS], Mure of Caldwell Papers, MS. 5003, 1r–16v; and see William Mure, ed., *Selections from the Family Papers preserved at Caldwell* (Glasgow, 1874), 1:260.

7. On the religious conflicts of the seventeenth and eighteenth centuries, see Kidd, *Union and Unionisms*; on the Jacobite movement, see Bruce Lenman, *The Jacobite Risings in Britain 1689–1746* (London, 1984).

8. On the "economic revolution" that preceded the industrial revolution, see Wrigley, *People, Cities and Wealth*. On the "industrious revolution," see De Vries, *Industrious Revolution*. On Scotland's relative backwardness until the late eighteenth century, see N. T. Phillipson and Rosalind Mitchison, eds., *Scotland in the Age of Improvement: Essays in Scottish History in the Eighteenth Century* (Edinburgh, 1996) and T. M. Devine, C. H. Lee and G. C. Peden, eds., *The Transformation of Scotland: The Economy since 1700* (Edinburgh, 2005).

9. Elizabeth Mure, "Some Remarks" and see William Mure, *Selections from the Family Papers*, 1:270.

10. On the expansion of Britain's overseas connections in the eighteenth century, see Marshall, *Making and Unmaking of Empires*, and T. M. Devine, *Scotland's Empire, 1600–1815* (London, 2003).

11. Smith, *Theory of Moral Sentiments*, pp. 183–84.

12. Estimates of slaves embarked by national flag and by broad disembarkation region, available on the Trans-Atlantic Slave Trade Database, at wilson.library.emory.edu:9090/tast/assessment/estimates.faces. On the Atlantic slave trade and the economic expansion of the eighteenth century, see Barbara L. Solow, ed., *Slavery and the Rise of the Atlantic System* (Cambridge, 1991), and Bernard Bailyn, "Considering the Slave Trade: History and Memory," *William and Mary Quarterly*, 3rd ser., 58, no. 1 (Jan. 2001): 245–52.

13. On the English East India Company in the eighteenth century, see Lucy S. Sutherland, *The East India Company in Eighteenth-Century Politics* (Oxford, 1952), Peter Marshall, *East Indian Fortunes: The British in Bengal in the Eighteenth Century* (Oxford, 1976), K. N. Chaudhuri, *The Trading World of Asia and the English East India Company, 1660–1760* (Cambridge, 1978), and H. V. Bowen, *The Business of Empire: The East India Company and Imperial Britain, 1756–1833* (Cambridge, 2006). On the French East India Company, see Henry Weber, *La compagnie française des Indes (1604–1875)* (Paris, 1904).

14. On the Indian conflicts of the eighteenth century, see Sanjay Subrahmanyam and Muzaffar Alam, *The Mughal State, 1526–1750* (Delhi, 1998), Sudipta Sen, *Empire of Free Trade: The East India Company and the Making of the Colonial Marketplace* (Philadelphia, 1998), Jon E. Wilson, *The Domination of Strangers: Modern Governance in Eastern India, 1780–1835* (Basingstoke, 2008), and Bayly, *Birth of the Modern World*.

15. *Observations on a Late State of the Nation* (1769), in *The Writings and Speeches of Edmund Burke*, ed. Paul Langford, 9 vols. (Oxford, 1981–2000), 2:175, 194–95.

16. On the Seven Years' War, see Fred Anderson, *A People's Army: Massachusetts Soldiers and Society in the Seven Years' War* (Williamsburg, VA, 1984) and Fred Anderson, *The Crucible of War: The Seven Years' War and the Fate of Empire in British North America, 1754–1766* (New York, 2000); on the British navy, see N.A.M. Rodger, *The Command of the Ocean: A Naval History of Britain, 1649–1815* (London, 2004). On the French army in the eighteenth century, see André Corvisier, *L'armée française de la fin du XVIIe siècle au ministère de Choiseul: Le soldat*, 2 vols. (Paris, 1964).

17. Letter of May 25, 1767, from David Hume to Trudaine de Montigny, in *New Letters of David Hume*, ed. Raymond Klibansky and Ernest C. Mossner (Oxford, 1969), p. 235.

18. "The revolution of 1757 was the foundation and the model of all the subsequent revolutions" (or at least of the revolutions in India), one of the Johnstones' friends said in the House of Commons in 1773. Speech of Colonel Burgoyne, reported in Sir John Malcolm, *The Life of Robert, Lord Clive*, 3 vols. (London, 1836), 3:340.

19. See below, chapter 3.

20. Complaint of John Gibson, September 14, 1719, NAS, GD1/510/64. Clandestine and disorderly marriages included those that did not follow the established procedures of the Church of Scotland for the reading of banns on three successive Sundays. James Johnstone was liable to a prison sentence, which was waived, and to paying a fine of fifteen hundred pounds, based on the rank of Barbara's father. On the history of clandestine marriages in Scotland, see Leah Leneman and Rosalind Mitchison, "Clandestine Marriage in the Scottish Cities 1660–1780," *Journal of Social History* 26, no. 4 (Summer 1993): 845–61.

21. Letter of April 14, 1746, from Henry Home (later Lord Kames) to Sir James Johnstone, in *Letters of David Hume, and Extracts from Letters Referring to Him*, ed. Thomas Murray (Edinburgh, 1841), p. 57.

22. "The Testament Testamentar and Inventary of the debts and sums of mony . . . owing and adebted to the deceast Sir William Johnstone,"

dated October 5, 1727, and proved December 10, 1728, Dumfries Commissary Court, CC5/6/9, available at www.scotlandspeople.gov.uk. The title of baronet of Nova Scotia was granted by the British Crown to 297 Scottish families between 1625 and 1707, of which the Johnstones of Westerhall were the 265th, in 1699. Robert Beatson, *A Political Index to the Histories of Great Britain & Ireland*, 3 vols. (London, 1806), 3:70–77. The titles were associated initially with the colonization of Nova Scotia in modern Canada and later with royal revenues more generally. Sir Crispin Agnew, "Who were the Baronets of Nova Scotia?," *The Scottish Genealogist* 27, no. 3 (September 1980): 90–111. On the ancestry of the Johnstones, see C. L. Johnstone, *History of the Johnstones, 1191–1909, with Descriptions of Border Life* (Edinburgh, 1909), pp. 175–83.

23. On the family of Barbara Murray's father and mother, the 4th Lord Elibank and his wife Elizabeth Stirling, see John Burke, *A Genealogical and Heraldic Dictionary of the Peerage and Baronetage of the British Empire*, 14th ed. (London, 1852) p. 364, and Arthur C. Murray, *The Five Sons of "Bare Betty"* (London, 1936).

24. "A Character of the Hon. Dame Barbara Murray, as given in a sermon, from 2d. Sam. XIV.14 preached in her Ladyship's parish church soon after her death," undated, in NAS, GD477/440.

25. The Old Parish Register for Scotland, available through www.scotlandspeople.gov.uk, gives the following places and dates of birth or baptism for the children of James Johnstone and Barbara Murray: William, April 12, 1720 (Aberlady); Elizabeth, April 17, 1721 (Edinburgh); Henreta, August 31, 1722 (Edinburgh); Barbara, November 8, 1723 (Edinburgh); Margaret, November 6, 1724 (Edinburgh); James, January 23, 1726 (Edinburgh); Alexander, July 18, 1727 (Edinburgh); Elizabeth, September 8, 1728 (Edinburgh); William, October 19, 1729 (born), October 31, 1729 (baptised) (Edinburgh); George, December 5, 1730 (Edinburgh); Charlet, November 2, 1732 (Westerkirk); John, June 28, 1734 (Edinburgh); Patrick, July 12, 1737 (Westerkirk); Gideon, June 24, 1739 (Westerkirk). Barbara and James Johnstone's oldest three children, William, Elizabeth, and Henretta, appear to have died in infancy.

26. Letter of September 1, 1757, from James Johnstone to William Johnstone, Huntington Library, San Marino, CA, Pulteney Collection [HL-P], PU 564 [484]. The Pulteney letters have been classified twice and have both a "PU" number and an older number written in hand on the face of the letters; the older number, in what follows, is given in square brackets.

27. On the earlier Lady Kinnaird, who "wore pillows upon her belly," see William Anderson, *Speeches and Judgement upon the Douglas Cause*

(Edinburgh, 1768), p. 615, and John Burke, *Genealogical and Heraldic Dictionary*, p. 575. In the more celebrated Douglas case of the 1760s, in which William Johnstone was involved as a legal expert, Lady Jane Douglas, the sister of the Marquess of Douglas, was accused by Andrew Stuart, the friend of William, David Hume, and Adam Smith, of having purchased two infants in France, of whom one was brought up as the family's heir. See Ernest Campbell Mossner, *The Life of David Hume* (Edinburgh, 1954), pp. 550–52.

28. Charles Kinnaird and "Walter Scot, servant to Sir James Johnstone of Westerhall," were reported to have been arrested on November 27, 1745, and released on December 19, 1745. *St. James's Evening Post*, December 3, 1745, no. 5598 and December 24, 1745, no. 5607. The family stories "of Lord Kinnaird eating his commission in prison—Of Westerhall being a refuge for the fugitives & of Lady Ogilvie's escape"—were recounted by Betty Johnstone, many years later, to her great-niece Elizabeth Caroline Johnstone. Mrs. Hamilton Gray, "Sketch of My Life" (1833–67), Gray of Carntyne Papers, NLS, Acc. 8100, 155, unpag.

29. Letters of August 18, 1758, from Charles Kinnaird to William, and of August 28, 1758, from Barbara to William, HL-P, PU 767 [744] and 768 [745].

30. Letters of October 9, and 19, 1759, from Betty to William, HL-P, PU 405 [397], 406 [398].

31. *Lloyd's Evening Post*, no. 1298, November 1, 1765.

32. Letter of December 24, 1751, from George Churchill to the Duke of Newcastle, National Archives, Kew [TNA], SP54/41/289r.

33. *The Female Rebels: Being some Remarkable Incidents of the Lives, Characters, and Families of The Titular Duke and Dutchess of Perth, the Lord and Lady Ogilvie, and of Miss Florence M'Donald. Containing Several Particulars of these Remarkable Persons not hitherto published* (Edinburgh, 1747), pp. 43, 48.

34. Letter of November 25, 1746, from the Earl of Albemarle in Edinburgh to the Duke of Newcastle in London, TNA, SP54/34/130r–131r (30A), "Sir Peter Halkett's Examination of John Martin, Lady Ogilvie's Servant," TNA, SP54/34/134r–134v (30C), letter of December 15, 1746, from the Earl of Albemarle in Edinburgh to the Duke of Newcastle in London, TNA, SP54/34/195r–196r (42B); letter of January 10, 1747, from Henry Fox to the Earl of Albemarle, TNA, WO4/43/25r; and see the Rev. William Wilson, *The House of Airlie*, 2 vols. (London, 1924), 2:187–91.

35. Letter of March 29, 1749, from Margaret to Barbara Johnstone (her mother), Edinburgh University Library, Laing Manuscripts [EUL-L], La.II.502/12; letter of April 7, 1757, from William to Charles Kinnaird,

Kinnaird Family, Rossie Muniments Perth and Kinross Council Archives, Perth [KR-PKA], MS100/2, Bundle 48.

36. Letter of September 23, 1743, from Alexander Boswell to Sir James Johnstone (the father), Houghton Library, Harvard University, Ms. Hyde 52 (1).

37. Alexander Carlyle, *Autobiography of the Rev. Dr Alexander Carlyle Minister of Inveresk* (Boston, 1861), pp. 147–48.

38. Letter of early 1759 from Barbara (the mother) to George, EUL-L, La.II.73/71.

39. *The Historical and the Posthumous Memoirs of Sir Nathaniel William Wraxall 1772–1784*, ed. Henry B. Wheatley, 5 vols. (London, 1884), 3:404, 5:111.

40. Copy, in James's hand, of a letter of June 8, 1759, from James to William, Norfolk Record Office (NRO), NRS 8347 24D5.

41. Unsigned letter of February 23, 1759, to William, sent from Schenectady, New York, HL-P, PU 1790 [1839]; letter of January 29, 1763, from Anne Ferguson to General James Murray, NAS, GD32/24/14. The unsigned letter appears to be from William's friend, Colonel Simon Fraser; see the later undated letter from Fraser to William, apparently of 1775, HL-P, PU 270 [296], and Stuart Reid, "Fraser, Simon, Master of Lovat (1726–1782)", ODNB, article 10124.

42. Contract between Alexander Johnstone and Margaret Graeme of December 23–24, 1764, "An Abstract of the Title of Alexander Johnstone Esq. to a Plantation and Estate called the Baccaye," Joseph Banks, Lincolns Inn, included in mortgage documents of May 6, 1772; Bristol University Library, West India Papers [BUL-W], Westerhall Estate Papers, DM 41/31. There is an excellent account of Scottish property in the West Indies in Douglas J. Hamilton, *Scotland, the Caribbean and the Atlantic World, 1750–1820* (Manchester, 2005).

43. Letter of October 30, 1773, from Betty to William, HL-P, PU 435 [422].

44. Letter of January 19, 1752, from Adam Smith to James Oswald, in *The Correspondence of Adam Smith*, ed. E. C. Mossner and I. S. Ross, 2nd ed. (Oxford, 1987), p. 7.

45. Letter of April 26, 1759, from Patrick Murray, 5th Lord Elibank to William, HL-P, PU 1425 [220]; letter of January 19, 1752, from Adam Smith to James Oswald, in Smith, *Correspondence*, p. 7.

46. Letter of July 21, 1763, from David Hume to Adam Smith, in Smith, *Correspondence*, p. 90. The reference was to the Douglas case, discussed above.

47. William Pulteney was elected for the Perth Burghs and for Cromartyshire in 1768, and he represented Cromartyshire from 1768 to 1774.

From 1775 to 1805, he was Member of Parliament for Shrewsbury. Sir Lewis Namier and John Brooke, *The History of Parliament: The House of Commons 1754–1790*, 3 vols. (London, 1964).

48. Speech of Sir William Pulteney of February 28, 1805, debate in the House of Commons on the second reading of the Bill for the Abolition of the Slave Trade, *The Parliamentary Debates, from the Year 1803 to the Present Time, first series*, 41 vols. (London, 1812–20), vol. 3, col. 660, and see below, chapter 5.

49. "Obituary, with Anecdotes, of remarkable Persons," *Gentleman's Magazine* 75, pt. 1 (June 1805): 587–88.

50. George, who was baptised in December 1730, recalled in the House of Commons that "I first went to sea, in 1744." Speech of George Johnstone of March 22, 1779, debate in the House of Commons on Mr. Fox's motion of censure, PH, vol. 20. col. 343. "Historical Memoirs of Commodore George Johnstone," in J. Rolfe, *The Naval Biography of Great Britain*, 4 vols. (London, 1828), 1:364–73. George is the only one of the eleven Johnstones to have been written about in any detail, and his naval career is described in Robin F. A. Fabel's biography, *Bombast and Broadsides: The Lives of George Johnstone* (Tuscaloosa, 1987).

51. Martha Ford was the daughter of Richard and Martha Ford, and was christened in 1744 at the church of Saint Martin in the Fields, Westminster. Her mother, the older Martha Ford, who died in 1794, described herself in her will as the widow of "Richard Ford late of the Haymarket Auctioneer." She left bequests to her daughters, Martha and Ann Ford, and to her three grandsons and her granddaughter; to her grandson George Lindsay Johnstone she gave the diamond ring which "my late husband used to wear." Wills of Richard Ford, proved June 27, 1775, PROB 11/1008, and of Martha Ford, proved February 21, 1794, PROB 11/1241; dates of the christening of Ann and Martha Ford, www.family search.org.

52. *Letters of John Ramsay of Ochtertyre, 1799–1812*, ed. Barbara L. H. Horn (London, 1966), p. 295.

53. Postscript by Charlotte in a letter of February 22, 1758, from Betty to William, HL-P, PU 400 [392].

54. On the excise in eighteenth-century Britain and the presumed "hardness of character" of the excise officers, see Adam Smith, *An Inquiry into the Nature and Causes of the Wealth of Nations*, ed. R. H. Campbell and A. S. Skinner (Oxford, 1976), pp. 898–99.

55. Old Parish Register for Scotland, available at www.scotlandspeople .gov.uk.

56. *Public Advertiser*, April 13, 1773, no. 11862; letter of December 29, 1772, from John to William, HL-P, PU 658 [652].

57. "This day is published, Price 6d. Dido to Aeneas, from Ovid, By Miss Elizabeth Caroline Keene." *Public Advertiser*, April 4, 1758, no. 9, p. 4. The introduction to an earlier translation—of Horace's Ode to Xanthias Phoceas—described it as "the work of a very ingenious young Lady of fourteen years of age." "Imitation of Horace. By Miss Elizabeth Caroline Keene." *Lloyd's Evening Post and British Chronicle*, December 28–30 1757, no. 70, p. 558.

58. John died on December 10, 1795. *Oracle and Public Advertiser*, December 26, 1795, no. 19200.

59. Unsigned letter of August 15, 1751, from the family's (unnamed) tutor to William, marked "Dr G——," HL-P, PU 503 [517].

60. Petition of Patrick Johnstone to be admitted as a writer in the East India Company's settlements, British Library, Oriental and India Office Collection (OIOC), IOR/J/1/2/104–7. He was approved as a writer for Bengal on October 31, 1753. Minutes of the Court of Directors of the East India Company, October 31, 1753, OIOC, IOR/B/72, p. 490.

61. A Journal of the Proceedings of His Majesty's Ship the Adamant Kept by Captain Gidion Johnstone, TNA, ADM51/8, entries for June 8 and October 18, 1780, and June 23, 1781.

62. Will of Gideon Johnstone, dated February 19, 1786, proved July 4, 1788, TNA, PROB 11/1168. The marriage of "Gideon Johnston, Esq., commander of his majesty's ship the Adamant," to Miss Colquitt, eldest daughter of Scrope Colquitt, in Liverpool on March 13, 1780, was reported in *St. James's Chronicle*, March 18, 1780, no. 2968, and in *The New Annual Register, or General Repository of History, Politics, and Literature, For the Year 1780*, 3rd ed. (London, 1793), p. 84.

63. The will of Sir James Johnstone's father was an inventory of extremely complex debts. Testament of Sir William Johnstone, proved December 10, 1728, Dumfries Commissary Court, CC5/6/9. On the Johnstones of Westerhall as "successively employed as factors or otherwise on the affairs of the Earls and Marquises of Annandale," and on the Johnstones' grandfather, Sir William Johnstone, as "factor or commissioner," see Sir William Fraser, *The Annandale Family Book of the Johnstones, Earls and Marquesses of Annandale*, 2 vols. (Edinburgh, 1894), 2:354–55, 389.

64. Letters of March 29, 1746, and June 6, 1746, from David Hume to Sir James Johnstone, in *The Letters of David Hume*, ed. J.Y.T. Greig, 2 vols. (Oxford, 1969), 1:87, 93.

65. Murray, *Five Sons*, p. 22.

66. 20th May 1758 Attested Copy of Mrs Meyrick's Settlement on her Marriage with Captain Johnstone, NRO, NRS 8335 24D4, pp. 15–16.

67. The stipend of each of the five commissioners of the excise for Scotland was five hundred pounds in 1761. *The Court and City Kalendar: Or, Gentleman's Register, for the Year 1761* (London, 1761), pp. 224–25. James Balmain was appointed solicitor of excise in 1771, and commissioner of excise in 1785. *Middlesex Journal*, November 23, 1771, no. 414; *Public Advertiser*, July 1, 1785, no. 15945.

68. Letter of October 29, 1767, from Horace Walpole to Sir Horace Mann, in *Horace Walpole's Correspondence*, ed. W. S. Lewis, 48 vols. (New Haven, 1960), 22:560.

69. "Questions to Samuel Romilly Lincoln's Inn April 8 1799," BUL-W, Westerhall Estate Papers, DM 41/53/2.

70. Their mother "had a good taste for literature," one of William's acquaintances recalled, "which she encouraged and promoted amongst the intelligent Shepherds"; "a deputation of Shepherds waited on her Ladyship to ask her permission to rehearse a Prologue." "Memoir by Alexander Young regarding Sir William Pulteney," dated 1833 and 1837, NAS, GD214/163, p. 2. Alexander Young was William's lawyer and described him as "the best client I ever had" (pp. 4–5). Barbara Johnstone's taste for literature was, in his description, a family characteristic, "like all the family of Elibank" (p. 2). The parish minister, too, commented on her literary gifts: "It pleased God to endue her mind with quickness of apprehension, penetration, & clearness of understanding, with a rich & lively fancy: & these gifts of nature, improved by reflection, & extensive readg. & joined to an admirable power of elocution, she possessed in an uncommon degree." "A Character of the Hon. Dame Barbara Murray." On the education of the younger children, see the petition of John Johnstone to be admitted as a writer in the East India Company's settlements, read in court December 19, 1750, certification of Richard Hoge of October 3, 1750, presented with the petition, OIOC, IOR/J/1/1/151,154; certification of George Paterson, teacher of mathematics in Edinburgh, of June 28, 1753, presented with Patrick Johnstone's petition to be admitted as a writer in the East India Company's settlements, IOR/J/1/2/105; certification of William Brown of Edinburgh of October 3, 1764, presented with Gideon Johnstone's petition to be admitted as a writer in the East India Company's settlements, IOR/J/1/5/140.

71. Unsigned letter of August 15, 1751, to William, HL-P, PU 503 [517].

72. This was the description of the counsel for the London booksellers, in the celebrated legal case of 1774 about literary property; speech of Mr. Mansfield of May 13, 1774, proceedings in the House of Commons on the Booksellers' Copy-Right Bill, PH, vol. 17, col. 1099; and see below, chapter 5.

73. Letter of early 1759 from Barbara (the mother) to George, EUL-L, La.II.73/71.

74. "Inventory of the possessions of the late Sir James Johnstone, taken August 11 1797," "List of Books in the Library at Westerhall," NAS, CC8/8/130/1733–70. The total value of the books was estimated at fifty-five pounds, thirteen shillings, two pence, and many of the volumes were considered to be almost worthless: "Plato's works abridged first vol. wanting one volume two pence" or "The Cure of Diseases of Body & Mind one vol. fourpence."

75. Letter of December 7, 1749, from John Graham to Barbara Johnstone, EUL-L, La.II.73/58.

76. Letter dated "the last day of 1750" from Barbara (the mother) to William, HL-P, PU 497 [511].

77. Unsigned letter of August 15, 1751, to William, HL-P, PU 503 [517].

78. Letter of July 29, 1751, from Charlotte to William, HL-P, PU 450 [443].

79. "I am most sensible of Mr Smiths great Qualitys and the Advantages you have & must reap by his Company and therefore should be well satisfyed it Cou'd be Contrived you were together till October that he goes to Glasgow, where you Cou'd be masters of your Selves and might read what you thought proper—This I do not think Can be done at any Common goat whey quarter, and therefore I shou'd wish on that, & other accounts, he wou'd rather take up with the hamper'd accomodation this place affords, and come here immediately as the season is far advanced & there will be no goat whey after the middle of August—Mr Scot who continues here till the end of August has the Room off the drawing Room, So Mr Smith and [you?] Can have the two Rooms above Stairs and if Mr Wederburn cou'd Submit to be in the same room with you, he might Likewise be invited to come along, but as in this manner there will be no spare Room in the house you'll perceive there's no acomodating him otherwise till Mr Scot goes away." Letter of July 15, 1751, from James Johnstone (the father) to William, HL-P, PU 501 [515]. The visit was planned in advance; their father wrote to William in January 1751 that "Mr Smith will be most welcome here during the harvest vacance." Letter of January 14, 1750 [1751], from James Johnstone (the father) to William, HL-P, PU 496 [510].

80. Letter of May 1, 1758, from Betty to William, HL-P, PU 432 [420].

81. Unsigned letter of August 15, 1751, to William, HL-P, PU 503 [517].

82. "Memorand for Sandy May 1751," EUL-L, La.II.73/80.

83. Unsigned and undated letter from William to Sir James Johnstone, endorsed "Wm 25 feb 1752," EUL-L, La.II.73/65.

84. Letter of May 7, 1746, from Henry Seymour Conway to Horace Walpole, in Walpole, *Correspondence*, 37:245; on Margaret at the battle of Culloden in 1746 and the "led horse for her husband in case of accidents on the field," see J. Bernard Burke, *Family Romance; Or, Episodes in the Domestic Annals of the Aristocracy* (London, 1853), 2:265.

85. Letter of May 8, 1746, from Walter Johnstone in Inverness to Sir James Johnstone, *The Scottish Historical Review* 1, no. 4 (July 1904): 449–51, p. 450.

86. "Colonel Haldane is named Governor of Jamaica I have aply'd to him to accompany him either as Governor of any of the Forts or in any other way by this means I shall not only keep my Company but be certain of being appointed Collector of Jamaica on Tessels Death." Letter of September 1, 1757 from James to William, HL-P, PU 564 [484].

87. "To get a lether of Recomendation from Sir John Ligonier to the Engineer for Anapolis Royal that he may Employ me as an assist without Pay

One from Ld. Duplin to Governour Cornwallis to Employ me in any of the works that are carryd on at the Expence of the Colony

Ld. Halifax's letter of Recomendation

To wait on Colonel Lascelles in St. James's Street opposite Park Place

To wait on Col. Monkton uper Brook Street Right hand side of the way almost at the Head of it

On Mr. Calcraft Germain Street near the corner of Duke Street

On Col. Campbell to thank him for the letter He was so good as to promise to give me to Col. Cornwallis

a letter of recomendation from Sir Robt. Rich or any of the Family of the Riches to Col. Lawrence

one from Ld. George Sackville to Cornwallis."

"Memorand for Sandy May 1751," EUL-L, La.II.73/80.

88. Petition of John Johnstone to be admitted as a writer in the East India Company's settlements, read in court December 19, 1750, certification of Richard Hoge of October 3, 1750, presented with the petition, OIOC, IOR/J/1/1/151,154.

89. The security for Patrick's appointment was provided by Peter Leheup of St. George's Hanover Square and Alexander Grant of London, Merchant. Minutes of the court of directors of the East India Company, November 28, 1753, OIOC, IOR/B/72, p. 522. The brothers' maternal uncle Lord Elibank had apparently declined to provide security for Patrick. "I cannot get L. E to think of the East India scheme for Pate he [thinks] it impossible to be obtained I have views of bringing it about in

[another] way," William wrote to their father. Letter of February 25, 1752 from William to Sir James Johnstone, EUL-L, La.II.73/65.

90. Letter of September 15, 1755, from Patrick to William, HL-P, PU 713 [701]; H. James Rainey, *A Historical and Topographical Sketch of Calcutta*, ed. P. Thankappan Nair (Calcutta, 1986), p. 114, n. 131; petition of Gideon Johnstone to be admitted as a writer, OIOC, IOR/J/1/5/364.

91. Letter of June 9, 1757, from James to William, HL-P, PU 563 [483]; letter of early 1759 from Barbara (the mother) to George, EUL-L, La.II.73/71.

92. Elizabeth Mary Louisa Meyrick was described in her marriage settlement with James, dated May 20, 1758, as the widow of John Meyrick, late vicar of Edwinston in Nottinghamshire, and daughter of "Sir Thomas Jones Knight deceased by Dame Elizabeth Mary Louisa Jones his wife . . . mentioned to be the daughter of Sir Thomas Montgomerie late of the Kingdom of Ireland Knight by Dame Clemence Montgomerie his Wife." These apparently straightforward relationships were the manifestations of a remarkable sequence of matriarchies over more than a century. The drama began, as it can be reconstructed in the wills of Louisa Johnstone's ancestors, with Etheldred Hovell, the widow of Sir William Hovell of Hillingdon or Hillington in Norfolk, who died in 1683, leaving her estate to her three daughters, Clemence, the wife of Charles Stuart of Hampshire, Dorothy, the wife of Martin Folkes of Norfolk, and Etheldreda, who was unmarried at her mother's death, but later married William Wake, who became Archbishop of Canterbury, and who herself had six daughters. Clemence Stuart, later Clemence Montgomerie, was Louisa Johnstone's grandmother. Her marriage to Charles Stuart appears to have been unsuccessful, and she formed an attachment fairly early on to an Irish knight, Sir Thomas Montgomerie. She too had three surviving daughters—Elizabeth Mary Louisa, Clemence, and Dorothy—and a son, Hugh. In 1714, some years after Charles Stuart's death in 1706, she married Thomas Montgomerie, and her three daughters, as well as her son Hugh and another daughter who died young, were known by the name of "Montgomerie"; they are referred to in Sir Thomas Montgomerie's will and in Clemence Montgomerie's own will as "Elizabeth Mary Louisa commonly called Elizabeth Mary Louisa Montgomerie," "the child called Hugh Montgomerie," and "the children Clemence and Dorothy commonly called Clemence and Dorothy Montgomerie." Elizabeth Mary Louisa Montgomerie was Louisa Johnstone's mother. She was unmarried and an adult when she proved her mother's will as executrix in 1720. In 1721 she married Thomas Jones; in his will, which was proved on Janu-

ary 29, 1731, he left his estate to his wife Elizabeth Mary Louisa, together with a bequest of fifty pounds to a child by an earlier marriage or relationship, described as "my unhappy son." Louisa Johnstone's mother then "intermarried," as recounted in Louisa's own marriage settlement, with an Anthony Reynolds of Huntingdonshire. It was the children of all these resilient women who constituted Louisa Johnstone's immediate family, and who played an important role over more than half a century in the lives of the Johnstones and in the administration of their distant estates. Copy of Mrs Meyrick's Settlement on her Marriage with Captain Johnstone, NRO, NRS 8335 24D4; wills of Dame Etheldred Hovell, proved February 13, 1684, of Sir Thomas Montgomerie, proved April 10, 1716, of Dame Clemence Montgomerie, proved October 19, 1720, and of Sir Thomas Jones, proved January 29, 1731; TNA, PROB 11/377, 11/551, 11/576, and 11/642. The date of the marriage of Thomas Jones and Elisabeth Louisa Mary Montgomery in London was April 26, 1721; www.familysearch.org. Louisa Johnstone, like James Johnstone, was buried in Westminster Abbey, and the nineteenth-century scholar of the Abbey registers, Joseph Chester, made a resolute effort to investigate her early life, but concluded that "there was a considerable mystery about her antecedents which it has been somewhat difficult to solve." Joseph Lemuel Chester, ed., *The Marriage, Baptismal, and Burial Registers of the Collegiate Church or Abbey of St. Peter, Westminster* (London, 1876), p. 458, n. 4.

93. Letter of August 9, 1758, from Barbara (the mother) to William, HL-P, PU 1789 [541]. Louisa received the news of her husband's death on February 18, 1758; her marriage settlement with James was dated May 20, 1758. In January 1759, James wrote to his mother about sending a man from Norfolk to sow turnip seeds at the family home in Westerhall, and lamented that "My Affairs suffer immensly, and what vexes me more, I am afraid it will kill Mrs Johnstone." Letter of January 19, 1759, from James to Barbara (the mother), HL-P, PU 565 [485]. Louisa Jones appears to have married John Meyrick in December 1739 and to have separated from him a little over a year later. A bill from her lawyer, Edmund Lacon, dated May 25, 1756, in the Norfolk Record Office, refers to the costs incurred in preparing a "Fair copy of your Marriage articles dated 13th December 1739" and "The Like of the Deed Poll of the 11th January 1741 Executed by Mr Meyrick as a provision for your Separate Maintenance." There is also a reference to a bond of the same date of a Mr. Anthony Reynold, who was presumably the husband of Louisa's mother, "to Indemnify him against your Debts." In 1754 Louisa inherited a part of the estate of her grandmother Lady Montgomerie,

consisting of a property in Norfolk, near the family estate of the Hovells, which was now owned by the descendants of her great-aunt Dorothy (Hovell) Folkes. The property came to her following the deaths of her mother, her mother's brother Hugh Montgomerie, Hugh Montgomerie's two young sons, and his widow, who had meanwhile remarried to a man called Colclough; it was subject to two legacies of five hundred pounds each to her two aunts, Clemence (Montgomerie) Reynolds and Dorothy (Montgomerie) Lyons. Joseph Chester wrote that Louisa "appears to have been a daughter of a Mr. Colclough," an attribution reproduced in Namier and Brooke's *History of Parliament*. But "Colclough," it seems, was the name of her uncle's widow's second husband, the widow upon whose death she inherited the Norfolk estate. Chester, *Marriage, Baptismal and Burial Registers*, p. 458, n. 4; Namier and Brooke, *History of Parliament*, 2:685. The estate was valuable—the lawyers for her aunt Dorothy's husband estimated it to be worth "upwds of £10000"—and it became the subject of litigation of a sort worthy of *Bleak House*, concerning the date from which interest should have been paid on the legacies by Louisa to her aunts. The Rev. Meyrick also attempted to claim a part of the estate but agreed to "accept £60 a year for his life and thereupon to Relinquish all his Right and Tithe to the said Estate on your giving up your Right to the separate Maintenance." It was Edmund Lacon, Louisa's lawyer, who announced her husband's death to her, in an extraordinary letter sent from Gray's Inn on February 18, 1758: "Dear Madam, if you are in ye land of ye Living, I beg leave to inform you of two memorable Events: First: Your Cause is heard, and you are to pay Interest for the two 500 £ Legacys, only from the death of ye jointress (namely) from the 6th February 1754 at 4 per Cent Second: That I this day received a message from your old Sweetheart (Mr Travers) that Mr. Rob. Meyrick had just been with him & informed him that he had received a Letter out of Nottinghamshire with an account that your poor dear Husband departed this Life, on Monday last & was to be buryed last Wednesday. Alas poor dear Soul. So now you are a fine young widow: But to be serious a little: I must look into ye deeds of [illegible] 1754 & if there is nothing there that debars you (as I think there is not) Methinks you will then come into a Share (Half) of his personal Estates if he left any worth looking after, provided he dyed without a Will which is very likely he did, but that must be inquired into. These two important matters will (I hope) call you from your Retirement to ye Metropolis to shine away in your weeds. For you look extremely well in Mourning. I shd have waited upon you at Xmas, had you signifyed that it wd have been agreeable, but from yr total Silence I lookt upon it otherwise: Give me Leave to wish you Joy on these two Occasions & to subscribe myself (as I really am) Madam your most obedient and faithful [illegible] Edm. Lacon 18th Feb: 1758 Gray's Inn I hope you will receive this safe as it is not Frank't." It was this letter that precipitated Louisa and James Johnstone's marriage; it is superscribed, in Louisa's hand, "My Dr J.J. Monday febr. 27th 1758." The "Cause" was the litigation over Louisa's grandmother's estate and the interest owed to her aunts; the person referred to as "your old sweetheart" was Louisa's late husband's lawyer, who is mentioned in Edmund Lacon's bill. Louisa was meanwhile also in debt to a Henry Dickanson, a London surgeon, to whom she took out a bond, on April 15, 1758, that she was "held and firmly bound" with respect to a mortgage of six hundred pounds. Lacon appears in the Norfolk Record Office documents as a most sinister figure. His bill of May 25, 1756, in the careful hand of a clerk, is a model of the unreformed Gray's Inn: "My fee and trouble," six shillings and eightpence, "Duty and parchment," three pounds and six shillings, "paid for a Box to send the Writings in to be executed by Mr Meyrick in Nottinghamshire," one shilling and eightpence, "gave my clks on this Occasion as you desired," one guinea, and so forth. Then there are the importunate letters in his own hand, addressed to the "Fairest of ye Universe," and "my Dear Love," full of complaints—"Can you be (so refinedly) delicate that you won't write to a man?"—and elaborate compliments— "I have now read your charming Letter 28 times over, I like it, as I do Milton,—ye more I read him, the more I admire, and so it is with your fair Epistle," or, "I've read [it] over, oftner than I ever read any single page in Coke (tho' I frequently did read him some time agoe)." One of the lawyers for Louisa's opponents meanwhile wrote to James, soon after his and Louisa's marriage, to inform him that "a Client of Mr Lacon has a Mortgage on the Estate & that Mr Lacon will not let the [new owner] have the title deeds, if all Sollrs. were to proceed in this method not any Mortgage can be assigned to another, I think Mr Lacon acts in a very particular way." "Mr Lacon's Bill," May 25, 1756, Trinity Term 1754, pp. 1–2, Michaelmas Term 1754, p. 1, NRO, NRS 8349 24D5; bond of April 15, 1758 between Elizabeth Mary Louisa Meyrick and Henry Dickanson, NRO, NRS 8119 24B6; letters of November 9, [1754], December 7, [1754], and February 18, 1758, from Edmund Lacon to Louisa Meyrick, NRO, NRS 8349 24D5; three opinions on the case of Dame Clemence Montgomerie's will, one dated January 21, 1750, one dated July 15, 1755, and one undated, Duncombe Family Papers, Hertfordshire Archives and Local Studies, DE/B664/T13, DE/B664/29595, and DE/B664/29630.

94. Letter of August 18, 1758, from Alexander Wedderburn to William, Pierpont Morgan Library, New York City, Pulteney Collection, vol.

17, 951. It is possible that the "Miss Mendez" of the broken engagement was the same "Miss Mendez" or "Miss Mendes" who was a poet and novelist and wrote a well-known poem to Horace Walpole. Jael Henrietta Mendez married John Neil Campbell in 1762 and was remarried after his death to Robert Hampden Pye. Her collected poems, published in 1772, included a poem dated 1758 on the subject of blighted love. "Too soon we parted, and too soon I fear, / Thy vows of love to me forgotten all, / Another claims the heart that once was mine." *Poems, by Mrs. Hampden Pye*, 2nd ed. (London, 1772), pp. 36–38, 43; *London Chronicle*, February 25, 1762, no. 807; *London Magazine*, September 1766, p. 492; and see Tamar Hodes, "Pye, Jael Henrietta (1737?–1782)," ODNB, article 72235.

95. Letter of April 26, 1759, from Patrick Murray, 5th Lord Elibank to William, HL-P, PU 1425 [220].

96. His father wrote to him in 1751 with considered advice about the choice of the person to whom his thesis should be dedicated, and recommended the Duke of Queensberry: "your mother thinks some such compliment as the Inclosed will be fitt to be wrote to him. Pray don't forget the Morum Suavitas So conspicuous in his Character." William responded with a more elaborate strategy: "I went with L. E [their uncle, Lord Elibank] to call for the D. of Q who received me barely with Civility & spoke nothing at all of my dedication. I shall call of him again but I intend to get myself recommended to the Dutchess which is more material I am told. I think I could do a vast deal in the way of recommending myself to people here [presumably in London] especially to the Scotch if I stay for a month or two longer. . . . I intend to recommend myself as much as I can to Mr M—— that would be of more consequence than almost the whole Kingdom besides." Letter of June 21, 1751, from Sir James Johnstone (the father) to William, HL-P, PU 498 [512]; letter of February 25, 1752, from William to Sir James Johnstone, EUL-L, La. II.73/65.

97. Letters of October 31, 1767, from James Johnstone (the father) and of November 3, 1767, from Andrew Stuart to William, HL-P, PU 556 [569] and 1977 [1644]; and see M. J. Rowe and W. H. McBryde, "Pulteney, Sir William, fifth baronet (1729–1805)," ODNB, article 56208.

98. On the Seven Years' War, see Fred Anderson, *Crucible of War*.

99. Letters of November 25, 1746, and December 15, 1746, from the Earl of Albemarle in Edinburgh to the Duke of Newcastle in London, TNA, SP54/34/130r–131r (30A) and SP54/34/195r–196r (42B); letter of January 10, 1747, from Henry Fox to the Earl of Albemarle, TNA, WO4/43/25r. Margaret Ogilvie had been imprisoned on a warrant from

the Lord Justice Clerk, the Scottish law officer; Lord Albemarle, the British military commander, wrote to the Duke of Newcastle that "the Lord Justice Clerk has promised me to issue out warrants to take up Miss Hepburn, Mr Johnstone and Miss Johnstone, the Lady's Brother & Sister, who assisted her on this occasion" (SP54/34/131r). There is no indication in the correspondence about which of Margaret's brothers and sisters were involved or whether they were ever arrested. Lord Albemarle was not convinced by the zealousness of the Scottish law officers: "I hope the Lord Justice Clerk & Lord Advocate will do their duty in discovering and detecting those under their Jurisdiction that have aided & abetted her Ladyship in getting off." But he was by then desperate to leave Scotland, as he wrote in the same letter to the Duke of Newcastle: "[I] cannot help wishing that your Grace would intercede in my favour that some person might be named soon to relieve me, for no English man can wish to be in Scotland above a twelvemonth together." Letter of December 15, 1746, from the Earl of Albemarle to the Duke of Newcastle, SP54/34/196r–196v (42B). In the court-martial with respect to Margaret's escape, held on December 5, 1746, a Lieutenant Leonard Hewitson was sentenced to be cashiered and an Ensign William Robertson to be suspended for three months; the King confirmed the sentence against Robertson and pardoned Hewitson. Letter of January 10, 1747, from Henry Fox to the Earl of Albemarle, TNA, WO4/43/25r.

100. Letter of March 29, 1749, from Margaret to Barbara Johnstone (her mother), EUL-L, La.II.502/12.

101. Letter of August 1, 1749, from Margaret Ogilvie in France to Viscountess Kenmure, EUL-L, La.II.502.

102. In the description of one of the British government's intelligence officers, "she comes home with Child, in order to be delivered here, to the End, that her Child may be a Naturally born Subject." The government's lawyers were unsuccessful in locating the records of her earlier prosecution for "treasonable practices." "I have sent a fitt Person to the Castle of Edinburgh to have obtain'd a Copy of the Warrant of her Commitment, which it seems has not been preserv'd or is not to be found there," William Grant wrote. Letter of September 17, 1751, from William Grant to the Lord Advocate, TNA, SP54/41/150r–150v.

103. Letter of April 17, 1757, from Charles Kinnaird to William, HL-P, PU 765 [768]. The letter crossed with a letter from William in which he wrote that "Lady Ogilvy died at Paris the beginning of Last month having been ill some time before of a consumption. The first intimation I had of this melancholy event was by the Tuesdays news paper but it is now confirmed by Private letters. You will take the most prudent method of communicating this to my sister. I am extremely shocked

with it. It is very extraordinary that we never heard of her illness." Letter of April 7, 1757, from William to Charles Kinnaird, KR-PKA, MS100/2, Bundle 48.

104. Letter of early 1759 from Barbara (the mother) to George, EUL-L, La.II.73/71, citing an earlier letter from Gideon to Charlotte.

105. On the British navy and the system of prize money, see Rodger, *Command of the Ocean*, and on George's disputes of 1758, see Fabel, *Bombast and Broadsides*, pp. 5–6.

106. Copy, in George's hand, of a letter of November 24, 1759, from George to General Francis Murray, NAS GD32/24/11; the letter is a recommendation for a Captain Oswald, the brother of James Oswald of Dunnikier, to whom Adam Smith had recommended William in 1752.

107. Letter of October 2, 1759, from George to William, HL-P, PU 467 [450]. On the fishing vessels and privateers, see letters of February 18, 1761, and August 9, 1761, from George to William, HL-P, PU 469 [453] and 470 [454].

108. Letter of May 7, 1759, from Charles Kinnaird to William, HL-P, PU 774 [750].

109. Letters of October 9 and 19, 1759, from Betty to William, HL-P, PU 405 [397], 406 [398]. The arbitration that settled the alimony payable to Barbara was by Alexander Boswell of Auchinleck (who was James Boswell's father). It referred to "questions of a nature extreamly delicate" and concluded that the causes of the separation "were such as made that proceeding however disagreeable, proper and expedient." "Decreet Arbitral betwixt Charles Lord Kinnaird and Barbara Lady Kinnaird" of 1760, NAS, GD137/2833, pp. 3–5.

110. Letter of October 19, 1759, from Betty to William, HL-P PU 406 [398].

111. "My Dearest Sr what shall I say to you—how dare tell you the fresh Misfortune I have brought Uppon You—to tell you I am frightend to Deaths Door, is Small Recompence for what you will Suffer. . . . on all sides I am persecuted—& oh—what must I expect to hear from you on receipt of this—yet Sr I am—the person—who am already distressd—& Depressd—on the Spot—yet on me the Additional weight falls—indeed—the sharpest—to acquaint you of all," Louisa wrote to James on July 17, 1759. The crisis was precipitated by the continuing litigation over the two legacies of five hundred pounds in Louisa's grandmother's will, in the course of which Louisa's cousins secured an order from the chancery court to take both Louisa and James into custody: "oh God how shall I tell you but—I must—that they would send down a Serjant at Arms—to take you into custody & bring you up by force. . . . I told them you was a capt on Duty in the kings Service—they said was you a

Colonell they would seize you at the Head of your Regt." Letter of July 17, 1759, from Louisa to James, NRO, NRS 8348 24D5.

112. Letter of July 18, 1759, from James to Louisa; NRO, NRS 8194 24C2. This is in a bundle of letters marked "private letters of no consequence," in which James also described his hopes for a lieutenancy, for entering parliament, and for finding a lead mine in the Glendinning hills. Letters of June 17, July 18, and December 2, 1759, from James to Louisa, NRO, NRS 8194 24C2.

113. "I would advise that Sheens Lochmaben and the Houses in Edinr should be directly sold to what purpose keep them an Instant If those will not pay Ld. E. [Lord Elibank, their father's creditor and their mother's brother] let Bentheath be added and a hill or two more if the whole was sold I should for my Part like it better it would make my Father easier," James wrote to William in June 1759. "Is there any Dishonesty any Trick any Fraud in this? None I am sure. But perhaps a Crazzy Rocking house that labours with the least Puff of Wind worse than a Ship in a Storm surrounded with Trees and Rooks Nests under which my ancestors on their Hams have shit beararsed in all weathers ought to be preffered by one fill'd with a True Scotian Pride and a Proper Family Spirit to Beauty Elegance and Interest. If this is my crime I plead guilty I may be pitied as dead and insensible to that Noble Hereditary Clannish Enthusiasm that I willingly could submit to; but should be sorry to raise Abhorrence far less Resentment in the Breast of any Good Man and much more Ld. E." Copy, in James's hand, of a letter of June 8, 1759, to William; and on the quarrel, see also letters of March 10 and July 5, 1759, from William to George; NRO, NRS 8347 24D5. The bundle of letters includes an undated note from James in which he explains that the letter about the English and Scottish estates was written "at the Instigation of William." "The use William made of this Letter was not to show it to Ld. E. for whose Perusal it was wrote but to send it to my Dearest Father with the Opinion he had of me and his Advise to disinherit me and give the Remnant of the Estate to Him My Worthy Father sent me William Letter to Him and This Letter of Mine to William with His Paternal Advise to trust William in Time coming with as few of My Secrets as possible. . . . I would have destroyed the Letter but think it fairer that the Letter and the Reason of it and above all the Beautiful Behaviour of my Dearest Father should be known to his Posterity." Undated note by James, NRO, NRS 8347 24D5.

114. "A View of the Monument Erected at Calcutta, Bengal," in John Zephaniah Holwell, *India Tracts* (London, 1774), frontispiece; *The Military History of Great Britain, for 1756, 1757* (London, 1757), p. 84. On the period of John's and other East India Company officials' imprison-

ment in the French factory in Dhaka (Dacca), see the letter of July 18, 1756, from Richard Becher and others to the court of directors of the East India Company, in T. Raychaudhuri, ed., *Indian Records Series: Fort William–India House Correspondence*, 21 vols. (Delhi, 1949–85), 1:1030. On the history of the legend of the "black hole," see Brijen K. Gupta, *Sirajuddaulah and the East India Company, 1756–1757: Background to the Foundation of British Power in India* (Leiden, 1966), pp. 70–80.

115. Letter of June 9, 1757, from James to William, HL-P, PU 563 [483].

116. Letters of September 11, 1759, October 9, 1759, October 19, 1759, and May 30, 1760, from Betty to William, HL-P, PU 404 [396], 405 [397], 406 [398], 408 [400].

117. Letter of February 22, 1758, from Betty to William, HL-P, PU 400 [392]. Walter Johnstone was the half-brother of Sir James Johnstone, born in 1715 to "Sir William Johnston and Julian Meikle his lady." Westerkirk Parish Records, Old Parish Register, available at www .scotlandspeople.gov.uk. Only two of Sir William Johnstone's sons— James, the father of the brothers and sisters who are the subject of this book, and his younger brother John, who died in 1741—were listed in the records of the Scottish gentry; they were the sons of Henrietta Johnstone of Sheens. See Edmund Lodge, *The Genealogy of the Existing British Peerage and Baronetage* (London, 1859) p. 729; William Anderson, *The Scottish Nation*, 3 vols. (Edinburgh, 1867), 2:579. Walter was mentioned in Sir William Johnstone's will as "Walter Johnstone his son," together with another son, Archibald. Testament of Sir William Johnstone, proved December 10, 1728, Dumfries Commissary Court, CC5/6/9. "Archibald Johnstone natural son to James Johnstone" was baptised in Dumfries in 1706. St. Mungo Parish Records, Old Parish Register, available at www.scotlandspeople.gov.uk. A printed document prepared in 1794 stated that Sir William Johnstone "was married a second Time to *Giles Meikle,* by whom he had two sons, *Archibald* and *Walter.*" *Case of Sir James Johnstone, Baronet, claiming the titles, honours and dignities of Marquis and Earl of Annandale* (n.p., [1794]), NLS, Adv. MS.25.8.31, p. 5.

118. Letter of February 24, 1761, from Gideon to William, HL-P, PU 490 [476].

119. Letter of October 29, 1759, from Betty to William, HL-P, PU 407 [399].

120. Letter of October 9, 1759, from Betty to William, HL-P, PU 405 [397]. James Ferguson, an Edinburgh lawyer and later a judge, as Lord Pitfour, was the husband of Barbara (Murray) Johnstone's sister Anne.

He was the intermediary in the family's tribulations from the time of the "doubts difficulties objections Answers etc. etc." over James's education, to the legal cases of Bell or Belinda and Joseph Knight. Letter of September 23, 1743, from Alexander Boswell to Sir James Johnstone (the father), Houghton Library, Harvard University, Ms Hyde 52 (1).

121. Letters of February 22, 1758, and May 1, 1758, from Betty to William, HL-P, PU 400 [392] and 432 [420].

122. Letter of June 26, 1758, from George to Betty, HL-P, PU 463 [448].

123. Letters of March 30, 1760, from Charlotte to Betty and of April 18, [1761], from Walter Johnstone to William, HL-P, PU 451 [444], 719 [707].

124. Letters of October 23, 1761, from James Johnstone (the father) to Betty, and of November 2, 1761, November 17, 1761, and June 22, 1762, from Betty to William, HL-P, PU 527 [542], 416 [406], 418 [408], 428 [417]. "I have at last the pleasure to inform you that I am Returned to Westerhall," Betty told William in May 1762. Letter of May 3, 1762, from Betty to William, HL-P, PU 426 [415].

125. On the provisions of the Treaty of Paris, completed on February 10, 1763, see avalon.law.yale.edu/18th_century/paris763.asp.

126. Letters of October 7, 1759, and November 18, 1759, from Alexander to Thomas Gage, in William L. Clements Library, University of Michigan (UMWCL), Gage Papers. Betty wrote to William in 1761 to report the information, from Charlotte, "that Mama has got a Letter from Sandy and that Uncle James had offerd fifteen Hundred Pound for a Magonety to him but that he had not yet got it." Letter of November 2, 1761, from Betty to William, HL-P, PU 416 [406]. "Uncle James" was General James Murray, at the time the military governor of Quebec. A "Magonety"—Betty's version of Charlotte's version of Sandy's spelling—was presumably a "Majority," or the rank of major. As late as the end of 1762, Alexander was still in difficulties. "I grieve at the accounts you give me of poor Sandy J.," his aunt, Anne Ferguson, wrote in January 1763 to James Murray. Letter of January 29, 1763, from Anne Ferguson to General James Murray, NAS, GD32/24/14.

127. Letter of February 18, 1761, from George to William, HL-P, PU 469 [453].

128. George III succeeded to the British throne in 1760. His tutor was the Earl of Bute, a Scottish nobleman; Bute's secretary was the dramatist John Home, David Hume's kinsman and one of George's close friends. On John Home, see Henry Grey Graham, *Scottish Men of Letters in the Eighteenth Century* (London, 1901), pp. 60–77.

129. On the controversy over George's appointment, see *The North Briton* 3, nos. 62 and 64 (London and Dublin, 1763), pp. 136–37, 152–58. The Johnstones' uncle, General James Murray, was appointed governor of Quebec; General James Grant was appointed governor of East Florida; Colonel George Scott and later General Robert Melvill were appointed governors of Grenada. See Douglas Hamilton, "Robert Melville and the Frontiers of Empire in the British West Indies, 1763–1771," in *Military Governors and Imperial Frontiers c. 1600–1800: A Study of Scotland and Empires*, ed. A. Mackillop and Steve Murdoch (Leiden, 2003), 181–204.

130. Letter of April 24, 1765, from M. Aubry to the Minister of the Navy and the Colonies, Archives Nationales, France-Colonies (AN-Col.), Correspondance à l'arrivée en provenance de la Louisiane, C13A/15/48–49.

131. The Atlantic slave trade expanded very rapidly in the period immediately preceding the Seven Years' War, to a level of more than seventy thousand slaves embarked per year in 1749–55. It resumed at an even higher level of eighty-six thousand slaves in 1764 and reached its highest level of the century, of one hundred fifteen thousand slaves embarked, in 1792. Estimates of slaves embarked by national flag, available at the Trans-Atlantic Slave Trade Database, wilson.library.emory.edu:9090/tast/assessment/estimates.faces.

132. Grenada was described in a pamphlet of 1764 as "very improveable" and potentially "very inconvenient" to the Spanish fleet, "which pass this way into the Bay of Honduras and the Gulf of Mexico." William Young, *Some Observations; which may contribute to afford a just idea of the nature, importance, and settlement, of our new West-India colonies* (London, 1764), pp. 1, 3. On the history of Grenada, see Beverley A. Steele, *Grenada: A History of Its People* (Oxford, 2003).

133. "Heads of enquiry relating to the State of the Island of Grenada," May 14, 1763, in TNA, CO101/1/6v.

134. *Audi Alteram Partem, or A Counter-Letter, to the Right Hon. the E——l of H——ll——gh* (London, 1770), pp. 50, 117, 119 [121, mispag.].

135. "An Abstract of the Title of Alexander Johnstone Esq.," BUL-W, Westerhall Estate Papers, DM 41/31; and see Hamilton, *Scotland, Caribbean*. On William's support for Alexander, see letter of December 13, 1764, from Sir James Johnstone to William, in Betty's hand, HL-P, PU 431 [568].

136. Letter of September 13, 1765, from Governor Melvill to the Lords Commissioners for Trade and Plantations, TNA, CO101/1/315r–316r.

137. Alexander Johnstone et al., "Copy of a Memorial of the Proprietors of Land in the Island of Grenada," enclosed in the complaint of
Colonel Alexander Johnstone of December 1, 1769, TNA, Privy Council
Papers, PC1/60/7. The crises of 1764–69 in Grenada are described in
considerable and obscure detail in two long pamphlets published in
1770, *A Narrative of the Proceedings upon the Complaint against Governor Melvill* (London, 1770) and *Audi Alteram Partem*. On the circumstances of the publication of the pamphlets, and on the Johnstones' involvement in their content, see below, chapter 6.

138. "At the Council Chamber Whitehall the 20nd of February 1770
Complaints agst. the Govr. of the Grenada's," TNA, PC1/60/7, Colonial
Series of Bundles, B7, July 1769–May 1770; "Constitution of Grenada
decided at the Court of St. James's on September 7 1768," TNA,
CO101/3,1v–2v, "The Laws of the Legislature, of the Islands of Grenada
and the Grenadines," TNA, CO103/1/9.

139. "The Laws of Grenada and the Grenadines," TNA, CO103/1/25,
56.

140. *Narrative of the Proceedings*, p. 92.

141. On the Grenada Assembly, see *Audi Alteram Partem*, app. 9.

142. *Audi Alteram Partem*, p. 113.

143. Letter of March 1, 1768, from James to Sir James Johnstone,
NAS, GD1/499/3. The circumstances of Alexander's conviction for mutiny and departure for London are recounted, fairly obscurely, in his and
his friends' *Narrative of the Proceedings*, pp. 54–56, 76, 126–32, and in
Audi Alteram Partem, pp. 111–13.

144. "Inventory & Valuation of the plantation commonly called Bac-
caye," December 1, 1770, BUL-W, Westerhall Estate Papers, DM 41/32/1.
"Habitations de l'isle de la Grenade dont les propriétaires sont à
Londres," September 6, 1779, AN-Col., Correspondance à l'arrivée,
C10A, Carton 3-1.

145. On George's career in Florida, see Fabel, *Bombast and Broadsides*, pp. 25–57; on estimates of the population of the colony in 1763,
see Robin F. A. Fabel, *The Economy of British West Florida, 1763–1783*
(Tuscaloosa, 1988), p. 18.

146. In Panama, the correspondent added, "the wildernesses there
abound with wolves, tygers, and lions." *Gentleman's Magazine* 42 (April
1772): 169.

147. Letter of June 11, 1765, from George to Lord Halifax, TNA,
CO5/582/250v; letter of June 12, 1765, from George and John Stuart,
Superintendent of Indian Affairs, to Lord Halifax, TNA, CO5/582/187r;
letter of April 1, 1766, from George to John Pownall, TNA, CO5/574/673r.

148. Extract of a letter of December 3, 1763, from Lieutenant Forde, TNA, CO5/582/63r; letter of April 14, 1765, from David Wedderburn to Alexander Wedderburn, UMWCL, Wedderburn Papers.

149. Letter of October 6, 1763, from David Hume to Hugh Blair, in Greig, *Letters of David Hume*, 1:403; on the journey via Jamaica and the "Indian Presents," see the letters of August 4, 1764, and October 31, 1764, from George to Lord Halifax, TNA, CO5/582/131r and 133r, and a letter of January 6, 1776, from James Dallas in New Orleans to George, EUL-L, La.II.123. The oath of office that James Macpherson swore as "Secretary & Clerk of the Council for this His Majesty's Colony of West Florida" is among George Johnstone's papers, EUL-L, La.II.76. A young man called "James Johnstone," who was described as George's "nephew," became "provost marshal," or legal officer. On James Johnstone, the provost marshal, see "Declaration of the Account of George Johnstone Esq. Governor of the Province of West Florida Between September 1764 and January 1767," December 19, 1771, TNA, AO1/1261/152; letter of March 27, 1766, from Montfort Browne to H. S. Conway, and deposition of James Johnstone of March 31, 1766, in Dunbar Rowland, ed., *Mississippi Provincial Archives English Dominion* (Nashville, TN, 1911), pp. 300, 486–87.

150. Certification of baptism of George Lindsay Johnstone, son of Governor Johnstone, in Pensacola, December 10, 1764, dated January 27, 1781, and included in the application of George Lindsay Johnstone to be appointed as a writer to the East India Company, OIOC, IOR/J/1/10/83. Martha Ford was not named on George Lindsay Johnstone's certificate of baptism, although she was named on the baptism certificates of George's and her younger sons, James Primrose (baptised on July 9, 1772, at St. James's, Westminster, the son of "George Johnstone & Martha Ford") and Alexander Patrick (baptised on January 6, 1776, also in St. James's, Westminster, the son of "George & Martha-Ford Johnstone"); certificates included in the applications of James Primrose Johnstone and Alexander Patrick Johnstone to be appointed as writers to the East India Company, IOR/J/1/13/127 and IOR/J/1/16/219. George in his will, proved in 1787, left bequests to George Lindsay, James Primrose, and Alexander Patrick, described as his "natural sons or reputed natural sons," and to his daughter, Sophia. Martha Ford's mother, the older Martha Ford, also left bequests to the four children, describing them as her grandchildren. George Lindsay Johnstone died in 1813, leaving an annuity to his mother, Martha Ford, and his estate to his sister Sophia Johnstone. Will of George Johnstone, proved June 12, 1787, TNA, PROB 11/1154; will of Martha Ford, proved February 21, 1794,

TNA, PROB 11/1241; will of George Lindsay Johnstone, proved February 1, 1814, TNA, PROB 11/1552. The exact circumstances of George Lindsay Johnstone's birth and baptism are obscure. There are two different dates of birth or baptism given for him, in three different sets of records: the East India Company records, which give the date of baptism as 1764, in Pensacola; the records of Westminster Abbey, where he was buried, which describe him as having died in 1813 at the age of 46, and therefore born in 1767; and the records of St. James's, Westminster, which show George Lindsay Johnstone as having been born on November 26, 1767, and christened on January 2, 1768. Chester, *Marriage, Baptismal, and Burial Registers*, p. 486; City of Westminster Archives. George and Martha appear to have had five children, the three sons and one daughter to whom George and their grandmother left bequests, and another son, John, who died before his father. The two older sons, John and George (Lindsay), were educated in France and in Italy, and their Italian tour is described in detail in a remarkable collection of letters in the Clements Library of the University of Michigan, the correspondence of the eminent mathematician Walter Minto, later professor of mathematics at Princeton, who was employed by George as tutor to his sons (on the recommendation of "D. Hume Esqr. & Professor Ferguson of Edinburgh University"). Walter Minto was the boys' tutor from 1776 to 1778, and the correspondence includes three letters from George and two from Martha Ford, of which one was to Minto, signed "MF," and one to the boys, signed "Mother." It seems likely, from the letters, that George (Lindsay) was the younger of the two boys; Minto referred in November 1778 to "George's (a boy of 11 *yrs*) returning in the cold of winter to England." Letters of August 26, 1778, from [Martha Ford] to George [Johnstone] and John [Johnstone], signed "Your most affectionate Mother"; of September 12, 1778, from [Martha Ford] to Walter Minto, signed "MF"; of October 30, 1778, from George to Walter Minto (a copy, in Minto's hand); and of November 23, 1778, from Walter Minto to George, Minto-Skelton Collection, William L. Clements Library, University of Michigan (UMWCL-MS). This is consistent, too, with the information in Fabel's biography of George, that one of his sons was a naval lieutenant, recently promoted to captain, who was killed in a hurricane in the West Indies in 1780. Fabel, *Bombast and Broadsides*, p. 145. The older son, on this hypothesis, was John, and George (Lindsay) was the younger son, who was eleven in 1778, and was therefore born in 1767. It seems possible, in these circumstances, that it was George and Martha's oldest son, John, who was baptised in Pensacola in December 1764 and that George used or reconstructed the record of the baptism, after John's death, in order to expedite George Lindsay's application to join the East India Company. The certification provided to the East India Company was signed by a Church of England clergyman, Thomas Carwardine, "Curate of Duke Street Chapel Westminster," and Thomas Thomson, "Lieut. in Col. Fullartons Regt. of Foot"; it is possible that they remembered the baptism of a son of George's on the Pensacola frontier in winter 1764 but not the first name that the infant was given. I am most grateful to Professor Robert E. Lewis of the University of Michigan, who was cataloguing the Minto-Skelton collection in the summer of 2007, for his kindness in drawing the correspondence to my attention and for providing me with copies of the letters; and to Barbara DeWolfe of the Clements Library and Susanna Linley of the University of Michigan History Department for putting me in touch with Professor Lewis.

151. Grant of a garden lot in Pensacola to Mrs. Martha Ford, signed George Johnstone, January 9, 1766, TNA, CO5/602/136v–137r; grant to Martha Ford, signed Montfort Browne, January 28, 1768, "pursuant to a warrant" from George Johnstone of January 12, 1768, TNA, CO5/601/255v.

152. "Declaration of the Account of George Johnstone Esq.," TNA, AO1/1261/152.

153. "The Inhabitants (copying after the Pattern set them by their Principal) are Strangers to the Paths of Vertue, and sunk in Dissoluteness and Dissipation." Charles Woodmason, *The Carolina Backcountry on the Eve of the Revolution: The Journal and Other Writings of Charles Woodmason, Anglican Itinerant*, ed. Richard J. Hooker (Chapel Hill, 1953), p. 82; and see Milo B. Howard, Jr. and Robert Rea, "Introduction," in Montault de Montberaut, *The Mémoire Justificatif of the Chevalier Montault de Montberaut; Indian Diplomacy in British West Florida, 1763–1765*, trans. Milo B. Howard, Jr. and Robert Rea (Birmingham, AL, 1965), p. 56, n.122. There is no reason to suppose that Martha Ford was either dissolute or dissipated, and the family's home in London was apparently a model of domestic virtue. Of the few letters from her that survive, or which I have been able to identify, one was to reassure her sons that their "noble father," who was then in New York, was in good health—"in the midst of all his difficulties he mentions you all in the Tenderest manner. I had this news only yesterday and thought I could not too soon communicate it to you"—and the other was a very touching letter to her sons' tutor, Walter Minto, on hearing that George, John, and Minto were all ill, in Pisa: "my anxiety for my dear George is really beyond expression. At the same time I am very certain, Mr Minto, you will take all possible care of him. I can't tell you how kind I felt it, in your makeing him write the letter, which was the only thing you coul'd have done, to convince me of

his health, as a mothers fears are very soon rous'd. . . . No one can feel more sincerely than I did, for your Situation, it must be a heavy Charge, other People's Children." Letters of August 26, 1778, from [Martha Ford] to George [Johnstone] and John [Johnstone], and of September 12, 1778, from [Martha Ford] to Walter Minto, signed "MF," UMWCL-MS.

154. Copy of an undated letter of late 1764 from James Macpherson to George, enclosed in a letter of January 2, 1765, from George to General Thomas Gage, Gage Papers, UMWCL.

155. "Discourse of the Chiefs of the Ozages and Missouri," answer by "Tamaroa, chief of the Cascasquias in the Name of the Illinois Nation," in "Copy of a Council held at Illinois in April 1765," TNA, Letters from Admirals (Admiral Sir William Burnaby), Jamaica, ADM1/238, unpag. On the Indian congresses of the 1760s, see Richard White, *The Roots of Dependency: Subsistence, Environment, and Social Change among the Choctaws, Pawnees, and Navajos* (Lincoln, NE, 1983), Patricia Galloway, "'So Many Little Republics': British Negotiations with the Choctaw Confederacy, 1765," *Ethnohistory* 41, no. 4 (Autumn, 1994), 513–37, and Daniel K. Richter, *Facing East from Indian Country: A Native History of Early America* (Cambridge, MA, 2001). It is interesting that Tamaroa is reported to have used the metaphor of a balance: "All the Red men have a Ballance in which is the French and English, at any time whatsoever they lift it, the English weigh the most. Why? because they are full of bad Actions, and have not unspotted Hearts like our Father. . . . tell him that this Land is Ours, and that we love it, and nobody can pretend any Right to it, not even the other Red Men themselves; why will you come here?" Answer by Tamaroa, TNA, ADM1/238.

156. Letter of June 12, 1765, from George and John Stuart to Lord Halifax, TNA, CO5/582/188r; and see Galloway, "So Many Little Republics."

157. The colonel from Scotland was David Wedderburn, the younger brother of Alexander Wedderburn, William's old friend and fellow law student from the summer of 1751, who was by 1765 an established lawyer in Scotland and later Lord Chancellor. See Alexander Murdoch, "Wedderburn, Alexander, first earl of Rosslyn (1733–1805)," ODNB, article 28954, and below, chapter 4.

158. Letter of June 12, 1765, from George and John Stuart to Lord Halifax, TNA, CO5/582/190r.

159. "The Red Men on this Side of the Mississippi, should be considered as English Men & those on the other side as French, but as the French are now going to Leave New Orleans, which they have Ceded to

the Spaniards, the Inhabitants who remain there will be considered as Spaniards, while the french who remain here will be Considered as English;" "You are to look, upon all the frenchmen that Shall remain on the Island of New Orleans . . . as Spaniards, & all the Frenchmen who are now or shall hereafter be permitted by the Governor, to settle on this Side the Great River Mississippi; you must look upon as Brittish Subjects." Speeches of George of March 26, 1765, and of John Stuart of March 27, 1765, Report of the Congress of April 2, 1765, in *Mississippi Provincial Archives*, pp. 223, 232, 243; Galloway, "So Many Little Republics," p. 525.

160. "Nonsopretties" were apparently a kind of "pretties," or ladies' clothes. Speech of Governor Johnstone, May 27, 1765, Report of the Congress held in Pensacola, Arthur Gordon, Secretary, TNA, CO5/582/195r, 195v, 196r, 204r; Treaty for the Preservation & Continuance of a Perfect Peace, May 28, 1765, TNA, CO5/582/211v; letter of June 12, 1765 from George and John Stuart to Lord Halifax, TNA, CO5/582/189v. Report of the Congress held in Mobile on March 26, 1765, in *Mississippi Provincial Archives*, pp. 217, 219.

161. Report of the Congress held in Pensacola, TNA, CO5/582/199v, 200v, 201v.

162. Letter of November 1, 1764, from George Johnstone, *The Gazetteer and New Daily Advertiser*, February 6, 1765, no. 11212. "This House think[s] it extremely impolitic to defer marking out a spot of ground for a market-place because we cannot as yet raise for that purpose a capacious building upon Corinthian columns." Motion of the House of Assembly of West Florida of January 3, 1767, in Robert B. Rea, comp., with Milo B. Howard, Jr., *The Minutes, Journals, and Acts of the General Assembly of British West Florida* (Tuscaloosa, AL, 1979), p. 69.

163. Extract of a letter of February 19, 1765, from George to John Pownall, TNA, T1/437/224r.

164. Letter of May 3, 1766, from George to Don Antonio D'Ullua [Ulloa], TNA, CO5/583/61, 63. On George's relations to Ulloa, see Gabriel Paquette, "The Image of Imperial Spain in British Political Thought, 1750–1800," *Bulletin of Spanish Studies* 81, no. 2 (2004), 187–214.

165. Letter of April 24, 1765, from M. Aubry to the Minister of the Navy, AN-Col., C13A/15/48–49.

166. "Declaration of the Account of George Johnstone Esq.," TNA, AO1/1261/152; letter of June 11, 1765 from George to Lord Halifax, TNA, CO5/582/249r.

167. Town plan of Pensacola under the British, 1765–81, in Clinton N. Howard, *The British Development of West Florida 1763–1769* (Berkeley, CA, 1947), opposite p. 42, and analysis of land grants, pp. 57, 65;

James Munro, ed., *Acts of the Privy Council of England, Colonial Series, vol. 5 (1766–1783)* (London, 1912), p. 593; grant of a garden lot in Pensacola to Mrs. Martha Ford, signed George Johnstone, January 9, 1766, TNA, CO5/602/136v–137r. There was also a land grant to John; John asked his correspondent Samuel Hannay, in 1770, if he had "any advices lately from Pensacola" or news of "the Person my Grant was sent to." Copy of a letter of December 27, 1770, from John to Samuel Hannay in John Johnstone Letter Book, 1767-1771 [JJLB-CLA], Johnstone of Alva papers, deposited by Sir James Raymond Johnstone in the Clackmannanshire Archives, Alloa [JA-CLA], PD239/201/9.

168. Extracts from the Minutes of His Majesty's Council for the Province of West Florida, May 18, 1765, in TNA, CO5/583/175r–176v. "Who could have foretold at the landing of Julius Caesar in Britain, the glory which was to shower down in that favourite Spot under your Majesty's Reign, yet a Similar space in the time that is to come, can only be considered as a point in the Existence of Your Majesty's Fame. . . . We look up as to another Alfred for Assistance." Francis Pousset, Speaker, Address of the Assembly of the Province of West Florida, November 22, 1766, in TNA, CO5/584/383v.

169. Letter of November 3, 1764, from George to Captain Mackinen, in *Mississippi Provincial Archives*, p. 158.

170. Letter of June 11, 1765, from George to Lord Halifax, TNA, CO5/582/249r. Macpherson, identified as "the celebrated publisher of FINGAL," was reported to have arrived in Charleston from Pensacola in July 1765, with the Indian Superintendent John Stuart, on a ship called the *Moro Castle*; he "embarks here for England." *South-Carolina Gazette*, July 13–20, 1765; and see John Richard Alden, *John Stuart and the Southern Colonial Frontier: A Study of Indian Relations, War, Trade, and Land Problems in the Southern Wilderness, 1754–1775* (Ann Arbor, MI, 1944), p. 215. Macpherson was later recommended for the position of "Vendue-Master," with George's support. Once he was himself on the point of being sent home, George recommended Macpherson as someone who could speak on his behalf. The charge against Macpherson was that he had issued a warrant for arresting a soldier in the 35th regiment without informing the commanding officer. Letter of April 1, 1766, from George to John Pownall, TNA, CO5/574/687r; letter of March 13, 1766, from H. S. Conway to George, and Charge against Mr. Clifton of April 1, 1766, in *Mississippi Provincial Archives*, pp. 297, 468–69.

171. Letter of March 27, 1766, from Montfort Browne to H. S. Conway in *Mississippi Provincial Archives*, p. 298.

172. Letter of April 1, 1766, from George to John Pownall, TNA, CO5/574/685r–686v. George's endeavor, in these circumstances, was to

follow the "Example of Caesar," and to remember the bellicose conduct "of that Magnanimous Nation who thereby justly became the Masters of the World." Letter of April 1, 1766, TNA, CO5/574/686v; letter of September 30, 1766, from George to John Stuart, Gage Papers, UMWCL.

173. Letter of April 1, 1766, from George to John Pownall, enclosing a deposition of Robert Collins, TNA, CO5/574/686,693.

174. Letter of October 10, 1764, from George to John Pownall, TNA, CO5/582/167r.

175. Extract of a letter of February 19, 1765, from George to John Pownall, TNA, T1/437/221r.

176. Letter of September 14, 1765, from George to Lord Halifax, TNA, CO5/582/297r.

177. An Act for the Regulation and Government of Negroes and Slaves, January 3, 1767, in *Minutes, Journals, and Acts*, pp. 330, 332, 342–47, and see Fabel, *Economy of British West Florida*, pp. 25–26.

178. Letter of June 12, 1765, from George and John Stuart to Lord Halifax, TNA, CO5/582/186v.

179. Speech of Governor Johnstone, May 27, 1765, Report of the Congress held in Pensacola, TNA, CO5/582/196r.

180. "The English were like snakes who hide in the grass" or "like crayfish," a Choctaw chief said to one of the former French officials. Montberaut, *Mémoire Justificatif*, pp. 150, 152.

181. On the interaction of the commerce in liquor, the political failure of the Choctaw chiefs, the expansion of the deerskin trade, and the "ecological balance of the woodlands," see White, *Roots of Dependency*, pp. 82–89. On the aftermath of the peace treaty of 1763 as the end of the "accommodationist vision of native-European coexistence," see Richter, *Facing East*, pp. 187–88.

182. Copy of a letter of September 30, 1766, from George to John Stuart, enclosed in a letter of December 19, 1766, from Stuart to General Gage, Gage Papers, UMWCL.

183. "If the Cherokees could be induced, by any means, to fall at the same time upon the Creeks, I think it would be advisable, in Order that they may be severely chastised . . . without giving them the least Possibility of thinking we had any Share in it"; "it was difficult to bring Matters to this Point without appearing an Accessary." Copy of a letter of May 19, 1766, from George to John Stuart, enclosed in a letter of July 2, 1766, from Stuart to General Gage, Gage Papers, UMWCL.

184. "Every Hostile measure permitted by the Laws of Nations should be used against the Creek Indians." Letter of October 4, 1766, from George to Brigadier William Tayler, TNA, T1/458/103.

185. Letter of June 23, 1766, from George to H. S. Conway, in *Mississippi Provincial Archives*, pp. 511, 513.

186. Letter of September 30, 1766, from George to John Stuart, enclosed in a letter of December 19, 1766, from Stuart to General Gage. Gage Papers, UMWCL.

187. Letters of September 22, 1766, and February 19, 1767, to George from the Earl of Shelburne, TNA, CO5/618/1, 4.

188. Deed of freedom recorded February 3, 1770, TNA CO5/605/f.349; and see "Slave Transactions, 1764–1779," in Fabel, *Economy of British West Florida*, p. 215.

189. On Clive as "the founder of the British empire in India" and on his principles in relation to "the entire history of British India," see "Lord Clive" (1840), in Lord Macaulay, *Critical and Historical Essays contributed to the Edinburgh Review*, 4 vols. (London, 1889), 3:76, 124; and see H. V. Bowen, "Clive, Robert, First Baron Clive of Plassey (1725–1774)," ODNB, article 5697.

190. Speech of Lord Clive of March 30, 1772, debate in the House of Commons on the East India Judicature Bill, PH, vol. 17, cols. 354, 358. On the economy of eighteenth-century Bengal, see Kalikinkar Datta, *Studies in the History of the Bengal Subah, 1740–1770, vol. 1: Social and Economic* (Calcutta, 1936), and Tilottama Mukherjee, "The Co-ordinating State and the Economy: The Nizamat in Eighteenth-Century Bengal," *Modern Asian Studies* 43, no. 2 (2009), 389–436.

191. Thomas Pownall, *The Right, Interest, and Duty, of the State, As concerned in the Affairs of the East Indies* (London, 1773), pp. 19, 24, 29.

192. Smith, *Wealth of Nations*, p. 748.

193. Letter of February 5, 1772, from John to William, HL-P, PU 655 [648]; copy, in John's hand, of a letter of December 29, 1761, from John in Calcutta to James Balmain, HL-P, PU 671 [620].

194. Letter of December 29, 1761, from John in Calcutta to James Balmain, HL-P, PU 671 [620]. John's postings in India included Ballasore (Baleshwar in Orissa), Burdwan, Calcutta, Dhaka, Golconda (Golkonda in Andhra Pradesh), Jellasore (Jaleswar in Orissa), Midnapore, and Vizagapatam (Visakhapatnam in Andhra Pradesh).

195. Letter of September 30, 1765, from Lord Clive to the East India Company court of directors, Third Report from the Committee Appointed to enquire into the Nature, State, and Condition of the East India Company (April 8, 1773) in Sheila Lambert, ed., *House of Commons Sessional Papers of the Eighteenth Century* (Wilmington, DE, 1975), 135:395.

196. Gholam-Hossein, *Seir Mutaqharin*, 1:281.

197. William Bolts, *Considerations on India Affairs; particularly respecting the present state of Bengal and its Dependencies*, 3 vols. (London, 1772–75), 1:vi–vii, 85. On the transition in Bengal, see Ranajit Guha, *A Rule of Property for Bengal: An Essay on the Idea of Permanent Settlement* (1963) (London, 1996), and Travers, *Ideology and Empire*; on Bolts, see Holden Furber, "In the Footsteps of a German 'Nabob': William Bolts in the Swedish Archives," in Holden Furber, *Private Fortunes and Company Profits in the India Trade in the 18th Century*, ed. Rosane Rocher (Aldershot, UK, 1997), 7:7–18, and Willem G. J. Kuiters, *The British in Bengal, 1756–1773: A Society in Transition Seen through the Biography of a Rebel: William Bolts (1739–1808)* (Paris, 2002).

198. On the Seven Years' War in India "considered as the attack and defence of the outworks of Bengal," see H. H. Dodwell, ed., *The Cambridge History of India* (Delhi, 1963), 5:157–58.

199. Copy of letter of December 29, 1761, from John in Calcutta to James Balmain, HL-P, PU 671 [620].

200. *Treaties and Grants from the Country Powers, to the East India Company* ([London], 1774), p. 152. On Clive's Irish title, "Baron Clive of Plassey," which he received in 1762, see Bowen, "Clive."

201. Speech of Lord Clive of March 30, 1772, debate in the House of Commons on the East India Judicature Bill, PH, vol. 17, cols. 335, 343, 358.

202. Petition of John Johnstone to be admitted as a writer in the East India Company's settlements, read in court December 19, 1750; certification of Richard Hoge of October 3, 1750, presented with the petition, IOR/J/1/1/151,154.

203. Letter of January 31, 1766, from the Select Committee in Fort William (Calcutta) to the court of directors of the East India Company, letter of October 1, 1765, from John Johnstone to Lord Clive, Fourth Report from the Committee Appointed to enquire into the Nature, State, and Condition of the East India Company (April 21, 1773) in *House of Commons Sessional Papers*, 135:517, 540.

204. Abdul Majed Khan, *The Transition in Bengal, 1756–1775: A Study of Saiyid Muhammad Reza Khan* (Cambridge, 1969), p. xiii.

205. John Johnstone, *Letter to the Proprietors of East-India Stock* (London, 1766), pp. 3–6, 8–9. On the commercial economy of Burdwan, see Ratnalekha Ray, *Change in Bengal Agrarian Society c. 1760–1850* (New Delhi, 1979), Subhas Chandra Mukhopadhyay, *The Agrarian Policy of the British in Bengal (The Formative Period, 1698–1772)* (Allahabad, 1987), and John R. McLane, *Land and Local Kingship in Eighteenth-Century Bengal* (Cambridge, 1993).

206. Copy of letter of December 29, 1761, from John in Calcutta to James Balmain, HL-P, PU 671 [620].

207. "No doubt both you and George and James would all Explen to John the situation of the defirent partys at the India House," their father wrote to William in 1764. Letter of December 13, 1764, from James Johnstone (the father) to William, in Betty's hand, HL-P, PU 431 [568].

208. Bolts, *Considerations on India Affairs*, 1:211. On the constitution and politics of the East India Company, see Sutherland, *The East India Company* and Bowen, *Business of Empire*.

209. Gholam-Hossein, *Seir Mutaqharin*, 2:582.

210. Speech of Lord Clive of March 30, 1772, debate in the House of Commons on the East India Judicature Bill, PH, vol. 17, col. 365.

211. John Johnstone, *Letter to the Proprietors*, pp. 9, 12, 66.

212. Minute of Ralph Leycester, June 11, 1765, Third Report from the Committee, *House of Commons Sessional Papers*, p. 431.

213. Extract of the general letter from the court of directors of the East India Company to the president and council at Bengal, June 1, 1764, in Fourth Report from the Committee of Secrecy Appointed to enquire into the State of the East India Company (March 24, 1773), *House of Commons Sessional Papers*, 136:148. On the establishment of the Select Committee to enquire into the nature, state, and condition of the East India Company, and the smaller Committee of Secrecy to examine the Company's books, see Sutherland, *East India Company*, pp. 222–38.

214. John Johnstone, *Letter to the Proprietors*, p. 8.

215. Testimony of Major William Grant, in Third Report from the Committee, *House of Commons Sessional Papers*, p. 303.

216. John and four of his friends in India were obliged, for example, to send a power of attorney to their brothers in England, with respect to the absconding French agents of a bond for seven thousand pounds. Letter of February 19, 1766, from Samuel Swinton in London to General John Carnac in India, about the power of attorney brought home by Lieutenant Grant, "signed by you Mr Johnstone, Mr Amyatt, my Brother, & himself appointing Mr William Johnstone Mr Samuel Hannay, & me your joint Attorneys for the recovery of £7000 & its Proceeds from Messrs. Chevalier & De la Bat." OIOC, Carnac Papers, MSS Eur F128/156, unfol.

217. Letter of August 30, 1762, from Sir James Johnstone (the father) to William, HL-P, PU 541 [536].

218. Sale list of the effects of the Reverend Henry Butler, sold at auction on December 5–6, 1761, in Calcutta. Henry Barry Hyde, *Parochial Annals of Bengal* (Calcutta, 1901), pp. 124–25. Tysoe Saul Hancock, an

East India Company surgeon in Calcutta, married Philadelphia Austen, the sister of George Austen, Jane Austen's father, in 1753. Richard A. Austen-Leigh, *Pedigree of Austen: Austen Papers, 1704–1856* (London, 1995), pp. 34–38.

219. It "was, as it is said, to be received as a Wadah referring to the Rents of the Jagheer of the Nazim, and as an Elmaum referring to the Calso Lands." Minute of John of June 17, 1765, Third Report from the Committee, *House of Commons Sessional Papers,* p. 435.

220. General letter of April 26, 1765, from the court of directors, letter of September 29, 1765, from Lord Clive to Mr. Dudley, in Malcolm, *Lord Clive,* 2:344, 348.

221. The crisis of 1765 was precipitated by the death of the nawab or Mughal governor of Bengal, Mir Jafar Ali Khan, an ally of the East India Company, and the accession of his young son, Najm-ud-daulah. See Khan, *Transition in Bengal*, pp. 69–101.

222. John Johnstone, *Letter to the Proprietors*, pp. 19, 23; letter of March 6, 1765, from the Nawab Najm-ud-daulah, summarized in Imperial Record Department, *Calendar of Persian Correspondence* (Calcutta, 1911), 1:390; letter of September 30, 1765, from Lord Clive to the court of directors, Third Report from the Committee, *House of Commons Sessional Papers,* p. 398; Accounts of Presents, June 6, 1765, Third Report from the Committee, *House of Commons Sessional Papers,* pp. 411–13.

223. Letters of April 17, 1765, from Lord Clive in Madras to Thomas Rous, chairman of the East India Company, and of May 7, 1765, from Lord Clive to the Select Committee of the East India Company in Calcutta, Third Report from the Committee, *House of Commons Sessional Papers,* pp. 404, 406.

224. John Johnstone, *Letter to the Proprietors*, pp. 28–29.

225. Letter of June 7, 1765, from Lord Clive to the court of directors, translation of a letter of June 1, 1765, from the Nawab Najm-ud-daulah, Bengal Secret Consultations, OIOC, IOR, P/A/6/390, 407, 416; John Johnstone, *Letter to the Proprietors*, p. 28. On John's confrontation with Clive at the meeting of the council in Calcutta, in which Clive remained silent, see Gholam-Hossein, *Seir Mutaqharin*, 2:380, and for a very different view, see Macaulay, *Critical and Historical Essays*, "Lord Clive," 3:144–45. In Ghulam Husain's history, Clive "informed Djanson [Johnstone] and Middleton [the Company's chief representative in Murshidabad] . . . that they had acted very improperly and unjustly," to which they responded by resigning from the Company and stating that they would be prepared to refund the presents if Clive would refund the presents that he had himself received. "Lord Clive on hearing so reso-

lute and so undisguised an answer, and finding that they had resigned the service, did not dare to enter into any discussion with them, and he remained silent." It was Johnstone, in Macaulay's version, who remained silent: "Johnstone . . . made some show of opposition. Clive interrupted him, and haughtily demanded whether he meant to question the power of the new government. Johnstone was cowed, and disclaimed any such intention. All the faces round the board grew long and pale; and not another syllable of dissent was uttered." This was based on Clive's own account, in a letter of May 6, 1765, to General John Carnac, quoted in Malcolm, *Lord Clive*, 2:321–22: "there was an appearance of very long and pale countenances, and not one of the council uttered another syllable."

226. Minute of June 17, 1765, from John Johnstone, in Third Report from the Committee, *House of Commons Sessional Papers,* pp. 433, 434; letter of October 1, 1765, from John to Lord Clive, Fourth Report from the Committee, *House of Commons Sessional Papers*, pp. 536, 537; OIOC, Bengal Secret Consultations, IOR/P/A/6/625–40, Fort William Consultations, Range 1, vol. 38, IOR/P/1/38/746–68.

227. John Johnstone, *Letter to the Proprietors*, p. 32. On Reza Khan, the nawab's adviser, see Khan, *Transition in Bengal*.

228. Letter of October 1, 1765, from John to Lord Clive, Fourth Report from the Committee, *House of Commons Sessional Papers*, pp. 537–38. I am very grateful to Amartya Sen for the interpretation of the Hindustani expression *Kuch bolega nahi*, which John's partner Motiram was supposed to have used to the Seths, Marwari bankers long established in Bengal.

229. "Your ransacking the Accounts of the Country Governt. I look upon as a gross abuse of our Power, and what we have not a Shadow of right to, unless we mean to throw off the Mask and set up ourselves as Subahdars [subordinate revenue officials]. Mohabeet Jung, at the Time the Country Government was uppermost, might have produced an equal claim for . . . examining into the Company's Books." Letter of April 8, 1765, from John Carnac in Feyzabad to John Johnstone, OIOC, Carnac Papers, MSS Eur F128/11.

230. Letter of May 6, 1765, from Lord Clive to John Carnac, in Malcolm, *Lord Clive*, 2:322; letter of April 17, 1765, from Lord Clive in Madras to Thomas Rous, chairman of the East India Company, in Third Report from the Committee, *House of Commons Sessional Papers*, p. 404.

231. Letter of April 8, 1765, from John Carnac in Feyzabad to John Johnstone, OIOC, Carnac Papers, MSS Eur F128/11.

232. Malcolm, *Lord Clive*, 2:338. On Sir John Malcolm, whose brother was called "Pulteney Malcolm," after William, see Dipesh Chakrabarty, "Comments on 'The "Inner Lives" of Empires,'" Princeton University, April 20, 2006. The diwani had been urged on the East India Company by Mughal officials on previous occasions. On an earlier offer in 1761, see the examination of Major William Grant, in Third Report from the Committee, *House of Commons Sessional Papers,* p. 306, and Walter Kelly Firminger, "Historical Introduction to the Bengal Portion of 'The Fifth Report,'" in *The Fifth Report from the Select Committee of the House of Commons on the Affairs of the East India Company* (1917) (Calcutta, repr. 1969), pp. cliv–clvii.

233. Letter to Betty Johnstone of [January 13,] 1767, JJLB-CLA, PD239/201/9.

234. Letters of September 20, September 21, 1765, and October 1, 1765, from John to Harry Verelst, draft letter of September 21, 1765, from Harry Verelst to John, receipt from John dated October 1, 1765, OIOC, Verelst Collection, MSS Eur F218/96.

235. Keene, *Miscellaneous Poems*. There are two copies of the volume in the British Library, of which one (call number 992.h.15/1) has a title page, a second title page with the name of the author and bookseller ("S. Hooper, in the Strand"), and a dedication to the extremely wealthy East India shipowner Charles Raymond, in gratitude for "the many and weighty obligations which you have been pleased to confer both on me and my family" (p. i). The other copy (call number 11632.d.47/2) has only the first title page, with no author's name or dedication. Both have the names of 124 subscribers, of whom ten were associated with Trinity College, Cambridge, and one, Charles Raymond, subscribed for one hundred copies, on "royal paper." Elizabeth Carolina appears to have left for India at about the time the book was published, and the errata page suggests that she had little opportunity to correct the proofs: "for tears read fears," "for he, who," "for sacreotis, sacerdotis," "for sink, sunk."

236. Goldsmith's comment was in a review of recent translations of Ovid, and noted the propensity to "talk like a debauchee in that of Mrs —; but the sex should ever be sacred from criticism." In Goldsmith's collected works, the review is annotated, "[Mrs. Elizabeth Keene, who had recently published a translation of Dido's Epistle to Aeneas]". *Critical Review* 7 (January 1759), p. 32; *The Miscellaneous Works of Oliver Goldsmith*, ed. James Prior, 4 vols. (London, 1837), 4:431.

237. On October 8, 1760, Elizabeth Carolina received permission from the East India Company to go to India: "That Mrs Ann and Caroline Keene has liberty for proceeding to their friends at Madrass and be both

excused paying the sum of £12- each for permission." Minutes of the court of directors of the East India Company, October 8, 1760, OIOC, IOR/B/76, p. 201. Elizabeth Carolina (Keene) Johnstone's antecedents are even more difficult to identify than those of Louisa (Jones or Meyrick) Johnstone. She is described in a monument erected by her daughter in the Johnstone mausoleum in the Westerkirk (now Bentpath) churchyard as the daughter of "Colonel William Keene of Norfolk," and in Namier and Brooke's *History of Parliament* as daughter of "Col. Keene, and niece of Sir Benjamin Keene"; Namier and Brooke, *The House of Commons 1754–1790*, 2:687. But I have been unable to find records of a Colonel William Keene in eighteenth-century army or East Indian Army lists or of a brother of Sir Benjamin Keene and Edmund Keene named William (although Edmund Keene, at the time Bishop of Ely, is listed among the subscribers to *Miscellaneous Poems*). Elizabeth Carolina's father was probably the "Talbot William Keene" who made a will on February 19, 1746, "being now on my departure for a Voyage to East India," which was proved by his widow, Ann, soon after "Ann and Caroline Keene" received permission to leave for India. In his own will, made on Sepember 18, 1795, John referred to "the reversion of the settlement of ten thousand rupees made on Miss Anne Keene sister of the now deceased Mrs. Elizabeth Caroline Keene my wife." Will of Talbot William Keene, proved November 17, 1760, TNA, PROB 11/860; will of John Johnstone, proved March 6, 1796, TNA, PROB 11/1272. It is likely that the father of Elizabeth Carolina and her sister was the "Wm. Keene" who was listed among the ensigns leaving for Fort St. George (Madras) from Colchester on February 5, 1746; OIOC, IOR/H/82, "Ensigns to Fort St George," p. 21. He may also have been the Keene who was promoted in Fort William (Calcutta) in 1752, as reported in the East India Company council's letter to the court of directors: "The President . . . has thought proper to grant lieutenants' commissions to Messrs. Kempe and Keene." A "Lieutenant Keene" was reported in a subsequent letter as having died a few months later: "Lieutenant Keene having likewise deceased on the 16th September [1753]." The court of directors instructed the council in Calcutta, more than twenty years later, to pay the sum of one hundred pounds to "Miss Ann Keene," and then again in 1779 to pay one hundred pounds to "Mrs Ann Keene, daughter of William Talbot Keene, deceased," and in 1780 to pay two hundred pounds to "Mrs Anne Keene Daughter of Wm. Talbot Keene deceased." Letters dated January 1, 1753, and January 4, 1754, letters of the court of directors of March 7, 1777, April 14, 1779, and July 5, 1780, in *Fort William–India House Correspondence*, 1:620, 741, 8:82, 222, 275. A "lieutenant Keene" was reported to have taken part in the battle of Kaveripak (Covrepauk) in south India in 1752. [Robert Orme], *A History of the Military Transactions of the British Nation in Indostan, from the year 1745* (London, 1763), p. 215. There was also a William Keene who was said to have deserted from the British forces in South India in 1750. Ananda Ranga Pillai in his diary described a dissolute Englishman who was killed in a duel in Pondicherry in 1752; the editor of the diary, H. Dodwell, commented that "it is not clear who the deserter was. The only commissioned officers who deserted about this time, so far as I know, were Captain-Lieutenant Daniel Murray . . . and Lieutenant William Keene, who deserted about the end of 1750. The first of the two is most likely meant." H. Dodwell, ed., *The Diary of Ananda Ranga Pillai* 12 vols. (Madras, 1904–1922), 8:120–21, n.2.

238. Logbook of the *Earl of Holdernesse*, OIOC, IOR/L/MAR/B/604C. The ship sailed from Portsmouth on March 29, 1761, anchored at the Fort of Mozambique on July 25, and arrived in Kulpi (Culpee), on the Hooghly River south of Calcutta, on December 9. The passenger list for the ship included "Mrs Dorothy Northall," who left the ship in Madras, "Miss Ann Keene" and "Miss Caroline Keene," who left at Culpee, "Susannah, Mrs Northall's Black Servant," "sent from Madrass to Bengall on a Country Vessel," and three "Women belongg. to ye. Military," Mary Wickham, Jane Naylor, and Ann Hotchkins.

239. The only description of Elizabeth Carolina's period in India that I have been able to identify is in a series of letters of 1761 and 1762 by the East India Company official Harry Verelst, who was later John's bitter enemy. In a letter to his agents in Calcutta in December 1761, Verelst wrote from Islamabad (Chittagong) in East Bengal that a colleague, Captain Thomas Fenwick, had been informed "by a Calcutta packet yesterday" about the "arrival of the two Miss Keenes, who have a Letter of particular recommendation to him," and who were living "in the Europe Captain's house that brought them to Calcutta (probably owing to their want of a more convenient situation)." He instructed the agents to offer the ladies "my gardenhouse, if agreeable to them," "in Capt. Fenwick's name, as I do not personally know them." In a letter of the same day to William Bolts, who later became John's partner, he asked Bolts to "accommodate the Ladies with what money, & other necessaries they may want, which you will please to tender them in Capt. Fenwick's name, but charge to my account." He added that "the Miss Keene's being particularly recommended to Capt. Fenwick, and in a Letter expressing a very anxious desire, I understand, to see him either in Calcutta, or come to him here, you will please to tender them my compliments & let them know that if Chittigong, on that account, is more agreeable to them for a season than Calcutta, they shall meet with as hearty a welcome here as

the place can afford . . . I am to request the favor you will accommodate the Ladies with every conveniency for their passage up to Luckypore" [Lakshmipur, in the delta of the Brahmaputra]. Elizabeth Carolina and her sister did make the journey around the Bay of Bengal to Chittagong, where they were in August 1762, and where they denied ever having received any money from Bolts, as Verelst wrote in another letter. They were by now living in the "little Bungalo" of Captain Fenwick, who was himself in Lakshmipur; they eventually left Chittagong for Lakshmipur in late October 1762 to return to Calcutta. Letters of December 27, 1761, from Harry Verelst to Messrs. Beaumont and Watts, Calcutta, and of December 27, 1761, from Harry Verelst to William Bolts, of August 9, 1762, from Harry Verelst to William Bolts, of October 21, 1762, from Harry Verelst to Captain Fenwick, and of October 27, 1762, to Anselm Beaumont, OIOC, Verelst Collection, Verelst Letter Book 1761–62, MSS Eur F218/79, ff. 91r–91v, 116r, 128r, 145v, 148r. On Bolts, Verelst, and the Misses Keene, see Kuiters, *British in Bengal 1756–1773*, pp. 99–102. The relations between the Miss Keenes and Verelst were awkward by the time of their return to Calcutta: the "two Ladies have been determining and undetermining for so long that they have no determination left at last, if ever they had any," Verelst wrote of their impending departure for the delta of the Brahmaputra. "Miss Caroline 'till the very hour of their going away . . . most flatly denied their ever having received any sums of monies from Bolts," "for I got the question put to her on purpose . . . by a gentleman here." Letters to William Billers of October 21, 1762, and to John Carnac of October 26, 1762, Verelst Letter Book 1761–62, ff.144v, 147v.

240. Letters of August 9, 1762, from Harry Verelst to William Bolts, of October 21, 1762, from Harry Verelst to Captain Fenwick, and of October 27, 1762, to Anselm Beaumont, OIOC, Verelst Letter Book 1761–62, MSS Eur F218/79, ff. 128r, 145v, 148r.

241. Letter of April 5, 1762, from Harry Verelst in Islamabad to Colonel Eyre Coote, OIOC, Verelst Letter Book 1761–62, MSS Eur F218/79, f. 97v. "The year 1761 was a very unhealthy one in Calcutta, but 1762 was even worse: an epidemic raged, and the burials recorded in the English register amount to 241." Hyde, *Parochial Annals*, p. 128.

242. Letters of October 21, 1762 to William Billers, and of October 26, 1762 to John Carnac, OIOC, Verelst Letter Book 1761–62, MSS Eur F218/79, ff.144v, 147v.

243. On the suspension of the Calcutta chaplain who married John and Elizabeth Carolina in September 1765, see Hyde, *Parochial Annals*, pp. 134–35. Clandestine marriages in the British enclave in Calcutta, as

in Scotland, were conducted without the formal reading of banns, or without the permission of the Company.

244. Minute of September 9, 1765, OIOC, Fort William Consultations, Range 1, vol. 38, IOR/P/1/38/733; logbook of the *Admiral Stevens*, IOR/L/MAR/B/566A, entry for October 5, 1765.

CHAPTER TWO. COMING HOME

1. Logbook of the *Admiral Stevens*, OIOC, IOR/L/MAR/B/566A, entries for December 29 and 31, 1765, and January 2, February 4 and 7, March 15, April 2, and May 1 and 24, 1766. It is possible that John and Elizabeth Carolina returned to London from Lisbon before the *Admiral Stevens* was repaired. The *Expedition* packet left Lisbon for England "with our dispatches" on April 5, the *King George* packet on April 21, and the *Hampden* packet on April 25. The logbook of the *Admiral Stevens* records the passengers going on shore on April 2, but it does not record their coming on board again (as was done in Calcutta, the Cape of Good Hope, and St. Helena). Entries for October 5, January 6, February 4, and April 2, 5, 21, and 25. On the East India Company directors' view of the ship, "so crazy a vessel as she appears to be," see letter of May 17, 1766 from the court of directors, in *Fort William–India House Correspondence*, 4:170. The journal of the young merchant who bought the seaweed, and who also bought ten thousand toothpicks while the ship was being repaired in Lisbon, is in the Cheshire Record Office; Peter Downes, "Memorandum of my Voyage in Ship Adml. Stevens," n.d., unpag., Cheshire Record Office, DDS 4005. On the "little Horse and Mare," see *St. James's Chronicle*, May 22, 1766, no. 815 and *Lloyd's Evening Post*, May 23, 1766, no. 1385.

2. Letter of May 30, 1766, to John Johnstone from the Court of Directors, OIOC, minutes of the Court of Directors of the East India Company, IOR/B/82, p. 62; East India Company versus John Johnstone, Chancery Court, TNA, C12/2379/7.

3. Letter of June 11, 1766, to the Court of Directors from John Johnstone, OIOC, Minutes of the Court of Directors, IOR B/82/72; John Johnstone, *Letter to the Proprietors*, p. 67. "Suppose the regulation with regard to prizes taken by ships of war should be thought improper, and that it was resolved to alter it during a war, it is believed, that a very considerable indulgence would be given in fixing the period at which such a regulation should commence; because otherways a species of injustice would be done to those who had engaged in the service upon the faith of the regulation as it formerly stood."

4. On the repatriation, or the drain, of East Indian wealth to Britain, see Marshall, *East Indian Fortunes*. On the politics of the East India Company, see George McGilvary, *Guardian of the East India Company: The Life of Laurence Sulivan* (London, 2006), and George McGilvary, *East India Patronage and the British State: The Scottish Elite and Politics in the Eighteenth Century* (London, 2008).

5. "There are said to be upwards of two hundred thousand Pounds sterling value, in Jewels, on board the Admiral Stevens, lately put into Lisbon, from Bengal," the *Public Advertiser* reported soon after the news of the ship's arrival in Lisbon reached London; the *London Evening Post* reported, a few days later, that the ship had "brought over . . . a valuable box of jewels, for the Right Hon. Lady Clive." *Public Advertiser*, April 25, 1766, no. 9821; *London Evening Post*, April 29, 1766, no. 6007.

6. Letter of June 26, 1758, from George to Betty, HL-P, PU 463 [448].

7. Letter of September 6, 1768, from John to Samuel Hannay, JJLB-CLA, PD239/201/9.

8. Letter of October 8, 1767, from William Pulteney to David Hume, Hume Manuscripts (Royal Society of Edinburgh), NLS, MS 23155, no. 96, ff. 255–56.

9. Undated letters from John to William of 1767 and 1768, HL-P, PU 625 [622] and PU 640 [637.]

10. Letter of [July 10, 1767] from John to William, HL-P, PU 624 [623].

11. Letter of December 25, 1770, from John to the Revd. Mr. Talbot Keene, JJLB-CLA, PD239/201/9.

12. Letters of February 11, 1768, and [August] 1768 from John to William, HL-P, PU 632 [629] and PU 640 [637]; letter of April 17, 1771, from James to John, JJLB-EUL, p. 59. The "Improveable" estate was that of Lord Hume, the Hirsle, which in the end was not sold.

13. Letters of October 21, 1770, from John in Balgonie to Alexander, JJLB-CLA, PD239/201/9, and of May 19, 1771, from John in Balgonie to William, HL-P, PU 651 [644].

14. Letter of March 1, 1768, from James to Sir James Johnstone, NAS, GD1/499/3.

15. See above, chapter 1.

16. Letter of August 1, 1749, from Margaret Ogilvie in France to Viscountess Kenmure, EUL-L, La.II.502.

17. The family "left the thing entirely to the young lady herself." Letter of November 16, 1769, from Lord Elibank to Sir James Johnstone, EUL-L, La.II.73/104; letter of March 29, 1775, from George Kinnaird to William, HL-P, PU 784 [756]; letter of January 13, 1775, from John Wedderburn to William, HL-P, PU 1755 [1805]. Margaret Wedderburn, the

child born in France of proscribed parents, was an alien and therefore subject to restrictions on inheritance. John Wedderburn was a kinsman of the Wedderburns, who were such close friends of William, in his studies with Adam Smith, and of George in West Florida; he was a kinsman, too, of the extended families of Wedderburns in Jamaica. "It was impossible for me to go down to Savanna la mar or Lucia near which places our three Cousins live," David Wedderburn wrote to his brother when he was about to leave Jamaica for Pensacola. Letter of January 29, 1765, from David Wedderburn to Alexander Wedderburn, Wedderburn Papers, UMWCL.

18. Letter of July 2, 1768, from John to Gideon, in care of William, HL-P, PU 634 [631].

19. Petition of Major James Johnstone, October 10, 1764, enclosing a certificate of age, October 1, 1764, IOR/J/1/5/136, 141. James requested Gideon's admission as their brother John's earnest wish and "only reward." In the certificate of Gideon's age, David Balmain, the minister of Westerkirk parish, who was James Balmain's father, together with two apparently semi-literate elders of the parish, attested in an extraordinarily shaky hand that "it appears from the Register of Baptisms," that Gideon was born on the 24th and baptised on the 28th of June 1745, six years to the day after his actual birth and baptism (or the dates, at least, that appear in the surviving register). Nineteen was an acceptable age at the time for the young men who were setting out as "writers" or rulers of India; someone of twenty-five would have been unacceptably old. Extract of the Westerkirk records for 1739, available at General Register House, Edinburgh. On Gideon's movements, see letters of February 22, 1758, from Betty to William, of February 24, 1761, from Gideon to William, and of May 19, 1771, from John to William, HL-P, PU 400 [392], 490 [476], PU 651 [644].

20. "Had either been the case . . . it would certainly have been mentioned in the dispatches to the Board," William's informant concluded; there was no "particular thing said about Cap. Gideon Johnstone." Unsigned letter of October 18, 1773, from the Admiralty to William, HL-P, PU 1911 [477].

21. Letter of September 30, 1774, from John Macpherson in Madras to James Macpherson in London, transcribed in a letter of June 27, 1974, from James N. M. Maclean of Edinburgh University to M. M. Stuart, NLS, M. M. Stuart Manuscripts, Acc. 9260/22. M. M. Stuart was an official in the Indian Civil Service, who in retirement undertook extensive research in Scotland on "unpublished or unregarded documents on Scots who went to India." He published an article about John Johnstone: M. M. Stuart, "Lying under the Company's Displeasure," *South Asian Review* 8, no. 1 (October 1974): 43–52, p. 43.

22. Alexander, James, William, and John were joint owners of the plantation, and Alexander later took out a very large mortgage on the plantation and the slaves with a celebrated Amsterdam banker. Letters of December 13, 1764, from Sir James Johnstone to William and of August 12, 1767, from John to William, HL-P, PU 431 [568], and PU 626 [624]; mortgage "for 400,000 Holland Guilders with interest at 5 per cent," September 1, 1775, BUL-W, Westerhall Estate Papers, DM 41/49 and DM 41/52.

23. "I have an idea that Mr Macintosh & I may settle our Matters so, as that we may divide our concern now, by one of us taking the Estate in Tobago & the other the Estate in Dominica," William wrote in 1773 of his partnership with a man called Macintosh. Draft letter from William to Robert Young of August 24–27, 1773, HL-P, PU 1910 [1541]. Macintosh, who had large debts to William, later ran away to the island of Madeira, en route, apparently, to the French East Indies: "la Compagnie des Indes vient de recevoir une lettre de l'isle de Madeira qui lui mande que Monsr Macintosh mon debiteur y etoit arrivé dans une vaisseau Francois de l'Orient destinée pour Pondicherry dans les Indes Orientales," William wrote in another draft of 1778. Draft letter from William of June 20, 1778, HL-P, PU 1945 [1554]. William was listed in 1769 as the proprietor of land in Grenada. "Copy of a Memorial of the Proprietors of Lands in the Island of Grenada," October 3, 1769, TNA, Privy Council Papers, PC1/60/7. George Ferguson, the son of the Johnstones' aunt Anne (Murray) Ferguson, was lieutenant governor of Tobago in 1781, at the time of the capitulation of the island to the French. *Lloyd's Evening Post*, September 24, 1781, no. 3786.

24. On William's involvement in the tobacco trade, see Jacob M. Price, *France and the Chesapeake: A History of the French Tobacco Monopoly, 1674–1791, and of Its Relationship to the British and American Tobacco Trades* (Ann Arbor, MI, 1973), 2:691–700. William explained some of the mechanisms on lending on West Indian estates in a draft letter of 1773: "You know that besides my own Loan on Tobago & another purchase on Dominica I want one for Mr Douglas on his Jamaica estate. . . . If it were possible to purchase [illegible] Portugal [illegible] with the Dutch or fflemish money we might save more than the exchange & change by Lending them to the West Indies. They sell here by their weight & not by Tale." Draft letter of August 24–27, 1773 from William in London to Robert Young, HL-P, PU 1910 [1541]; and on selling by tale, or number, see Smith, *Wealth of Nations*, p. 41.

25. In Tobias Smollett's description of Bath, "Clerks and factors from the East Indies, loaded with the spoil of plundered provinces; planters, negro-drivers, and hucksters, from our American plantations, enriched

they know not how." Tobias Smollett, *The Expedition of Humphrey Clinker* (1771) (Oxford, 1984), p. 36.

26. Letter of January 29, 1763, from Anne Ferguson to General James Murray, NAS, GD32/24/14; "Sir James is dangerously ill, by last letters we have reason to expect the worst." James Balmain was an officer of the excise, as well as the son of the local minister. As John Ramsay of Ochtertyre related half a century later, "The famous Lady Johnston's favourite daughter having married a man in the excise her father took to his bed. Somebody asked the Lady what ailed him. Nothing she said but the *Gauger* fever which is not deadly." Ramsay, *Letters*, p. 295.

27. "Some time ago I wrote to Lady Kinnard, at Edinburgh, desiring a letter to her Brother, the said Governor; she returned for answer, she was pretty sure that any places he had to bestow were disposed of; but she gave me a very kind letter to introduce me to her brother, Major Johnstone, whose advice and recommendation, she said, would be of service to me; but unluckily when I went to call on him, which was about Christmas last, he was gone to reside in Norfolk, so I have never seen him, and have hitherto delayed writing. He has a brother in the East Indies who has been very fortunate." Letter of March 16, 1765, and undated letter of summer 1765 from William Julius Mickle to Lord Lyttelton, in [John Ireland], "Anecdotes of William Julius Mickle," in Mickle, *Poems, and a Tragedy* (London, 1794), xi–lii, pp. xxvi, xxx. "You no Doubt have heard how my appeal against Hunter went at London from Lord Mansfields speech, I can plainly discover, Lady Kinnairds friends have been particularly bussie in using their Influence in support of the Entail. . . . I understand your brother the major has been particularly active," Barbara's estranged husband wrote to William in 1762. Letter of March 29, 1762, from Charles Kinnaird to William, HL-P, PU 777 [753].

28. Undated summary of a letter of August 13, 1765, from Edmund Dana to his father about his marriage to Helen Kinnaird, Massachusetts Historical Society [MHS], Dana Family Papers, Ms. N-1088, Dana Family I, Box 2, Folder 1770–73. Helen Kinnaird was born in 1749, and she and Edmund married on July 9, 1765; see www.familysearch.org.

29. Barbara Kinnaird died on October 21, 1765. *Lloyd's Evening Post*, November 1, 1765, no. 1298.

30. Letter of December 13, 1764, from Sir James Johnstone (the father) to William in Betty's hand, in the midst of John's final dramas in Bengal, and George's earliest ventures in West Florida, HL-P, PU 431 [568]; letters of January 13, 1767, from John to Betty, of January 26, 1767, from Betty to John, and of April 7, 1769, from John to Betty, JJLB-CLA, PD239/201/9; letters of June 19, 1770, from James to John and August 18, 1770, from James to Betty, JJLB-EUL, pp. 6, 35; letter of

March 28, 1768, from Mr. Douglas in Annan to Betty in Carlisle, EUL-L, La.II.73/102.

31. Letters of March 3, 1771, from James to John, of January 22, 1772, from James to John, and of May 30, 1771, from James to James Balmain, JJLB-EUL, pp. 48, 79, 129.

32. Letter of November 14, 1771, from Louisa to John Irving, JJLB-EUL, pp. 102–3.

33. Letter of April 18, 1761, from Walter Johnstone to William, HL-P, PU 719 [707].

34. Letter of May 26, 1771, from James to John, JJLB-EUL, p. 67.

35. James also encouraged Alexander, whose heir he had become, to marry for the first time; "tho your Legs may be weak your Loins may be strong. Matrimony is the grand Specifick for Human Woes." Letter of May 30, 1771, from James to Gilbert Petrie, of August 20, 1772, from James to John, of August 22, 1772, from James to Alexander, and of November 1, 1772, from James to Betty, JJLB-EUL, pp. 71, 159, 165, 171–72.

36. Letters of April 29, 1772, and July 16, 1772, from James to John, JJLB-EUL, pp. 149, 154, 156. Sir James Johnstone died on December 13, 1772, and Lady Johnstone died on March 15, 1773. *Scots Magazine* 34 (December 1772), p. 696, and 35 (March 1773), p. 165.

37. Letter of April 18, 1761, from Walter Johnstone to William, HL-P, PU 719 [707].

38. Letter of 1767 from John to Betty, JJLB-CLA, PD239/201/9.

39. Letter of December 29, 1772, from John to William, HL-P, PU 658 [652].

40. He was elected in 1767 for the constituency of St. David's. See *Audi Alteram Partem*, app. 9.

41. On the British parliamentary system of the 1760s, see Sir Lewis Namier, *The Structure of Politics at the Accession of George III* (London, 1961).

42. "My brother John I believe will also be able to secure a seat for himself & I look upon my own election as certain," William continued. Letter of November 15, 1766, from William Johnstone to James Oswald, Oswald Papers, Chest IV, C. I am most grateful to the owners of the Oswald Papers for permission to consult and quote from the papers, of which a schedule is available through the National Register of Archives, Scotland.

43. Undated letter of 1766 or 1767 from John Home to James Oswald, in *Memorials of the Public Life and Character of the Right Hon. James Oswald of Dunnikier* (Edinburgh, 1825), p. 115.

44. Namier and Brooke, *History of Parliament*, 2:683–87, 3:341–43. George was in parliament from 1768 until shortly before his death in 1787 for four successive and spectacularly venal English constituencies: Cockermouth (in Cumberland), Appleby (in Westmoreland), Lostwithiel (in Cornwall), and Ilchester (in Somerset). William was in parliament from 1768 to 1774 for the Scottish county of Cromartyshire and from 1775 to his death in 1805 for Shrewsbury (in Shropshire), a constituency substantially dominated by his wife's family interests. John was in parliament from 1774 to 1780, after he was elected in a brutal contest with James Oswald's son for the Dysart Burghs in Fife, Adam Smith's home constituency. James was in parliament from 1784 to 1790 for the Dumfries Burghs and again from 1791 to 1794 for the English constituency of Weymouth (in Dorset), another of William's dependencies. Three of the brothers—William, George, and John—were in parliament from 1774 to 1780 and a different three—James, William, and George—in parliament from 1784 to 1787. There were several other constituencies in which the brothers were unsuccessful candidates, including James in St. Ives (in Cornwall) in 1768, George in Carlisle (in Cumberland) in 1768, John in Haslemere (in Surrey) in 1768, Alexander in Wootton Bassett (in Wiltshire) in 1771, and John in Dumfriesshire in 1790. William was elected in 1768 in the Perth Burghs, as well as in Cromartyshire. See letters of March 28, 1768, from Mr. Douglas in Annan to Betty, EUL-L, La. II.73/102; of March 24, 1768, from James Murray to William Pulteney, Pulteney Collection, Pierpont Morgan Library, New York City, vol. 13: 746; of February 1, 1771, from John to Robert Mayne and William Pulteney, JJLB-CLA, PD239/201/9; and Namier and Brooke, *History of Parliament*, 1:238, 245, 386, 508–9, 2:687.

45. On the circumstances of the Haslemere election of 1768 and its relationship to the election of the same year in Shrewsbury, in which William lost to Lord Clive, see the letter of March 24, 1768, from James Murray to William, Pierpont Morgan Library, Pulteney Collection, vol. 13:746. William was a candidate in 1768 in Cromartyshire (where he was initially defeated but seated on appeal), the Perth Burghs (for which he was elected and later resigned), and Shrewsbury, where he was defeated. Namier and Brooke, *History of Parliament*, 1:363–64, 475–76, 508–9.

46. The "Dispute . . . relative to the late Election for Wootton Bassett" involved Alexander and Sir William Mayne. The brothers of the two protagonists, William and the banker Robert Mayne, were eventually accepted as arbiters. Letter of February 1, 1771, from John to Robert Mayne and William Pulteney, JJLB-CLA, PD239/201/9.

47. *Narrative of the Proceedings*, p. xlvi; letter of March 28, 1768, from Mr. Douglas in Annan to Betty in Carlisle, EUL-L, La.II.73/102.

48. Undated letter of [August] 1768 from John to William, HL-P, PU 640 [637].

49. [T.H.B. Oldfield], *An entire and complete History, Political and Personal, of the Boroughs of Great Britain*, 3 vols. (London, 1792), 3:108.

50. *Journals of the House of Commons*, 1774–76 (London, 1803), pp. 33–34 (December 9, 1774) and p. 301 (April 12, 1775).

51. On the politics of the 1760s and 1770s, see Paul Langford, "Introduction: Time and Space," in *The Eighteenth Century, 1688–1815*, ed. Paul Langford (Oxford, 2002), 1–32; Kathleen Wilson, *The Sense of the People: Politics, Culture and Imperialism in England, 1715–1785* (Cambridge, 1995).

52. Speech of George Johnstone of March 30, 1772, debate in the House of Commons on the East India Judicature Bill, PH, vol. 17, col. 376.

53. On the Select Committee and the Committee of Secrecy, see Sutherland, *East India Company*, pp. 222–38.

54. Letter of January 2, 1768 from Lord Clive to Dr. Adams, National Library of Wales, CR4/2; letter available on the Web site www.british onlinearchives.co.uk.

55. Letter of March 31, 1775, from George Dempster to William, HL-P, PU 162 [165].

56. Speech of William Pulteney of December 2, 1772, debate in the House of Commons on the Navy Estimates, PH, vol. 17, col. 538.

57. Speech of William Pulteney of April 29, 1772, debate in the House of Commons on the Bill for Encouraging Foreigners to Lend Money upon Estates in the West Indies, PH, vol. 17, cols. 483–85. These mortgages were the subject of the most intricate litigation and diplomatic representation, as in the complaints of the London merchants Bosanquet and Fatio with respect to a widow in Grenada, "la veuve Jacques," who sailed away one night to the French islands with all her slaves; and John's litigation against the same Fatio over bonds with respect to the East India Company and the French Compagnie des Indes. Complaint of John Johnstone and George Dempster of March 20, 1770, against Francis Philip Fatio, TNA, C12/392/73; copies of memorials enclosed in a letter of August 27, 1774, from Lord Dartmouth to Lord Rochford, TNA, SP78/293/125r–125v, 126r, 130r–130v. On the law of property in land and slaves in the eighteenth-century American and West Indian colonies, see Claire Priest, "Creating an American Property Law: Alienability and

Its Limits in American History," *Harvard Law Review* 120, no. 2 (December 2006), 386–459.

58. Speech of William Pulteney of June 3, 1774, proceedings in the House of Commons on the Bill for the Government of Quebec, PH, vol. 17, col. 1384.

59. Speech of William Pulteney of April 29, 1772, debate in the House of Commons on the Bill for Encouraging Foreigners to Lend Money upon Estates in the West Indies, PH, vol. 17, col. 484.

60. Speech of George Johnstone of May 8, 1770, debate in the House of Commons on an Address to the King on the Disturbances in America, PH, vol. 16, col. 996.

61. Speech of Lord George Germaine of December 14, 1770; report of a duel fought on December 17, 1770, between George Johnstone and Lord George Germaine over George Johnstone's observation on December 14 that "he wondered that the noble lord should interest himself so deeply in the honour of his country, when he had been hitherto so regardless of his own." PH, vol. 16, col. 1328, and fn., col. 1329.

62. George also reverted to the prospect of military despotism in the colonies and at home and to the logistical difficulties of "a war across the Atlantic": "have they thought of feeding an army with porter, sheep, and sour-crout across a tempestuous ocean?" Speeches of George Johnstone of February 6, 1775, on an Address to the King upon the Disturbances in North America, of October 26, 1775, on the Address of Thanks, and of April 24, 1776, on the Budget, in PH, vol. 18, cols. 256, 744, 747, 752, 756, 1323.

63. Letter of September 1, 1777, from Walter Minto to Alexander Waugh, UMWCL-MS.

64. Speech of John Johnstone of February 7, 1777, debate in the Commons on the Bill for suspending the Habeas Corpus Act, PH, vol. 19, cols. 5–6.

65. Speech of John Johnstone of February 25, 1777, debate in the House of Commons on Captain Blair's Petition, PH, vol. 19, col. 70.

66. This was the description of John's remarks in response to a comment by Henry Dundas "respecting the Principles of Liberty and manly feelings which prevailed in Scotland," in a letter of March 16, 1776, from Henry Dundas to the Duke of Buccleuch. Dundas added, "I hope you will not think me too vain if I tell you that I was desired by my Friends upon both sides of the House to return thanks to Mr Johnston for the opportunity he had given me of entering at large upon that subject." NAS, Papers of the Montague-Douglas-Scott Family, Dukes of Buccleuch, 1165–1947, GD224/30/1. The exchange, which was not reported

in the *Parliamentary History*, was apparently in the course of the Commons debate of March 14, 1776, on going into a committee on the Scotch Militia Bill; PH, vol. 18, cols. 1231–34.

67. "The whole country is under water." Letter of October 5, 1775, from Thomas Dundas M.P. to Sir Lawrence Dundas, North Yorkshire County Record Office, Zetland Papers, ZNK X 1/2/222. The meeting is discussed in Ian Adams and Meredyth Somerville, *Cargoes of Despair and Hope: Scottish Emigration to North America, 1603–1803* (Edinburgh, 1993), p. 140, and in Bernard Bailyn, *Voyagers to the West: A Passage in the Peopling of America on the Eve of the Revolution* (New York, 1988), p. 57, n.32.

68. Speech of George Johnstone of March 30, 1772, debate in the House of Commons on the East India Judicature Bill, PH, vol. 17, col. 379.

69. Speech of George Johnstone of March 30, 1772, debate in the House of Commons on the East India Judicature Bill, PH, vol. 17, cols. 377–78.

70. George's initial suggestion, in the General Court of Proprietors of the East India Company, was that parliament should remove the duties on tea in England, which "would enable them to send that commodity to several markets on the continent, and by these means convert the large quantities now in the warehouse to cash." It was his associate Mr. Creighton who added the proposal about the American duties—"this latter hint was immediately adopted by Governor Johnstone"—and the eventual motion, proposed by George, was the following: "That it be recommended to the Court of Directors *to obtain* an act of parliament, for them to export their surplus teas to foreign markets, clear of all drawbacks and duties, as well as to take off the three per cent. duty in America." *London Evening Post*, January 7, 1773, no. 7023, and see also *St. James's Chronicle or The British Evening Post*, January 9, 1773, no. 1856, and *Daily Advertiser*, January 11, 1773, no. 13121.

71. The "Resolutions allowing the East India Company to export Teas duty free" were debated and approved in the House of Commons on April 27, 1773. PH, vol. 17, cols. 840–41. On the Boston Tea Party, see Francis S. Drake, ed., *Tea Leaves* (Boston, 1884) and Benjamin Woods Labaree, *The Boston Tea Party* (New York, 1964). The term "Boston Tea Party" was not used, as Alfred Young has shown, until the 1830s. Alfred F. Young, *The Shoemaker and the Tea Party* (Boston, 1999), pp. 155–65.

72. *Portsmouth, New Hampshire, July 15, 1774* (Portsmouth, NH: Fowle, 1774); "A Letter from the Country, to a Gentleman in Philadelphia," December 4, 1773, in *The Writings of John Dickinson*, ed. Paul Leicester Ford, 2 vols. (Philadelphia, 1895), 1:462–63.

73. Speech of George Johnstone of March 25, 1774, debate in the House of Commons on the Boston Port Bill, PH, vol. 17, col. 1188.

74. A late Victorian account of the famine, by Sir William Hunter, estimated that ten million people had died in the space of nine months; Sir William Hunter, *Annals of Rural Bengal*, 7th ed. (London, 1897), p. 34. On the Bengal famine of 1770, see McLane, *Land and Local Kingship*, pp. 194–207.

75. Speech of George Johnstone of March 30, 1772, debate in the House of Commons on the East India Judicature Bill, PH, vol. 17, cols. 368–69.

76. Speech of Col. John Burgoyne, later Gen. John Burgoyne of the British Army in North America, of April 13, 1772, debate in the House of Commons on Colonel Burgoyne's Motion for a select committee on East India Affairs, PH, vol. 17, col. 459.

77. Letter of February 19, 1771, from John in Balgonie in Fifeshire to the East India Company Court of Directors in London, OIOC, IOR Miscellaneous Letters Received, 1771, IOR/E/1/55, ff.88r–88v. In the index of the minutes of the Court of Directors for 1771, the letter is registered as "Johnstone, Jno. Esq. desires to be Governor of Bengal." OIOC, IOR/B/86.

78. Letter of April 17, 1771, from James to John, JJLB-EUL, p. 64. The rumor of the week, reported in the *Middlesex Journal*, was that Thomas Rumbold, one of Clive's close friends, had been chosen as Governor of Bengal: "before the last Directors of the India Company quitted their office, they appointed Mr. Rumbold Governor of Bengal, and he is preparing to set out for that place." *Middlesex Journal or Chronicle of Liberty*, April 11, 1771, no. 317. Warren Hastings was appointed on April 9, 1771, to be second in council in Fort William (Calcutta) and to succeed John Cartier as governor. Minutes of the Court of Directors of the East India Company, OIOC, IOR/B/86, p. 457.

79. As George wrote, he had read "again & again" Hume's "discriptions of the Higher Scenes of Life, But that you could descend with equall ease from that elevation of thought into the simple engaging & domestick Situations of Mankind of this I was Ignorant before." Letter of March 22 [1763], from George Johnstone to David Hume, Hume Manuscripts, NLS, MS 23155, no. 94, f. 249; letter of April 2, 1759, from David Hume to Lord Elibank, in Ernest Campbell Mossner, ed., "New Hume Letters to Lord Elibank, 1748–1776," *Texas Studies in Literature and Language* 4, no. 3 (Autumn 1962): 431–60, p. 449.

80. Letters from David Hume of July 21, 1763 to Adam Smith, of March 10, 1769, to Jean-Baptise-Antoine Suard, of March 30, 1769, to Baron Mure of Caldwell, and of June 25, 1771, and January 2, 1772, to

William Strahan, in Greig, *Letters of David Hume*, 1:391, 2:195, 200, 243, 251. William's noble behaviour was in giving an annuity to Andrew Stuart, after he had lost the Douglas cause.

81. This was the account of his granddaughter, Elizabeth Caroline Gray. Gray, "Sketch of My Life," unpag.

82. Thomas Gainsborough, *Portrait of Sir William Johnstone-Pulteney*, Yale Center for British Art.

83. Henrietta Laura Pulteney was painted by Angelica Kauffmann in or around 1777. The painting is in the Holburne Museum of Art in Bath; see www.holburne.org/muse/search/item.cfm?MuseumNumber=1996.5.

84. The painting, now in the Tate Gallery in London, is identified as "Mrs Johnstone and her Son (?) circa 1775–80." It was bequeathed to the National Gallery in 1898 by Major General Julius Johnstone, who was Martha Ford's great-grandson and the grandson of George and her youngest son, Alexander Patrick, who died in India in 1803. OIOC, N/1/6 f.241. The painting, N01667, can be seen at www.tate.org.uk. George married Charlotte Dee in 1782, and their son, John Lowther Johnstone, was born in 1783. Alexander Patrick Johnstone was baptised in London in 1776. He and his wife, Maria D'Aguilar, had three children, George Buller Johnstone, Sophia Johnstone, and Emily Johnstone, who were left bequests in the wills of their uncle George Lindsay Johnstone and of the widower of their aunt Sophia Johnstone, the Duke of Cannizzaro. George Buller Johnstone was the father of John Julius Johnstone, who was christened in Leamington Spa on April 25, 1839. In the will of General John Julius Johnstone, dated November 12, 1898, and proved in Hong Kong in 1899, "my three quarters seated portrait of a lady and child and my circular sketch Head of Lady Hamilton (both which pictures are by George Romney)" were given to the trustees of the National Gallery. Wills of George Lindsay Johnstone, proved February 1, 1814, and Francis Platamone, Duke of Cannizzaro, proved November 27, 1841, TNA, PROB 11/1552 and 11/1953; probate of the Will of General John Julius Johnstone, January 11, 1899, Public Record Office of Hong Kong, H.K.R.S. no. 144/D. & S. no. 4/1211; christening information available at www.ancestry.co.uk. I am most grateful to Alex Kidson, author of the forthcoming complete catalogue of the paintings of George Romney (1734–1802), for confirming that the painting will be identified as being of Martha Ford and Alexander Patrick Johnstone.

85. David N. King, *Complete Works of Robert and James Adam* (Oxford, 2001), pp. 39–41, 359–61; David N. King, *Unbuilt Adam* (Oxford, 2001), pp. 181, 242–43.

86. Luis de Camöens, *The Lusiad; or, the Discovery of India. An Epic Poem*, trans. William Julius Mickle (Oxford, 1776), p. i; on Mickle's ap-

pointment to Lisbon, see undated letter from George to William Julius Mickle and undated copy of a letter from George to Mickle of early November 1780, Osborn Mickle Papers, Beinecke Library, Yale University [WJM-Y]. Mickle was the "Cousin German," or first cousin, of the Johnstones' Uncle Walter, the half-brother of their father. He was born in 1734 and was the son of Alexander Meikle, the minister of Langholm. J. J. Caudle, "Mickle, William Julius (1734/5–1788)," ODNB, article 18661; Rev. John Sim, "The Life of the Author," in *The Poetical Works of William Julius Mickle* (London, 1806); Ireland, "Anecdotes of Mickle." Walter Johnstone wrote to him, after they reencountered each other through James Balmain, as "Dear Cousin." "MR. JOHNSTONE, my Cousin German, who was Capt. of Marines, of the Edinburgh Man of War, and is uncle to the Governor of West Florida, has offered me letters to the West Indies, where his ship was long stationed," Mickle wrote to Lord Lyttelton in 1765. Letters of June 29, 1776, and July 2, 1778, from Walter to William Julius Mickle, in WJM-Y; Ireland, "Anecdotes of Mickle," p. xxx.

87. Letter of July 2, 1778, from Walter Johnstone to William Julius Mickle, WJM-Y.

88. When Bentham applied for the position of his secretary, George responded with an elaborate story about his dependence on William, "for he was so circumstanced that it was necessary for him not to quarrel with his brother." Letter of April/May 1778 from Jeremy Bentham to the Rev. John Forster, in *The Correspondence of Jeremy Bentham*, 12 vols., ed. Timothy L. S. Sprigge (London, 1968–2006), 2:104–5.

89. "The Strongest Citadel on the highest Summit is no longer tenable. The Isle of Britain can no longer place any security in the Sea that Surrounds her." Letter of December 24, 1783, from George in London to John Macpherson, Macpherson Correspondence, OIOC, Mss Eur F291/110; speech of Nassuba Mingo, Mobile, April 1, 1765, in *Mississippi Provincial Archives*, p. 242.

90. Letters of May 30, 1771, and January 25, 1772, from James to James Balmain, JJLB-EUL, pp. 77–78, 132–33.

91. Letter of May 18, 1779, from Alexander to William Julius Mickle, WJM-Y.

92. Letter of October 9, 1759, from Betty to William, HL-P, PU 405 [397]; letter of March 29, 1762, from Charles Kinnaird to William, HL-P, PU 777 [753].

93. Letter of May 30, 1776, from George to Walter Minto, in Minto's hand, UMWCL-MS.

94. Letter of March 9, 1777, from Walter Minto to David Minto, UMWCL-MS.

95. Smith, *Wealth of Nations*, p. 640.

96. "Only if he be inclined to mind future examinations and after-reckonings, he will be cunning enough to manage so as that the ruin he is likely to leave behind be not imputable to him"; Gholam-Hossein, *Seir Mutaqharin*, 2:581. Haji Mustafa, the translator of 1789, added that "the accusations brought in general against the English by the natives" include the charge that "of so many English that have carried away such princely fortunes from this country, not one of them has ever thought of shewing his gratitude to it by sinking a well, digging a pond, planting a public grove" (2:577, n. 27).

97. "Articles of Charge against Robert Melvill Esq.," December 1, 1769, TNA, Colonial Series of Bundles, PC1/60/7.

98. *Narrative of the Proceedings*, pp. ii, iii.

99. "Report presented to the Committee on February 20, 1770," TNA, PC1/60/7; *Narrative of the Proceedings*, pp. xlviii, 41, 53, 108, 114.

100. Steele, *Grenada*, p. 62.

101. In the words of the act, Augustine had "by his Activity, care and Ability, contributed greatly to the Seizing and Destroying many of the said Runaway Slaves." After he was freed, according to the complaint, Augustine lived for several months in the governor's own house, a measure that was necessary, the governor said, in order to protect him from the "jealousies" of his former owner. Alexander Johnstone, "Articles of Charge against Robert Melvill Esq.," December 1, 1769, Privy Council Bundle, TNA, PC1/60/7; "An Act to Free *Augustine*, a Negroe Man Slave belonging to *Couston* of the Parish of *St. John*, in this Island *Grenada*, Planter, or to whomsoever else belonging, passed April 29, 1767," in "The Laws of Grenada and the Grenadines," TNA, CO103/1/48r; *Narrative of the Proceedings*, pp. 3–4, 31, 40.

102. "The confusion arising in the minds of his Majesty's Counsellors of Granada, proceeds from this, that the majority of them cannot distinguish between the several capacities in which they act at different times and on different occasions, having (though the same men) very distinct and very different authorities." *Narrative of the Proceedings*, p. 87.

103. There was a Peter Gordon who was one of the justices of the peace who convicted Alexander of mutiny, and a Peter Gordon, justice of the peace, who tortured the five slaves, of whom three died from their injuries; a Peter Gordon who became commander of Alexander's regiment after he was convicted and who addressed the officers and soldiers on parade about the "protestant interest" and the "protestant religion"; and a Peter Gordon who was a member of the governor's council (or senate). On the multiple Peter Gordons, see *Narrative of the Proceedings*, pp. 4, 77, 83, 125–26.

104. "Copy of a Memorial of the Proprietors of Land in the Island of Grenada," TNA, PC160/7; *Narrative of the Proceedings*, p. xx.

105. *Narrative of the Proceedings*, pp. iii, xxx, 29, 40.

106. Bolts appears to have been in fairly close contact with John and William during his period in London. "I'm glad our friend Bolts prospects are so good," John wrote to a business associate in February 1771, and a few weeks later, to Alexander, "I hope you will immediately learn from Mr Hannay whether Mr Bolts will pay off his Bonds to Mrs Johnstone & Betty." When William wrote to John in 1772 with questions about the operation of the Mayor's Court in Calcutta, John answered some of the questions, and referred him to Bolts for the others: "Messrs. Bolts & Petrie can supply the defects." When Bolts was finally obliged to leave the country, in 1773—"Poor Bolts is gone"—John described his departure as "a heavy stroke." Letters of February 8, 1771, from John to Samuel Hannay and of March 23, 1771, to Alexander, JJLB-CLA, PD239/201/9; letters of February 5, 1772, and October 16, 1773, from John to William, HL-P, PU 655 [648] and PU 660 [654].

107. "Tagoor" was carried to the "Cutcherry" court and "without any examination, enquiry, or form whatever, tied up, severely flogged, and beat on the head with his own slippers," a "very ignominious punishment." Bolts, *Considerations on India Affairs*, 1:93–94, 2:59; 3:113–14.

108. Bolts, *Considerations on India Affairs*, 1:vi, 109, 202, 217, 228. Of the "Mogul government," Bolts wrote, "it does not appear, that they ever much concerned themselves about the religion either of their own Indian subjects, or of those who traded with them" (p. 13).

109. See Michael H. Fisher, *Counterflows to Colonialism: Indian Travellers and Settlers in Britain, 1600–1857* (Delhi, 2004).

110. Speech of Edmund Burke of December 18, 1772, debate in the House of Commons on preventing the East India Company from sending out Supervisors to India, PH, vol. 17, col. 671.

111. "Account of the late Famine in India," *Gentleman's Magazine* 41 (September 1771): 402–4; "Cruelties practised by the English in Bengal," *Gentleman's Magazine* 42 (February 1772): 69.

112. Speech of George Johnstone of March 30, 1772, debate in the House of Commons on the East India Judicature Bill, PH, vol. 17, col. 369.

113. Speech of George Johnstone of March 30, 1772, debate in the House of Commons on the East India Judicature Bill, PH, vol. 17, col. 377; Petition of Gregore Cojamaul and Johannes Padre Rafael, September 12, 1769, Second Report from the Committee Appointed to enquire into the East India Company, *House of Commons Sessional Papers* (May 26, 1772), 135:282.

114. John Johnstone, Evidence in behalf of the Plaintiff Rafael (1774), OIOC, Verelst Collection, MSS Eur F218/73. The significance of the rukah in the merchants' case was that the order for their imprisonment, on the grounds that "this tribe are of a bad cast, and their principles only falsehood and imposition," was given by the East India Company official Harry Verelst in the form of a rukah. See Kuiters, *British in Bengal*, p. 244.

115. "I had a letter from Gideon dated the 30 December from Bussorah.... I had also a letter by the last Packet dated 17 April from George, he was then confined to his bed unable to write himself by Sciatic Pains, which he said was much easier than they had been & made light of. The Phisical Phrase for it was a Flatus, the pains of his breast however was greatly relieved." Letter of May 19, 1771, from John to William, HL-P, PU 651 [644].

116. Letters of May 30, 1771, from James to James Balmain, of September 1, 1771, from James to Betty, and of October 2, 1771, from James to Walter Johnstone, JJLB-EUL, pp. 75–79, 84, 88.

117. "Declaration of Bell or Belinda a black Girl belonging to John Johnstone Esq.," Cupar, July 4, 1771, NAS, JC26/193/3. The declaration and the other papers relating to the case, prior to the circuit court session of September 1771, are included in the box identified in the NAS as High Court of Judiciary Processes Main Series, 1771, third box. The box was previously classified as JC26/193 and has also, apparently, been mislabelled as JC27/193/5; the document "Petition for Bell or Belinda a Black Girl" is marked both "EXJC27/193/5" and "exJC26/193." The Bell or Belinda case, together with other cases of black men and women in eighteenth-century Scotland, is discussed in the important forthcoming work by Professor John Cairns of the University of Edinburgh, *The Scottish Law of Slavery*. On infanticide in eighteenth-century Scotland, see the excellent book by Deborah A. Symonds, *Weep Not for Me: Women, Ballads, and Infanticide in Early Modern Scotland* (University Park, PA, 1997).

118. "Indictment agt Bell or Belinda a Negroe Girl," Porteous Roll for Fifeshire, Autumn 1771, NAS, JC26/193/3. On the "Act Anent Child Murder," which was in force from 1690 to 1809, see Symonds, *Weep Not For Me*, pp. 127–60. Under the provisions of the act, "if any woman shall conceal her being with child dureing the whole space and shall not call for and make use of help and assistance in the birth, the child being found dead or amissing the mother shall be holden and reputed the murderer of her own childe" (p. 128). On domestic slavery in Anglo-Indian families in a slightly later period, and the elusive identifications of slaves or servants, see Finn, "Slaves out of Context."

119. The Northern Circuit on September 3, 1761, convicted Mary Burgess, "late servant to John Sprunt," of child murder and condemned her to death. She was sent to Edinburgh, where her case was considered by the Lord Justice Clerk and Commissioners of Justiciary and the sentence confirmed. She was sent back to the Tolbooth in Perth, to be hanged on January 15, 1762, "her body thereafter to be delivered to Neil Menzies Surgeon in Perth to be by him Publickly Dissected & anatomized." "Dead Warrant agt. Mary Burgess," November 27, 1761, signed W. Grant, Ch. Areskine, Alexr. Boswel, Gilb. Elliot, Andr. Pringle and Alexr. Fraser, PKA, Royal Burgh of Perth, Burgh Records, B59/26/11/1, Bundle 6.

120. The expression "Intran" or "Intran." was used to indicate the presence of the defendant, or "Pannel," in the courtroom: "thereafter the Clerk writes in the Book thus, Intran. That is, The Prisoner enters the Pannal." John Louthian, *The Form of Process before The Justiciary Court in Scotland*, 2nd ed. (Edinburgh, 1752), p. 46. The late Latin "intraneus" means "that is within, inward." Nathan Bailey, *An Universal Etymological English Dictionary* (London, 1770).

121. "Petition for Bell or Belinda a Black Girl," September 13, 1771, NAS, JC26/193/3.

122. North Circuit Minute Book, Perth, September 12–13, 1771, no. 25, May 9, 1771–October 15, 1772, NAS, West Register House (WRH), JC11/28, unpag. On transportation from Scotland, see A. Roger Ekirch, "The Transportation of Scottish Criminals to America during the Eighteenth Century," *The Journal of British Studies* 24, no. 3 (July 1985): 366–74, and A. Roger Ekirch, *Bound for America: The Transportation of British Convicts to the Colonies, 1718–1775* (Oxford, 1987). Approximately seven hundred people were transported to America from all Scottish jurisdictions between 1718 and 1775, in Ekirch's estimate. Almost half of all the people prosecuted in the High Court of Justiciary in Edinburgh, which considered only serious crimes, were ordered to be transported; of the 181 people ordered to be transported, 22 had been charged with murder or infanticide. Ekirch, "Transportation of Scottish Criminals," pp. 368–71.

123. Bonds for the transportation of George Phelp, William Brown, Janet Abernethy, and "Belinda," or "the person of Bell alias Belinda a native of Bengal in the East Indies," signed by Patrick Colquhoun in Glasgow, December 4, 1771, NAS, JC26/193/3.

124. Certificate of the landing of George Phelp, Janet Abernethy, William Brown, and "Bell alias Belind a black girl," Port of James River Upper District, John Earnshaw, Collr., Jacob Bruce, Compr., Lewis Burwell, Naval Officer, April 29, 1772, NAS(WRH), JC41/12; "A List of all Ships and Vessels which have entered Inwards in the Upper District of

James River in Virginia between the fifth day of January and the fifth day of April 1772," TNA, CO5/1350. The trials of Phelp, Abernethy, and Brown are recorded in the North Circuit Minute Book, Aberdeen, September 20–23, 1771, NAS(WRH), JC11/28, and in NAS, JC26/193/1 (Phelp) and JC26/193/2 (Abernethy and Brown).

125. Letter of January 13, 1775, from John Wedderburn to William, HL-P, PU 1755 [1805].

126. Allan Maconochie, Information for Joseph Knight, a native of Africa, pursuer, April 25, 1775 [Lord Kennet Reporter], p. 1; James Ferguson, Information for John Wedderburn, Esq; of Ballandean, Defender, July 4, 1775 [Lord Kennet Reporter], pp. 1–2; Advocates' Library, Edinburgh, Court of Session Papers, Campbell Collection, vol. 33, papers 24 and 25. The owner of James Somerset, Charles Steuart, whose brother was a lawyer and printer in Edinburgh, was cashier and paymaster-general of the Customs office in Boston. In 1762 he was a Virginia merchant seeking to trade with the French colony of Saint-Domingue on the basis of a recommendation from William (Johnstone) Pulteney's friends in the tobacco business, and by 1765 he had become surveyor general of Customs for the Eastern Middle District of North America; he was a friend of Benjamin Franklin's son, the governor of Pennsylvania, and of the Johnstones' maternal uncle, James Murray, the former governor of Quebec. Letter of June 20, 1762, from A. J. Alexander, statement of August 9, 1765, Port of Perth Amboy, letter of August 25, 1769, from Governor Franklin, letter of November 27, 1769, from Governor Murray, NLS, Steuart Mss. 5025/8r–9v, 34r, 177r, 240r. On Steuart's brother James, "our printing house," and the project that his son should "set up a Shop as a Bookseller," see letter of May 9, 1770, NLS, Steuart Mss. 6404/21r. On the background to the Somerset case, see James Oldham, "New Light on Mansfield and Slavery," *Journal of British Studies* 27 (January 1988), 45–68; Steven M. Wise, *Though the Heavens May Fall: The Landmark Trial That Led to the End of Human Slavery* (Cambridge, MA, 2005).

127. Ferguson, Information for John Wedderburn, pp. 2–3; Maconochie, Information for Joseph Knight, April 25, 1775, p. 1; and see Cairns, *Scottish Law of Slavery* and Iain Whyte, *Scotland and the Abolition of Black Slavery, 1756–1838* (Edinburgh, 2006). Joseph Knight is the subject of a remarkable historical novel by James Robertson, *Joseph Knight* (London, 2003).

128. Petition of December 14, 1773, Memorandum of November 15, 1774 for John Wedderburn Esquire, NAS, CS235/K/2/2, p. 4; Ferguson, Information for John Wedderburn, p. 3; John Swinton, Perth, decision of May 20, 1774, NAS, SC 49/6/134/3/3.

129. A copy of "this paragraph in a letter from John Johnston at Bengal to his brother, Governor Johnston, in London," dated December 14, 1763, was kept by John Swinton; A. C. Swinton, *Concerning Swinton Family Records and Portraits at Kimmerghame* (Edinburgh, 1908), pp. 93–94. Samuel Swinton was the friend to whom John and Archibald sent a power of attorney from India in the matter of the absconding French agents and the bond for seven thousand pounds. Letter of February 19, 1766, from Samuel Swinton to General John Carnac in India, OIOC, Carnac Papers, MSS Eur F128/156, unfol. On the Johnstones and the Swintons, see below, chapters 5 and 6.

130. Letter of January 15, 1775, from John Wedderburn to William, HL-P, PU 1757 [1807]; letters of March 24, 1775, and August 26, 1775, from Betty to William, HL-P, PU 436 [423], 437 [424].

131. Ferguson, Information for John Wedderburn, pp. 13, 22; Robert Cullen, *Additional Information for John Wedderburn of Ballendean, esq; defender; against Joseph Knight, a Negro of Africa, pursuer June 1777* (n.p., 1777), pp. 14, 26, 35, 74, 78; the copy of Cullen's *Information* in the New York Public Library (KF p.v.4, no. 3) bears the stamp, "Adam Smith" and is identified as being Smith's copy.

132. Ferguson, Information for John Wedderburn, p. 18.

133. Cullen, *Additional Information*, pp. 12, 51, 76.

134. Manuscript summary, NAS, CS235/K/2/2; Ferguson, Information for John Wedderburn, p. 37.

135. *Edinburgh Advertiser* 18, no. 888 (June 30–July 3, 1772); *Caledonian Mercury*, January 17, 1778.

136. North Circuit Minute Book, Perth, September 12–13, 1771, no. 25, May 9, 1771–October 15, 1772, NAS (WRH), JC11/28, unpag.

CHAPTER THREE. ENDING AND LOSS

1. Letter of December 22, 1764, from Barbara (their mother) to John, UMWCL-MS.

2. Barbara Murray Johnstone died at Westerhall on March 15, 1773. *Scots Magazine* 35 (March 1773), p. 165, and "A Character of the Hon. Dame Barbara Murray," p. 120. She was a woman of extraordinarily robust health, which she attributed to the fact that she, like her brother Lord Elibank, had "continued so long on the breast, she for two years & he for 22 months." Letter of February 18, 1768, from Sir James Johnstone to William, HL-P, PU 557 [570]. Charlotte Johnstone Balmain died in Edinburgh on April 2, 1773. *Public Advertiser*, April 13, 1773, no. 11862. John wrote to William, on December 29, 1772, that he and Betty

were going to visit "poor sister Charlotte" after their father's death: "her own long Illness, a consumptive Cough, since the death of her favorite child last year, had reduced her so low she could barely walk when I came here." HL-P, PU 658 [652].

3. Letters of April 23, 1772, from Sir James Johnstone to William and of June 18, 1772, from John to William, HL-P, PU 562 [577], 656 [649].

4. Letters of July 29, 1751, from Charlotte to William, HL-P, PU 450 [443], of May 19, 1771, from John to William, HL-P, PU 651 [644], and of November 1, 1772, from James to Betty, JJLB-EUL, p. 171.

5. Letters of November 22, 1771, and August 20, 1772, from James to John, and of August 28, 1772, from James to John Irving, JJLB-EUL, pp. 108, 159, 168–69. Letters of September 13 and December 6, 1778, from John to James Balmain, JA-CLA, Bundle 6, PD239/6/24,32.

6. Letter of July 20, 1772, from Walter Johnstone to Walter Ogilvy, HL-P, PU 751 [725].

7. Letter of February 12, 1778, from Walter Johnstone to James Balmain, JA-CLA, Bundle 6, PD239/6/2.

8. Letters of October 5, 1773, and October 30, 1773, from Betty to William, HL-P, PU 434 [421], 435 [422].

9. Letter of December 28, 1773, from James to John Irving, in JJLB-EUL, p. 178; "Pulteney Esqr. and others . . . agt. Johnstone Esqr. Award," and "Release William Pulteney and John Johnstone Esqr. to Alexander Johnstone Esqr.," April 28, 1774, BUL-W, Westerhall Estate Papers, DM 41/38 and DM 41/48/1. The "Release" required the payment of thirty thousand pounds by Alexander to William and John.

10. Will of Alexander Johnstone, dated May 23, 1775, and proved January 24, 1783, TNA, PROB 11/1099. The sequence was as follows: James and his possible future sons, "lawfully begotten or to be begotten"; James's possible sons' "heirs male"; George; William's sons by a different wife; George's son George in case he were to become legitimate; George's second son, James, also in case he were to become legitimate; John; John's son James Raymond Johnstone; Gideon; Gideon's possible future sons; whoever should in the future succeed to James's title of baronet and to the title of Marquis of Annandale.

11. Alexander's granddaughter, who was also described as his great-granddaughter, was called Ann or Anne Sutherland and was in service with a grocer in the Canongate in Edinburgh. She was married to Alexander Sutherland, a drover. She wrote to John's grandson in 1839 that "being a relation of the Johnstones of Westerhall I hope and trust you will look into my unfortunate situation owing to my Husband being badly in London for upwards of three months in consequence of a severe hurt that reduced [us] into actual starvation therefore I hope you

will have the kindness to render a small assistance as we are in great Distress." The letter is endorsed, "Case of Anne Sutherland daughter of Jane Castino Johnstone a mulato daughter of Col. Alexander Johnstone" and "Her mother Jane Castino Johnstone (Granado) married a sailor who name was William Wilson (Jane being Grand daughter of Col. Alexr. Johnstone)—whose daughter here is the application Jane the mother lived with James Johnstone Hangingshaw—her mother yet lives at Bexly-heath. Alexr. Sutherland is a drover. She was in service with one [illegible] in the Canongate a grocer." In an undated letter, endorsed "Case of Ann Sutherland Grand daughter illegitimate of Col. Alexr. Johnstone," Alexander Sutherland wrote that "my wife called upon your Honour two years ago and received one pound sterling" and that they had "endeavoured to see the late Sir Frederick Johnstone," George's grandson, "but unfortunately I got my Leg broken and otherwise Dreadfully crushed on the body"; they were "next to Starvation." Letter from Ann Sutherland of May 11, 1839, in JA-CLA, Bundle 7, PD239/7/11, and undated letter from Alexander Sutherland and Ann Wilson, JA-CLA, Bundle 5, PD239/5/27.

12. Will of Scrope Colquitt, signed July 26, 1780, codicil signed July 4, 1781, proved January 27, 1783, TNA, PROB 11/1099. The interest and income on the sum of 1,500 pounds was by the codicil payable to Gideon for his lifetime, if he survived his wife.

13. "A Journal of the Proceedings of His Majesty's Ship the Adamant Kept by Captain Gidion Johnstone," TNA, ADM51/8.

14. One of the very few sources for Gideon and Fanny's life in England and Scotland, other than her father's will, is a letter from John to Fanny, available on a public history and philately Web site. The letter, in John's handwriting, is dated "Denovan, 2nd August" and indicates an affectionate friendship between John and Fanny: "ye love and attention you have shown him during so long an illness deserve a high place in the character of the Good Wife you wont to tantalise me with." The rest of the letter is concerned with gardening—"I am now at Denovan which grows every day more beautiful. . . . Of your neatness & attention to my ornamentals, I have dayly proof"—and furniture: "I sent a list inclosed to Gideon of such things as I thought might be worth sending down, the other articles would be very expensive in Freight. . . . If there be any of them that could be of use to my brother George I would be glad he had them . . . & remainder might be committed to the care of Mr Dingwall the upholsterer . . . to put up in one of my houses in Leadenhall Street." Letter of August 2, [1785 or 1786,] from John to Fanny (Colquitt) Johnstone, available at http://www.victorianweb.org/previctorian/letters/johnston.html. The "Good Wife" was a familiar figure in the comedy of

the times; as in *The Good Wife's New Year's Gift. Picture of Mock Trumps; Or, The Schools of Scandal lectrified by the School of Science, In a general Display of the Muscles, Complexion, and Passions for Gambling* (London, 1784). The other observation on Gideon and Fanny's circumstances is in a letter of 1786, from Martha Ford to William Julius Mickle. Martha Ford was in Edinburgh, where she had gone with her daughter Sophia to visit her younger sons, and "had the Happiness of meeting my two beloved Children in perfect Health." She and her companion, the children's governess, were "much Delighted with the Prospects of Scotland which struck us amazingly on our entry to Edinburgh." She reported that John had written her "a very kind letter," and was going to take Sophia to visit Alva; "poor Captain Gideon is much to be Pitied his wife being in a Melancholy Situation." Letter of July 10, 1786, from Martha Ford to William Julius Mickle, WJM-Y.

15. Will of Gideon Johnstone, proved July 4, 1788, TNA, PROB 11/1168.

16. Speech of George Johnstone of February 25, 1777, debate in the House of Commons on Captain Blair's Petition, *Parliamentary Register*, 17 vols. (London, 1775–80), 6:281. Equiano's account of the expedition to the Musquito shore is in Olaudah Equiano, *The Interesting Narrative and Other Writings*, ed. Vincent Carretta (London, 2003), pp. 198–218. On the central American Gulf coast in the eighteenth century, see Troy S. Floyd, *The Anglo-Spanish Struggle for Mosquitia* (Albuquerque, NM, 1967) and Vincent Carretta, *Equiano the African: Biography of a Self-Made Man* (Athens, GA, 2005), pp. 179–92.

17. On the Carlisle Commission, chaired by Lord Carlisle, see Frederick B. Tolles, "Franklin and the Pulteney Mission: An Episode in the Secret History of the American Revolution," *Huntington Library Quarterly* 17, no. 1 (November 1953): 37–58.

18. The three letters were to Joseph Reed, a general in the Revolutionary army who was the brother-in-law of a London merchant; Robert Morris, a business associate of William's; and Francis Dana, the brother of Barbara Kinnaird's medical student son-in-law. Letters of June 10, 1778, from George to Francis Dana, of April 11, 1778, to General Joseph Reed, and of June 16, 1776, to Robert Morris, in Charles Stedman, *The History of the Origin, Progress and Termination of the American War*, 2 vols. (Dublin, 1794), 2:55–58.

19. *London Chronicle*, October 15, 1778, no. 3412. George was described by a Scottish acquaintance as having acquired the "hatred of the Army," the "detestation" of the navy, and "the contempt of both our Friends and Foes in America." Letter of October 7, 1778, from Colonel Stuart to Lord Bute, in Mrs. E. Stuart Wortley, ed., *A Prime Minister and*

*His Son: From the Correspondence of the 3rd Earl of Bute and of Lt.-
General the Hon. Sir Charles Stuart, K.B.* (London, 1925), p. 137.

20. Letter of August 26, 1778, from Martha Ford to "My dear George
and John," UMWCL-MS.

21. Letters of October 30, 1778, from George to Walter Minto, and of
November 23, 1778, and December 10, 1778, from Walter Minto to
George, UMWCL-MS.

22. Letter of January 15, 1779, from John Udny, British Consul in
Leghorn (Livorno) to John Traill, TNA, FO335/38/14; letter of Febru-
ary 1, 1779, from Thomas Robinson, Lord Grantham, in Madrid to
Lord Weymouth, TNA, SP94/207/188; letter of March 5, 1779, from
Josiah Hardy, British Consul in Cadiz, to Lord Weymouth, TNA,
SP94/207/402. Letter of February 9, 1779, from Frederick Robinson in
London to Lord Grantham in Madrid, and draft letter of March 1,
1779, from Lord Grantham to George, Wrest Park (Lucas) Manuscripts,
Bedfordshire and Luton Archives [WP-BLA], L30/14/333/177 and L30/
14/201. The boy from Bengal was another passenger: "A black boy from
Bengal, who was a passenger on board the Westmoreland, Captain Wil-
lis Machell, from Leghorn, is now in London, and ready to be restored
to his master, whose name is understood to be Home, or Hume." *Morning Chronicle and London Advertiser*, May 18, 1779, no. 3118.

23. The most detailed account of the expedition is in G. Rutherford,
"Sidelights on Commodore Johnstone's Expedition to the Cape," *The
Mariner's Mirror* 28 (1942), pp. 189–212, 290–308; and see Admiral Sir
Thomas Pasley, *Private Sea Journals, 1778–1782*, ed. Rodney M. S. Pas-
ley (London, 1931), Vincent T. Harlow, *The Founding of the Second Brit-
ish Empire, 1763–1793*, 2 vols. (London, 1952), 1:106–25, and Fabel,
Bombast and Broadsides, pp. 144–64.

24. George was married to Deborah Charlotte Dee on January 31,
1782. Records of the British Factory Chaplaincy, Lisbon, available at
www.familysearch.org, and see also Fabel, *Bombast and Broadsides*,
p. 164.

25. *The Annual Register, Or a View of the History, Politics, and Literature, For the Year 1782* (London, 1783), p. 111.

26. Pasley, *Private Sea Journals*, pp. 170, 202.

27. William Pulteney, *Considerations on the question lately agitated in
Westminster-Hall* (London, 1787).

28. Will of George Johnstone, proved June 12, 1787, TNA, PROB
11/1154. George's youngest son was brought up in Scotland by Adam
Ferguson, to whom George left fifty pounds, describing him as the "most
worthy of the human race"; his other trustees included John Wedderburn, the former owner of Joseph Knight, described as "my beloved and

respected friend." William Julius Mickle, who had married and retired on "what he had acquired when with Commodore Johnstone," wrote a lavish eulogy to George's public life: from Jamaica ("as childhood closed thy ceaseless toils began"), to Parliament ("unaw'd, unstain'd! / By private aim unwarpt as generous youth, / Thy ear still listening to the voice of Truth"), and to the final decision of the House of Lords: "And rescued Honour on thy death-bed smiled." John was overcome, as he wrote to Mickle a few weeks after George's death, at this recollection of the "pleasing Instructive awfull Scene": "I cannot find words to convey the emotions of my Soul on reading the Tribute your Genius has paid to that Character which I contemplate as the most finished I have known or read of—Tho I have read It again & again, It commands my Tears to flow every time as fully as at the first." James, he anticipated, would be similarly affected: "I mean to read it to Sir James today as his Soul loved George above any other living." Letter of August 8, 1787, from John Johnstone to William Julius Mickle, WJM-Y; Ireland, "Anecdotes of Mickle," p. xlviii, and "To the Memory of Com. Geo. Johnstone," in Mickle, *Poems, and a Tragedy*, pp. 206, 207, 208 [misprinted as 212].

29. Letter of December 29, 1772, from John to William, HL-P, PU 658 [652].

30. Catherine Murray, the housekeeper, was paid twenty pounds per year, the two footmen were paid eighteen guineas and sixteen guineas (a guinea was one pound and one shilling), the cook was paid ten guineas, the housemaid seven guineas, and the coachman seventeen pounds: "Besides the £17 in money Sir James found his Coachman in washing, which he did not do to his Footmen." List of Servants living with Sir James Johnstone at the time of his death in London with an acct. of the Yearly Wages of each. BUL-W, Westerhall Estate Papers, DM 41/67/1.

31. Letter of March 10, 1792, from A. Pearson in the Excise Office, Edinburgh, to Sir James Johnstone, among the Westerhall West Indies papers; BUL-W, Westerhall Estate Papers, DM 41/70/4.

32. Louisa was presumably in her mid-thirties when she and James married in 1758; her mother was unmarried at the time when her grandmother's will was proved in 1720, and she herself married the Rev. Meyrick in 1739. Louisa and James's marriage settlement provided for the "Child and Children of the Body of the said James Johnstone on the Body of the said Elizabeth Mary Louisa Meyrick to be begotten." Copy of Mrs. Meyrick's Settlement on her Marriage with Captain Johnstone, NRO, NRS 8335 24D4.

33. James Murray Johnstone was described in James's will, dated March 12, 1790, and in a codicil dated January 28, 1794, as the child of Jean Swanston of Rumford in Essex, and he appears to have been born

some time after 1773. James left the sum of one hundred pounds a year to "Richard Murray Captain of the Ship Hankey and Catherine Murray my housekeeper" until James Murray Johnstone reached the age of twenty-one; there was a separate annuity to Jean Swanston, contingent on the provision that she should have "paid such attention or care to the bringing up of her said son as to meet with the approbation of the said Richard Murray and Catherine Murray." James also left a legacy to Catherine Murray "whether she shall be living with me at the time of my death or not" and "independent of . . . any husband or husbands she may have at my decease." After James's death, Louisa's secretary, William Otto, asked her cousin Sir Martin Folkes, "At the desire of Mrs Murray," for an introduction to the banking house of Neave for "her Brother Richard Murray late Commander of the Norfolk from London to Grenada." Will of Sir James Johnstone, proved March 21, 1796, TNA, PROB 11/1272; letter of July 31, 1798, from William Otto to Sir Martin Folkes, NRO, Folkes of Hillington Mss. (Additional) [FHA-NRO], MC50/53/11.

34. Speeches of James Johnstone in debates of July 21, 1784, February 1, 1785, May 9, 1785, June 13, 1785, and May 15, 1787, comment of Richard Brinsley Sheridan of April 4, 1787, in PH, vol. 24, col. 1169, vol. 25, cols. 124, 560, 888, and vol. 26, cols. 907, 1182. The episode of the apology was on May 14, 1788: "*Sir JAMES JOHNSTONE* said, that he understood, that a few nights ago, he had been guilty of improper conduct, for which the *Chair* had reprimanded him; but he had not yet reprimanded himself. He now begged pardon of Mr. *Speaker*, of the House, and of the Noble Lord, whom he had been so unfortunate as particularly to offend. He acknowledged he had been drunk, and hoped that would excuse him. *Lord* MORNINGTON said, the *Chair*, and House, would witness for him, that, perceiving the Hon. Baronet's situation, he had declared at the time, that he received no offence from what passed. *Mr.* SPEAKER said, he was sure the whole House admitted, with pleasure, Sir *James Johnstone*'s apology. After this Gentleman-like explanation, equally manly, liberal and honourable, on both sides, the House *adjourned*, in perfect good humour." *World*, May 15, 1788, no. 430.

35. Dedication to Sir James Johnstone in William Dickson, *Letters on Slavery* (London, 1789), p. 1; *The Star*, February 24, 1792, no. 1194, and see Whyte, *Scotland and Abolition*, pp. 113–17.

36. "In all European colonies the culture of the sugar-cane is carried on by negro slaves. The constitution of those who have been born in the temperate climate of Europe could not, it is supposed, support the labour of digging the ground under the burning sun of the West Indies; and the culture of the sugar-cane, as it is managed at present, is all hand labour,

though, in the opinion of many, the drill plough might be introduced into it with great advantage." Smith, *Wealth of Nations*, p. 586.

37. Speech of James Johnstone of April 23, 1792, debate in the House of Commons on Mr. Dundas's resolutions for the gradual abolition of the slave trade, PH, vol. 29, cols. 1265–66. The speech is also cited in Thomas Clarkson, *The History of the Rise, Progress, and Accomplishment of the Abolition of the African Slave Trade by the British Parliament*, 2 vols. (London, 1808), 2:458. Clarkson's report is slightly more explicit about the question of the plough: "he found the land produced more sugar than when cultivated in the ordinary way by slaves."

38. William Dickson, "Letters to Thomas Clarkson, Esq. M.A.," in Joshua Steele and William Dickson, *Mitigation of Slavery, in Two Parts* (London, 1814), pp. 287–88, 291. "The Negroes became expert plough-men in about six months," Dickson wrote, and "the canes on the ploughed land, were the finest and best yielding ever seen on that estate, or indeed in Grenada"; "I must own that, in no part of my abolition labours, was my anxiety greater, or of nearly so long continuance. A failure would probably have condemned the plough to a long oblivion, and might even have been held up as a *proof* (and it would have been as good a one as most which were given) that the Abolition itself, from which the experi-ment emanated, was a wild and pernicious project," pp. 292–93.

39. Letter of May 16, 1793, from R. Keith in Westerhall, Grenada, to Sir James Johnstone, BUL-W, Westerhall Estate Papers, DM 41/70/10–11.

40. Will of Sir James Johnstone, proved March 21, 1796, TNA, PROB 11/1272.

41. Alex McCracken, "The Glendinning Antimony Mine (Louisa Mine)," *Transactions of the Dumfriesshire and Galloway Natural History and Antiquarian Society*, 3rd ser., vol. 42 (1965), 140–48; "The Par-ish of Westerkirk," in Sir John Sinclair, *The Statistical Account of Scot-land, Drawn up from the Communications of the Ministers of the Different Parishes*, 21 vols. (Edinburgh, 1791–94), 11:525–26. On the use of antimony in the casting of cannon balls, see *Encyclopaedia Britan-nica; or, a dictionary of arts, sciences, and miscellaneous literature*, 20 vols. (Dublin, 1790–98), 2:87.

42. Westerkirk Kirk Sessions for November 12, 1778, March 4, 1781, and March 11, 1781, available on microfilm at the National Archives of Scotland, CH2/368/2/171–73. The Kirk and the Presbytery to which the matter was referred appear to have been deeply confused by the entire business; their conclusion, on March 11, 1781, was to appoint "James Johnstone to make satisfaction according to his Confession & leave it to the civil law to determine whether he was the Father of Henrietta Allens Child or not."

43. Will of Sir James Johnstone, proved March 21, 1796, TNA, PROB 11/1272.

44. Entries for January 20, 1793, August 1, 1793, October 1, 1793, April 1, 1794, January 13, 1795, July 7, 1795, January 16, 1797, and April 4, 1797, Westerkirk Library Minute Book, Bentpath Library, Dumfries and Galloway. I am most grateful to Mrs. Margaret Sanderson of Bentpath for showing me the minute book and the library, for which a building was constructed with a donation from Thomas Telford, the great engineer who grew up near the site of the Louisa Mine.

45. Letter of September 18, 1773, from John to William, HL-P, PU 659 [653]. We are "now moving to Denovan," he wrote a few weeks later; letter of October 16, 1773, from John to William, HL-P, PU 660 [654]. John and Elizabeth Carolina lived on the estate of Denovan in Stirling for less than four years. John's purchase of the Alva estate was completed in 1775, and he was living there at the time of Elizabeth Carolina's death in 1778. On the circumstances surrounding the purchase of Alva, see the letters of July 25, 1775, and July 17, 1775, from Alexander Robertson to Alexander Wedderburn, NAS, Papers of the Sinclair family, Earls of Rosslyn (NAS-SR), GD164/1089.

46. "A true Copy of the Register of the parish Church of Kirkandrews upon Esk for the year of our Lord 1773," Cumbria Record Office. I was led to this register by a fading photocopy of part of a printed document, in the M. M. Stuart papers in Edinburgh, NAS, Acc. 9260/22, and an accompanying letter to Stuart from Miss E. Talbot Rice of the National Army Museum, dated September 10, 1774, in which she says that "I am afraid, however, I can't throw any light on . . . the mulatto."

47. Letter of October 16, 1773, from John to William, HL-P, PU 660 [654]; letter of April 3, 1776, from Robert Walpole in Lisbon to Lord Weymouth, in TNA, SP89/81/199r.

48. East India Company versus Johnstone, TNA, C12/2379/7; complaint of Johnstone and Dempster against Francis Philip Fatio, TNA, C12/392/73.

49. They were "Molly a black Girl, the Slave or Servant of John Johnstone," "Molly Sommerville servant and Cookmaid," "David Youll servant," and "Sarah Ross servant & dairymaid." "Indictment agt Bell or Belinda a Negroe Girl," Porteous Roll for Fifeshire, Autumn 1771, NAS, JC26/193/3.

50. Female Servants Tax, Stirlingshire, August 1789, NAS, E326/6/18/183; Male Servants Tax, Stirlingshire, August 1792, NAS, E326/5/19/187. There were three gardeners for whom John paid the male servants tax in 1792, one at Alva, one at the estate of Denovan, where Gideon had lived, and one at the estate of Hawkhill, outside Edinburgh, where Betty lived.

John's earliest return for male servants at Alva, in 1778, was for five servants; his earliest return for female servants, in 1785, was for three people, NAS, E326/5/1/165 and E326/6/2/126. He declared eighteen female servants over the entire period from 1785 to 1791 and sixteen male servants in 1778 and 1791–92.

51. Gray, "Sketch of My Life," unpag.

52. Letter of May 14, 1778, from John to James Balmain, JA-CLA, Bundle 6, PD239/6/13.

53. Letter of October 5, 1785, from John to William, HL-P, PU 664 [656]; letter of August 8, 1787, from John to William Julius Mickle, WJM-Y.

54. Letter of August 8, 1787, from John to William Julius Mickle, WJM-Y; letter of March 3, 1771, from James to John, JJLB-EUL, p. 49; letter of January 7, 1773, from Walter Johnstone to William, HL-P, PU 739 [727]; on John as curator of Barbara's older son and tutor of her younger children, see "Testament Dative and Inventary of Charles Lord Kinnaird," April 13, 1768, available at www.scotlandspeople.gov.uk.

55. I am most grateful to Susan Mills of Clackmannanshire Council Heritage for showing me the mausoleum in Alva, and to John Packer of Canonbie for showing me the mausoleum in Westerkirk.

56. "The Negro's Complaint, A Poem, By the celebrated Mr Cooper," in *Two of the Petitions from Scotland, Which were presented to the Last Parliament, Praying the Abolition of the African Slave Trade* (Edinburgh, 1790), p. 9. James Balmain and "John Johnston, Esq; of Alva" are identified in the printed list at the end of the volume as subscribers for one and two guineas respectively, and "James Johnston Esq. Yr. of Alva" is written in by hand as a subscriber for three guineas. Goldsmiths' Library copy, available on the Web site, Gale Cengage Making of the Modern World, Goldsmiths'-Kress Library of Economic Literature 1450–1850 (MOME).

57. The Johnstone of Alva papers in Clackmannanshire contain letters from, among others, Elizabeth Carolina's nephew Talbot William Keene (in a debtor's prison in Northampton), George and Martha Ford's daughter Sophia, and Alexander's illegimate granddaughter. Letters of August 2, 1813, from Talbot William Keene, of January 7, 1833, from Sophia Cannizzaro, and of May 11, 1839, from Ann Sutherland, JA-CLA, Bundle 7, PD239/7/1, 2, 11.

58. There was another settlement of ten thousand rupees on Elizabeth Carolina's sister, with whom she had travelled to India in 1762. Will of John Johnstone, proved March 6, 1796, TNA, PROB 11/1272.

59. Letter of December 3, 1795, from Adam Ferguson to John Johnstone. It "will be difficult for me to resist the desire of seeing you," Fergu-

son wrote; his letter arrived shortly before John's death on December 10, 1795. Vincenzo Merolle, ed., *The Correspondence of Adam Ferguson*, 2 vols. (London, 1995), 2:375. Five of John's six brothers died before him, Patrick, Sandy, George, Gideon, and James; Adam Ferguson was a close associate of George as well as of John.

60. Questions to Samuel Romilly, Lincoln's Inn, April 8, 1799, BUL-W, Westerhall Estate Papers, DM 41/53/2.

61. This was with respect to a private act of parliament involving William, Louisa, Joan Osy (the Dutch mortgage holder from 1775), and the aftereffects of a new slave revolution in Grenada. Letter of March 24, 1796, from John Forster to Sir Martin Browne Folkes, FHA-NRO, MC50/51/3.

62. Will of Louisa Mary Elizabeth Johnstone, proved April 15, 1797, TNA, PROB 11/1289.

63. Letter of February 1, 1797, from Louisa to Sir Martin Browne Folkes, FHA-NRO, MC50/52/2.

64. *London Chronicle*, June 8, 1782, no. 3982.

65. *Whitehall Evening Post*, July 10, 1784, no. 5781.

66. "Madam . . . You followed, with my approbation, a plan of coertion with her which we both thought the best method of correcting several bad habits which had been the consequence of too much indulgence; that we were mistaken & instead of doing good we did harm, that she has conquered these habits & tho' she may entertain no doubt of the good intentions of those who pursued the first plan, yet it may require some time & more maturity of understanding, to think of the past with perfect indifference." Undated draft letter, possibly of 1785, from William to an unnamed correspondent, HL-P, PU 1874 [1518].

67. "Mr Pulteney would forego his whole fortune, except 5000l. per annum, to the young couple, provided he was created Earl of Bath, with remainder to Mr. Pitt's children. By this marriage the Minister would have enjoyed a neat 25,000l. per annum. Miss Pulteney, it is now said, is to be married to the Duke of Marlborough's eldest son." *New-York Daily Gazette*, July 28, 1789. An earlier report in a New York newspaper recounted that "Mr. Pulteney is gone over to Paris, to bring over his only daughter, a buxom lass, (*flavis capillis*) [red haired] to bestow her hand upon the Right Hon. W. Pitt, and with it a reversionary fortune of not less than 25,000l. per annum." *Independent Journal*, May 19, 1784. On the negotiations about Henrietta Laura's projected marriage to William Pitt, see *Morning Post and Daily Advertiser*, September 14, 1784, no. 3616, *London Chronicle*, September 28, 1784, no. 4355, *Morning Herald and Daily Advertiser*, October 1, 1784, no. 1227, and *Whitehall Evening Post*, January 11, 1785, no.

5876. On negotiations with Lord Morton, see *Public Advertiser*, May 25, 1786, no. 16227, and with the Marquess of Tichfield, *General Evening Post*, June 10, 1786, no. 8208.

68. See R.N.W. Thomas, "Pulteney, Sir James Murray-, seventh baronet (c.1755–1811)," ODNB, article 19620.

69. *Le Trésorier (Sir William Pulteney)* by James Gillray is in the National Portrait Gallery, London; see www.npg.org.uk/collections.

70. Letter of April 13, 1805, from Edmund Dana to Francis Dana, MHS, Dana Family Papers, Box 4, folder 1805.

71. "Obituary, with Anecdotes, of remarkable Persons," *Gentleman's Magazine* 75, part 1 (June 1805): 587–88.

72. "List of Slaves belonging to Port Royal 13 July 1798 Now rented to Westerhall Estate," BUL-W, Westerhall Estate Papers, DM 41/21/10. William was involved in the transaction at the level of extreme detail, as an earlier letter from the Grenada agents to Louisa's heir suggests. "We have this morning received another letter from Sir William Pulteney on the subject of the removal of his Negroes to Westerhall Estate—Sir William seems anxious before he writes decisively on the matter to his attorney in Grenada to receive the approbation of his co Trustees. . . . Sir William Pulteney proposes that the Negroes previous to their being removed should be regularly appraised and agrees to accept as their hire what is usually paid on similar occasions which may be from 10 to 12 pct. of their value yearly." Copy of a letter of October 16, 1797, from J. Petrie Campbell & Co. to Sir Martin Browne Folkes, FHA-NRO, MC50/52/30.

73. Letter of August 8, 1797, from William to Forster & Cooke, Lincoln's Inn, BUL-W, Westerhall Estate Papers, DM 41/62/14.

74. "But, the Inundations of the Mississippi being irregular, sometimes sudden, & violent they cause great inconvenience & distress to the Inhabitants, who are not yet sufficiently numerous, nor rich, to make proper Banks and Canals to remedy in some measure the Evil." Letter of May 22, 1780, from Lewis Rose in New Orleans to William Pulteney, HL-P, PU 1662 [1616].

75. Colquhoun, who was born in Scotland and went to Virginia as a young merchant, returned to Glasgow in 1766, where he "soon after formed connections of the very first respectability," becoming chief magistrate in 1782 and Lord Provost in 1783. Iatros [G. D. Yeats], *A Biographical Sketch of the Life and Writings of Patrick Colquhoun, Esq., LL.D* (London, 1818); "Mr Colquhoun—Family and Public Services," n.d., London Metropolitan Archives, acc. 1230/7; and Ruth Paley, "Colquhoun, Patrick (1745–1820)," ODNB, article 5992.

76. Barbara's son-in-law Edmund Dana wrote to his brother Francis Dana, who was one of George's ill-fated correspondents from the mission of reconciliation of 1778, that William was "coldhearted & severe. . . . You have probably heard he has at the age of 76 married a widow of 35, with two daughters. Not knowing what to do with his immense property, he has in view undoubtedly, an heir." Letter of May 9, 1804, from Edmund Dana to Francis Dana, MHS, Dana Family Papers, Box 70, folder 1804.

77. On the parliamentary history of Wilberforce's Bill, see Robert Isaac Wilberforce and Samuel Wilberforce, *The Life of William Wilberforce*, 5 vols. (London, 1838), and Clarkson, *Abolition of the African Slave Trade*.

78. Clarkson, *Abolition of the African Slave Trade*, 2:499.

79. Estimates of slaves embarked by national flag, the Trans-Atlantic Slave Trade Database, wilson.library.emory.edu:9090/tast/assessment/estimates.faces.

80. Speech of Sir William Pulteney of February 28, 1805, debate in the House of Commons on the second reading of the Bill for the Abolition of the Slave Trade, *Parliamentary Debates*, vol. 3, col. 660; Clarkson, *Abolition of the African Slave Trade*, 2:495–500.

81. Margaret Pulteney died on November 1, 1849. *Morning Chronicle*, November 3, 1849, no. 24973.

82. On the applications of George Lindsay Johnstone, James Primrose Johnstone, and Alexander Patrick Johnstone to be appointed as writers to the East India Company, see above, chapter 1. In the papers of John and Elizabeth Carolina's daughter Anne Elizabeth, there is a touching copy of a letter of condolence from a "Mr Walker of Perth" about the "afflicting accounts from India" of the death of "your Nephew," presumably addressed to Betty, in which he writes of the consolation that "the short period of his life should be past in such purity & consequent happiness. . . . I think the shock was Amongst the greatest which fate had it in its power to make me feel." Letter of August 17, 1794, from Mr. Walker, NAS, GD477/440.

83. Patrick Kinnaird left Spithead in April 1770 and arrived in Madras, after an arduous journey via Rio de Janeiro and the Cape of Good Hope, in April 1771. In Madras, he met Gideon, who had been reconfirmed as a naval officer, and "is just the old man. He is very well and seems to be very happy at his appointment. He and I hits it off very well as I am very humble." John recounted the circumstances of Patrick's death to his older brother George Kinnaird a few months later: "The last letter I had from him was dated the night before he embarked on a Coun-

try vessel from Madras for Bengal, in Company with another writer named Fitzgerald, both being tired with their long stay at Madras, & too impatient to arrive at their destined settlement to wait till the Morse should sail. By what accident we have not yet learnt, but the vessel was Cast away in entering the River at Bengal, & my dear Patie with his Companion & several others who could not swim, were lost. . . . What to me affords the greatest Consolation under this Lot of humanity, is the Reflection that he died uncorrupted, & probably as well prepared as he ever would have been from a longer Acquaintance in this fluctuating & unsatisfactory Stage of Existence." Letters of March 8, 1770, and June 15, 1771, from Patrick Kinnaird to George Kinnaird, KR-PKA, MS100/2, Bundle 60, and of April 15, 1772, from John to George Kinnaird, Bundle 75. Logbook of the *Morse*, OIOC, L/MAR/480A; letter of August 30, 1771, from the East India Company Council in Calcutta to the Court of Directors, *Fort William–India House Correspondence*, 6:308. Patrick Kinnaird's death was reported more than usually inaccurately in reference works on the Scottish nobility: "Patrick, the younger son, an officer in the East India Company's service, was killed by a tiger on the coast of Coromandel in July 1771," or "Patrick, who was unfortunately killed by a tiger, on the coast of Africa." William Anderson, *Scottish Nation*, 2:609; John Debrett, *Peerage of the United Kingdom*, 2 vols. (London, 1814), 2:837.

84. Letter of December 4, 1787, from James Balmain to Henry Dundas, NAS, GD51/4/38.

85. Mrs. Hamilton Gray, *Tour to the Sepulchres of Etruria, in 1839* 3rd ed. (London, 1840), p. 254. "The connexion of the polished nations of remote antiquity with each other, is one of the most interesting speculations of the present day; and each fresh discovery leads us to suppose, that long before the people of the ancient world were bound together under the leaden yoke of universal empire, very distant lands were intimately united by colonization, commerce, and political alliance."

86. Letters of September 6, 1796, from Francis Dana in Cambridge, Massachusetts, to Frances Shirley Western in London, of July 4, 1802, from Francis to Edmund Dana, and of August 12, 1802, from Edmund to Francis Dana, MHS, Dana Family Papers, Ms. N-1088, Dana Family I, Box 4, Folder 1796, Dana Family Papers, Box 70, Folder 1802.

87. Philip Dundas was born on September 5, 1806, on Prince of Wales Island (Penang); Margaret (Wedderburn) Dundas died in Calcutta on November 7, 1806; Philip Dundas, her husband, died on Prince of Wales Island on April 8, 1807; his brother-in-law, John Hope Oliphant, died there on March 23, 1807. OIOC, India Office Family History Search,

indiafamily.bl.uk; E. G. Cullin and W. F. Zehnder, eds., *The Early History of Penang, 1592–1827* (Penang, 1905), p. 26.

88. Will of Philip Dundas, proved January 26, 1808, TNA, PROB 11/1472.

89. *In the Court of Chancery, Between Sir John L. Johnstone, Complainant, and Sir James Pulteney* (Geneva, NY, 1811), pp. 3, 5, 12, 19.

90. Letters of January 5, 24, and 30, 1809, from Mrs. Anne Elizabeth Gordon to Colonel Aaron Burr, Aaron Burr Papers, PHi:4787–90.

91. Letter of December 4, 1805, from Charlotte Nugent, formerly Charlotte (Dee) Johnstone, to Sir James Murray Pulteney, HL-P, PU 1633 [1497].

92. On *La Comédie Humaine* as "this endless series of incidents in which souls are fatally at cross-purposes with one another," and in which "the outside world is a purely human one and is essentially peopled by human beings with similar mental structures, although with completely different orientations and contents . . . the danger of an abstract, 'bad' infinity is avoided by a great concentration of events (as in a novella) and a genuinely epic significance is thus attained," see Georg Lukács, *The Theory of the Novel: A Historico-Philosophical Essay on the Forms of Great Epic Literature* (1920), trans. Anna Bostock (London, 1971), pp. 108–9.

93. *In the Court of Chancery*, p. 12; Will of Henrietta Laura Pulteney, Countess of Bath, proved August 22, 1808, TNA, PROB 11/1483. *Report of the Proceedings, upon an Inquisition of Damages, in a cause between The Rev. George Markham, Plaintiff, and John Fawcett, Esq. Defendant: for Criminal Conversation with the Plaintiff's Wife Taken at the King's-Arms Tavern, Old Palace Yard, on Tuesday, May 4, 1802* (London, 1802), pp. 33, 37, 51; Pulteney v. Fawcett, Bill and Four Answers, TNA, C13/132/16.

94. Henrietta Laura's old friend was Adrienne de Lezay-Marnésia, whom she came to know in France before the Revolution. "J'attache un très grand prix à L'Amitié de Mademoiselle votre fille et je ne desire rien autant que de pouvoir lui donner des preuves de Mon Attachement Mon bonheur depends beaucoup du sien elle ne sauroit éprover aucun Chagrin sans que je le partage c'en est un bien grand pour moi que d'être separée d'elle et j'attends avec bien de l'impatience Un tems ou nous pourions esperer de nous revoir," she wrote in a letter to Adrienne's mother. Letter from Henrietta Laura Pulteney to the Marquise de Marnésia, July 7, [1786], HL-P, PU 1341 [83]. Adrienne de Lezay-Marnésia married Claude de Beauharnais, a cousin of the Empress Josephine. Her daughter Stéphanie Laure Adrienne de Beauharnais was adopted by Na-

poleon; letter of February 21, 1806, from Napoleon to the Elector of Baden, and message of March 4, 1806, to the Senate, in *Correspondance de Napoléon I* (Paris, 1863), 12:81–82, 129. The only extended study of Stéphanie's life suggests that Napoleon was indignant at the idea of a relation of Josephine being taken care of by an Englishwoman. Françoise de Bernardy, *Stéphanie de Beauharnais, (1789–1860), Fille adoptive de Napoléon Grande-duchesse de Bade* (Paris, 1977), pp. 22, 26. In 1806 Stéphanie was married by imperial treaty to the grandduke of Baden. She was later a spirited observer of the transformation of Germany's fortunes, as she wrote to a friend in France in 1814: "If you only knew what a state of uncertainty this poor Germania is in! Everyone's head has been turned, no one dreams of anything but constitutions, a return to ancient ideas; according to these hopes, we will find ourselves back in the fifteenth century. There is to be a national customary law more or less like that of the age of chivalry. All this is very fine if it lasts, but it is easier to restore customary law than gothic ideas. It is rare that men retrogress of their own volition. It takes many generations to forget that one has been in a good condition, and comfortable. One can begin again, but to go backwards is impossible." Letter of November 1814 from the Grand Duchess of Baden to Annette de Saint-Alphonse, in Chantal de Tourtier-Bonazzi, ed., *Correspondance d'Annette de Mackau Comtesse de Saint-Alphonse Dame du palais de l'impératrice Joséphine, (1790–1870)* (Paris, 1967), p. 393.

95. Will of George Lindsay Johnstone, proved February 1, 1814, TNA, PROB 11/1552.

96. Sophia Johnstone's husband, Francis Platamone, inherited the title of Duke of Cannizzaro. See the wills of Martha Ford, proved January 1, 1831, Sophia Duchess of Cannizzaro, proved April 3, 1841, and Francis Platamone, Duke of Cannizzaro, proved November 27, 1841, TNA, PROB 11/1780, 11/1944, and 11/1953.

97. Burial of Mrs. Martha Ford, aged 86, December 23, 1830. Copy of the Register of Burials in the Parish of St. Marylebone, Royal Society of Medicine.

98. Will of Martha Ford, proved January 1, 1831, TNA, PROB 11/1780.

99. In 1784 Ferguson made an effort to sublet the house to a General Fletcher Campbell and described it as "a Storey in a Land. The Rooms are a Dining Room Small drawing Room two bed Chambers & a Kitchen as I am told very well furnished. The Neighbours that is to Say the People over head are two Old Women who neither Spin nor make any noise whatever." Letter of October 27, 1784, to General Fletcher Campbell, in Merolle, *Correspondence of Adam Ferguson*, 2:307.

100. Entry for January 24, 1809, in William K. Bixby, ed., *The Private Journal of Aaron Burr* (Rochester, NY, 1903), 1:64.

101. Letter of August 3, 1809, from Betty to Anne Elizabeth Gordon, NAS, GD477/440.

102. Will of Miss Betty Johnstone, proved December 24, 1813, available at www.scotlandspeople.gov.uk, pp. 318–29. The "Plate Trinkets wine and Spirits China Books Horses house and Garden aliments &c.," and cash, were valued at £307 14s 11.1/2d; the rest of the estate consisted of a "Principal Sum in Bond," dated November 11, 1777, from John to Betty, of four hundred pounds, the interest on the bond, and part of an annuity to Betty from John's son-in-law, James Gordon of Craig. At the very end of her life, Betty's niece Anne Elizabeth Gordon recorded in a memorandum, she "called me to her Bedside and said if any money remained after paying her debts and other Expences that she wishes £10 to be given to the poor of the parish of Westerkirk and £10 to the poor of the parish of Alva."

CHAPTER FOUR. ECONOMIC LIVES

1. On the tragedy of history and the sequence of historical understanding of great events, from the heroic to the inexorable and eventually to the tragic, in which even the American Revolution can be seen "as it was—an event full of accident, uncertain in outcome," see Bernard Bailyn, *The Ordeal of Thomas Hutchinson* (Cambridge, MA, 1974), pp. ix–xi. To paraphrase what Bailyn wrote of Thomas Hutchinson, the loyalist governor of Massachusetts, whom George denounced in the House of Commons in October 1775 and who visited George, much later, after George had himself become a "loyalist," "it is essential to understand the efforts that had no future if one is to explain the victory of what, in the retrospect of later history, became the forces [of empire]." Bailyn, *Thomas Hutchinson*, p. x; speech of George Johnstone of October 26, 1775, debate in the House of Commons on the Address of Thanks, PH, vol. 18, cols. 744–45. "I called this forenoon upon Govr. Johnstone at Kensington Gore. . . . I found him very civil, polite, and obliging; and as he has altered his sentiments on American affairs, I hope he will alter his opinion of me," Hutchinson wrote after his visit to George. Entry for February 9, 1779, Peter Orlando Hutchinson, ed., *The Diary and Letters of His Excellency Thomas Hutchinson, Esq.*, 2 vols. (New York, 1884–86), 2:242.

2. Macaulay, *Critical and Historical Essays*, "Lord Clive," 3:169.

3. William Pulteney, *Thoughts on the Present State of Affairs with America, and the Means of Conciliation* (London, 1778), p. 63.

4. J. R. Seeley, *The Expansion of England: Two Courses of Lectures* (London, 1888), p. 137; and see Christopher Leslie Brown, *Moral Capital: Foundations of British Abolitionism* (Williamsburg, 2006), pp. 8–9.

5. Jean-Baptiste Say, "Discours préliminaire," in Jean-Baptiste Say, *Traité d'Economie Politique, ou simple exposition de la manière dont se forment, se distribuent, et se consomment les richesses* (Paris, 1803), p. i.

6. John Stuart Mill, "On the Definition of Political Economy; and on the Method of Investigation Proper to It" (1836), in Mill, *Collected Works* (Toronto, 1967), 4:309–39, p. 310.

7. Bailyn, *Thomas Hutchinson*, pp. ix–x.

8. Letter of August 22, 1761, from John in Ajudagar to the East India Company's Council in Calcutta, OIOC, IOR, H/47/65; letter of June 12, 1765, from George and John Stuart to Lord Halifax, TNA, CO5/582, 189v. On discussions of free trade in the early period of the East India Company's dominion in India, see Marshall, *East Indian Fortunes*.

9. Letter from George to John Pownall of October 31, 1764, TNA, CO5/582/167r; speech of George Johnstone of May 27, 1765, TNA, CO5/582/195v.

10. David Hume, *The History of England*, 6 vols. (Indianapolis, 1983), 3:78. Hume uses the expressions "ordinary course," "common course," and "natural course" more than fifty times in his published writings; Smith uses them more than seventy times.

11. Keene, *Miscellaneous Poems*, pp. 10, 69, 105.

12. Undated letter from John to William of 1767, HL-P, PU 625 [622]; letter of April 29, 1772, from James to John, JJLB-EUL, p. 148.

13. Letter of November 1, 1772, from James to Betty, JJLB-EUL, p. 171.

14. Speech of George Johnstone of March 30, 1772, debate in the House of Commons on the East India Judicature Bill, PH, vol. 17, col. 379; speech of John Johnstone of February 10, 1777, debate in the House of Commons on the Bill for suspending the Habeas Corpus Act, PH, vol. 19, col. 6; speech of George Johnstone of February 25, 1777, debate in the House of Commons on Captain Blair's Petition, PH, vol. 19, col. 62.

15. "Copy of a Memorial of the Proprietors of Land in the Island of Grenada," TNA, PC1/60/7; *Narrative of the Proceedings*, p. v.

16. "The English have been so little used to making conquests, or rather to keeping what they have made, that it is no wonder they have not till lately adopted any steady plan," Alexander's friends wrote in one of the pamphlets produced in support of his petition over oppression and torture in the island of Grenada. There were three possible destinies: first, of "utterly exterminating the original inhabitants," second, of "themselves adopting their laws, customs, and manners" (much as "the

conquerors of China are now become Chinese"), or third, of inducing "the conquered to adopt theirs . . . to assimilate and make them the same people as themselves." The first destiny was "so cruel and barbarous, so shocking to humanity, as well as repugnant to good policy, that it can only be justifiable by divine command, which we all know was the case with the Jews, the only people who steadily pursued that method of conquest." The second destiny was that of "Alexander the Great, in his conquest of Persia" and of "the Tartars in China." The third destiny, of "conquest and colonization," "seems to have been pursued by the Greeks" and "was invariably followed by the Romans." *Audi Alteram Partem*, pp. 115–16.

17. Letter of March 3, 1764, from George Johnstone to James Townsend Oswald, Oswald Papers, Chest IV, C.

18. Letter of September 30, 1766, from George to John Stuart, Gage Papers, UMWCL. There was Tacitus, James II, and the Duke of Alva, or "gladiators, pimps, sharpers, parasites, and buffoons." Speeches of George Johnstone of May 8, 1770, on an Address to the King on the Disturbances in America, of February 6, 1775, on an Address to the King on the Disturbances in North America, and of December 11, 1775, on the American Prohibitory Bill, PH, vol. 16, cols. 995–96, vol. 18, cols. 260, 1061.

19. "The transactions of the Portugese in India are peculiarly the wars and negociations of commerce, and therefore offer instructions to every trading country, which are not to be found in the campaigns of a Caesar or a Marlborough." Mickle, "Introduction," in Camöens, *Lusiad*, i–clxxxvi, p. clv; letter of May 25, 1774, from William Julius Mickle to George, WJM-Y.

20. Speeches of William Pulteney and of an unnamed opponent of the bill, April 29, 1772, debate in the House of Commons on the Bill for Encouraging Foreigners to Lend Money upon Estates in the West Indies, PH, vol. 17, cols. 482, 484. Texel was the island near Amsterdam where large Dutch trading ships arrived.

21. On anxiety and empire, see Ranajit Guha, "Not at Home in Empire," *Critical Enquiry* 23, no. 3 (Spring 1997), 482–93, and Jon E. Wilson, "Anxieties of Distance: Codification in Early Colonial Bengal," *Modern Intellectual History* 4, no. 1 (April 2007): 7–23.

22. Speech of George Johnstone of May 18, 1774, debate in the House of Commons on the Budget, PH, vol. 17, col. 1346.

23. Speech of John Johnstone of February 25, 1777, *Parliamentary Register*, 6:291.

24. Pulteney, *Present State of Affairs*, pp. 63, 67.

25. Pasley, *Private Sea Journals*, pp. 167, 205.

26. Speech of George Lindsay Johnstone of November 25, 1801, debate in the House of Commons on Sir William Pulteney's Motion for a committee on the Trade between India and Europe, PH, vol. 36, col. 297.

27. On the connections between the eastern and western British empires, see Marshall, *Making and Unmaking of Empires*, H. V. Bowen, "Perceptions from the Periphery: Colonial American Views of Britain's Asiatic Empire, 1756–1783," in *Negotiated Empires: Centers and Peripheries in the Americas, 1500–1820*, ed. Christine Daniels and Michael V. Kennedy (New York, 2002), pp. 283–300, and Philip Stern, "British Asia and British Atlantic: Comparisons and Connections," *William and Mary Quarterly* 63, no. 4 (October 2006), 693–712.

28. "Between India and America no analogy can be drawn," William declared in the House of Commons in 1801: "Above all, America is uninhabited, and boundless tracks of fertile land were presented to the industry of the planter. India is one of the most populous countries on the globe, and every inch of ground is appropriated." "It was true," another orator added, "in America, every thing was wild and uncultivated. In India, every thing was made." Speeches of Sir William Pulteney and Mr. Tierney of November 25, 1801, debate in the House of Commons on Sir W. Pulteney's Motion for a Committee on the Trade between India and Europe, PH, vol. 36, cols. 288, 307–8.

29. On the maritime organization of the Mississippi delta economy, see Walter Johnson, *River of Dark Dreams* (forthcoming, 2012).

30. Speech of George Johnstone of February 24, 1779, debate in the House of Commons on the Budget, PH, vol. 20, col. 162.

31. "Petition for Bell or Belinda a Black Girl," September 13, 1771, NAS, JC26/193/3.

32. One of William's partners in his estates in Tobago, with whom he later quarrelled, escaped to the island of Madeira, en route to Pondicherry in the French East Indies; and see above, chapter 2.

33. It was "to the honour of John Swinton," the *Caledonian Mercury* wrote, that the highest court in Scotland had affirmed his judgement that the slavery of Joseph Knight was inconsistent with the principles of the kingdom. *Caledonian Mercury*, January 17, 1778. Swinton was an expert on the law of entails and a "thinking, dull man," in Lord Cockburn's description. Cockburn, *Examination of the Trials*, 1:85, 289.

34. Receipt of January 13, 1766, from General John Carnac in Bengal to Samuel Swinton, OIOC, Carnac Papers, MSS Eur F128/11; and see Swinton's correspondence with David Anderson and Robert Keith in Calcutta, British Library, Anderson Papers, vol. 13, Add. Ms. 45429. On Swinton's publishing career, see "Swinton, Samuel (?–1797)," in Jean Sgard, *Dictionnaire des journalistes, 1600–1789* (Oxford, 1999), 2:940–

42, and on his long and turbulent friendship of more than twenty years with Pierre Augustin Caron de Beaumarchais, see Gunnar Von Proschwitz and Mavis Von Proschwitz, eds., *Beaumarchais et le Courier de l'Europe: Documents inédits ou peu connus* (Oxford, 1990).

35. Swinton, *Swinton Family Records*, pp. 93–94. I'tesamuddin described a journey with Archibald Swinton to "a town in the Highlands, where his elder brother John was chief Magistrate"; in London "Captain Swinton took me to his brother's house in Coventry Street, near Haymarket." Mirza Sheikh I'tesamuddin, *The Wonders of Vilayet Being the Memoir, Originally in Persian, of a Visit to France and Britain in 1765*, trans. Kaiser Haq (Leeds, 2002), pp. 54, 141. On Archibald Swinton's evidence as an expert before George and William's Select Committee, see below, chapter 5, and on I'tesamuddin (I'tisam al-Din), see Fisher, *Counterflows to Colonialism*, pp. 87–90.

36. Letter of June 13, 1775, from Patrick Tonyn to Alexander Wedderburn, enclosing a survey and estimate of costs, NAS-SR, GD164/1713.

37. David Wedderburn arrived in Florida after an arduous journey involving an English vessel bound from Leghorn to the Bay of Honduras that lost its rudder off Saint-Domingue, where he was accused of being "the Governor of Jamaica in disguise." His companion was a captain "who had been in the East Indies, in Africa, in N. America, in France, and in Flanders." He had several different prospects in this postwar period of opportunity: "to fix my residence at Genl Gage's (if I like him) at N. York"; to lead an expedition against the Illinois, "as I see at present in this peaceful time, no other opening"; or to devote himself to "making rich" in the upper Mississippi ("Monsr. D'Abbadie, late Governor of New Orleans got the Ilinois trade into his hands, and died after one year only, worth 60,000 pounds Sterg."). Letters of June 3, 1764, October 12, 1764, January 1765, and April 14, 1765, from David Wedderburn to Alexander Wedderburn, Wedderburn Papers, UMWCL.

38. Letters of December 31, 1771, and March 17, 1772, from David Wedderburn to Janet Erskine, NAS-SR, GD164/1698.

39. On Peter Leheup, a merchant of Huguenot descent who in the same year that he provided security for Patrick was the projector of the lottery for the purchase of Sir Hans Soane's Museum—for which he was later convicted of fraud—see the debate in the Commons on the Enquiry into the Management of the Last Lottery, December 4, 1753, PH, vol. 15, cols. 192–249, and Jacob M. Price, "The Excise Affair Revisited: The Administrative and Colonial Dimensions of a Parliamentary Crisis," in *England's Rise to Greatness, 1660–1763*, ed. Stephen B. Baxter (Los Angeles, 1983), 257–322. On Alexander Grant, a merchant of Invernessshire descent and owner of a plantation in East Florida, see David Hancock,

Citizens of the World: London Merchants and the Integration of the British Atlantic Community, 1735–1785 (Cambridge, 1995), pp. 48–59, 153–85.

40. His cousin John Macpherson, with whom he corresponded (in Gaelic) about Indian affairs, and about Gideon's enterprises in Benares, was an East India Company official in Madras and later in Calcutta. Macpherson Correspondence, OIOC, Mss Eur F291/122; Paul J. deGategno, "Macpherson, Sir John, first baronet (c.1745–1821)," ODNB, article 17730.

41. Letters of August 11, 1770, and May 30, 1771, from James to Gilbert Petrie, JJLB-EUL, pp. 37–38, 71–73. John Malcolm, in his description of John Petrie, refers to "his friends the Johnstones"; John recommended William to "Messrs. Bolts & Petrie" for detailed information about the Mayor's Court in Calcutta. "I was in hope that in the Scramble for Power & Perquisites we might have had the satisfaction of being useful to our friend Petrie," John wrote to a business associate in February 1771. A few weeks later, he wrote to Alexander about "poor Petrie who has been at Deaths door." Malcolm, *Lord Clive*, 3:22; letter of February 5, 1772, from John to William, HL-P, PU 655 [648]; letters of February 8, 1771, from John to Mr. Hannay and of March 23, 1771, from John to Alexander, JJLB-CLA, PD239/201/9. On John Petrie in Bengal, see Bolts, *Considerations on India Affairs*, 2: app., pp. 81–97, 3:449. On John and William Petrie, see R. G. Thorne, *The History of Parliament: The House of Commons, 1790–1820*, 5 vols. (London, 1986), 1:781–83.

42. Deed of freedom recorded February 3, 1770, TNA, CO5/605/f.349.

43. Letter of Lieutenant Governor Montfort Browne of May 13, 1769, to the Board of Trade, TNA, C05/620/29–35. "The state of man never was more truly wretched and distressing than mine at present," Browne wrote in the same letter; his two secretaries had both died, and the new governor, George's successor, "on the second of May, hanged himself in his study. I had the honour of dining and spending the preceding day with him, when he seemed chearful and composed, and shewed me the utmost politeness."

44. Will of Thomas Thomson, proved March 5, 1787, TNA, PROB 11/1151. On Primrose Thomson's salary, "for acting as Secretary to the Governor for Copying the Dispatches and keeping the Publick Accounts for 3 1/2 years," see "Declaration of the Account of George Johnstone Esquire," TNA, AO1/1261/152. Thomas Thomson signed the certification of George Lindsay Johnstone's baptism in Pensacola; see above, chapter 1.

45. "Distancing Oneself from the Eighteenth Century," in Hendrik Hartog, *Law in the American Revolution and the Revolution in the Law:*

A Collection of Review Essays on American Legal History (New York, 1981), pp. 242, 250. On earlier disputes over the dominion of the law, the state, and the corporation, see Otto Gierke, *Political Theories of the Middle Ages*, trans. F. W. Maitland (Cambridge, 1900), and Maitland, "Translator's Introduction."

46. "Of Interest," in David Hume, *Essays Moral, Political, and Literary*, ed. Eugene F. Miller (Indianapolis, 1987), p. 304.

47. Smith, *Wealth of Nations*, pp. 405, 610, 722–23.

48. Ibid, pp. 55, 630.

49. J. Z. Holwell, *Interesting Historical Events, Relative to the Provinces of Bengal, and the Empire of Indostan* (London, 1765), p. 181. John Zephaniah Holwell was an expert on Indian cosmogony and the embroiderer of the myth of the black hole. His daughter, a Mrs. York, was one of John's close friends in Calcutta; John described her departure for England in 1761, together with her sister, a Mrs. Playdel, as "so Great a Loss" of ladies whose "Intimacy & friendship" had "warmed my heart." Letter of December 24, 1761, from John to James, HL-P, PU 672 [621].

50. Undated letter of 1772 from Adam Ferguson to John Macpherson, in Merolle, *Correspondence of Adam Ferguson*, 1:95.

51. Speech of Alexander Wedderburn of May 10, 1773, debate in the House of Commons on General Burgoyne's Motions relating to the Conduct of Lord Clive in India, PH, vol. 17, col. 865.

52. Speech of William Pulteney of November 25, 1801, debate in the House of Commons on Sir W. Pulteney's Motion for a Committee on the Trade between India and Europe, PH, vol. 36, col. 282.

53. See Rothschild, *Economic Sentiments*, chapter 1.

54. It was not the practice, he wrote, "for persons of the rank I then held, to receive money themselves: It is delivered to their Bannians, who, as silver money is very bulky, and the coin much adulterated, take the trouble of examining, weighing, and reckoning it over." John Johnstone, *Letter to the Proprietors*, pp. 43–44.

55. Testimony of Major William Grant, in Third Report from the Committee, *House of Commons Sessional Papers,* p. 303; letter of December 29, 1761, from John Johnstone in Calcutta to James Balmain, HL-P, PU 671 [620]. On John's army career, see Orme, *Military Transactions*, 2:176, and John Johnstone, *A Letter to the Proprietors*, p. 2.

56. John Johnstone, *Letter to the Proprietors*, p. 21. On Gideon's later career in the navy, see "A Journal of the Proceedings of His Majesty's Ship the Adamant Kept by Captain Gidion Johnstone," TNA, ADM51/8.

57. Letter of March 17, 1772, from David Wedderburn in Bombay to the chairman of the court of directors of the East India Company in

London, OIOC, IOR/H/768/199–200, in a discussion of the East India Recruiting Bill. The "temptation" of these benefits, he concluded, "would make recruits flock to the Company's standard, while the King's troops would find it very difficult to get a man." On the East India Company's army, see Raymond Callahan, *The East India Company and Army Reform, 1783–1798* (Cambridge, MA, 1972).

58. James's aspiration, when he had any access to money, was to buy himself an army position; he asked Louisa, early in their marriage, to ascertain "the very lowest Terms on which I can get a Lieutcy. in the Gaurds." Letter of June 17, 1759, from James to Louisa, NRO, NRS 8194 24C2.

59. "In respect to the 1000£ you state against the Colonel in your Private account with him, I should Imagine as matters Stand settled betwixt us two, you cannot do otherwise—It is certain you Paid that Money for his Commission two Years before I took up your Bond to Drummond: & as I had no Authority on the part of the Colonel to pay this sum of 1050 on his Account, to extinguish any Debt he might be owing you, I dont see how I could Constitute my Claim against him without either Security or Voucher—It is evident you would be giving up the 50£ of Interest paid by you the first year were you to omit stating the 1000£ advanced on his Account." Letter of September 18, 1773, from John to William, HL-P, PU 659 [653].

60. "I had the good fortune to take a Brigg from Martinique," he reported a few months later. Letters of February 18, 1761, and August 9, 1761, from George to William, HL-P, PU 469 and 470 [453 and 454].

61. William Julius Mickle was George's "joint agent for the disposal of the prizes," and George's servant, Louis Lacelle, was entitled to a share of his "prize money" (and "to Expect all his masters old Cloathes"). "Form of agreement between Captn George Johnstone of his Majty Sloop Hornett & Louis Lacelle," 15 February 1760, EUL-L, La.II.73/78. Sim, "Life of the Author," p. lii.

62. Letter of July 2, 1768, from John to Gideon, in care of William, HL-P, PU 634 [631].

63. Notes by Charles Ferrier, Accountant in Edinburgh, May 2, 1809, JA-CLA, Bundle 17, PD239/17/22/2.

64. Speech of Lord Clive of March 30, 1772, debate in the House of Commons on the East India Judicature Bill, PH, vol. 17, col. 355.

65. Speech of Colonel Barré of May 10, 1773, debate in the House of Commons on General Burgoyne's Motions relating to the Conduct of Lord Clive in India, PH, vol. 17, col. 867.

66. On Clive's presents, see Bruce Lenman and Philip Lawson, "Robert Clive, the 'Black Jagir,' and British Politics," *The Historical Journal* 26, no.

4 (Dec. 1983), 801–29. On political gifts and patronage in late Mughal India, see McLane, *Land and Local Kingship*, pp. 96–121; Kumkum Chatterjee, *Merchants, Politics, and Society in Early Modern India: Bihar, 1733–1820* (Leiden, 1996); Mridu Rai, *Hindu Rulers, Muslim Subjects: Islam, Rights, and the History of Kashmir* (Delhi, 2004); and Kumkum Chatterjee and Clement Hawes, eds., *Europe Observed: Multiple Gazes in Early Modern Encounters* (Lewisburg, PA, 2008).

67. John Johnstone, *Letter to the Proprietors*, pp. 61, 62, 64 [mispr. as 46], 66.

68. Undated letter from John to William of 1767, HL-P, PU 625 [622]; letter of August 22, 1772, from James to Alexander, JJLB-EUL, p. 164.

69. Opinion of July 4, 1764, from John Johnstone in Burdwan, Fort William Select Consultation, Fourth Report from the Committee, *House of Commons Sessional Papers*, p. 498; on the miners' library, see the Westerkirk Library Minute Book, Bentpath Library, and on Stéphanie de Beauharnais, see letter of November 1814, in *Correspondance d'Annette de Mackau*, p. 393, and above, chapter 3.

70. Letter of December 29, 1761, from John in Calcutta to James Balmain, HL-P, PU 671 [620]; minute of June 17, 1765, from John to the Select Committee of the East India Company in Calcutta, in Third Report from the Committee, *House of Commons Sessional Papers*, p. 434; letter of October 5, 1775, from Thomas Dundas M.P. to Sir Lawrence Dundas, North Yorkshire County Record Office, Zetland Papers, ZNK X 1/2/222.

71. "Articles of Charge against Robert Melvill Esq.," "Replies for Lieut. Col. Johnstone," TNA, PC1/60/7.

72. "Now I would gladly hope, that this last Illegal Action is as little Anté constitutional, as the other Anté constitutional Action was Illegal. Of which last Fact You may be convinced by looking at the 17th Geo: 2. Chap. 34th Sect. 22d." Letter of October 5, 1765 from George to General Thomas Gage, in *Mississippi Provincial Archives*, pp. 407–8.

73. Letter of April 1, 1766, from George to John Pownall, TNA, CO5/574/3/739–40, letter of January 28, 1766, from George to John Pownall, the Governor's Complaint of the Chief Justice, April 1, 1766, in *Mississippi Provincial Archives*, pp. 347, 450.

74. Letter of April 1, 1766, from George to John Pownall, TNA, CO5/574/704; *Narrative of the Proceedings*, pp. xlii–xliii.

75. Letter of March 9, 1765, from James Macpherson to Major Robert Farmar, enclosed in a letter of March 21, 1765, from Farmar to Gage; Gage Papers, UMWCL. An Act Appointing where the Laws of this Province shall be Lodged, January 3, 1767, in *Minutes, Journals, and Acts*, pp. 322–23.

76. See Lauren Benton, *Law and Colonial Cultures: Legal Regimes in World History, 1400–1900* (Cambridge, 2002).

77. Letter of July 2, 1766, from George to M. Aubry, *Mississippi Provincial Archives*, pp. 316–18.

78. Speech of George Johnstone of March 26, 1765, Congress in Mobile, *Mississippi Provincial Archives*, p. 223.

79. Alexander's friends' version of the story was that he had arrested (for drunkenness) the wife of a reduced sergeant in the regiment, who might or might not have been subject to martial law, on the grounds that she had "enlisted into the 70th regiment when it embarked at Corke for the West Indies, in the quality of Leagerlady; one of those females who are allowed to follow the camp in order to wash the mans cloaths, cook their victuals, and minister to their other necessary occasions [and] though she had no pay, yet she was entitled to, and received the common allowance of provisions." *Audi Alteram Partem*, pp. 111–13.

80. "Our Servants are as likely, at least, to make an ill Use of their Power as the Nabob's are, but are not so easily to be restrained." Opinion of Warren Hastings of March 1, 1763, Fort William Consultation, Fourth Report from the Committee, *House of Commons Sessional Papers,* p. 486.

81. Maconochie, Information for Joseph Knight, p. 20, Ferguson, Information for John Wedderburn, p. 14; Cullen, *Additional Information.*

82. Minute of June 17, 1765, from John Johnstone, in Third Report from the Committee, *House of Commons Sessional Papers,* p. 433.

83. "From the first settlement of the colony of Virginia to the year 1778, (Oct. Sess.) all negroes, Moors, and mulattoes, except Turks and Moors in amity with Great Britain, brought into this country by sea, or by land, were slaves." *Hudgins v. Wrights*, Supreme Court of Virginia 11 Va. 134; 1806 Va. LEXIS 58; 1 Hen. & M. 134.

84. Bolts, *Considerations on India Affairs,* 1:93–94; speech of John Johnstone of February 10, 1777, debate in the House of Commons on the Bill for suspending the Habeas Corpus Act, PH, vol. 19, col. 6.

85. Hartog, "Distancing Onself from the Eighteenth Century," in *Law in the American Revolution,* pp. 234–35, 242–43; speech of James Johnstone of February 1, 1785, proceedings in the House of Commons relating to the Westminster Scrutiny, PH, vol. 25, col. 124.

86. Smith, *Wealth of Nations,* p. 37.

87. Speech of George Johnstone of March 26, 1765, *Mississippi Provincial Archives*, pp. 220, 221.

88. Smith, *Wealth of Nations,* p. 627. Smith described the book as the "very violent attack I had made upon the whole commercial system of Great Britain." Letter of October 1780 from Smith to Andreas Holt in Smith, *Correspondence,* p. 251.

89. [William Julius Mickle], *A Candid Examination of the Reasons for Depriving the East-India Company of its Charter, contained in "The His-*

tory and Management of the East-India Company, from its Commencement to the Present Time." Together with Strictures on some of the Self-Contradictions and Historical Errors of Dr. Adam Smith, in his Reasons for the Abolition of the said Company (London, 1779), advertisement, unpag., p. 17; Mickle, "Introduction," in Camöens, *Lusiad*, p. clxxvii.

90. Letter of February 8, 1771, from John to Samuel Hannay, JJLB-CLA, PD239/201/9.

91. Pulteney, *Present State of Affairs*, p. 62.

92. "Lord Kinnaird has lately married a Lady (Miss Ransom) of the most engaging accomplishments & great Fortune not less than 120,000 £. He was quite well when I left London and I heard from him that your Brother & his numerous family were all in good Health." Letter of June 10, 1778, from George in Philadelphia to Francis Dana, MHS, Dana Family Papers, Ms. N-1088, Dana Family I, Box 2.

93. Speech of Lord North of February 25, 1777, debate in the House of Commons on Captain Blair's Petition, *Parliamentary Register*, 6:292.

94. Brian Edwards, "Some account of the British settlement on the Musquito shore, drawn up for the use of government, in 1773," submitted as one of the "authentic papers" in support of Captain Blair's Petition, presented in the House of Commons by George in February 1777; *Parliamentary Register*, 6:336. On the Cartagena expedition of 1740, and the "expedition into the south seas," see George's speech of February 25, 1777. *Parliamentary Register*, 6:282–83, 302.

95. *Audi Alteram Partem*, pp. 50, 119 [121, mispag.]; Edwards, "Some account of the British settlement on the Musquito shore," *Parliamentary Register*, 6:328; Patrick Colquhoun, *A treatise on the wealth, power and resources of the British empire, in every quarter of the world, including the East Indies* (London, 1814), p. 363.

96. On the "shift of the Atlantic slave trade southward," the British settlement of newly conquered islands in 1763–1806, and the "effort to establish plantation economies where they had not existed before," see Christopher Leslie Brown, "Slavery and Antislavery, 1760–1820," in *Oxford Handbook of Atlantic History*, ed. Nicholas Canny and Philip Morgan (Oxford, forthcoming). On the "increasing and unprecedented extension of credit to the West Indies in the later eighteenth century," see S. G. Checkland, "Finance for the West Indies, 1780–1815," *Economic History Review*, new ser., 10, no. 3 (1958): 461–69, p. 461.

97. Speech of William Pulteney of February 28, 1805, debate in the House of Commons on the second reading of the Bill for the Abolition of the Slave Trade, *Parliamentary Register*, 5 vols. (London, 1805–7), 1:389. The model statesman was the duke of Marlborough.

98. Speech of William Pulteney of February 28, 1805, debate in the House of Commons on the second reading of the Bill for the Abolition of the Slave Trade, *Parliamentary Debates*, vol. 3, col. 659.

99. George was one of hundreds of minor British officials who appeared in George Bancroft's ten-volume *History of the United States*: a "fiery and half-frantic governor of West Florida," whose participation in the Commission of Conciliation was a "mere device." George Bancroft, *The History of the United States*, 10 vols. (Boston, 1860–74), 5:235, 10:122–23.

100. Even the Johnstones' friend and neighbor Sir John Malcolm alluded to John's "delinquency." Macaulay, *Critical and Historical Essays*, "Lord Clive," 3:144–45; Malcolm, *Lord Clive*, 3:340.

101. "Warren Hastings" (1841), in Macaulay, *Critical and Historical Essays*, 3:287–421, p. 295.

102. Letter of September 29, 1765, from Lord Clive to Mr. Dudley, in Malcolm, *Lord Clive*, 2:344.

103. John Johnstone, *Letter to the Proprietors*, and see Firminger, "Historical Introduction," pp. cxlv–cxlvii.

104. Letter of August 26, 1765, from John to the president and council of the East India Company in Calcutta, Fourth Report from the Committee of Secrecy, *House of Commons Sessional Papers*, p. 207.

105. "Part of the uncultivated Tracts may be offered, upon easy terms, to any Raits, or Weavers, that would undertake to labour them." Letter of August 22, 1761, from John in Ajudagar to the East India Company's council in Calcutta, OIOC, IOR, H/47/65.

106. Letter of September 30, 1765, from Lord Clive to the Court of Directors, Third Report from the Committee, *House of Commons Sessional Papers*, p. 391. Clive's proposed regulation of commerce was like one of the political economists' parodies of the times about over-elaborate public monopoly: five shares to be allocated to "the Governor," three shares to "The General," a two-thirds share to "One Chaplain," a one-third share to "One Sub Export Warehouse Keeper," and "One *Persian* translator." Fort William Select Committee Proceedings, September 18 1765, in Fourth Report from the Committee, *House of Commons Sessional Papers*, p. 511.

107. Letters of September 30, 1765, November 28, 1765, and January 31, 1766, from Lord Clive to the Court of Directors, Third Report from the Committee, *House of Commons Sessional Papers*, pp. 391, 393, 454, and of January 31, 1766, from Lord Clive to the Court of Directors, Fourth Report from the Committee, p. 519. "The factious Spirit which lately blazed out so violently in Council, hath reached the lower Classes," Clive lamented in his answer of January 31, 1776, to John's defense (p. 519).

108. General letter from the Court of Directors of April 26, 1765, in Malcolm, *Lord Clive*, 2:348.

109. Bolts, *Considerations on India Affairs*, 1:vi. East India Company officials did settle in India in John and Gideon's lifetimes; of the 508 young men appointed to Bengal from 1762 to 1784, only 37 had "returned home" by the end of the period, 150 were dead, and 321 were still in Bengal. Speech of Major Scott of July 16, 1784, debate in the House of Commons on Pitt's India Bill, *Parliamentary Register*, 45 vols. (London, 1782–96), 16:100.

110. One of the defining conditions of the East India Company's later dominion in India was that "no Covenanted Servant, or Englishman" should "hold any Land." Extract of the Company's letter to the Select Committee at Bengal, May 17, 1766, in Fourth Report from the Committee of Secrecy, *House of Commons Sessional Papers*, p. 254. John was involved in the exchanges that were a part of enduring commercial relationships in the inland trade in salt: "incurring bad Debts, by supplying Money to the Molungees, as we have done very large Sums, when distressed by their Losses, whether by Cheapness of Grain, Overflowings, or Caterpillars in their Farms." Letter of August 26, 1765, from John to the president and council of the East India Company in Calcutta, in Fourth Report from the Committee of Secrecy, *House of Commons Sessional Papers*, p. 207.

111. Gholam-Hossein, *Seir Mutaqharin*, 2:583–84. As Robert Travers has written, "The British in India were destined to remain a society of temporary exiles rather than settlers, and a class of rulers rigidly separated from those they ruled." Travers, *Ideology and Empire*, p. 29. John was a transitional figure, as this destiny unfolded, and the figure of a different future.

112. Letter of May 30, 1765, from Lord Clive to General Carnac, in Malcolm, *Lord Clive*, 2:360.

113. On laissez-faire when it was new, see Rothschild, *Economic Sentiments*, pp. 1–6.

114. Speech of William Pulteney of May 1, 1788, debate in the House of Commons on the Wool Export Bill, PH, vol. 27, col. 386.

115. This was in an obituary of James Wilson, the founder of *The Economist* and Bagehot's father-in-law. See Emma Rothschild, "Political Economy," in *Cambridge History of Nineteenth-Century Political Thought*, ed. Gareth Stedman Jones and Gregory Claeys (Cambridge, 2011).

116. Mickle, "Introduction," in Camöens, *Lusiad*, p. clxxviii; Mickle, *Candid Examination*, pp. 8, 17, 26.

117. On early critics of Smith, see Emma Rothschild, "Adam Smith in the British Empire," in *Empire and Modern Political Thought*, ed. Sankar Muthu (Cambridge, 2012).

118. Letter of May 30, 1765, from Lord Clive to General Carnac, in Malcolm, *Lord Clive*, 2:360.

119. Adam Smith, *An Inquiry into the Nature and Causes of the Wealth of Nations, with notes, supplementary chapters, and a life of Dr. Smith*, 11th ed., ed. William Playfair, 3 vols. (London, 1805), 2:253, note p.; William Playfair, *Letter to Sir W. Pulteney Bart. M.P. on the establishment of another public bank in London* (London, 1797). Playfair and Patrick Colquhoun corresponded in the 1780s about the interest on money and the British constitution. Glasgow University Library, Special Collections, Copy Letter Book, Patrick Colquhoun, Ms Murray 551 [GUL-PC], letters of January 30, 1786, from Patrick Colquhoun to George Dempster, and undated letter of 1786 from Patrick Colquhoun to William Playfair, 52v, 109r–110r.

120. Letters of August 8, 1802, and April 13, 1805, from Edmund Dana to Francis Dana, MHS, Dana Family Papers, Box 70, folder 1802, Box 4, folder 1805.

121. Carlyle, *Autobiography of Carlyle*, p. 547. Mickle denounced Hume at great length in a long pamphlet on deism, and as the "modern Midas," in a poem written on the occasion of Hume's death. [William Julius Mickle], *Voltaire in the Shades, or Dialogues on the Deistical Controversy* (London, 1770); "On the Death of David Hume," in *The Poetical Works of William Julius Mickle*, collated by Thomas Park (London, 1808), p. 144 [mispag.; 162].

122. Robert Southey, "On the state of the Poor, the principle of Mr. Malthus's Essay on Population, and the Manufacturing System" (1812), in Southey, *Essays, Moral and Political* (London, 1832), p. 112.

123. Felicité de Lamennais, *Essai sur l'indifférence en matière de religion*, 3 vols. 6th ed. (Paris, 1820), 1:375.

124. Letter of July 2, 1778, from Walter Johnstone to William Julius Mickle, WJM-Y.

125. John Stuart Mill, *On Liberty* (1859) (London, 1974), p. 69; and see Rothschild, "Political Economy," and Karuna Mantena, *Alibis of Empire: Henry Maine and the Ends of Liberal Imperialism* (Princeton, 2010).

CHAPTER FIVE. EXPERIENCES OF EMPIRE

1. "In general, I must also observe, that masters are kind to their slaves." Speech of George Johnstone of October 26, 1775, debate in the House of Commons on the Address of Thanks, PH, vol. 18, col. 747.

2. Letter of March 13, 1756, to the Freemen of Liverpool from James Gordon, John Welch, and S. Colquitt, in *An Entire and Impartial Collec-*

tion of all the Papers &c. Published on Both Sides, concerning the Late Election at Liverpool (Liverpool, 1761), p. 14. On the *Adlington*, the *Reyton*, and the *Lord Strange*, of which Scrope Colquitt was a part owner, see the Trans-Atlantic Slave Trade Database, wilson.library. emory.edu:9090/tast/database/search.faces.

3. Gray, "Sketch of My Life," unpag.

4. Logbook of the *Earl of Holdernesse*, OIOC, IOR/L/MAR/B/604C, entry for July 19, 1761.

5. Will of Philip Dundas, proved January 26, 1808, TNA, PROB 11/1472.

6. Letter of May 11, 1839, from Ann Sutherland, in JA-CLA, Bundle 7, PD239/7/11, and undated letter from Alexander Sutherland and Ann Wilson, Bundle 5, PD239/5/27; and see above, chapter 3.

7. Letters of January 16, 1793, and April 15, 1794, from R. Keith in Grenada to James, BUL-W, Westerhall Estate Papers, DM 41/70/9 and DM 41/70/14; will of Sir James Johnstone, proved March 21, 1796, TNA, PROB 11/1272.

8. Letter of August 12, 1767, from John to William, HL-P, PU 626 [624].

9. Extract, Process Joseph Knight against Sir John Wedderburn of Ballendean Bart., 1774, NAS, CS235/K/2/2, p. 8.

10. Letter of July 20, 1770, from William Colhoon or Colqhoun in Senegal to Betty Colqhoun in Glasgow, Glasgow City Archives (GCA), Mitchell Library, TD 301/6/1/6. The name "Colhoon" was also spelled as Colqhoun or Colquhoun. William Colhoon's sister was described in the register of her marriage as "Eliz: Col:houn S D of Robt. Colqhoun." Old Parish Register, Glasgow, April 16, 1771, available at www.scotlands people.gov.uk.

11. Letter of September 18, 1773, from John to William, HL-P, PU 659 [653].

12. Will of Alexander Johnstone, proved January 24, 1783, TNA, PROB 11/1099.

13. Letters of September 17, 1796, from William Otto to Sir Martin Browne Folkes and of October 24, 1797, from J. Forster to Sir Martin Browne Folkes, FHA-NRO, MC50/51/15 and MC50/52/30.

14. Wills of Sir Thomas Montgomerie, proved April 10, 1716, and of Sir Thomas Jones, proved January 29, 1731, TNA, PROB 11/551, 11/642.

15. Letter of June 13, 1775, from Patrick Tonyn to Alexander Wedderburn, enclosing a survey and estimate of costs, NAS-SR, GD164/1713.

16. Letters of October 12, 1764, from St. Christopher, of January 29, 1765, from Kingston, Jamaica, and of April 14, 1765, from Mobile, from

David Wedderburn to Alexander Wedderburn, Wedderburn Papers, UMWCL.

17. Letter of December 31, 1771, from David Wedderburn to Janet Erskine, NAS-SR, GD164/1698. Nothing is "so fâde, so bête, so perfectly ennuyante, as the conversation of that motley class of beings, that, stile themselves, the modest women of Bombay. It is true, I sometimes allow them to come & sup with me, but that is much more from a certain pomp & impertinence in me, more from the ridicule of seeing a parcel of Blockheads, in velvet Mantuas, & Garden Stuff brocades, with large Hoops, & enormous Wigs, than from any sort of pleasure I find in their Society. I tried at first to assort them properly, but finding that no benefit accrued to me from this, I look no further now, than to the proper shading of my partys, from the Jet black, to the Jaunâtre."

18. "Inventory of the Estate and Effects of the late Brigadier General Wedderburn," Bombay, December 15, 1773, NAS-SR, GD164/231.

19. On Samuel Swinton's black servant, see The Proceedings of the Old Bailey, 19 February 1766, www.oldbaileyonline.org. This was a case involving the "simple grand larceny" of a silver spoon from the house in Coventry Street, by the brother of Samuel Swinton's servant. "I brought his brother from the West-Indies; they are both blacks," Swinton told the court. In a later case, of July 3 1771, a silver teapot and a silver sugar dish were stolen from the Coventry Street house, and Swinton was described as a "wine merchant;" the teapot was recovered by "a little tawney boy belonging to Mr. Swinton."

20. *Bill of Advocation, Mrs Stewart-Nicolson, against Houston Stewart-Nicholson, Esq.* (Edinburgh, 1770), p. 11; *Replies for Mrs Stewart-Nicolson to the Answers of Mr Stewart-Nicolson, November 27, 1770* (Edinburgh, 1770), p. 22. John Swinton, who was so involved in the cases of Bell or Belinda and Joseph Knight, was one of Mrs. Stewart-Nicholson's lawyers, as John Cairns has pointed out. Cairns, *Scottish Law of Slavery*.

21. Letters of March 10, 1765, from Robert Hay in Fort Marlboro (Bengkulu, on the west coast of Sumatra) to Sir John Hall, and of August 5, 1767, from Henry Idell in London to Miss Isabella Hall, Receipt from Thomas Nilson to Henry Idell of August 26, 1767. NAS, GD206/4/33. Robert Hay, of the East India Company's Council in Benkulen, was taken prisoner by the French during the Seven Years' War and sent on parole to Calcutta at the time when John was a newly promoted member of the Company's Council in Calcutta. Letter of November 12, 1761, from the East India Company's Council in Calcutta to the Court of Directors in London, *Fort William–India House Correspondence*, 3:374, 380. William Colhoon or Colqhoun was once again closer to the daily life of en-

slavement. "I have a very fine girl about twelth years of age I have had her Eighteen M: with me," and "I never shall sell her she has been more serves to me than Any White Woman that Ever I honour'd except my Mother," he wrote to his sister's husband from Sierra Leone in 1775; "if my sister Betty will except of her I shall send her home." Letter of April 1, 1775, from William Colhoon in Sierra Leone to Archibald Patterson in Glasgow, GCA, TD 301/6/3/1.

22. "I should esteem a Visit from a Man of your worth and of your Sentiments," James wrote to Gilbert Petrie in August 1770, "congratulating you on your Return to Brittain, to your Family, your Friends, and Relations." The present was to be brought to Norfolk by "a Gentleman going to London, who promised to take Care of the Animal." "Putrid fever" was a name given to typhus, and the rue or ruta plant was considered to have medicinal properties. Letters of August 11, 1770, and May 30, 1771, from James to Gilbert Petrie, JJLB-EUL, pp. 37–38, 72.

23. Speeches of John Petrie and George Canning of March 1, 1799, debate in the House of Commons on Mr. Wilberforce's Motion for the Abolition of the Slave Trade, PH, vol. 34, cols. 529, 552.

24. Letter of August 18, 1804, from Francis Dana to Edmund Dana, MHS, Dana Family Papers, Box 70, folder 1804.

25. "Permission Granted to British Prisoners in Rhode Island to Depart for Great Britain," November 15, 1776, William James Morgan, ed., *The Naval Documents of the American Revolution* (Washington, DC, 1976), 7:165. See also *Morning Chronicle and London Advertiser*, February 3, 1777, no. 2405.

26. Letter of September 15, 1778, from Lord Carlisle to Lady Carlisle, Royal Commission on Historical Manuscripts, *The Manuscripts of the Earl of Carlisle, Preserved at Castle Howard, Fifteenth Report, Appendix, Part VI* (London, 1897), p. 366. "Frederick" was a member of Carlisle's household in New York.

27. Seeley, *Expansion of England*, p. 137.

28. See Christopher Brown, "Slavery and Antislavery."

29. Estimates of slaves embarked by national flag, the Trans-Atlantic Slave Trade Database, wilson.library.emory.edu:9090/tast/assessment/estimates.faces.

30. I am most grateful to Walter Johnson and David Todd for helpful discussions of the history of the imagined futures of slavery.

31. Smith, *Wealth of Nations*, pp. 25, 43, 148, 266, 574.

32. Ferguson, Information for John Wedderburn, p. 22.

33. "They are generally false, designing, treacherous, knavish, impudent and revengeful." Edwards, "Some account of the British settlement on the Musquito shore," p. 334.

34. Speech of William Pulteney of February 28, 1805, debate in the House of Commons on the second reading of the Bill for the Abolition of the Slave Trade, *Parliamentary Debates*, vol. 3, col. 658.

35. Minute from John Johnstone of June 17, 1765, in Third Report from the Committee, *House of Commons Sessional Papers,* pp. 433–34, 436, letter of October 1, 1765, from John to Lord Clive, Fourth Report from the Committee, *House of Commons Sessional Papers,* pp. 539, 541; John Johnstone, *Letter to the Proprietors*, p. 32.

36. The peace settlements of the 1760s marked the end, in Daniel Richter's description, of a "shared Euro-Indian transatlantic world," and of the decorous politics of negotiation, which were replaced, in the new American Republic, by a "far simpler, racially defined frontier line." Richter, *Facing East*, pp. 187–88.

37. "Declaration of the Account of George Johnstone Esquire," TNA, AO1/1261/152.

38. Letters of January 28, 1766, from George to H. S. Conway, and of July 2, 1766, from George to M. Aubry, in *Mississippi Provincial Archives*, pp. 294, 317–18.

39. An Act for the Regulation and Government of Negroes and Slaves, January 3, 1767, An Act for the Order and Government of Slaves, June 6, 1767, in *Minutes, Journals, and Acts*, pp. 330–31, 342, 344.

40. "Mr P——y, who was the near neighbour, intimate friend, and inseparable companion of his Excellency Governor M——ll . . . had a pretty extraordinary taste in his amours, even in those countries. His first mistress was a black wench, a near relation to the famous Augustin; by her he had a daughter; and by that daughter another, or rather a granddaughter, who, at the time of his intimacy with his Excellency, was the favourite mistress, conducted his domestic affairs, and sat at the head of his table." This pamphlet, described as a collective production by "the authors of these sheets, for they are the work of many," was apparently published before the outcome of the case in the Privy Council, and is followed by ninety-one pages of appendices. *Audi Alteram Partem*, pp. 3, 78–79, 114.

41. Letter of August 12, 1767, from John to William, HL-P, PU 626 [624]; "Habitations de l'isle de la Grenade dont les propriétaires sont à Londres," September 6, 1779, AN-Col., Correspondance à l'arrivée, C10A, Carton 3-1.

42. James's associate William Dickson wrote of the revolution in Grenada in 1795 that "very few, however, of Sir James's Negroes joined the *brigands* (not one voluntarily) in consequence, no doubt, of the good treatment they experienced. Another good consequence of this, was the preservation of their health and lives; one proof of which was that Sir

James lost but 3 of his people, out of 340, by an epidemic flux which prevailed in 1793, and carried off 30 out of 400, on a neighboring estate, situated in all respects like Westerhall." Dickson, "Letters to Thomas Clarkson," in Steele and Dickson, *Mitigation of Slavery*, p. 294. On Julien Fédon, a plantation owner in Grenada and the son of a French colonist and a free black woman from Martinique, see Steele, *Grenada*, pp. 108–48.

43. James MacQueen, *The Colonial Controversy, containing a Refutation of the Calumnies of the Anticolonists* (Glasgow, 1825), pp. 36–37, 86; James MacQueen, *The West India Colonies; the Calumnies and Mispresentations circulated against them* (London, 1824), p. 350. MacQueen was appointed to Westerhall at the age of 19, when William inherited the plantation after Louisa's death: "I had the charge of it for several years, when it belonged to the late Sir William Pulteney. I knew it from 1797 . . . The estate 'passed,' first, 'into the hands' of Lady Johnstone; and at her death, in 1797, it came into the hands of Sir William Pulteney." *Colonial Controversy*, pp. 36–37. See Gordon Goodwin, "MacQueen, James (1778–1870)," rev. Elizabeth Baigent, ODNB, article 17736.

44. On politics, resistance, and agency, see Walter Johnson, "On Agency," *Journal of Social History* 37, no. 1 (Fall 2003): 113–24.

45. Letter of September 13, 1765, from Governor Melvill to the Board of Trade, TNA, CO101/1/315r–316r; "An Act for the better Government of *Slaves*," Grenada, December 11, 1766, CO103/1/53r; An Act for the Regulation and Government of Negroes and Slaves, January 3, 1767, in *Minutes, Journals, and Acts*, pp. 330, 342–43, and see above, chapter 1.

46. Léon Vignols, "Études négrières de 1774 à 1928: Pourquoi la date de 1774," *Revue d'histoire économique et sociale* 3, no. 1 (1928): 5–11, pp. 8–9; Emma Rothschild, "A Horrible Tragedy in the French Atlantic," *Past and Present*, no. 192 (August 2006): 67–108. On the mortgage discussions of 1772 and 1774, see above, chapter 2. "Marooning" was more generally a synonym for lawlessness. One of the projects for the ill-fated expedition of 1781, off the Cape of Good Hope, was to harass the Dutch settlers, to the dismay of George's friends: "a paultry, Shameful, Sheep-stealing, Marooning party on shore." Pasley, *Private Sea Journals*, p. 170.

47. "An Act for Vesting certain Estates, in the Island of Grenada, late of Sir James Johnstone, Baronet, in Trustees, to raise Money by Mortgage for repairing the Damage done thereto in the late Insurrections." 36 Geo. III. Private. c. 118 (1796).

48. Simon Schama, *Rough Crossings: Britain, the Slaves, and the American Revolution* (London, 2005), p. 24.

49. Wilberforce and Wilberforce, *William Wilberforce*, 3:213.

50. Speeches of William Pulteney and of General Gascoyne, on "the minds of the negroes," February 28, 1805, debate in the House of Commons on the second reading of the Bill for the Abolition of the Slave Trade, *Parliamentary Debates*, vol. 3, cols. 644, 658. "In treating of this important question, the hon. mover [Wilberforce] has contented himself with saying, that there is nothing new in it," another of the bill's opponents, Sir William Young, declared: "Nothing new, sir! Has nothing new happened in the situation of St. Domingo? . . . Is there nothing new in the situation of Jamaica?" (col. 646).

51. Speech of William Wilberforce of February 28, 1805, debate in the House of Commons on the second reading of the Bill for the Abolition of the Slave Trade, *Parliamentary Debates*, vol. 3, col. 672; speech of George Lindsay Johnstone of November 25, 1801, debate in the House of Commons on Sir W. Pulteney's motion for a committee on the trade between India and Europe, PH, vol. 36, col. 297.

52. Speech of William Wilberforce of February 28, 1805, *Parliamentary Register*, 1:392–93.

53. See letters of May 9, 1764, November 21, 1764, and February 15, 1765, from the Directors of the East India Company in London to the Company's Council in Calcutta, and letters of September 30, 1765, and March 24, 1766, from the Council in Calcutta to the directors in London, *Fort William–India House Correspondence*, 4:39, 40, 60, 71, 357, 404.

54. See Indrani Chatterjee, *Gender, Slavery, and Law in Colonial India* (Oxford, 1999), and Finn, "Slaves out of Context," pp. 199–203.

55. It was "a commerce established of the most barbarous and cruel kind that ever disgraced the transactions of any civilized people. The traders on the Musquito shore were accustomed to sell their goods at very high prices and long credit, to the Musquito Indians, and the mode of payment set on foot by the British settlers, was to hunt the other surrounding tribes of Indians, and seize them by stratagem or force, from whence they were delivered to the British traders as slaves, at certain prices, in discharge of their debts." Speech of George Johnstone of February 25, 1777, debate in the House of Commons on Captain Blair's Petition, *Parliamentary Register*, 6:283.

56. Johnson, "On Agency," p. 115.

57. Extract, Process Joseph Knight against Sir John Wedderburn, 1774, NAS, CS235/K/2/2, pp. 3–4, 19; Ferguson, Information for John Wedderburn, p. 5.

58. Letter of March 3, 1771, from James to John, JJLB-EUL, p. 50.

59. Fraser, *Annandale Family Book*, 2:354–55, 384–85.

60. Letter of October 29, 1767, from Horace Walpole to Sir Horace Mann, in Walpole, *Correspondence*, 22:560.

61. Letter of October 2, 1759, from George to William, HL-P, PU 467 [450].

62. Smith, *Wealth of Nations*, p. 130.

63. Letter of May 14, 1778, from John to James Balmain, JA-CLA, Bundle 6, PD239/6/13. On the Carron Works, see R. H. Campbell, *Carron Company* (Edinburgh, 1961).

64. Letter of January 29, 1763, from Anne Ferguson to General James Murray, NAS, GD32/24/14.

65. Vicesimus Knox, "On Preaching and Sermon Writers," in *Essays Moral and Literary*, 2 vols. (London, 1779), 2:157. The context is a discussion of Sunday sermons, considered as "the establishment of public lectures." "It is certainly true, that since the acquisition of books has been facilitated by their numbers, oral instruction is rendered less necessary. But though books are easily procured, yet even in this age of information, there are thousands in the lower classes who cannot read. Besides, it is a well known truth, that the same precepts inculcated by a living instructor, adorned by a proper oratory, enforced by a serious and authoritative manner, produce a powerful effect, not to be experienced in solitary retirement. There is likewise a sympathy communicated in a numerous audience, which attaches the mind more strongly to the speaker."

66. Jane Austen, *Mansfield Park* (1814) (London, 1996), chapter 43, p. 346.

67. Smith, *Wealth of Nations*, pp. 131, 454, 619.

68. [Thomas Pownall], *A Memorial, most humbly addressed to the Sovereigns of Europe, on the present state of affairs, between the Old and New World*, 2nd ed. (London, 1780), pp. 42–43.

69. Letter of March 23, 1779, from Frederick Robinson in London to Lord Grantham in Madrid, WP-BLA, L30/14/333/190.

70. Letter of September 15, 1755, from Patrick to William, HL-P, PU 713 [701]. The letter from Patrick almost certainly arrived after his death, the following June. There were no East India Company ships that left Bengal after September 15, 1755, and arrived in England before June 20–21, 1756; Anthony Farrington, *Catalogue of East India Company Ships' Journals and Logs, 1600–1834* (London, 1999).

71. "My Lord imploys me now for all the little favours he has to ask for the Regt." Letter of March 29, 1749, from Margaret to Barbara Johnstone (her mother), EUL-L, La.II.502.12.

72. Letter of October 19, 1759, from Betty to William, HL-P, PU 406 [398].

73. Letter of April 14, 1771, from David Wedderburn to Janet Erskine, NAS-SR, GD164/1698; undated letter of January 1765 from David Wedderburn to Alexander Wedderburn, Wedderburn Papers, UMWCL.

74. Letter of October 19, 1759, from Betty to William, HL-P, PU 406 [398].

75. Speech of William Pulteney of December 2, 1772, debate in the House of Commons on the Navy Estimates, PH, vol. 17, col. 540; speech of Sir William Pulteney of February 28, 1805, debate in the House of Commons on the second reading of the Bill for the Abolition of the Slave Trade, *Parliamentary Debates*, vol. 3, col. 659.

76. Robert Darnton, "An Early Information Society: News and the Media in Eighteenth-Century Paris," *American Historical Review* 105, no. 1 (February 2000), 1–35.

77. See William St. Clair, *The Reading Nation in the Romantic Period* (Cambridge, 2004), Richard B. Sher, *The Enlightenment and the Book: Scottish Authors and Their Publishers in Eighteenth-Century Britain, Ireland and America* (Chicago, 2006), Robert Darnton, *The Business of Enlightenment: A Publishing History of the "Encyclopedie," 1775–1800* (Cambridge, MA, 1979).

78. Speech of Edmund Burke of December 18, 1772, debate in the House of Commons on preventing the East India Company from sending out Supervisors to India, PH, vol. 17, col. 671.

79. Speeches of Lord Clive and of George Johnstone of March 30, 1772, debate in the House of Commons on the East India Judicature Bill, PH, vol. 17, cols. 341, 376.

80. Letters of May 2, 1794, and June 11, 1794, from Samuel Swinton to Henry Dundas, TNA, HO42/30/5r–5v and HO42/31/168r. On Swinton's newspapers, see the will of Samuel Swinton, proved June 19, 1797, TNA, PROB 11/1293.

81. Carlyle, *Autobiography of Carlyle*, p. 173.

82. "TO THE PUBLIC. Mr Bolts takes this method of informing the public that the want of a printing press in this city being of great disadvantage in business, and making it extremely difficult to communicate such intelligence to the community as is of the utmost importance to every British subject, he is ready to give the best encouragement to any person or persons who are versed in the business of printing to manage a press, the types and utensils of which he can produce. In the meantime, he begs leave to inform the public that having in manuscript many things to communicate, which most intimately concern every individual, any person who may be induced by curiosity or other more laudable motives, will be permitted at Mr Bolt's house to read or take copies of the same. A person will give due attendance at the hours of from ten to twelve any morning." Paper affixed to the door of the Council House in Calcutta and other public places, September 1768. H. E. Busteed, *Echoes from Old Calcutta* (Calcutta, 1888), p. 171, and see Miles Ogborn, *Indian Ink: Script and*

Print in the Making of the English East India Company (Chicago, 2007), pp. 203–5.

83. "Six American Monthly Papers for which I am obliged," as Elizabeth Carolina's host in Chittagong wrote to a commercial correspondent, in the summer of 1762. Letter of June 26, 1762 from Harry Verelst to John Wood, OIOC, Verelst Letter Book 1761–62, MSS Eur F218/79, f. 114v.

84. Logbook of the *Earl of Holdernesse*, OIOC, IOR/L/MAR/B/604C, entry for September 4, 1761.

85. "Here nothing is spoke of but the Superb marriage of Mons. Le Dauphin with the Queen of Hungary's Daughter. "The marriage of Marie-Antoinette, daughter of the Empress Maria Theresa, and the Dauphin Louis, grandson of Louis XV, took place in Vienna, by proxy, in April 1770, and in Versailles in May 1770." Letters of May 30, 1770, from John Haliburton in Dunkirk and of March 20, 1771, from William Rooke, BL, Anderson Papers, vol. 13, Add. Ms. 45429, ff. 59, 179.

86. Robert Darnton, "Early Information Society," pp. 2, 7.

87. Speech of Sir William Pulteney of August 4, 1784, debate in the House of Commons on the Resolution Respecting the Method to be observed by Members in Franking of Letters, PH, vol. 24, col. 1332. A letter of October 22, 1771, from John to William, addressed to "Monsieur Pulteney a Spa Allemagne," was marked "not to be found Returned to Mr Jno. Johnstone in London to pay 1 Shilling Postage." HL-P, PU 652 [645].

88. Copy of a letter of September 4, 1785, from George Johnstone to Henry Dundas, OIOC, IOR/G/17/5 ff.127–28. The project was "œconomical," in George's description—which was "a necessary ingredient to constitute good Government"—and would "induce a saving of £25,000 a year in our paquets round the Cape of Good Hope . . . as well as being the first link in the Chain of our power in India."

89. Undated letter of 1745 or 1746 from David Hume to Sir James Johnstone, in Greig, *Letters of David Hume*, 1:82.

90. The letters of 1776 from James Macpherson in London to John Macpherson in Madras were partially in Gaelic; OIOC, Macpherson Correspondence, Mss Eur F291/122. The cipher Bolts devised for his correspondence with Sweden is described in Furber, "In the Footsteps," p. 13.

91. Letter dated April 8, 1762, to the Court of Directors, in *Fort William–India House Correspondence*, 3:419. On the information order in eighteenth-century India, see C. A. Bayly, *Empire and Information: Intelligence Gathering and Social Communication in India, 1780–1870* (Cambridge, 1996).

92. Bayly, *Empire and Information*, p. 40.

93. Imperial Record Department, *Calendar of Persian Correspondence*, 1:400.

94. Fifth Report from the Committee Appointed to enquire into the Nature, State, and Condition of the East India Company (June 18, 1773), *House of Commons Sessional Papers*, 135:547.

95. William arranged for the translation into French of various pamphlets on the politics of the English East India Company, by an abbé who was embarrassed not to have recognized, in the name of "Pulteney," that of "Jonhston which I know very well." Letter of March 2, 1768, from [Pierre Joseph André] Roubaud to William, HL-P, PU 1666 [1620]. Roubaud's *Le politique indien* refers to the observation of "F. T. Holwel ce bon & brave patriote," that "Une Compagnie commerçante & militaire tout ensemble, est un monstre à deux têtes, dont l'existence ne sauroit être de longue durée." [Pierre Joseph André Roubaud], *Le politique indien, ou considerations sur les colonies des indes orientales* (Amsterdam, 1768), pp. 88, n.(a), 89.

96. Letter of April 14, 1765, from David Wedderburn to Alexander Wedderburn, Wedderburn Papers, UMWCL.

97. "When I went ashore they flocked down to the beach, and, on their knees, begg'd to be taken any where from the Island, I think I never saw joy more strongly painted on human faces, than when I spoke german to them, & told them I would take as many on board as we could make room for. I shall make a set of unfortunate creatures happy, & shall get some very good soldiers for my Masters." Letter of May 8, 1770, from David Wedderburn to Janet Erskine, NAS-SR, GD164/1698.

98. This was an aversion that Ghulam Husain contrasted to the earlier assimilation of Muslim conquerors and Hindu inhabitants, who "have come to coalesce together into one whole, like milk and sugar that have received a simmering." Conversations were extremely dire, in his description. "So soon as an Englishman could pick-up any thing relative to the laws or business of this land, he would immediately set it down in writing, and lay it up in store for the use of another Englishman." The "Hindians," meanwhile, were, in conversation with the English, "very much like a number of pictures set up against the wall"; "they are unable to have a communication of ideas." Gholam-Hossein, *Seir Mutaqharin*, 2:404, 584, 587–88, and see Travers, *Ideology and Empire*, and Kumkum Chatterjee, "History as Self-Representation."

99. Letter of April 8, 1765, from John Carnac in Feyzabad to John Johnstone, OIOC, Carnac Papers, MSS Eur F128/11.

100. Letter of June 17, 1765, from John to the Council of the East India Company in Calcutta, in Third Report from the Committee, *House of Commons Sessional Papers*, p. 436.

101. Report of the Congress held in Pensacola, TNA, CO5/582/199v, 200v, 201v.

102. Speech of George Johnstone of March 30, 1772, debate in the House of Commons on the East India Judicature Bill, PH, vol. 17, col. 373.

103. Letter of October 1, 1765, from John to Lord Clive, Fourth Report from the Committee, *House of Commons Sessional Papers*, pp. 536–37.

104. Edmund Burke, "Second Letter on a Regicide Peace," in *The Works of the Right Honourable Edmund Burke*, 12 vols. (London, 1899), 5:380. On the commercial and financial press, see John J. McCusker, *Essays in the Economic History of the Atlantic World* (London, 1997), Ogborn, *Global Lives*, and Ogborn, *Indian Ink*; and see Will Slauter, "Forward-Looking Statements: News and Speculation in the Age of the American Revolution," *Journal of Modern History* 81 (December 2009): 759–92.

105. On affective knowledge, see Bayly, *Empire and Information*, p. 17.

106. Letter of December 13, 1764, from James Johnstone (the father) to William, in Betty's hand, HL-P, PU 431 [568].

107. Letter of August 18, 1770, from James to Betty, JJLB-EUL, p. 35.

108. "I can assure you I neither stirr'd from my Desk, nor shall quit It till they are finished." Letter of February 5, 1771, from John to William, JJLB-CLA, PD239/201/9.

109. "The loss of one eye, and the delicate situation of the other, make all searches for papers a very great trouble to me," the Johnstones' father wrote to Hume. "I am very desirous to spare you such a disagreeable task, as looking for old papers," Hume responded. Letters of December 29, 1760, from Sir James Johnstone to David Hume and of January 1, 1761, from David Hume to Sir James Johnstone, in Murray, *Letters of David Hume*, pp. 72, 74, 75.

110. Letter of December 29, 1772, from John to William, HL-P, PU 658 [652]; letter of August 8, 1787, from John to William Julius Mickle, WJM-Y; letters of May 15, 1797, and May 19, 1797, from J. Forster to Sir Martin Brown Folkes, FHA-NRO, MC50/52/10 and MC50/52/11.

111. Will of William Bolts, proved September 7, 1808, TNA, PROB 11/1485.

112. Letter of November 11, 1768, from John to William, HL-P, PU 644 [641].

113. "The defendants, who are respectable sugar brokers . . . had received the sugar for the purpose of being sold, not directly from Sir William, but from Petrie and Campbell, West-India merchants, to whom it

had been consigned. . . . Although a person authorised by him promised he would pay them all the money they had advanced in a few days, they said they had nothing to do with Sir William Pulteney, and actually sold off the whole of the sugar. For about a week between the time of the sale and when the action was brought, sugar had been 3s. a hundred dearer than when the sugar was sold, and this action was brought to recover the difference between the two prices, which amounted to 1600 l." The suit was unsuccessful. Court of Common Pleas, *Pulteney v. Kymar and M'Tagart. Caledonian Mercury*, June 16, 1800, no. 12284.

114. John Johnstone, *Letter to the Proprietors*, p. 67, and see above, chapter 4.

115. John had complained that his salt had been stopped by Clive, and Clive responded, "In consequence of your Letter, I have sent for Cojimaul [his associate], to enquire, who gave him the authority to make use of my name in arresting your Salt. I shall order him to go to You. In the meantime I desire You will apply to Mr. Sumner [another official] upon this occasion, as I have no Concern in Salt, or any other Trade whatsoever." Letter of October 1, 1765, from Clive to John, National Library of Wales, CR2/4, available at britishonlinearchives.co.uk.

116. Letters of April 17, 1765, from Lord Clive in Madras to Thomas Rous, the chairman of the East India Company, and to John Walsh, in Third Report from the Committee, *House of Commons Sessional Papers*, pp. 404–5; examination of Lord Clive and Mr. Walsh by the committee, pp. 313–14. Clive's letter to John Walsh arrived in London on March 30, 1766, and his attorneys immediately bought shares for him at the price of 165-1/4; when the "public Advices" of the events of the summer of 1765 reached London on April 20, 1766 (in letters that had been sent from the *Admiral Stevens* in Lisbon) the price of stock rose to 190. Examination of John Walsh, Third Report from the Committee, p. 314.

117. "Governor Johnstone's Speech in the General Court of Proprietors," n.d., in NAS, GD105/679, p. 17.

118. Marshall, *East Indian Fortunes*, pp. 22–24, Bowen, *Business of Empire*, pp. 262–75.

119. Dickson, "Letters to Thomas Clarkson," in Steele and Dickson, *Mitigation of Slavery*, p. 293.

120. Bailyn, *Voyagers to the West*, p. 26.

121. "Nay, should the pale figures of my departed friends present themselves to my imagination in all the horrors of their inhuman massacre, I will remove them from my mind, and cover their bodies with a pall till this subject is decided," George announced, although he went on to pay tribute to "that gallant and generous youth, who was the last to forsake his friend, or his station," identified in a footnote in the printed

version of the speech as "Patrick Johnstone, who was killed in the black hole." He also evoked "the brother of Mr Ellis, the brother of Mr Hay, the brother of Mr Lushington, the widow of Mr Amyat, and the father of Mr Chalmers, all now before you begging for justice." "Governor Johnstone's Speech in the General Court of Proprietors," n.d., in NAS, GD105/679, pp. 3, 17, 38.

122. On the "multiplier effect" in the economists' sense of "projects which directly increase the income of workers and start a round of expenditures (multiplier effect) throughout the economy," see Alvin H. Hansen, "Keynes and the General Theory," *The Review of Economics and Statistics* 28, no. 4 (November 1946): 182–87, p. 186.

123. On John's comments on his own disbursements, see the letter of December 29, 1772, from John to William, HL-P, PU 658 [652], and above, chapter 2.

124. Smith, *Wealth of Nations*, p. 768.

125. Copy, in James's hand, of a letter of June 8, 1759, to William, and see above, chapter 1. NRO, NRS 8347 24D5.

126. Naomi Tadmor, *Family and Friends in Eighteenth-Century England: Household, Kinship and Patronage* (Cambridge, 2001), chapters 1, 3, and 4. Tadmor "takes seriously concepts of the family used by people in the past" in exploring the experience of a number of English families: families, as she observes, who "did not know that they were taking part in a grand terminological transformation. For them the language of kinship, with its diverse and pluralistic usages, was a living reality" (p. 156).

127. Letter of December 29, 1772, from John to William, HL-P, PU 658 [652].

128. North Circuit Minute Book, Perth, September 12–13, 1771, no. 25, May 9, 1771–October 15, 1772, NAS (WRH), JC11/28, unpag. "A List of all Ships" TNA, CO5/1350.

129. Their ship was struck by "a very large Ball of Fire" off the west coast of Africa; the ship's surgeon was "extremely Ill of a violent fever"; a British naval officer came on board and pressed (or forced into military service) "four of our people"; to the east of Mozambique, the captain "put all our chest down . . . so as to have all the guns clear." Logbook of the *Earl of Holdernesse*, OIOC, IOR/L/MAR/B/604C, entries for April 15, May 31, August 22, and October 2, 1761; and see above, chapter 1.

130. Letter of August 4, 1764, from George Johnstone to the Board of Trade, TNA, CO5/582/131r. George was in Jamaica on September 25, 1764, and in West Florida on October 31, 1764; TNA, CO5/582/166,170. Certification of baptism in Pensacola, December 10, 1764, included in the application of George Lindsay Johnstone to

be appointed as a writer to the East India Company, OIOC, IOR/J/1/10/83; and see above, chapter 1.

131. Letter of February 9, 1779, from Frederick Robinson to Lord Grantham, WP-BLA, L30/14/333/177.

132. Letters of March 8, 1770, and March 20, 1770, from Patrick Kinnaird to George Kinnaird, KR-PKA, MS100/2, Bundle 60.

133. Proceedings before the Justices, Joseph Knight, Sir Jn. Wedderburn, 1773, NAS, SC49/6/134/3/3. The house in Jamaica was some years into the future: "Sir John about the time he was baptized said he would give him his freedom 7 years hence if he behaved well for that now he was only begining to be of use to him."

134. According to John Wedderburn, Joseph Knight "first cohabited with her as his Mistress when she was a Servant in the . . . house unknown to any person till at last her being with Child made the discovery." He "further wanted she should have a house near to the Complainers house at Bandean. The objections he had to such a near neighbour of this kind will easily occur to every Considerable person." Complaint of John Wedderburn, November 15, 1774, NAS, CS235/K/2/2.

135. Letter of October 9, 1759, from Betty to William, HL-P, PU 405 [397].

136. Letter of April 25, 1762, from Betty to William, HL-P, PU 425 [414].

137. When William later advanced money to Alexander to buy the Grenada plantation, their father assured him, in a letter in Betty's hand, that "should any misfortune befall him which God avert you need not doubt but that all your Brothers will Contribute to Relive you." Letters of August 30, 1762, and December 13, 1764, from James (the father) to William, HL-P, PU 541 [536], 431 [568].

138. Letters of October 5, 1773, and October 30, 1773, from Betty to William, HL-P, PU 434 [421], 435 [422].

139. Letter of June 19, 1770, from James to John, JJLB-EUL, p. 5.

140. "Which to Purchase out of my Privy Purse I might as well attempt to Pay off the National Debt." Letter of November 14, 1771, from Louisa to John Irving, JJLB-EUL, p. 102.

141. Letter of April 12, 1771, from John to Alexander Alison, JJLB-CLA, PD239/201/9.

142. Letters of September 2, 1769, and October 16, 1773, from John to William, HL-P, PU 646 [642], 660 [654].

143. Letter of September 6, 1768, from John to William, HL-P, PU 641 [638].

144. Letter of February 12, 1778, from Walter Johnstone to James Balmain, JA-CLA, Bundle 6, PD239/6/2.

145. Undated letter of 1777 from Walter Johnstone to William, HL-P, PU 736 [710].

146. Letter of July 11, 1768, from John to William, JJLB-CLA, PD239/201/9; letter of September 6, 1768, from John to William, HL-P, PU 641 [638]. "I am at a loss to understand Georges answer; you say you told him you & I proposed £400 each, & that he said he thought he could do very well upon 400—do you mean that he agreed to your proposal, or wd. accept of only 400 from you & I together? I wish I could accommodate George with Land instead of Houses, but undoubtedly I meant that he should receive from me £400 neat including the rent from the Houses; if that Rent be absorbed in the repairs I must make it good."

147. Letter of September 1, 1771, from James to Betty, JJLB-EUL, p. 84.

148. Letter of July 29, 1751, from Charlotte to William, HL-P, PU 450 [443].

149. "My father says George is generosity to Charlotte and me is great but my mother would not alow him to show us the Letter," she wrote to William in 1758, and in 1761, "Papa after Reading over a great many Letters of Jocks is Clear that the fifty Pound does not belong to us. . . . this I own I think Extremely hard as Im sure Jock would never have wrote me he had sent it if it had not been true and more so as my Father will show me non of the Letters." Letters of May 1, 1758, and November 17, 1761, from Betty to William, HL-P, PU 432 [420], 418 [408].

150. Letter of April 18, 1761, from Walter Johnstone to William, HL-P, PU 719 [707].

151. Letter of May 30, 1771, from James to James Balmain, JJLB-EUL, p. 75.

152. Elizabeth Carolina and her sister travelled from Calcutta to Chittagong at some point between December 1761 and August 1762, on a route that Harry Verelst expected to take them via Lakshmipur. He wrote of the journey to another traveller in the same season, "The rains being now set in . . . you will find the road over to the Fenny very disagreeable and difficult. . . . There are three Elephants gone to Luckypore to assist in bringing your baggage." To one of John's friends he wrote of "several shocks of earthquakes . . . so violent as to rend and shatter the only strong brick building we had." Letters of April 5, 1762, from Harry Verelst to Colonel Eyre Coote, and of May 14, 1762, from Harry Verelst to John Carnac, OIOC, Verelst Letter Book 1761–62, MSS Eur F218/79, ff. 97v, 105v–106r; and see above, chapter 1.

153. Of her son, she wrote that "I shall have much more enjoyment in having him pushed on by your interest, or even your Purse, than by having him promoted by the first minister in Britain." Letter of January 29, 1763, from Anne Ferguson to General James Murray, NAS, GD32/24/14.

154. Letters of December 31, 1771, and March 17, 1772, from David Wedderburn to Janet Erskine, NAS-SR, GD164/1698.

155. Letter of April 16, 1767, from David Wedderburn to Janet Erskine, NAS-SR, GD164/1693.

156. Letter of early 1759 from Barbara (the mother) to George, EUL-L, La.II.73/71.

157. Letter of March 4, 1764, from James (the father) to William, in Betty's hand, HL-P, PU 552 [566].

158. Letter of April 17, 1757, from Charles Kinnaird to William, HL-P, PU 765 [768]; letter of June 9, 1757, from James to William, HL-P, PU 563 [483]; unsigned letter of October 18, 1773, from the Admiralty to William, HL-P, PU 1911 [477].

159. Letter of December 22, 1764, from Barbara (the mother) to John, in UMWCL-MS.

160. Letter of April 1, 1771, from George Malcolm to William, HL-P, PU 917 [980]. Of George Malcolm's seventeen children, several, including Sir John Malcolm, Admiral Sir Pulteney Malcolm, and Sir Charles Malcolm, later became ornaments of the British empire in India and elsewhere. George Malcolm was almost destitute in the 1760s, following a series of "misfortunes," or financial speculations; see J. W. Kaye, *The life and correspondence of Major-General Sir John Malcolm*, 2 vols. (London, 1856), 1:2–5. As he wrote to William later in 1771, in a letter about planting Italian poplars, "I have now five Boys & four Girls. How to get them Porridge & Plaiding gives me often very strong Quams." Letter of December 7, 1771, from George Malcolm to William, HL-P, PU 923 [985]. The "lads" in India about whom he was concerned in 1771 were the sons of his brother-in-law John Maxwell, William's other factor. See letters of April 22, 1771, from George Maxwell to William and of May 3, 1771, from John Maxwell to William, HL-P, PU 918 [981] and PU 1554 [1186]; on Malcolm's and Maxwell's activities as William's factors, see Michael B. Moir, "Estate Papers from Dumfriesshire, 1764–1872," available at www.lib.uoguelph.ca/resources/archival_&_special_collections/collection_update/07/Pulteney/summary.html.

161. Letter of March 22, 1771, from William Colhoon in London to Betty Colqhoun in Glasgow, GCA, TD 301/6/1/8.

162. Letters from William Brown to Andrew Davidson and John More, in NAS, JC26/193/2.

163. As James Johnstone wrote to James Balmain, when Balmain had begun to search the archives in Edinburgh for records of the Johnstones' claim to the Annandale peerage, "My Dear James I do know you and know that the Sincerest affection for me are not words of Course but the

real Sentiments of your Soul not of yesterday, but long before we took our Solitary walk from Shiells to Westerhall, it began in our Infancy and will Stand I hope the Utmost Efforts of Old Age. Mine for you is Strong as ever, tho I am both Bald & Grey. I am none of those, who will have hoards of Secrets come out against Them at the last Day, Sure I am that I would not desire to have any with you, besides in the Present Case it would be Folly because you could not Serve me unless you knew what I was desirous should be Searched after." Letter of May 30, 1771, from James to James Balmain, JJLB-EUL, p. 75.

164. Speech of Lord Clive of March 30, 1772, debate in the House of Commons on the East India Judicature Bill, PH, vol. 17, cols. 356, 363–65.

165. Letter of November 1, 1772, from James to Betty, JJLB-EUL, p. 171.

166. Speeches of William Pulteney of December 2, 1772, on the Navy Estimates and of George Johnstone of May 18, 1774, on the Budget, PH, vol. 17, cols. 538, 1346.

167. Letter of June 7, 1769, from John to James, JJLB-CLA, PD239/201/9.

168. Letter of early 1759 from Barbara (the mother) to George, EUL-L, La.II.73/71.

169. "It will be a very good employment for your numerous attendants who have little to do to gather shells dry seaweeds catch Butterflies & stuff dead Birds, your Presents too have a chance of coming in better condition than the Cash. . . . Mrs W. desires me however to add, that she is by no means tired of living birds, & that she would rather take her chance of their coming safe, & stuff them herself when they happen to die." Letter of April 1, 1772, from Alexander Wedderburn to David Wedderburn, NAS-SR, GD164/1700; on British collections in India, see Maya Jasanoff, *Edge of Empire: Lives, Culture, and Conquest in the East, 1750–1850* (New York, 2005). David Wedderburn died outside the fortified city of Baruch in November 1772. His death was described in detail in a letter to his sister; letter of February 20, 1773, from John Mackenzie to Janet Erskine, NAS-SR, GD164/1705.

170. Letter of December 13, 1764, from James (the father) to William, in Betty's hand, HL-P, PU 431 [568].

171. Receipt of January 13, 1766, from General John Carnac in Bengal to Samuel Swinton, OIOC, Carnac Papers, MSS Eur F128/11; and see Swinton's correspondence with David Anderson and Robert Keith in Calcutta, British Library, Anderson Papers, vol. 13, Add. Ms. 45429.

172. Letter of December 13, 1764, from James (the father) to William, in Betty's hand, which becomes bigger and bigger as she transcribes page

after page of details of prices and rents, HL-P, PU 431 [568]; letter of December 29, 1761, from John to James Balmain, HL-P, PU 671 [620].

173. Letters of June 11, 1766, and April 11, 1771, from David Wedderburn to Janet Erskine, NAS-SR, GD164/1693 and GD164/1698.

174. Letter of March 13, 1761, from the East India Company's Court of Directors in London to the Council in Calcutta, letter of April 8, 1762, from the Council in Calcutta to the Court of Directors in London, *Fort William–India House Correspondence*, 3:77, 423. The new groves of willow trees were intended, eventually, for warlike purposes: "we hope in time you may raise trees for the making of proper charcoal to be used in your manufacturing gunpowder" (p. 77).

175. Letter of October 21, 1762, to William Billers, Verelst Letter Book 1761–62, OIOC, Mss Eur F218/79, 145r.

176. Letter of April 12, 1771, from David Wedderburn to Janet Erskine, NAS-SR, GD164/1698.

177. The *Jupiter*, of the expedition to Rio Plata, was a menagerie of bulls, cows, turkeys, and singing birds, en route to settling "Fort Johnstone," in the description of George's friend Captain Pasley: "my *Jupiter* is at present a perfect Noah's Ark: Bulls, Cows, Rams, Ewes, Ram Goats, Ewe Goats, Lambs and Kids in variety—Calves of both species, Boar and Sow Pigs with old and young—Turkeys, Geese, Ducks, Fowls—Singing Birds of different kinds to turn loose—All kinds of Trees to Plant and Grasses of every kind—Seeds both Cape and European without number and without name—Water Cresses, Sorrel, Water Dock, Purcelean, Will'd Mint, Time—and the Lord knows what. How my Commodore's scheme may be relished at home I know not; but he is indefatigable in every project he attempts." Pasley, *Private Sea Journals*, p. 184, and, on the "new-constructed Battery" on the island of Trinidada, to be known as "Fort Johnstone," p. 193.

178. "Arbres Fruitiers du Midi de la France," October 12, 1784, in Von Proschwitz and Von Proschwitz, *Beaumarchais*, p. 856.

179. Letters of December 19, 1767, and December 31, 1771, from David Wedderburn to Janet Erskine, NAS-SR, GD164/1693 and GD164/1698.

180. He "often declared his intention of providing for her, as no Will was found, no provision was made. Mr Mackenzie & me immediatly consider'd ourselves bound by every tye of Honor & Gratitude to protect & support her decently & properly till your orders cou'd reach us; We propose, show'd you aprove of it, that 2,000 rups. show'd be settled on her, the interest of this money will barely enable her to live comfortably nor do we think any less sum will do it." Letter of April 20, 1773,

from Alexander Maclellan in Bombay to Alexander Wedderburn, NAS-SR, GD164/1709. On the relations between East India Company officials and "Mogull" women, see Ghosh, *Sex and the Family*.

181. "Inventory of the Estate and Effects of the late Brigadier General Wedderburn," Bombay, December 15, 1773, NAS-SR, GD164/231.

182. Laurel Thatcher Ulrich, *The Age of Homespun: Objects and Stories in the Creation of an American Myth* (New York, 2001), p. 414.

183. The exchange was denominated in "half dressed Deer skins." Treaty for the Preservation & Continuance of a Perfect Peace, May 28, 1765, TNA, CO5/582/210v, 211v.

184. Letter from John to James of December 24, 1761, HL-P, PU 672 [621].

185. "There is a gentleman, now in England, who . . . has purchased in the Dacca province in one morning eight hundred pieces of muslin at his own door, as brought to him by the weavers of their own accord." Bolts, *Considerations on India Affairs*, 1:194, 206.

186. Cape Coast Ledger no. 27 (July 1 to December 31, 1764), TNA, T70/738, pp. 1, 23, 28, 29, 37. Captain John Knight was the captain of six slaving voyages, on two vessels, the *Phoenix* and the *King George*. Two of the voyages on the *Phoenix*, in 1759–60 and 1764–65, were from Cape Coast Castle in modern Ghana to Jamaica. "List of voyages," voyage identification numbers 17465 and 17601, available at the Trans-Atlantic Slave Trade Database, wilson.library.emory.edu:9090/tast/database/search .faces. On the Cape Coast Castle, see William St. Clair, *The Grand Slave Emporium: Cape Coast Castle and the British Slave Trade* (London, 2006).

187. "And a new outfit for a three years Station is very Expencive." Letters of December 21, 1759, from Gideon to George, EUL-L, La. II.73/75, and of December 23, 1759, from Gideon to William, HL-P, PU 489 [475].

188. Will of George Johnstone, proved June 12, 1787, TNA, PROB 11/1154.

189. His stock included Indian cloth reexported from London; "the Cassimere is a thin light Cloth conseqently fit for a warm Climate." Letters of March 21, 1770, and of March 23, 1770, from Samuel Swinton to David Anderson and Robert Keith in Calcutta, British Library, Anderson Papers, vol. 13, Add. Ms. 45429, 37, 41.

190. Letters of February 16, 1761, from Harry Verelst in Islamabad to Messrs. Beaumont and Watts and of April 27, 1761, to John Cartier in Dhaka. OIOC, Verelst Letter Book 1761–62, MSS Eur F218/79, ff.4v, 20v.

191. A cardinal was "a short cloak worn by ladies, originally of scarlet cloth with a hood," as in, from 1745, "You are capering about in your fine cardinals." *Oxford English Dictionary*.

192. A family of "rich Asiatics" was described satirically by "John Homespun" in *The Lounger*: "my neighbour *Mushroom*'s son" who "had sent a trunk full of fineries to dress up his mother and sisters," and who eventually returned home from India with "flowered muslins and gold muslins, white shawls and red shawls." In Homespun's conclusion, "I must try to find out some new place of residence, where Nabobs, Rajahs, and Lacks of Rupees, were never heard of, and where people know no more of Bengal than of the Man in the Moon." "Influence of the neighbour-hood of a rich Asiatic, in a letter from JOHN HOMESPUN," in [Henry Mackenzie], *The Lounger. A Periodical Paper, Published at Edinburgh in the Years 1785 and 1786*, 3 vols. (London, 1787), 1:iv, 147, 148, 151.

193. Will of George Johnstone, proved June 12, 1787, TNA, PROB 11/1154; will of Etheldred Bennet, proved May 28, 1766, TNA, PROB 11/918. Etheldred Bennet was the daughter of Louisa's maternal great-aunt, Etheldred (Hovell) Wake.

194. Extract, Process Joseph Knight against Sir John Wedderburn of Ballendean Bart. 1774, NAS, CS235/K/2/2.

195. North Circuit Minute Book, Aberdeen, September 23, 1771, NAS(WRH), JC11/28.

196. Porteous Roll for Fifeshire, Autumn 1771, NAS, JC26/193/3; "Declaration of Bell or Belinda a black Girl," Cupar, July 4, 1771, NAS, JC26/193/3.

197. "Declaration of Bell or Belinda a black Girl," Cupar, July 4, 1771, NAS, JC26/193/3.

198. Report of the examination of Joseph Knight at Balindean on November 15, 1773, in Copy of Proceedings before the Justices, 1773, NAS, SC49/6/134/3/3.

199. Letter of August 8, 1797, from William to Forster & Cooke, Lincoln's Inn, BUL-W, Westerhall Estate Papers, DM 41/62/14; "List of slaves belonging to Westerhall," July 13, 1798, which includes "Pierre / carré to England," Accounts of Westerhall Estate January 1, 1796, to December 31, 1797, BUL-W, Westerhall Estate Papers, DM 41/21/10; undated letter from Alexander Sutherland and Ann Wilson and letter from Ann Sutherland of May 11, 1839, JA-CLA, Bundle 5, PD239/5/27 and Bundle 7, PD239/7/11; "A true Copy of the Register of the parish Church of Kirkandrews upon Esk for the year of our Lord 1773," Cumbria Record Office; Westerkirk Kirk Sessions for November 12, 1778 and March 4, 1781, NAS, CH2/368/2/171–73; will of Sir James Johnstone, proved March 21, 1796, TNA, PROB 11/1272.

200. "Declaration of Bell or Belinda a black Girl," NAS, JC26/193/3.

201. "Declaration of Bell or Belinda a black Girl," NAS, JC26/193/3; "Indictment agt Bell or Belinda a Negroe Girl," Porteous Roll for Fifeshire, Autumn 1771, NAS, JC26/193/3; "Petition for Bell or Belinda a Black Girl," September 13, 1771, JC26/193/3. The emphasis on "or" and "alias" is added.

202. One Company servant asked to "send back to Bengal two Black Women named Lizerda and Theodora"; Warren Hastings asked to "return to India a Black servant named Monick who came with me from thence." Petitions of December 19, 1750, by William Barwell and of January 29, 1766, by Warren Hastings, OIOC, IOR/B/71, p. 262 and IOR/E/1/48, Miscellaneous Letters Received, Letter 7. By the early 1770s, these requests were numerous; see, for example, the letters with respect to "Martha," "Domingo," "Caesar," "Patna," and others in IOR/E/1/55, ff. 242–453. The two logbooks of the *Admiral Stevens*, IOR/L/MAR/B/566A and IOR/L/MAR/B/566B, were kept by James Angus and Captain Griffin. On Indian servants and slaves in Britain, and on the new regulations introduced in 1769 to require bonds for servants "sent to England," see Fisher, *Counterflows to Colonialism*, pp. 53–65, 216–21.

203. Minute of September 9, 1765, OIOC, Fort William Consultations, Range 1, vol. 38, IOR/P/1/38/733.

204. North Circuit Minute Book, no. 25, 1771–72, NAS(WRH), JC11/28.

205. Certificate of Landing, April 29, 1772, NAS(WRH), JC41/12; "A List of all Ships and Vessels," TNA, CO5/1350. Notice about James Patteson, *Virginia Gazette* (Purdie & Dixon), Williamsburg, April 23, 1772, available at the University of Virginia's Web site "The Geography of Slavery in Virginia," www2.vcdh.virginia.edu/gos/search.

206. Complaint of John Wedderburn, November 15, 1774, NAS, CS235/K/2/2.

207. List of Witnesses, Porteous Roll for Fife Shire, Autumn 1771, "Declaration of Bell or Belinda a black Girl," July 4, 1771, "Petition for Bell or Belinda," September 13, 1771, NAS, JC26/193/3.

208. Letter of December 8, 1770, from John to Alexander, JJLB-CLA, PD239/201/9.

209. James wrote to John in January 1772 to express his sympathy with "Mrs Johnstone's misfortune" and his hopes for the continuation of the family: "your Children I must consider as my own," and "the Thorn Tree [the emblem of the Johnstones] is too weak to admit the loss of a Single Branch." Letter of January 22, 1772, from James to John, JJLB-EUL, p. 128. John wrote to William from Balgonie in May 1771, and in a later letter recalled that he was in Kirkaldy, a few miles away, in early

June of the same year. The later letter was concerned, as so often, with the records of the Grenada plantation: "upon examining my Papers I find the Original Draft of my Letter to the Colonel dated the 12th June 1771 is wrote in my own hand, nor am I certain whether the Copy sent was wrote from this Draft by my own hand, or by Mr Kay my Clerk, but I am apt to believe It was by my own hand as I was at Kirkaldie at that time." Letters of May 19, 1771, and September 18, 1773, from John to William, HL-P, PU 651 [644] and PU 659 [653].

210. "Mr Balmain & family are just arrived & join in Compliments to you," John wrote to a business acquaintance. Letter of April 12, 1771, from John in Balgonie to Alexander Alison, JJLB-CLA, PD239/201/9. Charlotte and James Balmain's son George was born in Edinburgh on February 25, 1772, while Bell or Belinda was on the *Betsey*, on her way to Virginia. Old Parish Register, www.scotlandspeople.gov.uk.

211. "Complaint of John Wedderburn," May 30, 1774, NAS, CS235/K/2/2; Cairns, *Scottish Law of Slavery*.

212. "Indictment agt Bell or Belinda a Negroe Girl," Porteous Roll for Fifeshire, Autumn 1771, NAS, JC26/193/3.

CHAPTER SIX. WHAT IS ENLIGHTENMENT?

1. William Pulteney, *Present State of Affairs*, p. 68.

2. Ferguson, *Moral and Political Science*, 1:266, 268.

3. On the Scottish science of man, see J.G.A. Pocock, *Barbarism and Religion*, pp. 199–221, Phillipson, *Hume*, esp. pp. 137–41, and Phillipson, *Adam Smith*.

4. Ferguson, *Moral and Political Science*, 2:281.

5. "Beantwortung der Frage: Was ist Aufklärung?" (1784), in Immanuel Kant, *Werkausgabe*, ed. Wilhelm Weischedel (Frankfurt, 1968), 11:53–61; "What is Enlightenment?" in Hans Reiss, ed., *Kant's Political Writings* (Cambridge, 1970), 54–60; Ian Simpson Ross and David Raynor, "Adam Smith and Count Windisch-Grätz: New Letters," *Studies on Voltaire and the Eighteenth Century* 358 (1997): 171–87, 172.

6. Ferguson, *Moral and Political Science*, 1:164, 208, 235.

7. On enlightenment and empire, see Rothschild, "Global Commerce," Michèle Duchet, *Anthropologie et histoire au siècle des lumières* (1971) (Paris, 1995), Jennifer Pitts, *A Turn to Empire: The Rise of Imperial Liberalism in Britain and France* (Princeton, 2005), and Sankar Muthu, *Enlightenment against Empire* (Princeton, 2003).

8. Hume, "My Own Life," in Hume, *Essays*, xxxi–xli, p. xxxvi; Hume, "Of Interest," in Hume, *Essays*, p. 304; and see Emma Rothschild, "The

Atlantic Worlds of David Hume," in *Soundings in Atlantic History: Latent Structures and Intellectual Currents, 1500–1830*, ed. Bernard Bailyn and Patricia L. Denault, 405–48 (Cambridge, MA, 2009).

9. See, on Ferguson, Fania Oz-Sulzberger, *Translating the Enlightenment: Scottish Civic Discourse in Eighteenth-Century Germany* (Oxford, 1995).

10. See Rothschild, "Adam Smith in the British Empire."

11. [Arthur Lee], *An Essay in Vindication of the Continental Colonies of America, From A Censure of Mr Adam Smith, in his Theory of Moral Sentiments. With some Reflections on Slavery in general. By an American* (London, 1764), pp. iv, 10.

12. "Well has Dr Smith in treating of this subject expressed the Indignation of a generous mind at that Cruelty & oppression which is the disgrace of modern times," Allan Maconochie wrote in the manuscript "Memorial for Joseph Knight" (1775), p. 34; NAS, CS235/K/2/2. The sentence does not appear in the printed version of the memorial, although the same passage from *The Theory of Moral Sentiments* is quoted; Maconochie in the printed version also modifies the effect of Smith's criticism of the colonists with the qualification, "However worthy and respectable individuals of the Americans may be found . . ." Maconochie, Information for Joseph Knight, p. 37.

13. "Of National Characters," in Hume, *Essays*, p. 208, n.10 and p. 629. On the uses of Hume's footnote by Samuel Estwick, "Assistant Agent for the Island of Barbados," arguing for slavery, and Granville Sharp, arguing against slavery, see Rothschild, "Atlantic Worlds." James Beattie of Aberdeen, in particular, the "bigotted silly fellow" who was such an object of ridicule to Smith and Hume, was an eloquent critic of Hume. See, on Beattie, the letters from Smith to Hume of May 9, 1775, in Smith, *Correspondence*, p. 182, and from Hume to William Strahan of October 26 1775 in Greig, *Letters of David Hume*, 2:301; and James Beattie, *An Essay on the Nature and Immutability of Truth; in Opposition to Sophistry and Scepticism* (Edinburgh, 1770), pp. 480–81.

14. The abolition map is reproduced in Christopher Brown, *Moral Capital*, pp. 6–7.

15. Mickle, *Candid Examination*, p. 8.

16. Mickle, "Introduction," in Camöens, *Lusiad*, p. clxxv; speech of William Pulteney of February 28, 1805, debate in the House of Commons on the second reading of the Bill for the Abolition of the Slave Trade, *Parliamentary Debates*, vol. 3, col. 658.

17. [Richard Clarke], *The Nabob: or, Asiatic Plunderers* (London, 1773), p. 3.

18. The declaration in the English Court of Chancery that Lord Annandale had become a lunatic, who "doth not enjoy lucid Intervals," on December 17, 1744, and the "Brieve of Furiosity" of 1757 in Scotland, together with the involvement of a "Clerk in the Petty Bag Office," are described in *The Sessional Papers of the House of Lords, Annandale, Fitzwalter and Sussex Peerages*, 2 vols. (London, 1844), 1:75–79. Hume wrote to Sir James Johnstone of Lord Annandale's novel that "we were oblig'd to print off thirty copies, to make him believe that we had printed a thousand, and that they were to be disperst all over the kingdom. My Lady Marchioness will also receive a copy, and I am afraid it may give her a good deal of uneasiness, by reason of the story alluded to in the novel, and which she may imagine my Lord is resolv'd to bring to execution." Letter of June 18, 1745, from David Hume to Sir James Johnstone, in Greig, *Letters of David Hume*, 1:61. The novel may have been *The Triumph of Love and Virtue. A Novel Wrote by a Gentleman* (London, 1745). The story turns on a young nobleman from an unnamed "Northern Country, where the Hearts and Understandings are so moderate and cool," who rescues a poor but virtuous opera dancer in the Venetian countryside, conducts her respectfully home in his gondola, returns to his own country where he becomes "desperately ill" in a "little Country House," and eventually marries his beloved after she has been naturalized and ennobled by the magnanimous king of his country (pp. 40, 48). The title page of the work does not identify a printer or publisher, and contains the text "London: Printed in the Year MDCCXLV."

19. Letter of October 22, 1745, from David Hume to the older Sir James Johnstone, in Greig, *Letters of David Hume*, 1:64. "I have some dark remembrance," the Johnstones' father wrote to Hume, at a time when he was almost blind; "I require to have circumstances brought into my mind by others, in order to recollect with distinctness, the true state of these transactions." Letter of December 29, 1760, from Sir James Johnstone to David Hume, in Murray, *Letters of David Hume*, pp. 72, 74. The letter is dated from Weldehall, which was presumably a mistaken transcription of "Westerhall." Weldehall was the house in Hertfordshire in which Hume and Lord Annandale had lived so unhappily fifteen years before. The manuscripts transcribed by Murray were apparently dispersed in the course of the nineteenth century; see J.Y.T. Greig, "Introduction," in Greig, *Letters of David Hume*, 1:xxix. The Johnstones of Westerhall were very distant relatives of the Annandale Johnstones. Sir James Johnstone's younger brother, Colonel John Johnstone, married the widow of the late marquis of Annandale, the mother of the "lunatic." John Johnstone was killed in 1741 in the unsuccessful British siege of

Cartagena, in what is now Colombia. James Johnstone's own involvement in the case was as a friend of his widowed sister-in-law, as a legal adviser to the family, and eventually as a claimant to the peerage. John Debrett, *The Baronetage of England*, rev. George William Collen (London, 1840), p. 316.

20. The uncles were the Johnstones' mother's brother Lord Elibank and her brother-in-law "Jemmy Ferguson," or Lord Pitfour (the presiding judge in Bell's trial). Letter of August 14, 1764, from Hume to Lord Elibank, in Mossner, "New Hume Letters to Lord Elibank," p. 455.

21. Letter of March 22, [1763,] from George to Hume, Hume Manuscripts, NLS, MS 23155, no. 94, f. 249; letter of April 2, 1759, from Hume to Lord Elibank, in Mossner, "New Hume Letters to Lord Elibank," p. 449; letters from Hume to Adam Smith of July 21, 1763, and of June 25, 1771, and January 2, 1772, to William Strahan, in Greig, *Letters of David Hume*, 1:391, 2:243, 251. The sister in question, in the letter of 1763, was presumably Charlotte, who had eloped a few weeks before. Barbara had been legally separated from her husband since 1760, and Betty had returned to Westerhall after the crisis over the muslins, in the summer of 1762.

22. Letter of October 8, 1767, from William Pulteney, Hume Manuscripts, NLS, MS 23155, no. 96, ff. 255–56; letters of February 22, 1772, and January 25, 1774, to William Strahan in Greig, *Letters of David Hume*, 2:260, 283.

23. William was "a young gentleman I have known intimately these four years," Smith wrote in 1752. Letter of January 19, 1752, from Adam Smith to James Oswald, in Smith, *Correspondence*, p. 7, and see above, chapter 1.

24. "I shall ever consider it as the most agreeable Letter I ever received," Andrew Stuart wrote of William's letter about the settlement made by Frances Johnstone's cousin General Pulteney, who had recently died; "it was brought to me at the Poker Club when in company with Ferguson, Smith, Robinson [Robertson?], Blair, and many others of your friends. . . . You may easily imagine what joy it diffused over the whole company, we got all into such spirits that the meeting continued longer than usual and as the Post was gone before we broke up there was no opportunity of writing you that night." Letter of November 3, 1767, from Andrew Stuart to William, HL-P, PU 1977 [1644]. The Johnstones' father's letter of congratulations to William, on receiving the news of General Pulteney's death, was less convivial: "may we be all sensibly impressed with gratitude to God for the manifold blissings he has So bountifully bestowed on me, & mine." Letter of October 31, 1767, from Sir James Johnstone (the father) to William, HL-P, PU 556 [569].

25. Letter of September 3, 1772, from Adam Smith to William, in Smith, *Correspondence*, p. 163.

26. On the British Coffee House, see Sher, *Enlightenment and the Book*, pp. 128–31.

27. Letter of March 25, 1776, from James Macpherson to John Macpherson, Macpherson Papers, OIOC, Mss Eur F291/122; letters from Edmund Burke and Henry Dundas to Smith of December 7 and December 20, 1786, and March 21, 1787, and of Smith to Alexander Ross of December 13, 1786, in Smith, *Correspondence*, pp. 297–302. "I have written a Note to Smith to remind him of trying to bring Bourke again upon the Subject & to get him to speak decisively about it if he does so even to an acquaintance like Smith he is an honourable man & wont go back," Simon Fraser wrote to William, in an undated letter, probably from 1775, HL-P, PU 270 [296].

28. The letter was concerned with electoral votes in the vicinity of Westerhall, and John's purchase of the estate of Hangingshaw near the Ettrick Forest. Byken was a village near Westerhall, of which the Duke of Buccleuch was the landowner, as he was of the lands around Hangingshaw; Smith was at this time actively involved in the management of the Duke's estate. Letter of April 17, 1771, from James to John, in Louisa's hand, JJLB-EUL, p. 61, and see Phillipson, *Adam Smith*, pp. 202–8.

29. On James Townsend Oswald's appointment as secretary for the Leeward Islands, see List of the House of Commons, 1768, PH, vol. 16, col. 453.

30. Letters of October 8, 1767, September 6, 1768, and September 18, 1773, from John to William, HL-P, PU 629 [626], PU 641 [638], PU 659 [653].

31. Betty wrote again a week later, "I wish you would let us know what Doctor Cullen says about the Copper," and on April 25, "Im affraid Doctor Cullen has said nothing good about the Copper other wise you would have wrote." Letters from Betty to William of March 6, March 14, and April 25, 1762, HL-P, PU 422 [412], 423 [390], and 425 [414].

32. Letters of August 6, 1770, and November 1, 1772, from James to Betty, JJLB-EUL, pp. 25, 172.

33. "Dr Hunter beged I would send you this Memorandum that he might not give you the Trouble of a visit the Election for St Georges Hospital comes on friday next where you are requested to attend the Ballot for his brother," John wrote to William in 1768. From Westerhall, in the midst of his anxieties over the "affair" at Kirkaldy, he wrote, "In our last Strugle for the Restitution [of East Indian property] Dr Hunter acted the kindest part & attended three days to give us his Vote. I wish you could return this obligation in furthering his Brothers pretensions as

succeeding to the St Georges Hospital with your own Vote and as many friends as you can engage. George & I have qualified in order to give him our Votes & he is a man of that Stamp as makes me think him worthy to be ranked in the number of our friends; perhaps he may assist us with some stock on Security to replace it." Letters of September 6, 1768, and undated letter of 1768 from John to William, HL-P, PU 641 [638] and 649 [618]. The Dr. Hunter who acted the kindest part was Dr. William Hunter; Dr. John Hunter, his younger brother, was elected to St. George's Hospital in 1768. See Helen Brock, "Hunter, William (1718–1783)," and Jacob W. Gruber, "Hunter, John (1728–1793)," ODNB, articles 14221, 14234. Dr. William Hunter's transactions in East India Company shares in 1766–70 are described in C. Helen Brock, ed., *The Correspondence of Dr. William Hunter, 1740–1783*, 2 vols. (London, 2008), 1:288, 297–98.

34. "One of the first Commoners in Great Britain, in point of property and talents, I mean William Pulteney, Esq. has paid particular attention to the Vegetable Syrup; and, by his desire, Dr. Black of Edinburgh did me the honour of calling on me. . . . Mr. Pulteney omits no opportunity of recommending the medicine." Isaac Swainson, Sole Proprietor of the Medicine, and only Successor to Mr. De Velnos, *An Account of Cures by Velnos' Vegetable Syrup* (London, 1789), pp. 13–14.

35. See H. S. Torrens, "Benett, Etheldred (1775–1845)," ODNB, article 46424, and Jean Jones, "Hall, Sir James, of Dunglass, Fourth Baronet (1761–1832)," ODNB, article 119635.

36. Luther P. Eisenhart, "Walter Minto and the Earl of Buchan," *Proceedings of the American Philosophical Society* 94, no. 3 (June 20, 1950): 282–94, p. 282.

37. Copy in Walter Minto's hand of a letter of November 23, 1778, to George, in UMWCL-MS; commencement oration by Walter Minto of September 24, 1788, quoted in Eisenhart, "Walter Minto," p. 291.

38. "I have not wrote you for some time. I suppose that your book is printing. Lord Shelburne told me one day that he supposed Governor Johnson would not perhaps return to West Florida, as he is coming home, and sayd, that he saw no reason why he should not offer the government of it to you," one of Hume and Ferguson's old friends wrote to Ferguson in 1766. Lord Shelburne was at the time the secretary of state for the Southern Department, which included the North American colonies. Letter of October 10, 1766, from Robert Clerk to Adam Ferguson, Merolle, *Correspondence of Adam Ferguson*, 1:68.

39. Letter of April 4, 1772, from Andrew Stuart to William, enclosing a letter of March 1772 from Adam Ferguson, in which he provided information about the Dutch empire in the Indies, derived from one of his

wife's relations, "who lived long in Batavia in quality of English Consul."
HL-P, PU 2008 [1674], PU 210 [1674x]. Letters of July 30, 1772, from
David Hume to an unidentified recipient, Merolle, *Correspondence of
Adam Ferguson*, 2:548, and of November 23, 1772, to Adam Smith, in
Greig, *Letters of David Hume*, 2:266; letters of Adam Ferguson to John
Macpherson of March 31, 1774, and June 19, 1778, and to David Hume
of June 6, 1774, Merolle, *Correspondence of Adam Ferguson*, 1:105,
112, 171.

40. Will of George Johnstone, proved June 12, 1787, TNA, PROB
11/1154. "I will that he should be removed there before the age of four
years," George wrote of his youngest son, and expressed his "unalterable
desire" that the boy "should be educated in Scotland until he shall attain
his age of fourteen years at the least." He relented in part in a later codicil, on the grounds that his wife "had expressed her wish to be that my
said son . . . should remain with her till he hath compleated his sixth year
after which time she is willing that he should be brought up in Scotland."
"My whole Flock little Johnston and all have been at Leith for Sea bathing," Ferguson wrote to Sir John Macpherson in July 1790. "I have never
ceased to think of an excursion to Italy; but the charge of George Johnstones Son forbids it." To Alexander Carlyle in 1796 he wrote of "the
little Johnston" that "the time must come at which he will either bear
himself up on feelings of a Gentleman or be lost to his Friends. . . . The
dissappointment may draw tears from those who had the happiness of
intimacy with his Family or who even are acquainted with himself in his
more pleasant and better moments in which he has scarcely an equal
among Boys." Letters of July 31, 1790, to Sir John Macpherson and November 23, 1796, to the Rev. Alexander Carlyle, Merolle, *Correspondence of Adam Ferguson*, 2:340–41, 407–8.

41. Letters of October 27, 1784, from Adam Ferguson to General
Fletcher Campbell, of December 3, 1795, to John Johnstone, and of July
7, 1796, and August 1, 1798, to Sir John Macpherson, in Merolle, *Correspondence of Adam Ferguson*, 2:307, 375, 400–401, 442.

42. In 1766 David Wedderburn escaped with Adam Smith and his young
pupil, the Duke of Buccleuch [Buccleugh], from an unfortunate love affair
in the French countryside. "Madame . . . wrote a letter to her Daughter
explaining that she had many objections to our union," David Wedderburn
wrote to his brother from Soissons, in August 1766, about the end of a
romance in which "the Mother kept me three days in her house allow'd
me to be with her Daughter as formerly sent her Daughter to town in the
Coach with me and allow'd me to see her as much as I pleased at home
but forbid my going to the play or appearing in publick with her." "I took
the resolution yesterday to leave Paris with Smith & the Duke of Buc-

cleugh." Letter of August 9, 1766, from David Wedderburn to Alexander Wedderburn, NAS-SR, GD164/1696. The members of the Select Society on October 17, 1759, are listed in "Appendix to the Life of Dr Robertson," Dugald Stewart, ed., *The Works of William Robertson*, 8 vols. (London, 1827), 1:xci–xcii. The connections of other members of the society to the Johnstones and their friends were multiple; they included Andrew Stuart, whose widow William married in 1804, Harry Erskine, who married Alexander and David Wedderburn's sister Janet, and Alexander Boswell, Lord Auchinleck, James Boswell's father, who in 1760 was the arbitrator in the separation of Barbara (Johnstone) Kinnaird.

43. Members of the Poker Club in 1774, in Alexander Fraser Tytler, ed., *Supplement to the Memoirs of the Life and Writings of the Hon. Henry Home of Kames* (Edinburgh, 1809), pp. 33–35.

44. Anonymous, *A Specimen of the Scots Review* (n.p., 1774), pp. 9, 18. On the publishing and printing industry in Scotland, see Sher, *Enlightenment and the Book*.

45. Letter of October 2, 1747, from David Hume to James Oswald, Greig, *Letters of David Hume*, 1:107.

46. Unsigned letter of August 15, 1751, to William, HL-P, PU 503 [517].

47. Letter of April 17, 1757, from Charles Kinnaird to William, HL-P, PU 765 [768], inscription, verso, in James's hand. The reference is to the translations of Horace by the Rev. Philip Francis, the father of the politician in India and the teacher of Edward Gibbon.

48. "Inventory of the Household Furniture Linnens and Books In Lord Kinnairds House at Drimmie 1767," available at www.scotlandspeople. gov.uk; "Inventory of the possessions of the late Sir James Johnstone, taken August 11, 1797," "List of Books in the Library at Westerhall," available at NAS, CC8/8/130/1733–70. The reference to "Muncaster on the Slave Trade" is to *Historical Sketches of the Slave Trade, and of its Effects in Africa* (1792), a fervent denunciation of slavery by Lord Muncaster, the Cumberland abolitionist politician and close associate of William Wilberforce.

49. Will of George Johnstone, proved June 12, 1787, TNA, PROB 11/1154.

50. Will of Miss Betty Johnstone, proved December 24, 1813, available at www.scotlandspeople.gov.uk.

51. "List of Subscribers," in Camöens, *Lusiad*, trans. Mickle, unpag.

52. Letter of December 13, 1764, from James Johnstone (the father) to William, in Betty's hand, HL-P, PU 431 [568].

53. Sale list of the effects of the Rev. Henry Butler, sold at auction on December 5–6, 1761, in Calcutta. Hyde, *Parochial Annals*, pp. 124–25.

54. "Your Books are all safe with me viz. at my Lodgings in London." Letter of December 14, 1759, from Samuel Swinton to George; EUL-L, La.II.73/74. "I need not tell you how disagreeable this Service is, as you had your share of it," Swinton wrote of the impress: "I have had two or three out Trips of 15 or 20 Mile with a Gang, being the youngest Officer."

55. Letter of February 17, 1768, from William Colhoon in Port Glasgow to Betty Colqhoun in Glasgow, GCA, TD 301/6/1/1.

56. Bolts, *Considerations on India Affairs*, 2:119.

57. Will of William Bolts, proved September 7, 1808, TNA, PROB 11/1485.

58. Entries for October 4, 1796, and April 4, 1797, Westerkirk Library Minute Book, Bentpath Library.

59. Speeches of Mr. Attorney General Thurlow and Mr. Mansfield, proceedings of March 24 and May 13, 1774, on the Booksellers' Copy-Right Bill, PH, vol. 17, cols. 1086, 1099; speeches of George Johnstone and of Edmund Burke of May 13 and May 16, 1774, cols. 1101–6.

60. Letter of March 17, 1772, from David Wedderburn to Janet Erskine, NAS-SR, GD164/1698. "Your caution about them is quite unnecessary," he wrote in a letter that is an interesting illustration of the passage to India, with uncertain letters of recommendation and into an uncertain future: "Your freind Donaldson the bookseller, hoped I would take them under my immediate care, if their father should be dead when they arived, but, I bless God, the old fool was in good health when they landed, and I hope will continue so."

61. Letter of March 17, 1770, from Samuel Swinton to David Anderson and Robert Keith, British Library, Anderson Papers, vol. 13, Add. Ms. 45429, 37.

62. Letters of March 16, 1765, and November 23, 1765, from William Julius Mickle to Lord Lyttelton, and undated letter of spring 1765, in Ireland, "Anecdotes of Mickle," pp. xxvi, xxx, xxxiii; Sim, "Life of the Author," pp. ix, xv, xxxiv.

63. A. P. Woolrich, "Ruddiman, Thomas (1674–1757)," ODNB, article 24249; George Chalmers, *The Life of Thomas Ruddiman* (London, 1794).

64. Letters of November 22, 1769, December 8, 1769, January 12, 1770, May 9, 1770, and September 30, 1776, from James Steuart to Charles Steuart, NLS, Steuart Mss. 6404/5r, 7r, 11v, 21r, 21v, 67r. A "Mr Johnstone" appears in the brothers' letters in 1770, but there is no indication that he was one of the Johnstones of Westerhall: "Inclosed receive a letter from Mr Johnstone he is in raptures with your last to him & anxious to keep up the correspondence." James Steuart was not particu-

larly well informed about events in London, and he wrote in July 1772, a month after the decision in the Somerset case, that "I did not 'till of late know that you were the person concerned in the Negro cause, shal be sorry if you have been at the whole charge of the decision which I hope is not the case as it appears to be a general concern." Letters of December 3, 1770, and July 23, 1772, NLS, Steuart Mss. 6404/37r, 57r–v.

65. Letter of January 21, 1772, from James Steuart in Edinburgh to Charles Steuart, NLS, Steuart Mss. 5027/106r. James Somerset had by then already escaped.

66. The older James Johnstone qualified as an advocate on June 18, 1720, Barbara (Murray) Johnstone's brother Patrick Elibank qualified on June 22, 1723, and her brother-in-law James Ferguson on February 17, 1722; William Johnstone qualified on July 13, 1751, and his first cousin, the younger James Ferguson, on July 30, 1757. *The Minute Book of the Faculty of Advocates*, vol. 2 (1713–50), ed. John Macpherson Pinkerton (Edinburgh, 1980), pp. 31, 49, 61; vol. 3 (1751–83), ed. Angus Stewart (Edinburgh, 1999), pp. 6, 75. One of the Johnstones' maternal uncles was governor of Quebec, and another was a naval officer in the south Atlantic, whose two-year-old daughter was described in 1763 as precociously patriotic; "she is a fine child & sings Hearts of Oak." Murray, *Five Sons*, p. 149; John Ramsay, *Scotland and Scotsmen in the eighteenth century, from the MSS. of John Ramsay, of Ochtertyre*, ed. Alexander Allardyce (1888, repr. Bristol, 1996), 1:150.

67. Patrick Ferguson, who invented the repeating rifle, united, in Ferguson's epitaph, the "calm judgement" of his father, with "the vivacity and genius of his mother's family." Adam Ferguson, *Biographical Sketch or Memoir, of Lieutenant-Colonel Patrick Ferguson: originally intended for the British Encyclopaedia* (Edinburgh, 1817), pp. 6, 11. Letter of February 19, 1765, from Anne Ferguson to General James Murray, in Murray, *Five Sons*, p. 150; she added that "my George has begun the Education of a merchant & must remain in the practice & study of it here for some years, when I wrote you formerly I truely thought that no part of particular instruction belonged to the Business. I'm now better informed" (p. 153).

68. "I don't find this climate so very hot as I imagined," he added. Letter of June 3, 1764, from David Wedderburn to Alexander Wedderburn, Wedderburn Papers, UMWCL.

69. Mossner, *Life of David Hume*, p. 386. Estimate of costs, enclosed in a letter of June 13, 1775, from Patrick Tonyn to Alexander Wedderburn, NAS-SR, GD164/1713.

70. Entry for January 6, 1826, in W.E.K. Anderson, ed., *The Journal of Sir Walter Scott* (Edinburgh, 1998), p. 66. "My heart always warms to

that Swinton connection. So faithful to old Scottish feelings," Scott wrote on June 6, 1826 (p. 177).

71. "Memoir of the Early Life of Sir Walter Scott, written by himself" (1808), in John Gibson Lockhart, *The Life of Sir Walter Scott*, 5 vols. (Edinburgh, 1902), 1:3, 12, 14; Lockhart, *Sir Walter Scott*, 1:165, 315.

72. "Memoir of the Early Life of Sir Walter Scott," 1:45.

73. Will of George Johnstone, proved June 12, 1787, TNA, PROB 11/1154; will of William Julius Mickle, proved March 14, 1789, TNA, PROB 11/1177.

74. Will of John Johnstone, proved March 6, 1796, TNA, PROB 11/1272.

75. Will of Martha Ford, proved February 21, 1794, TNA, PROB 11/1241; Will of Samuel Swinton, proved June 19, 1797, TNA, PROB 11/1293.

76. *Songs in the Justiciary Opera, Composed Fifty Years ago* (Auchinleck, 1816), pp. 2, 4. The *Justiciary Opera* was composed, for the most part, by James Boswell and the lawyer Andrew Crosbie, during a journey to London in 1778. "The Journal of James Boswell, 1777–1779," in Geoffrey Scott and Frederick A. Pottle, eds., *Private Papers of James Boswell from Malahide Castle*, 18 vols. (Mount Vernon, NY, 1928-34), 13:106.

77. The case of Agnes Walker of Dumfries, for whom the jury in Dumfries recommended compassion in 1762, is discussed in the remarkable "Information for Janet Gray" presented on August 6, 1798, in connection with the case of Janet Gray before the Court of Session in Edinburgh; NAS, JC3/49, unpag. The case of Christian Crawford is reported in *The Acts of Sederunt of the Lords of Council and Session, from the 15th of January 1553, to the 11th of July 1790* (Edinburgh, 1790), pp. 525-26; the sentence was signed by Robert Dundas, who argued for perpetual servitude in the case of Joseph Knight.

78. *Scots Magazine* 33 (September 1771), pp. 449, 498. Bell or Belinda was not a criminal, in that she had not been convicted of the crime for which she was indicted. The report in the circuit court minute book was more circumspect: "the advocate Depute Represented that from the particular Circumstances of this he Consented to the pannells being banished." North Circuit Minute Book, no. 25, NAS, JC11/28.

79. *Caledonian Mercury*, September 14, 1771, no. 7717.

80. *Public Advertiser*, September 19, 1771, no. 11479.

81. *Scots Magazine* 34 (June 1772), p. 299.

82. *Caledonian Mercury*, Febuary 21, 1776.

83. Extract, Process Joseph Knight against Sir John Wedderburn of Ballendean Bart., NAS, CS235/K/2/2, p. 10; memorandum of 15 Novem-

ber 1774 for John Wedderburn Esquire, NAS, CS235/K/2/2, p. 3. "Mr
Donaldson's news paper" was the *Edinburgh Advertiser*; *Edinburgh Advertiser* 18, no. 888 (June 30–July 3, 1772).

84. *Caledonian Mercury*, February 21, 1776.

85. Cairns, *Scottish Law of Slavery*.

86. "Petition for Bell or Belinda a black Girl," September 13, 1771, in JC26/193/3.

87. "Act & Warrant by the Sherif of Fife for opening the Seals on the Charter Room &c at Leslie House," November 1, 1774, NAS, GD86/969. The decision was the culmination of "a competition for the estate of Rothes, between [the] sister of the Earl last deceased . . . [and the] brother of the last Earl's father," and turned on the meaning of the word "or" in an entail of 1694; it was resolved by the High Court of Justiciary in favour of the Countess or the female heir, "this not being a *male fief.*" *Scots Magazine* 36 (March 1774), p. 165.

88. The unpleasant matters involved "Liquors Alledged to have furnished" to a Miss Margaret Scott; letter of June 14, 1792, from William Stewart to Sir James Johnstone about the "affair of Miss Scots" and Submission between Sir James Johnstone and Miss Margaret Scott of July 12, 1793, BUL-W, Westerhall Estate Papers, DM 41/70/8 and DM 41/40/13. Three years later, after James's death, John Tait wrote to William Otto, Louisa's secretary, about "Miss Scot's suit": "it will be necessary that Lady Johnstone, as well as you, give immediate instructions." Letter of June 9, 1795, from John Tait to William Otto, BUL-W, Westerhall Estate Papers, DM 41/70/16.

89. On John Tait's description of the missing writings as having been "received up by me writer to the signet doer for the marquis of Annandale" on May 16, 1766, see *The Sessional Papers of the House of Lords, Annandale Peerage* (London, 1877), 11:575. "How long the bond of entail and resignation remained with Sir James Johnstone cannot be determined. But he must have returned it prior to 16th May 1766 when John Tait, as agent for George, Marquess of Annandale, got up from the clerk to the law-suit the resignation and other writs, as appears from a contemporary copy of Mr Tait's receipt found in the same collection of Annandale papers." Fraser, *Annondale Family Book*, 2:385.

90. Letter of August 30, 1762, from James (the father) to William, HL-P, PU 541 [536].

91. Statement of Mr. John Tait Junior, W.S. of January 4, 1819, NAS, SC70/1/18/561, 563. There were at least two, unrelated John Taits who were writers to the signet, or solicitors, in eighteenth-century Edinburgh. The older John Tait, who as Tait of Harviestoun was John's neighbor in Clackmannanshire, died in 1800. Randall Thomas Davidson, *The Life of*

Archibald Campbell Tait, 2 vols. (London, 1891), 1:2–5. The younger John Tait, who died in 1817, was an aspiring poet before qualifying as a lawyer in 1781. Charles Rogers, *The Modern Scottish Minstrel*, 6 vols. (Edinburgh, 1857), 1:70–72.

92. Letter of October 19, 1759, from Betty to William, HL-P, PU 406 [398].

93. "The Belief, the Sentiment of a Mexican a Mahometan, a Worshiper of the Sun, whom we call Idolaters, Infidells, & Heathen, what could, our Worthy, Good, Relation, Ci Devant Archbishop Wake, have said, more, or Juster," she wrote to her cousin in 1797. Letter of February 1, 1797, from Louisa to Sir Martin Browne Folkes, FHA-NRO, MC50/52/2.

94. "I have ever esteemed It a particular happiness that God bestowed upon me so worthy a Father & enabled me the means & opportunity of expressing my Duty & affection for him. His dying blessing & the marks of his Concern for me & mine will be a Source of grateful pleasure to me while I live," John wrote to William. Letter of December 29, 1772, from John to William, HL-P, PU 658 [652]; letter of October 31, 1767, from James Johnstone (the father) to William, HL-P, PU 556 [569]; letter of December 3, 1795, from Adam Ferguson to John, Merolle, *Correspondence of Adam Ferguson*, 2:375.

95. Inscription in the memorial to John Johnstone, in the mausoleum in Westerkirk churchyard, Bentpath, Dumfries and Galloway; Keene, *Miscellaneous Poems*, p. 22–23, 142–45. The memorial was erected by John and Elizabeth Carolina's daughter: "within the mausoleum which he erected over his parents and brother, this tablet is placed, to express the veneration and filial piety of his daughter, Anne Elizabeth Gordon, 1824."

96. "If you do not come home soon I shall never have the pleasure of seeing you," she wrote to John in India, "but my Dear I can assure you that upon a frequent and narow examination I feel no steps in my life that gives death any additional horror and I bless God I am quit content with the part I have acted nor can I see anything I could have mended & I think Im even rewarded in this life for since this time two year I have had a peaceable & happy life." Letter of December 22, 1764, from Barbara (their mother) to John, UMWCL-MS.

97. *The principal acts of the General Assembly of the Church of Scotland, conveened at Edinburgh the 20th day of May, 1756* (Edinburgh, 1756), p. 13, representation of the Presbytery of Langholm. On the religious history of eighteenth-century Scotland, see Callum G. Brown, *Religion and Society in Scotland since 1707* (Edinburgh, 1997).

98. See above, chapter 1.

99. "My brother who is curate to my Father at Tadmorton in Oxfordshire has some idea of going abroad again as Chaplain to some ship," Elizabeth Carolina's nephew wrote to her son, in 1813, in a letter from the debtors' prison in Northampton. "I did not know your proper address untill I was informed by a person of Dumfrys in Scotland who unfortunately, as I am sorry to say a *Prisoner for Debt* in this place *with myself* I am only here for the trifling [crossed out] Sum of £75." After their father's death, his brother, the Rev. John Wroe Keene, was described as "mentally unhappy on account of his prospects"; he later wrote of his hope to "sell all my fathers books," "I have Humes and Smollets history of England." Letters to James Raymond Johnstone of August 2, 1813, from Talbot William Keene, of October 21, 1824, from Edward Daniell, and of May 17, 1827, from John Wroe Keene, in JA-CLA, Bundle 7, PD239/7/2, Bundle 30, PD239/30/29, and Bundle 52, PD239/52/8.

100. Letter of March 29, 1775, from George Kinnaird to William, HL-P, PU 784 [756]. Edmund Dana and Helen Kinnaird married in 1765, when she was sixteen, and his decision to abandon medicine for the clergy was carefully considered: "my living has been magnified beyond measure, but I have great privileges in it wh. no other person ever had upon acct. of its being upon an Estate of Mr. Pulteney. I really understood before I took ye gown that whatever deficiencys it labord under Mr. Pulteney wd. make good," he wrote to his father in Cambridge, Massachusetts from his first clerical position in Brigstock in Northamptonshire, the same parish where Elizabeth Carolina's brother Talbot William Keene was later rector. The names of Edmund and Helen Dana's children were an extended recognition of their great-aunts, great-uncles, grandmother, uncles, and cousins: Frances Johnstone Dana (who died in infancy), Elizabeth Caroline Dana, another Frances Johnstone Dana, George Kinnaird Dana, William Pulteney Dana, Barbara Dana, Henrietta Laura Dana, Charles Patrick Dana, Maria Dana. Letter of December 22, 1770, from Edmund Dana to Richard Dana, MHS, Dana Family Papers, Ms. N-1088, Dana Family I, Box 2; Box 57, Folder Dana Genealogy—Notes and Letters. Talbot William Keene was at Brigstock when his son, also Talbot William Keene, wrote to James Raymond Johnstone from the debtors' prison in Northampton, and he was still there in 1822, when his daughter Hester wrote to thank James Raymond for "your very affectionate Letter with its acceptable contents." "My Father was order'd by our apothecary, to take Red Wine, his bowels being in a weak state, & his Answer was, he cou'd not *afford* it. . . . He is now drinking your Health." Letters of August 2, 1813, from Talbot William Keene and of December 10, 1822, from Hester Amey Keene, in JA-CLA, Bundle 7, PD239/7/2 and Bundle 25, PD239/25/14.

101. The older Mickle was also the entrepreneur of a brewery in Edinburgh, "having obtained permission to reside in Edinburgh, and to have his parochial duty performed by a substitute." Sim, "Life of the Author," pp. ix–xi.

102. *Inquisition of Damages*, and see above, chapter 3.

103. Davidson, *Archibald Campbell Tait*, 1:2–5.

104. Certification of Richard Hoge, OIOC, IOR/J/1/1/154.

105. Fraser, *Book of the Johnstones*, 2:354–55, 384–85.

106. Unsigned letter of August 15, 1751, to William, HL-P, PU 503 [517].

107. Letter of February 16, 1775, from John Wedderburn to William, HL-P, PU 1759 [1809]. There were writers in the Johnstones' lives in the sense of lawyers (or solicitors) and Indian officials, and also, in this existence without the mechanical reproduction of correspondence, in the sense of copyists and clerks. John, Patrick, and Gideon were all educated in "writing." They were in a position to be writers themselves, like the young Walter Scott, who paid for his books from the circulating library out of "copy-money" ("I remember writing upwards of 120 folio pages with no interval either for food or rest"), or like the father of Laura's friend's father-in-law, the archbishop of York, a half-pay officer who "wrote a very good hand" and supported his son by writing and engrossing for "two eminent solicitors." "Memoir of the Early Life of Sir Walter Scott," in Lockhart, *Sir Walter Scott,* 1:46 Sir Clements Markham, *A Memoir of Archbishop Markham, 1719–1807* (Oxford, 1906), p. 5.

108. Undated letter of 1762 or 1763 from David Wedderburn in Edinburgh to Janet Erskine, NAS-SR, GD164/1693.

109. Certification of Richard Hoge that John studied "under my Tuition for Writing, Arithmetick, & Merchants accompts" from November 1748 to May 1749, Edinburgh, October 3, 1750; OIOC, IOR/J/1/1/154, and for Patrick, IOR/J/1/2/105 and Gideon, IOR/J/1/5/139,140.

110. Letters of June 12, 1789, from William Laidlaw and of June 13, 1789, from James Robertson about James Primrose Johnstone, OIOC, J/1/13/128,129. George wrote to the East India Company that the two older boys had been given the "best education in my power to bestow." Letter of January 6, 1781, from George to the directors of the East India Company about George Lindsay Johnstone, OIOC, J/1/10/175. The excellent education was with Walter Minto, and prior to that in the household of a schoolmaster near Boulogne; letter of M. Lacombe of Montreuil sur Mer to George of July 2, 1776, in which he looks forward to receiving a young relative of a friend of George's, "Monsieur Burgess tresorier De La Compagnie des Indes orientales," and expresses his elaborate good wishes for George's sons: "these two children will always be dear to me,

and I will never forget them. I invoke all the powers which command the sea that they may calm the waves of the Mediterranean, and that the most favourable winds may carry them happily to the port where their desires tend." EUL-L, La.II/73/129.

111. Letter of February 14, [1767,] written in French, from David Wedderburn to Janet Erskine, NAS-SR, GD164/1693.

112. The daughter, Jeanie Ferguson, was by then a "good decent girl of sixteen"; "for a soul & genious, Ill sett her loose with any she that ever stept in Petticoats." Letter of January 29, 1763, from Anne Ferguson to General James Murray, NAS, GD32/24/14.

113. "Betty Kinnaird stays at Bromley in Kent with Mrs Hawksworth," Betty wrote to William after Barbara's separation. Letter of October 9, 1759, from Betty to William, HL-P, PU 405 [397]. Will of George Lindsay Johnstone, proved February 1, 1814, TNA, PROB 11/1552.

114. Notebooks of Miss E. C. Johnstone, Alva, 1816 and 1824, NLS, Acc. 8100/120,121.

115. "You know the shrewdness with which the most unlettered farmer will treat when he has an advantage," Edmund Nelson wrote of the turnip farmer. Letter of March 26, 1777, from Edmund Nelson to James, NRO, NRS 8348 24D5; bundle of bills paid by the Rev. Edmund Nelson, over the period from 1776 to 1792, in NRO, NRS 8386 24E1; will of Sir James Johnstone, proved March 21, 1796, TNA, PROB 11/1272. The Johnstones' Edmund Nelson was the first cousin of the other Rev. Edmund Nelson, who at the same time, and a few miles to the east, was sending his son Horatio to serve in the navy in Jamaica. William White, *History, Gazetteer and Directory, of Norfolk* (Sheffield, 1836), pp. 274, 451; obituary of the Rev. James Edmund Rose Nelson, *Gentleman's Magazine* 11 (August 1839): 208.

116. Letters of March 3, 1771, from James to John and of May 30, 1771, and January 25, 1772, from James to James Balmain, JJLB-EUL, pp. 49–50, 77–78, 132–33.

117. Walter Scott, *Guy Mannering; or, The Astrologer* (1815) (London, 2003), p. 104. Dominie Sampson, who had been successively a "probationer of divinity," a country schoolteacher, and a copier of accounts, had been asked for his "assistance to catalogue and put in order the library of my uncle the bishop, which I have ordered to be sent down by sea. I shall also want him to copy and arrange some papers." The period of most of the novel is "near the end of the American war," in the early 1780s. Adam Ferguson and John Home, George's friend, make fleeting appearances, and the dénouement turns on the return of a former "clerk in a Dutch house" from the East Indies to the west of Scotland (pp. 12, 104, 201, 228, 309).

118. "Of Refinement in the Arts," in Hume, *Essays*, p. 271.

119. Unsigned letter of August 15, 1751, to William, HL-P, PU 503 [517].

120. Letter of June 9, 1746, from Henry Home (Lord Kames) to Sir James Johnstone, in Murray, *Letters of David Hume*, pp. 68–69; and on Hume as "a gentleman born," letter of June 22, 1745, from Philip Vincent to Sir James Johnstone, p. 13. The salary in question was either £75 or £37.10s.

121. Ferguson, *Moral and Political Science*, 2:266. "Of Essay-Writing," in Hume, *Essays*, p. 534.

122. John's son James Raymond was sent to him in Dumfries, and so was Charlotte's daughter: "Caroline is a sweet tempered giddy lively agile creature full of health." "It puts me in mind of a German poem I was struck with many years ago. The writer complains that the Almighty comes against him who is but a worm with Thunder lightning & tempest & the rhyme always made me laugh for Donder Blixom & Storm answer to worm & leave a dreadful idea in the mind from their rough sound," Walter wrote to James Balmain, of the weather in Dumfries in the winter of 1778. Letters of November 19, 1778, from John to James Balmain and of September 4, 1778, and December 18, 1778, from Walter to James Balmain, JA-CLA, Bundle 6, PD239/6/6,22,33.

123. Letter of April 18, 1761, from Walter Johnstone to William, HL-P, PU 719 [707].

124. Letter of May 25, 1774, from William Julius Mickle to George Johnstone, WJM-Y.

125. Louisa's grandmother, when she signed the last codicil to her will with a "mark," insisted on a "memorandum" of explanation, "for that every body knew she writ a good hand but now being weak could not write so well." Charlotte assured William that "my love & gratitude to you equals that of my Sisters tho greatly her inferiore in expressing or in any way acknowledging the favours I owe you." Codicil to the will of Clemence Montgomerie, September 10, 1720, PROB 11/576; postscript by Charlotte in a letter of February 22, 1758, from Betty to William, HL-P, PU 400 [392].

126. "Copy of three Deeds &ct," November 30, 1771, JJLB-EUL, pp. 116–20.

127. Letters of April 7, 1769, from John to Betty, of February 8, 1771, from John to an unnamed associate, and of March 9, 1771, from John to "Mr Waugh Collector of Land Tax," in JJLB-CLA, PD239/201/9.

128. Letter of August 3, 1809, from Betty to Anne Elizabeth Gordon, NAS, GD477/440.

129. Iatros, *Patrick Colquhoun*, p. 5.

130. "I did inform Mr Grant that I was willing to undertake the Business of transporting all the Felons that might occasionally be cast for transportation in Scotland," Patrick Colquhoun wrote to John Davidson in 1770. In 1774 he was still involved in the details of the business, writing to Walter Miller, the town clerk of Perth, that "you will therefore be very speedily freed of those who are at present in Perth Jail Indeed it is always my wish, & I exert every endeavour to render the Public Burthen as easy as possible by sending off every Convict the moment I can after Sentence is pronounced. . . . I presume Frazer cant be forwarded with the rest as you say he is to be whipt upon the 15th proximo." Letter of November 30, 1770, from Patrick Colquhoun to John Davidson, NAS, GD214/726/2; letter of May 20, 1774, from Patrick Colquhoun to Walter Miller, PKA, B59/24/11/166.

131. Letters of April 26, 1786, to George Dempster and April 9, 1787, to Henry Brisbane, GUL-PC, Ms Murray 551, 79v, 145v.

132. Letter of May 29, 1797, from Patrick Colquhoun to William, GUL-PC, Ms Murray 551, 166v, Paley, "Colquhoun."

133. "Mr Colquhoun—Family and Public Services," n.d., London Metropolitan Archives, acc. 1230/7.

134. Iatros, *Patrick Colquhoun,* pp. 4–8; David G. Barrie, "Patrick Colquhoun, the Scottish Enlightenment and Police Reform in Glasgow in the Late Eighteenth Century," *Crime, History & Societies* 12, no. 2 (2008): 59–79, p. 74.

135. Copy, in George's hand, of a letter of November 24, 1759, to General Francis Murray, NAS, GD32/24/11.

136. *Titus Andronicus,* 2.1.126–27. "Memorand for Sandy May 1751," EUL-L, La.II.73/80; letter of February 25, 1752, from William to Sir James Johnstone, EUL-L, La.II.73/65.

137. Letter of March 29, 1749, from Margaret to Barbara Johnstone (her mother), EUL-L, La.II.502/12.

138. Copy of a letter of September 4, 1785, from George Johnstone to Henry Dundas, OIOC, IOR/G/17/5 ff.127–28.

139. The secretary was George and John's friend and David Hume's cousin, the dramatist John Home.

140. Bolts, *Considerations on India Affairs,* 1:211.

141. Copy of letter of December 29, 1761, from John in Calcutta to James Balmain, HL-P, PU 671 [620], and see above, chapter 2.

142. Letter of December 31, 1771, from David Wedderburn to Janet Erskine, NAS-SR, GD164/1698.

143. On the parliamentary politics of the later eighteenth century, see Namier, *Structure of Politics.*

144. *Narrative of the Proceedings*, p. xlvi, and see above, chapter 2; on George's dinner with Alexander Wedderburn and Alexander Carlyle, see Carlyle, *Autobiography of Carlyle*, pp. 482–84.

145. George was the unsuccessful candidate in Carlisle, on March 23, 1768, in the interest of his patron and friend Sir James Lowther; he was chosen in May to replace the successful candidate in Cockermouth (who had himself, also in the Lowther interest, been elected to two different constituencies). The Stewarts were to be sent, subject to Betty's instructions, to "attend the Cockermouth Ellections." Letter of March 28, 1768, from Mr. Douglas in Annan to Betty, EUL-L, La.II.73/102; Namier and Brooke, *History of Parliament*, 1:242–48, 403–6.

146. Speech of George Johnstone of May 8, 1770, debate in the House of Commons on an Address to the King on the Disturbances in America, PH, vol. 16, col. 995.

147. Speeches of George Johnstone of October 26, 1775, on the Address of Thanks and of November 20, 1775, on the American Prohibitory Bill, PH, vol. 18, cols. 745, 748, 1000; and see also debates of February 6, 1775, on an Address to the King on the Disturbances in North America, of February 10, 1775, on the Bill for Restraining the Trade and Commerce of the New England Colonies, of October 31 and November 3, 1775, on employing Foreign Troops without the Consent of Parliament, and of December 8, 11, and 21, 1775, on the American Prohibitory Bill, PH, vol. 18, cols. 253–62, 301, 817, 819–30, 1058, 1061–62, 1106.

148. The passions that "are the great incitement to human actions" consisted, in George's account, of ambition, avarice, and "the power of devising or executing any plan or project, which the mind in the heat of emotion or sentiment may propose to itself, according to the various succession of ideas which resolve, and this passion I shall call *whim*"; "the effects of the last mentioned passions, have been fully and masterly considered, by some late writers on government; but no author that I know of, has ever attended to the effects of *whim*." [George Johnstone], *Thoughts on our Acquisitions in the East Indies; particularly respecting Bengal* (London, 1771), pp. 3–4, 8.

149. Daniel T. Rodgers, *Contested Truths: Keywords in American Politics since Independence* (Cambridge, MA, 1998), pp. 4–7.

150. Speech of George Johnstone of October 26, 1775, debate in the House of Commons on the Address of Thanks, PH, vol. 18, col. 749; George Johnstone, *Thoughts on our Acquisitions*, p. 2.

151. Extracts from the Minutes of His Majesty's Council for the Province of West Florida, May 18, 1765, TNA, CO5/583/175r–176v.

152. *Narrative of the Proceedings*, p. ii.

153. Namier, *Structure of Politics*, p. 18. The earlier description was from the older Pitt's grandfather, writing to his son from Madras in 1706, and the later description was from Edward Gibbon, writing to his father, and in his father's assumed voice, in 1760.

154. "Of the Original Contract," in Hume, *Essays*, p. 465.

155. Gholam-Hossein, *Seir Mutaqharin*, 2:582, and see above, chapter 1.

156. John Johnstone, *Letter to the Proprietors*, pp. 28–29.

157. "I pass all the Forenoon in the Secretary's House from ten till three, where there arrives from time to time Messengers, that bring me all the Secrets of this Kingdom, and indeed of Europe, Asia, Africa and America," Hume wrote to Hugh Blair. Letter of April 1, 1767, in Greig, *Letters of David Hume*, 2:133. On Hume's earlier letters from the British embassy in Paris, see Klibansky and Mossner, *New Letters of David Hume*, pp. 89–130.

158. Letter of January 21, 1762, from Henry Vansittart, Peter Amyatt, Culling Smith, Warren Hastings, and John Johnstone to the Court of Directors, in *Fort William–India House Correspondence*, 3:400.

159. Speech of Governor Johnstone, May 27, 1765, Report of the Congress held in Pensacola, TNA, CO5/582/195r.

160. Letter of April 1, 1778, from John to James Balmain, JA-CLA, Bundle 6, PD239/6/7; speech of Colonel Barré of March 23, 1778, debate in the House of Commons on Colonel Barré's Motion for a Committee to enquire into the Public Expenditure, PH, vol. 19, col. 973. The disgraceful war was the war against the American Revolution.

161. Letter of October 29, 1767, from Horace Walpole to Sir Horace Mann, in Walpole, *Correspondence*, 22:561. William's lawyer, who described him as "the best client I ever had," recalled an exchange in the House of Commons in which Pitt charged William with niggardliness, and William responded with "a very spirited speech, some sentences of which I shall never forget and they were these, 'If I am fond of money . . . it is my own money I am fond of, and not that which the unbounded cupidity and extravagance of the Right Honourable Gentleman wrings from the hard hands of every Peasant of this devoted country.' " "Memoir by Alexander Young regarding Sir William Pulteney," NAS, GD214/163, pp. 4, 9.

162. Speech of George Johnstone of March 30, 1772, debate in the House of Commons on the East India Judicature Bill, PH, vol. 17, col. 376.

163. Speech of George Johnstone of February 6, 1775, debate in the House of Commons on an Address to the King on the Disturbances in North America, PH, vol. 18, cols. 258, 262.

164. Speech of William Pulteney of May 18, 1772, debate in the House of Commons on the East India Judicature Bill, PH, vol. 17, cols. 471–73; letter of February 5, 1772, from John to William, HL-P, PU 655 [648]; Bolts, *Considerations on India Affairs*, 1:85.

165. Letter from George Johnstone, *Public Advertiser*, January 25, 1773, no. 11805; Pulteney, *Considerations*.

166. Letter of March 2, 1768, from [Pierre Joseph André] Roubaud to William, HL-P, PU 1666 [1620]; undated letter from J. Dalrymple to George, EUL-L, La.II.73/165; "I wish you would form an equitable constitutional scheme between the company & Government & put George Johnstone on the title page."

167. *Narrative of the Proceedings*, pp. i, vii, xix, xliii–xlv, 1.

168. *Narrative of the Proceedings*, pp. ii, iv.

169. *Audi Alteram Partem*, pp. 78, 114; *Narrative of the Proceedings*, p. 40.

170. *Narrative of the Proceedings*, pp. 40–42. "The fact is, their thumbs were tied together behind their backs, to which the Rope was attached, and they were hoisted up and lowered down four several times in this agony; this *slight* method of torture (according to Mr. Melvill's expression) is reckoned among the cruellest used in the inquisition" (p. 40). See also *Audi Alteram Partem*, pp. 85–86.

171. *Audi Alteram Partem*, p. 3.

172. Letter of March or April 1734 from David Hume to Dr. George Cheyne, in Greig, *Letters of David Hume*, 1:18; "My Own Life," in Hume, *Essays*, p. xxxiii; report of Josiah Tucker to the antiquarian and lawyer David Dalrymple, Royal Commission on Historical Manuscripts, *Fourth Report of the Royal Commission on Historical Manuscripts, Part 1* (London, 1874), p. 532.

173. See Rothschild, "Atlantic Worlds."

174. *Specimen of the Scots Review*, pp. 8, 9, 27. David Hume commented on the pamphlet, which was in part an attack on "about twenty" of his own critics, in a letter to his cousin and George's friend John Home. Letter of June 4, 1774, from David Hume to John Home, in Greig, *Letters of David Hume*, 2:291.

175. "This he illustrated by a humourous instance from the Jesuits, Jansenists, and Molinists, which sat the House in a laugh." Speech of Alexander Wedderburn of May 10, 1773, debate in the House of Commons on General Burgoyne's Motions relating to the Conduct of Lord Clive in India, PH, vol. 17, col. 865; "Of Superstition and Enthusiasm," in Hume, *Essays*, p. 79 and "Of Refinement in the Arts," Hume, *Essays*, p. 273.

176. Hume discusses the political influence of whim in "Of the Rise and Progress of the Arts and Sciences," in Hume, *Essays*, p. 112; George

Johnstone, *Thoughts on our Acquisitions*, pp. iv, 1, 5, 10, 11, 15, 17, 27, 28.

177. Maconochie, "Memorial for Joseph Knight," p. 34, NAS, CS235/K/2/2, Maconochie, Information for Joseph Knight, p. 37; *Narrative of the Proceedings*, p. ii.

178. The principle of "sub-dividing the empire into many parts" was the only one on which the American colonies could be governed "at so great a distance from the seat of empire," George said. "The distance of America from the seat of government," Smith wrote, was unlikely to endure, and "the seat of the empire" would move, eventually, to the new world. Speeches of George Johnstone of May 18, 1774, on the budget and of October 26, 1775, on the Address of Thanks, PH, vol. 17, col. 1346, vol. 18, cols. 740, 741, 749–50; Smith, *Wealth of Nations*, pp. 625, 946–47.

179. Bolts, *Considerations on India Affairs*, 1:vii–viii; Smith, *Wealth of Nations*, p. 819.

180. [Charles Johnstone], *Chrysal: Or, the Adventures of a Guinea*, 4th ed. (London, 1764), 1:xi–xii, xxiii. Sir Walter Scott, who described Charles Johnstone as a "prose Juvenal," wrote that he "was an Irishman by birth, though it is said a Scotsman by descent, and of the Annandale family." "Charles Johnstone," in *The Miscellaneous Prose Works of Sir Walter Scott, Bart.*, 6 vols. (Boston, 1829), 3:316, 319.

181. Speech of Lord Camden of February 22, 1774, proceedings in the House of Lords on the question of literary property, PH, vol. 17, col. 997.

182. On the disposition of enlightenment, see Rothschild, *Economic Sentiments*, chapter 1.

183. "Lime," n.d., "Cyclises," n.d., "The Indian Method of making Stucco," n.d., "Carrots," May 13, 1766, JJLB-EUL, unpag.

184. "Dare to be wise! Begin! The present hour / Is all that man can boast within his pow'r." Keene, *Miscellaneous Poems*, p. 97.

185. Adam Smith, *Lectures on Jurisprudence*, ed. R. L. Meek, D. D. Raphael, and P. G. Stein (Oxford, 1978), p. 540.

186. "Your obliging Letter & Lucky Tickett arrived safe (Lucky it must be) for I have the Sattisfaction from it (even preferable to Money) to be Convinced I have a Share in the Friendship of a Man of your real Merit. . . . I have Relations of my own Undoubtedly would have done this for me, But them I would not be obliged to as few very few have your generous way of Thinking & Believe me no Situation ever so Inconvenient But I would rather go through than recieve a Benefit & an Upbraiding together." Letter from Louisa to John Irving of November 20, 1771, JJLB-EUL, pp. 105–6.

187. Elizabeth Mure, "Some Remarks," p. 270.

188. Kant, "What is Enlightenment?" in Reiss, *Kant's Political Writings*, p. 54.

189. Letters of October 5, 1773, and October 30, 1773, from Betty to William, HL-P, PU 434 [421], 435 [422], and see above, chapter 3.

190. Letter of March 29, 1775, from George Kinnaird to William, HL-P, PU 784 [756]. The portrait is in Nicholas Phillipson's description "remarkable for being a family conversation piece dominated by a characterful young woman to whose conversation her elders are listening politely. Even more striking, her uncle and aunt both possess the new, feminine quality of complaisance that the moralists believed to be so necessary for the improvement of manners." Nicholas Phillipson, "Manners, Morals and Characters: Henry Raeburn and the Scottish Enlightenment," in Duncan Thomson, *Raeburn: The Art of Sir Henry Raeburn 1756–1823* (Edinburgh, 1997), 29–28, p. 37.

191. Letter of August 3, 1809, from Betty to Anne Elizabeth Gordon, NAS, GD477/440; letter of January 29, 1763, from Anne Ferguson to General James Murray, NAS, GD32/24/14.

192. Letter of October 31, 1791, from William to Henrietta Laura, HL-P, PU 1876 [1578]. "I see, in your case that this want of consciousness [of Henrietta Laura's own merits] may be pushed too far & that your great diffidence of yourself not only prevents you from observing your own merit, but leads you to magnify every little want of attention to small & inferior matters, as if they were capital faults & imperfections. This is pushing an admirable quality too far."

193. Hartog, *Man and Wife in America*, p. 115.

194. Will of Sir James Johnstone, proved March 21, 1796, TNA, PROB 11/1272; will of Henrietta Laura Pulteney, proved August 22, 1808, TNA, PROB 11/1483; will of Martha Ford, proved February 21, 1794, PROB 11/1241; will of George Lindsay Johnstone, proved February 1, 1814, TNA, PROB 11/1552; will of Martha Ford, proved January 1, 1831, TNA, PROB 11/1780.

195. Diary entry of January 19, 1768, in Frederick A. Pottle, *James Boswell: The Earliest Years, 1740–1769* (New York, 1996), pp. 349–50. On Boswell's "infection," see William B. Ober, "Boswell's Gonorrhea," *Bulletin of the New York Academy of Medicine* 45, no. 6 (June 1969): 587–636.

196. Letters of April 17, 1771, from James to John and of February 17, 1772, from James to Betty, JJLB-EUL, pp. 64, 138.

197. Letter of May 9, 1778, from John Wedderburn to William, HL-P, PU 1762 [1811].

198. Speech of George Johnstone of March 30, 1772, on the East India Judicature Bill, PH, vol. 17, col. 377.

199. "Answers of the Members of Assembly, to the accusations of the Council," *Narrative of the Proceedings*, p. 89.

200. Bolts, *Considerations on India Affairs*, 1:ix.

201. *Star*, June 25, 1789, no. 354. The occasion was the decision on relief to Episcopalians in Scotland and the prospects for the "Roman Catholic Petition."

202. "The rebellion in Ireland did not arise out of Jacobinical principles, but partly from religious views, and partly from oppression. There never was a period since the beginning of the French Revolution when there was less reason to adopt a measure like the present than now," George Lindsay Johnstone said; and was accused, with his allies, of being "as ignorant of the internal policy of Ireland as they were of that of Kamschatska or Mesopotamia." Speeches of William Pulteney of June 5, 1801, and of George Lindsay Johnstone and Mr. Ogle of June 11, 1801, debates in the House of Commons on the Habeas Corpus Suspension Indemnity Bill, in PH, vol. 35, cols. 1526–27, 1530. Speeches of George Johnstone of February 7, 1775, on an Address to the King upon the Disturbances in North America and of John Johnstone of February 7, 1777, debate in the House of Commons on the Bill for suspending the Habeas Corpus Act, PH, vol. 18, col. 257, vol. 19, cols. 5–6. On habeas corpus, see Paul D. Halliday, *Habeas Corpus: From England to Empire* (Cambridge, MA, 2010).

203. Letter of October 5, 1775, from Thomas Dundas M.P. to Sir Lawrence Dundas, North Yorkshire County Record Office, Zetland Papers, ZNK X 1/2/222, and see above, chapter 2.

204. "Account of the late Famine in India," *Gentleman's Magazine* 41 (September 1771): 402; "Cruelties practised by the English in Bengal," *Gentleman's Magazine* 42 (February 1772): 69.

205. Letter of June 12, 1765, from George and John Stuart to Lord Halifax, TNA, CO5/582/186v, and see above, chapter 2.

206. The calculations were made in a memorandum of justification for the ordinance, passed by the new governor-general of Grenada, the Comte de Durat, on July 7, 1779, which discharged the inhabitants of Grenada from paying any of their obligations to creditors in London or elsewhere in the British empire. The calculation, described as a "proof," was that there had been 16,000 negroes in the island at the time of the British conquest in 1762, and that the British "commerce" (the slave trade) had imported an additional 155,000, for a total supply of 171,000 individuals. At the time of the reconquest, there were 36,000 negroes on the island. A maximum of 40,000 negroes had been "exported" to the French colonies, and the expected loss was "evaluated at 5 percent per year," or a total of 8,500. It was on this basis that the "excess loss"—"perte excessive

de negres"—was evaluated at 86,500. The anonymous author of the memorandum attributed the mortality of the slaves to the "odious calculations" and "speculations of interest" of the British slave trade with respect to conditions on the passage from Africa, in particular the slaves' having to drink sea water, which extinguished the "germ of life" to such an extent that many thousands died within one to three years of arriving in the island. "Réflexions sommaires au soutien de l'ordonnance rendüe par M. le Comte de Durat le 7 Juillet 1779," undated and unpag., in AN-Col., Correspondance à l'arrivée, C/10a/carton 3-1.

207. "By an official return, made in the year ending the 31st of January 1812, on a black population of 23,602 the deaths were 819, and the births only 339; and in domestic and other labour the deaths were 206 and the births 139, making a decrease upon the whole of 553 after deducting the births." Over the four-year period since 1809, deaths had exceeded births by 2,519: "according to this scale of mortality, the population would be annihilated in less than 40 years." Colquhoun, *Wealth, power and resources*, p. 375.

208. Emphasis added. *Caledonian Mercury*, Febuary 21, 1776.

209. "Petition for Bell or Belinda a Black Girl," September 13, 1771, NAS, JC26/193/3.

210. Maconochie, "Memorial for Joseph Knight," p. 13, NAS, CS235/K/2/2.

211. This is the phrase used by Condorcet in a polemic of 1791 in opposition to slavery; "Sur l'instruction publique," in A. Condorcet O'Connor and M. F. Arago, eds., *Oeuvres de Condorcet*, 12 vols. (Paris, 1847–49), 7:198.

212. Speeches of George Johnstone of October 26, 1775, debate in the House of Commons on the Address of Thanks, PH, vol. 18, col. 747, and of February 25, 1777, debate in the House of Commons on Captain Blair's Petition, *Parliamentary Register*, 6:283.

213. *Narrative of the Proceedings*, p. 48; letter of October 1, 1765, from John to Lord Clive, Fourth Report from the Committee, *House of Commons Sessional Papers*, p. 541.

CHAPTER SEVEN. HISTORIES OF SENTIMENTS

1. "Petition for Bell or Belinda a Black Girl," September 13, 1771, JC26/193/3; *Caledonian Mercury*, September 14, 1771, no. 7717.

2. Letter of November 22, 1771, from James to John, JJLB-EUL, p. 108; letter of December 6, 1778, from John to James Balmain, JA-CLA, Bundle 6, PD239/6/32.

3. George Cheyne, *The Natural Method of Curing the Diseases of the Body, and the Disorders of the Mind Depending on the Body,* 3rd ed. (London, 1753), which was listed in the inventory of the library at Westerhall, prepared after James's and Louisa's deaths, as "Cheyne . . . The Cure of Diseases of Body & Mind." "Inventory of the possessions of the late Sir James Johnstone," NAS, CC8/8/130/1733.

4. Cheyne, *Natural Method,* p. 154.

5. "The whole man is distinguished into *Body, Soul* and *Spirit.*" George Cheyne, *Philosophical Principles of Religion Natural and Revealed,* 5th ed. (London, 1736), p. 104.

6. Keene, *Miscellaneous Poems,* pp. 142–43.

7. Letter of December 10, 1822, from Hester Amey Keene to James Raymond Johnstone, in JA-CLA, Bundle 25, PD239/25/14, and see above, chapter 6.

8. Speech of George Lindsay Johnstone of November 25, 1801, debate in the House of Commons on Sir W. Pulteney's Motion for a Committee on the Trade between India and Europe, PH, vol. 36, col. 297; speech of George Johnstone of November 20, 1775, debate in the House of Commons on the American Prohibitory Bill, PH, vol. 18, col. 1000.

9. Letter of September 15, 1755, from Patrick to William, HL-P, PU 713 [701].

10. "Commencement Oration" of September 24, 1788, in Eisenhart, "Walter Minto," pp. 290–91. In a letter of May 24, 1788, to the Earl of Buchan about Minto's appointment as professor of mathematics, the philosopher John Witherspoon concluded, in the same spirit, that "there are many Classes of Ideas sentiments habits and practices which arise from the Newness of the Country which europeans either cannot understand or will not believe." Eisenhart, "Walter Minto," p. 290.

11. William Pulteney, *The Effects to be Expected from the East India Bill upon the Constitution of Great Britain, If passed into a Law* (London, 1783), p. 22.

12. "[If] you could convince the negroes in our islands, that their state was much more shocking than ever they had before considered it, the only consequence would be, that they would be more ripe for insurrection." Speech of Sir William Pulteney of February 28, 1805, debate in the House of Commons on the second reading of the Bill for the Abolition of the Slave Trade, *Parliamentary Debates,* vol. 3, col. 660.

13. Hume, *Enquiries,* p. 228.

14. "Einleitung zu den Vorlesungen über die Römische Geschichte October 1810," in *Kleine historische und philologische Schriften von Barthold Georg Niebuhr* (Bonn, 1828), pp. 92–93; Barthold Georg Nie-

buhr, *Römische Geschichte*, 3 vols., 3rd ed. (Berlin, 1828), 1:6; letter from Goethe of November 23, 1812, in Susanna Winkworth, ed. and trans., *The Life and Letters of Niebuhr*, 3 vols. (New York, 1852), 1:358.

15. Bernard Bailyn, *History and the Creative Imagination* (St. Louis, MO, 1985), pp. 10, 13; Bernard Bailyn, "The Challenge of Modern Historiography," *American Historical Review* 87, no. 1 (February 1982): 1–24, p. 22. The Atlantic slave trade database is in Bailyn's description an "extraordinarily perceptive eye" like the space telescope, which "has led to a degree of precision and a breadth of vision never dreamed of before and has revealed, and continues to reveal, not only new information but also new questions never broached before." Bernard Bailyn, "Considering the Slave Trade," p. 245.

16. This is Anthony Grafton's translation of Leopold von Ranke's celebrated description, inspired by Niebuhr, of the object of historical inquiry: "'wie es eigentlich gewesen,' 'how it really was.'" Anthony Grafton, *The Footnote: A Curious History* (Cambridge, MA, 1999), pp. 44, 69.

17. R. G. Collingwood, *The Idea of History* (Oxford, 1961), p. 215.

18. As Ranajit Guha asked, "Can we afford to leave anxiety out of the story of the empire?" Guha, "Not at Home in Empire," p. 487.

19. "Of Refinement in the Arts," "Of Interest," in Hume, *Essays*, pp. 271, 274, 304; and see Rothschild, "Atlantic Worlds."

20. *Esquisse d'un tableau historique des progrès de l'esprit humain*, in O'Connor and Arago, *Oeuvres de Condorcet*, 6:232–34.

21. Ibid.

22. John Johnstone, *Letter to the Proprietors*, pp. 28–29. Administrative history was described by G. R. Elton as the history of the machinery of authority, and also a history of ideas and of "personality." G. R. Elton, "The Problems and Significance of Administrative History in the Tudor Period," *Journal of British Studies* 4, no. 2 (May 1965): 18–28, pp. 18–19.

23. Hartog, *Man and Wife in America*, pp. 2, 5.

24. G. W. Leibniz, *The monadology and other philosophical writings*, trans. Robert Latta (Oxford, 1898), p. 248.

25. Letter of April 25, 1762, from Betty to William, HL-P, PU 425 [414].

26. Letter of October 2, 1759, from George to William, HL-P, PU 467 [450].

27. Letters of August 26, 1778, from Martha Ford to George [Johnstone] and John [Johnstone], signed "Your most affectionate Mother," and of September 12, 1778, from [Martha Ford] to Walter Minto, signed "MF," UMWCL-MS.

28. "Carrots," May 13, 1766, in JJLB-EUL, unpag.

29. The letters are not immediate in any metaphysical sense. Some of the most interesting of the Johnstones' letters have survived in the form of letter books, or copies of letters; others are mediated in the sense that they are the letters of James about woe and anxiety, for example, in the hand of Louisa, or their father's letters about the revenue administration of Burdwan, in Betty's hand. They are immediate, rather, because of their ordinariness. They convey an unusual sense of how these brothers and sisters lived: of the boys having to share a room if Adam Smith came to stay, or of Betty's kitchen (in Adam Ferguson's real estate letter), or of James and Louisa moving into one room to save the rent, or of John, in Balgonie in December 1770, explaining to Alexander that he had finally found the missing roll of maps (presumably of the Westerhall plantation in Grenada), which he had carefully wrapped up with his own hands and which Elizabeth Carolina had as carefully tidied away.

30. Letter of May 7, 1759, from Charles Kinnaird to William, HL-P, PU 774 [750]; letter of early 1759 from Barbara (the mother) to George, EUL-L, La.II.73/71.

31. Letter of October 1, 1765, from John to Lord Clive, Fourth Report from the Committee, *House of Commons Sessional Papers*, pp. 537, 541.

32. "You know that in Law I am the son of nobody, and if I die intestate the King is my Heir, it is therefore the more necessary to have a Will, indeed ever since I have been possessed of any Property I could call my own I have kept one by me." Letter of September 10, 1785, from William Young in Patna to General James Murray, in Murray, *Five Sons*, p. 200.

33. On Louisa's family history, see above, chapter 1, notes 92 and 93.

34. "I beg my Respects to Mrs. Mickle—& Mrs. Ford if she & my Dear Miss Sophia be still with you. I shall be glad to know how they do & when they return to Town." Letter of August 8, 1787, from John to William Julius Mickle, WJM-Y.

35. Letter of December 29, 1772, from John to William, HL-P, PU 658 [652].

36. Note of April 27, 1815, from James Raymond Johnstone to Anne Elizabeth Gordon, NAS, GD477/440.

37. Letter of July 8, 1819, from James Raymond Johnstone to Anne Elizabeth Gordon, NAS, GD477/440. "Aunt Gordon was specially friend to us," her niece Elizabeth Caroline Gray wrote in her own autobiographical memoir: "she dressed very oddly & had very odd impulsive manners & laughed immensely & loudly. . . . She was one of the kindest the wittiest & the happiest women that ever breathed." Gray, "Sketch of My Life," unpag.

38. Old Parish Register for Westerkirk, at www.scotlandspeople.gov.uk.

39. Lord Blackburn on the Annandale Peerage Case, reported in the *Glasgow Herald*, June 1, 1881, no. 130, and July 19, 1881, no. 171.

40. "Declaration of Bell or Belinda a black Girl," July 4, 1771, "Indictment agt Bell or Belinda a Negroe Girl," NAS, JC26/193/3.

41. "Adieu my dear John . . . And may mens sibi conscia Recti digna ferant Praemia." Letters of September 1, 1771, to Betty and of October 30, 1771, to John, JJLB-EUL, pp. 84, 96; Virgil, *Aeneid*, book 1: 604–5.

42. Extract, Process Joseph Knight against Sir John Wedderburn of Ballendean Bart., 1774, NAS, CS235/K/2/2, pp. 8–10; "Memorial for Joseph Knight late servant to Sir John Wedderburn of Ballendean Bart. In the proces of Advocation at Sir John's instance ag. him, 1775," NAS, CS235/K/2/2, p. 1.

43. List of voyages, voyage identification numbers 17465 and 17601, the Trans-Atlantic Slave Trade Database, wilson.library.emory.edu:9090/tast/database/search.faces.

44. The history of the Johnstones is the opposite sort of history, in several respects, from the history of an unknown man, Louis-François Pinagot, which is the subject of Alain Corbin's extremely interesting study, *Le monde retrouvé de Louis-François Pinagot: Sur les traces d'un inconnu (1798–1876)* (Paris, 1998). A large number of things happened to the Johnstones, who were continually on the move, elaborately literate, and who made a great noise in the world; Louis-François Pinagot was a poor shoemaker who lived and died in the periphery of the Bellême forest in Normandy and of whom the only "manuscript trace, and even the only individual trace," was a single cross, in the register of a petition about a road, inscribed at the very end of his life (p. 287). But even in the Johnstones' lives, and especially in the lives of their servants and slaves, there are vast spaces of silence. There is no manuscript trace of Bell or Belinda, except the manuscript written by the two notaries public in Perth on September 13, 1771, with the pen which she touched, or which they wrote that she touched.

45. David Hume, *A Treatise of Human Nature* (Oxford, 1978), p. 140; Henry Mackenzie, *The Man of Feeling* (1771) (Oxford, 2001), p. 4.

46. This is the annotation on a bundle of family letters in the Johnstone of Alva Papers in the Clackmannanshire Archives, JA-CLA, Bundle 9, PD239/9. Almost everything that historians will ever be able to find out about the Johnstones is there to be found out because somebody, at some point in the long eighteenth century, made the choice that a particular letter, or newspaper, or linen cloth, or mortgage, or receipt, was not to be thrown away; and because other individuals, granddaughters, or officers of the court, or lawyers' clerks, collected the records and transported them to somewhere else. Everything that all these eigh-

teenth-century and nineteenth-century individuals chose to preserve was preserved, in turn, by other individuals over subsequent generations between their times and ours. The warrant for Margaret's commitment could not be found in 1751, and the record of the court martial of the soldier who was on duty when she escaped from Edinburgh Castle, which was sent to London in 1746, is no longer there, or no longer in the state papers for Scotland. But the record of Bell or Belinda's statement of July 4, 1771, was carried from Cupar to Perth, as part of the Porteous Roll for the county of Fife, and her petition of September 13, 1771, the petition that was signed by James Ross and Thomas Mitchell, when she touched the pen, was carried from Perth to Edinburgh; the receipt of her arrival in America, on March 31, 1772, was sent to Edinburgh from Williamsburg, Virginia. The private records of the Johnstones' lives, too, are the outcome of choices and conflicts, over all the intervening generations. There are the legal opinions and mortgages and bills for "fee and trouble" that were conserved in connection with the conflicts over James's and Louisa's and Henrietta Laura's estates. There is a bundle of documents about William's anxiety with respect to the rental value of the slaves on the Westerhall plantation in the legal papers of Louisa's great-aunt's grandson, who was her heir, in the Norfolk Record Office; and in a different collection in Norfolk, a bundle of Louisa's own legal papers, the transgressive bundle that contained the agreement of her separation from her first husband, the notification of his death, her lawyer Mr. Lacon's bill, and Mr. Lacon's love letter, "Fairest of ye Universe." FHA-NRO, MC50/52/30; NRO, NRS 8349 24D5, and see above, chapter 1. In Bristol, there are more legal papers, conserved by the solicitors on William's side of the dispute over the inheritance of the Westerhall plantation in the 1790s: the mortgage with the names of the slaves called "Johnston" and "Fashonable," a list of the servants living with James at the time of his death, and a note of whose laundry he paid for; and William's letter to Louisa's great-aunt's grandson's solicitor about the exchange of "another seasoned negro for Pierre." "Abstract of the Title of Alexander Johnstone," May 6, 1772; "List of Servants living with Sir James Johnstone at the time of his death in London"; letter of August 8, 1797, from William to Forster & Cooke, Lincoln's Inn, in BUL-W, Westerhall Estate Papers, DM 41/31, DM 41/67/1, DM 41/62/14.

47. Ginzburg and Poni, "Il nome e il come," pp. 185–89. It is possible to look for a name, "Martha Ford," for example, in a database that is the union of the catalogue of the National Archives in London and the "A2A" or "Access to Archives" catalogue of four hundred other English archives; or in a Web site of the Church of Latter Day Saints, www

.familysearch.org, which has been consulted more than fifteen billion times; or in the transcripts of all the criminal cases at the Old Bailey in London between 1674 and 1834, which are available at www.old baileyonline.org (and in which the "little tawney boy" who lived with Samuel Swinton ran into the street in 1771); or in the online collection of digitized images of all wills proved in the Prerogative Court of Canterbury between 1384 and 1858, or in a database of digitized and searchable images of every book published in England, or with an English imprint, between 1700 and 1800, the Gale Cengage Eighteenth Century Collections Online (ECCO) database. The name is itself elusive enough, in the images of eighteenth-century texts, searchable on the basis of optical character recognition, and inscribed in the Johnstones' world of multiple empires and multiple transliterations. John appears as "Mr Djonson (Johnstone)" in Ghulam Husain's and Haji Mustafa's *Seir Mutaqharin*, and as "Djanson"; he can also be discovered, in the ECCO database, by a search for "Djanfon" and "Djonfon." Gholam-Hossein, *Seir Mutaqharin*, 2:377, 380, 381. Katy Giannini and Greg Hatch, "Family History Library of the Church of Jesus Christ of Latter-day Saints," *Serials Review* 32, no. 2 (June, 2006), 137–42.

48. See Revel, "L'institution et le social."

49. Richard Avedon, "Borrowed Dogs," in *Richard Avedon Portraits* (New York, 2002), unpag.

50. On the "multi-resolution experience" of "super-smooth zooming over billions of pixels," a "seamless web of images and information, allowing you to browse a virtual universe of interconnected scenes that constantly evolves and changes over time," see http://churmura.com/general/photosynth-technology/18846/ and http://www.ted.com/talks/blaise_aguera_y_arcas_demos_photosynth.html. I am most grateful to Professor Anthony Grafton for conversations about Seadragon and Blaise Aguera y Arcas.

51. See Jacques Revel, "Présentation," in Georges Lefebvre, *La grande peur de 1789* (Paris, 1988), 7–23.

52. This is the annotation on a bundle of James's letters in the Norfolk Record Office, NRO, NRS 8194 24C2.

53. In the great compendium of eighteenth-century British political life, Namier and Brooke's *History of Parliament*, there were four brief biographies: of James, William, George, and John (with even briefer and, in the end, unenlightening references to Louisa and to Elizabeth Carolina). In the Edinburgh University Library's Manuscripts Room, I then asked, in 2002, to see a document that turned out to be James's letter book, and was to a great extent about women: letters to sister Betty, letters in Louisa's hand, Louisa's own letter about the lottery and

having expectation at least. The history of the Johnstones has been a story, or so I hope, that has both women and men in it; a story of colonial administration and parliamentary oratory, that is also a story of damask and alimony, and a story, above all, of an eighteenth-century family. James's letters were a window into this world of family relationships. It seemed possible, all at once, to follow the thread of the name beyond the four brothers who were in public or parliamentary life, to all the Johnstone brothers and sisters, and to at least some of the other individuals with whom they lived. It was the Johnstone sisters, in the end, who were at the heart of many of the family's crises: Margaret's imprisonment for treason in 1746, Barbara's separation, Betty and their mother's estrangement over the Indian textiles. It was Elizabeth Carolina and Martha Ford who were the most adventurous of all the extended family, in the sense that they set out for the empire as unconnected individuals, and not as officers in the army or navy or officials in the service of the East India Company. But the brothers' and sisters' own letters, including James's letters, the extraordinary collection of William's letters in the Huntington Library in California, and the letters in so many other public and private archives, were only one among multiple sources of information about the family, and in particular about the sisters and sisters-in-law, with their unsettled identities and their unsettled names. The list I gave earlier, of the dates of birth or christening of the Johnstones' parents' fourteen children, was compiled from the Old Parish Register of the Church of Scotland, which is available on the Web site described as the "official government source of genealogical data for Scotland," www.scotlandspeople.gov.uk. The family reconstitution of their marriages and friendships was far more circuitous: a journey through wills, bundles of lawyers' papers, family history Web sites, death certificates, and disputes over inheritance, over two or three or four generations. Arnaldo Momigliano wrote of Ronald Syme's evolution into "a moralist historian," that prosopography reaches individuals without explaining them: that the "spiritual interests of people are considered much less than their marriages." The history of the Johnstones has been a story of family relationships, in Syme's sense of "the bare facts of origin, blood and propinquity," and of individual choices, which were also moral choices. Ronald Syme, *Tacitus*, 2 vols. (Oxford, 1958), 2:561, Momigliano, "Ronald Syme," pp. 75-76.

54. There is a passing reference in Namier and Brooke's *History of Parliament* to James's opposition to the slave trade, as well as to the candle tax and the duties on hawkers and peddlers; there is no mention of the brothers' slave holdings or of their West Indian estates. William, in the *History of Parliament*, as in histories of the Scottish enlightenment,

appears as "the friend of Adam Smith and David Hume." Namier and Brooke, *History of Parliament*, 2:686, 3:341, and Brooke, "Introductory Survey," 1:1–204, p. 172.

55. This was one of the "entries on the source list," listed online in 2002 by a shortlived project of public history called CASBAH (Caribbean Studies Black and Asian History), and provided to CASBAH by the National Archives of Scotland; it was this reference that led me to the North Circuit minutes of Bell or Belinda's trial, to distinguished historical scholarship on the Scottish law of slavery and on infanticide, and eventually to the receipt for Bell or Belinda's arrival in Virginia. The CASBAH "Progress Report 17" for October–November 2001, which includes the reference to Bell alias Belinda, was still available online in 2010, although a note dated 2004 states that CASBAH "was a demonstrator project. . . . All members of the project team have moved on to new challenges elsewhere." www.casbah.ac.uk//reports/progressreport17.stm, and www.casbah.ac.uk/contact.stm.

56. Ranajit Guha, "Chandra's Death," in Ranajit Guha, ed., *Subaltern Studies: Writings on South Asian History and Society* 5 (Delhi, 1987): 135–65, pp. 138–39.

57. On the "bad" or the "spurious" infinity, see Georg Wilhelm Friedrich Hegel, *Hegel's Science of Logic*, trans. A. V. Miller (New York, 1969), p. 137. The "discrete, unlimited nature of the material of the novel . . . has a 'bad' infinity about it," which is resolved by the biographical form, in Lukács's account; and, in the case of *La Comédie Humaine*, by the psychological unity of the characters. Lukács, *Theory of the Novel*, pp. 81, 108–9.

58. This is the historian's endless illusion: in Alain Corbin's expression, "il ne serait pas absurde de songer à une enquête collective, à la création d'un 'Centre de recherches pinagotiques' en quelque sorte." Corbin, *Le monde retrouvé*, p. 15.

59. I am extremely conscious, all the same, of having used a different figurative language, which is also an eighteenth-century idiom. This is the language of the story, or the narrative, of historical fiction. The first part of the book was in the form, explicitly, of a narrative (setting out, coming home, family portraits) that began with the birth of Barbara and James Johnstone's first child and ended with the death of Betty, the last and longest-lived of their children. It was a story in E. M. Forster's sense, in *Aspects of the Novel*, of a "narrative of events arranged in their time-sequence." It was not a plot ("a narrative of events, the emphasis falling on causality"). But it was a narrative with at least something, or so I hope, of the condition of a story, which "can have only one fault: that of making the audience not want to know what happens next." E. M. For-

ster, *Aspects of the Novel* (1927) (London, 2005), pp. 42, 87. I am very conscious, too, that the book has been full (full to bursting, from time to time) of individuals with names, who have been characters in the story and characters, too, in the sense of the interior and exterior dispositions with which the Johnstones and their friends were so preoccupied. The character of the individuals has been important both in the narrative and in the second part of the book (about empire and enlightenment), which was not a narrative but a vista or observation of the past. The book has been filled, above all, with details. It is a historical treatise, in this respect (in Tocqueville's sense of the historian as one who knows almost everything about the details of events in the past and almost nothing about the real relations between past individuals, or the real conditions of the mind). But the description of details is the technique of the novelist as well. It is the most familiar technique, in particular, of the nineteenth-century novel, or of nineteenth-century realism. It is a technique of verisimilitude, in which the novelist, who knows everything and who chooses to describe a diamond ring or a conversation about the slave trade, conveys the impression that the individuals in a novel, who are no more than "characters," are almost real, or lifelike. The historians' details that were for Tocqueville so dull, the duty of posterity ("it is for the latter to do the history of details") are also a technique and an illusion. The art of the novelist, in Balzac's description, consisted in "amassing so many facts and depicting them as they are." But "I have done better than the historian, I am more free," he wrote in the introduction to *La Comédie humaine*: "The novel must be the better world. . . . But the novel will be nothing if, in this imposing lie, it is not true in its details." Alexis de Tocqueville, *L'ancien régime et la révolution: fragments et notes*, 2 vols. (Paris, 1952–53), ed. J. P. Mayer, vol. 2, pt. 2, p. 29; Honoré de Balzac, *L'avant-propos de 1842 sur la Comédie humaine* (Bournemouth, 1980), pp. 9–10. I am grateful to Professor Alexander Nehemas for discussion of these questions.

60. Smith, *Wealth of Nations*, p. 768. Inquisitiveness was for E. M. Forster "one of the lowest of the human faculties." Forster, *Aspects of the Novel*, p. 87.

61. "They sometimes amused me in a long voyage," George wrote; he had however "lost the original to which was notes Explaining some allusions Peculiar to each story." The romance had some general resemblance to George's own and his parents' lives: "The first story was begun on a plan & intended to be Continued. In ye second book The Girl was to prove with Child . . . Physicians . . . depressd & dispised by her neighbours. The man Perswaded to marry her: She insolent to her neighbours & He henpeck't. In ye 3d. was the Birth & Christening Nurse Priest [il-

legible] In the fourth the follys of Education Sent to Sea. In the fifth a Lieut. Capt. Adml. beats the French is made an Alderman And speaks nonsense in ye House. dies The folly of a Funeral." Letter dated "Octr. 1st" from George to William, HL-P, PU 466 [461], and dated by the Huntington Library October 1, 1759. The visitor to Lord Camden was Sir George Colebrooke: "I waited on Lord Camden, then Chancellor, to point out to me a proper person to reside at Calcutta as standing counsel. . . . His fondness for novels was excessive. When I waited on him, I found the window-seats of his parlour heaped with books of that description." Sir George Colebrooke, *Retrospection: Or Reminiscences addressed to my Son Henry Thomas Colebrooke, Esq., Part 1* (London, 1898), pp. 170–71. On the Johnstones' intermittent friendship with Colebrooke, the chairman of the East India Company in 1772, see Sutherland, *East India Company*, pp. 189–90.

62. " 'If I had a turn for those things, I might know a great deal of his history, for the greatest part of it is still in my possession.' 'His history!' said I. 'Nay, you may call it what you please,' said the curate; 'for indeed it is no more a history than it is a sermon.'" Mackenzie, *Man of Feeling*, p. 4.

CHAPTER EIGHT. OTHER PEOPLE

1. Gray, *Tour to the Sepulchres of Etruria, in 1839*, 3rd ed. (London, 1843), pp. 2, 3, 6, 12, 73. Elizabeth Caroline Johnstone Gray was a very serious student of Barthold Niebuhr's ancient history. She explained in a later study that her references to Niebuhr's *Römische Geschichte* would be entirely to the footnotes, in order to avoid confusion on the part of the reader between the original and the English translation. Mrs. Hamilton Gray, *The History of Etruria*, 3 vols. (London, 1844), 2:v. "I thought her perfectly unpretending and unaffected; slight figure, a delicate woman, pretty dark hair and dark eyes, and pleasing expression of countenance. I never should have suspected her of being so learned or so laborious and persevering as she is," Maria Edgeworth wrote after meeting Elizabeth Caroline in Newcastle in 1843. *The Life And Letters Of Maria Edgeworth*, 2 vols. (Boston, 1895), 2:656.

2. Hume, *Treatise of Human Nature*, p. xix.

3. "Borrowed Dogs," in Avedon, *Portraits*, unpag.

4. "My Own Life," in Hume, *Essays*, p. xl.

5. Letter of April 13, 1805 from Edmund to Francis Dana, MHS, Dana Family Papers, Box 4, Folder 1805. Alexander's will was an extraordinary illustration of the relationship between money, inheritance, and male primogeniture, outlining the sequence of bequests that extended

from James and his "heirs male" to George, to "the first son of the Body of my Brother William Pulteney by any wife other than his present wife," to George Lindsay Johnstone "in case he is now or hereafter shall become the legitimate son of my said brother George Johnstone within and according to the Law of Scotland," and to John and Gideon's sons. Will of Alexander Johnstone, proved January 24, 1783, TNA, PROB 11/1099 and see above, chapter 3.

6. Undated letter from Betty to William, HL-P, PU 411 [388], and letter of May 30, 1762, from James Johnstone (the father) to William, HL-P, PU 533 [549].

7. Letter of October 30, 1778, from George to Walter Minto, UM-WCL-MS.

8. "Let her know from me the first of her furious or splenatick fits that apears visible here shall set her to the Door," their mother wrote. "My temper never was so gentel, tho I shall with great calmness befor her father hear all she has to say in her own vindication. . . . Youll see she will grow sick and Curse me for not sending her to Moffat to mend her Beauty in reality she is inraged at two things want of beauty and wealth and I can give her nather so miserable she must be but if she keeps it to her self I shall be easie." Letter dated "the last day of 1750" from Barbara (the mother) to William, HL-P, PU 497 [511].

9. Letter of early 1759 from Barbara (the mother) to George, EUL-L, La.II.73/71.

10. Letter of October 2, 1759, from George to William, HL-P, PU 467 [450].

11. Letters of July 8, 1770, and January 22, 1772, from James to John, and of February 17, 1772, from James to Betty, in JJLB-EUL, pp. 18, 128–29, 138. William Colhoon, on the point of going to sea on a slaving vessel in 1771, wrote to his sister in Glasgow with the most extraordinary conditional arithmetic of affection: "As for friends I have none but you and my sister Janny. . . . Dr Betty my love and reguard for you is unpossible for me to mention for since you was Born my heart was always for your welafare I love you as weal as I woud do my wife if I had on and if you was both put to distress I would not know which to assist first if my wife had no children for if I had only one shilling I could part it between us." He also urged her to "consider in your own Breast" her impending marriage: "you can get your own Bread very well and nobody to control you you will find it quite different in a marriage state where there his two people the have different tampers which makes it disagreeable. . . . Tell your own mind and do as you think proper." Letter of March 22, 1771, from William Colhoon in London to Betty Colqhoun in Glasgow, GCA, TD 301/6/1/8.

12. Letter of October 9, 1759, from Betty to William, HL-P, PU 405 [397].

13. Letter of March 9, 1777, from Walter Minto to David Minto, UM-WCL-MS.

14. Letter of October 14, 1786, from George Lindsay Johnstone in Lucknow to William Julius Mickle, WJM-Y.

15. Will of Alexander Patrick Johnstone, made in Benares on November 20, 1799, and proved in London on January 14, 1807. TNA, PROB 11/1454.

16. James W. Alexander, *Forty Years' Familiar Letters* (New York, 1860), 2:342.

17. Letters from Lord Clive to the Court of Directors of September 30, 1765, and January 31, 1766, in Third Report from the Committee, *House of Commons Sessional Papers,* p. 395, Fourth Report from the Committee, *House of Commons Sessional Papers,* pp. 517–18.

18. Letter of December 22, 1764, from Barbara (the mother) to John, UMWCL-MS; letter of January 7, 1773, from Walter Johnstone to William, HL-P, PU 739 [727].

19. Letter of November 15, 1766, from William Johnstone to James Oswald, Oswald Papers, Chest IV, C.

20. "I should be glad to know what is become of little George," he wrote to Alexander in 1771, letter of March 23, 1771, from John to Alexander, JJLB-CLA, PD239/201/9; and, on "my Dear Miss Sophia," letter of August 8, 1787, from John to William Julius Mickle, WJM-Y.

21. Letter of October 5, 1785, from John to William, HL-P, PU 664 [656].

22. Letters of June 3, 1769, from John to James Johnstone (the father) and of March 23, 1771, from John to Alexander, JJLB-CLA, PD239/201/9; letter of October 20, 1768, from John to William, HL-P, PU 643 [640]; letter of October 1, 1765, from John to Lord Clive, Fourth Report from the Committee, *House of Commons Sessional Papers,* p. 537.

23. Letter of January 7, 1773, from Walter Johnstone to William, HL-P, PU 739 [727].

24. Letter of February 19, 1771, from John to the East India Company Court of Directors, IOR/E/1/55; John Johnstone, *Letter to the Proprietors,* p. 61.

25. Draft letter of April 8, 1774, from William to Mr. R. Pemberton, HL-P, PU 1914 [1544].

26. Copy of a letter of October 24, 1759, from George to James Murray, NAS, GD32/24/11.

27. Speech of George Johnstone of May 27, 1765, letter of June 12, 1765, from George and John Stuart to the secretary of state, in *Mississippi Provincial Archives,* pp. 188, 194.

28. Speech of George Johnstone of October 26, 1775, debate in the House of Commons on the Address of Thanks, PH, vol. 18, col. 757.

29. Letters of February 17, 1772, from James to Betty and of August 22, 1772, from James to Alexander, in JJLB-EUL, pp. 139, 164; letter of June 7, 1769, from John to James, JJLB-CLA, PD239/201/9.

30. Letter of May 3, 1762, from Betty to William, HL-P, PU 426 [415].

31. Letter of August 8, 1787, from John to William Julius Mickle, WJM-Y.

32. Letter of October 30, 1771, from James to John, JJLB-EUL, p. 96.

33. Letter of February 24, 1761, from Gideon to William, HL-P, PU 490 [476].

34. Letter of 1766 or 1767 from John Home to James Oswald about George's return from West Florida, in Oswald, *Memorials*, p. 115.

35. Letter of December 22 1764 from Barbara (their mother) to John, UMWCL-MS.

36. The vexed word "representation" was taken in Bell or Belinda's lifetime to refer to the representation of land as well as persons. There is very distinguished scholarship on black people in eighteenth-century Scotland in the work of John Cairns on the Scottish law of slavery, on Scottish convicts (by Roger Ekirch) and on the Scottish law of infanticide (by Deborah Symonds). There is important work on slavery in eighteenth-century India and on East Indians in eighteenth-century Britain; there is work that could be done on East Indians in eighteenth-century Virginia. But after some years of trying to find out something more, or anything more, about Bell or Belinda, in the petitions to the East India Company with respect to servants to be brought to England, or in the advertisements for runaway indentured servants in the *Virginia Gazette*, or in the logbooks of the East India Company and merchant shipping, I am seriously doubtful that it will be possible to identify a population—any of these populations—with the degree of precision required of what the quantitative historian Ernest Labrousse described as "the stable relationship" or statistical "means," "representative situations," or "'characteristic,' 'significant,' 'typical' facts." C.-E. Labrousse, *La crise de l'économie française à la fin de l'ancien régime et au debut de la révolution* (Paris, 1943), pp. 122, 134, 171; C.-E. Labrousse et al., eds., *Histoire économique et sociale de la France* (Paris, 1970), 3:xii.

37. T. C. Howell, comp., *State Trials*, 34 vols. (London, 1809-1826), vol. 20, cols. 2, 22.

38. Extract, Process Joseph Knight against Sir John Wedderburn of Ballendean Bart., 1774, NAS, CS235/K/2/2. Ferguson, Information for John Wedderburn, pp. 1–2; Maconochie, Information for Joseph Knight, p. 1.

39. I am extremely grateful to Professor John Cairns for discussions of these cases, which will be considered in his forthcoming book on the Scottish law of slavery. There were several cases subsequent to *Somerset* and *Knight v. Wedderburn* in which English courts were complicit in slavery, and there were many cases in which English and Scottish lawyers were closely involved in the details of the slave economy. Mansfield's judgment in *Somerset* was "a masterpiece of decisive insubstantiality," in Ruth Paley's description, and "there can be little doubt that de jure slavery continued to exist" in England. But the public discussion of the Somerset case after 1772, and of the Knight case in Scotland after 1778, was so extensive that the recognition of slavery was ambiguous in later cases. There is no case subsequent to Bell or Belinda's, so far as I have been able to discover, in which an individual was judged to be a slave by a court in the British isles. See Ruth Paley, "After Somerset: Mansfield, Slavery and the Law in England, 1772–1830," in *Law, Crime and English Society, 1660–1830*, ed. Norma Landau (Cambridge, 2002), 165–84, esp. pp. 172, 181; John W. Cairns, "After *Somerset*: Some Scottish Evidence," in *Free Soil*, ed. Sue Peabody and Keira Grinberg, forthcoming.

40. List of Assize for the Circuit Court of Justiciary to be held at Perth in the month of May 1771, NAS, JC26/193/2.

41. Ferguson, Information for John Wedderburn, p. 3; John Swinton, Perth, decision of May 20, 1774, NAS, SC 49/6/134/3/3.

42. "Petition for Bell or Belinda a Black Girl," September 13, 1771, "Declaration of Bell or Belinda a Black Girl," July 4, 1771, NAS, JC29/193/3.

43. Abū al-Faẓl ibn Mubārak, *Ayeen Akbery: Or, the Institutes of the Emperor Akber*, trans. Francis Gladwin, 3 vols. (Calcutta, 1786), 3:272. Madho Sarup Vats, "Excavations at Harappa," in *Annual Bibliography of Indian Archaeology* 12 (1937) (Leyden, 1939), 1–9, p. 7; Jonathan P. Parry, *Death in Banaras* (Cambridge, 1994), p. 196.

44. I am very grateful to Professor Bhavani Raman for the suggestion that Bell or Belinda, in going into the deepest interior of the Johnstones' house to give birth, may have been seeking to repeat a different ritual, that of the *Khānazād*, by which a child born within a household, whose father was a member of the family of the household's owners or masters, would thereby become a member of the owners' family. Sir William Hay Macnaghten, *Principles and Precedents of Moohummudan Law* (Calcutta, 1825), p. 313.

45. "The prisons that I saw in Edinburgh, Glasgow, Perth, Stirling . . . &c. were old buildings, dirty and offensive, without court-yards and also generally without water," the prison reformer John Howard wrote after his tour of Scotland and Ireland in 1779–83, listing the "FEES payable to

the JAILOR" and "FEES payable to the CLERK of the TOLBOOTH." Of the Tolbooth in Glasgow, in 1787, where the "transports" were confined, he wrote that "most of the rooms were very offensive, and some very damp.—No endeavours are used to *reclaim* these unhappy objects; whose long *confinement*, together with the great severity of their *chains*, and their scanty *food* (being only two pennyworth of bread in a day) must reduce them to the extremity of misery and desperation." John Howard, *The State of the Prisons in England and Wales*, 3rd ed. (Warrington, 1784), pp. 195–200; John Howard, *An Account of the Principal Lazarettos in Europe* (Warrington, 1789), p. 75. John Swinton, when he was himself a lord in the Court of Justiciary, made recommendations to the magistrates of Perth "concerning the treatment of prisoners, and for preserving their health while confined in Jail," "keeping men separate from women," and "the regular cleaning the Prisoners' Clothes and keeping the Jail clean": "what are the Jailors fees, and by whom payable?" "Recommendation by Lord Swinton and Lord Dunsinnan to The Magistrates of Perth concerning the Jail," September 1795, PKA, Perth Burgh Records, B59/24/11/117.

46. John Swinton was sheriff depute of Perth at the time of the conviction of Mary Burgess for child murder exactly ten years earlier, and together with the Perth magistrates, was responsible for the transport of prisoners from county to county and the execution of sentences; see above, chapter 2. The case of Mary Burgess, who "had not the benefit of counsel," as well as the carrying out of the sentence of hanging and public dissection, was reported in *Scots Magazine* 23 (1761), pp. 554, 704; on John Swinton's appointment in 1758 as sheriff depute of Perth, see *The Universal Scots Almanack* (Edinburgh, 1758), p. 54.

47. *Virginia Gazette* (Purdie & Dixon) Williamsburg, October 1, 1772. The owner's name was Thomas Crauford, of Brunswick, who had bought Belinda from George Blair of Smithfield. It is interesting that a number of advertisements for runaway slaves and servants did mention that they were from the East Indies: "John Newton . . . an Asiatic Indian by Birth," "Tom, alias Caesar, born in the East-Indies," "an East India negro man called Jean, a slave born," or "a kind of Mulatto East-India Boy named Crispin." *Virginia Gazette* (Dixon & Hunter), July 13, 1776; *Virginia Gazette* (Hayes), June 26, 1784; *Virginia Gazette* (Nicolson), January 14, 1786; *The Herald and Norfolk and Portsmouth Advertiser* (Charles Willett), December 10, 1794; "The Geography of Slavery in Virginia," www.vcdh.virginia.edu/gos/search.

48. "I would therefore have you sell Kate to a good Master," a Boston merchant called James Murray, a British customs official and close friend of Charles Steuart, the owner of James Somerset, wrote in 1765. In 1766

he wrote, "I desire Dorinda may be sold as soon as you can get a good master and 50£," and in 1767, "If Kate will not fetch £80 proc & a good Master let her be sent hither—she will be fitter for us than a breeder." Letters of December 12, 1765, and September 26, 1766, from James Murray to Alexander Duncan and of January 6, 1767, from James Murray to Thomas Clark, MHS, Letters of James Murray 1764–69, Ms. N-571.

49. David Hume, *Dialogues concerning Natural Religion* (1779) (Cambridge, 2007), p. 34.

50. Smith, *Theory of Moral Sentiments*, pp. 75, 110.

51. Smith, *Theory of Moral Sentiments*, pp. 13, 135. Smith uses the words "eye" and "eyes" fifty-six times in the work, the words "imagine" and "imagination" 155 times, and the expression "other people" 84 times.

52. Gray, *Tour to the Sepulchres*, p. 2.

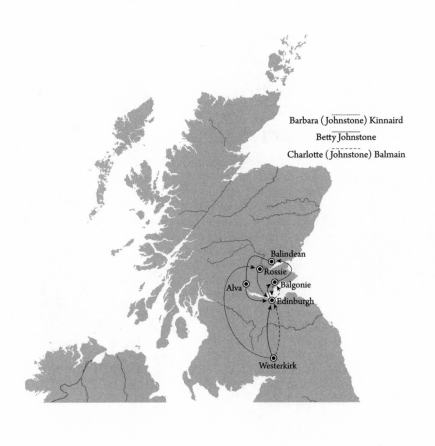

Barbara (Johnstone) Kinnaird
Betty Johnstone
Charlotte (Johnstone) Balmain

Balindean
Rossie
Alva
Balgonie
Edinburgh
Westerkirk

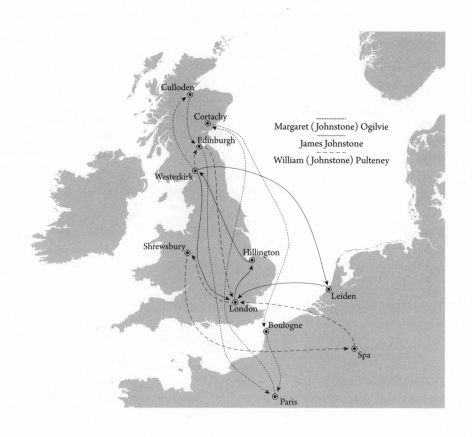

Culloden

Cortachy

Edinburgh

Westerkirk

Shrewsbury

Hillington

London

Boulogne

Leiden

Spa

Paris

Margaret (Johnstone) Ogilvie

James Johnstone

William (Johnstone) Pulteney

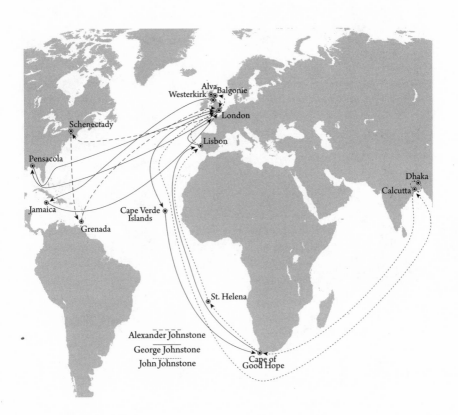

Alva
Balgonie
Westerkirk
London
Lisbon
Schenectady
Pensacola
Jamaica
Cape Verde
Islands
Grenada
Dhaka
Calcutta
St. Helena
Alexander Johnstone
George Johnstone
John Johnstone
Cape of
Good Hope

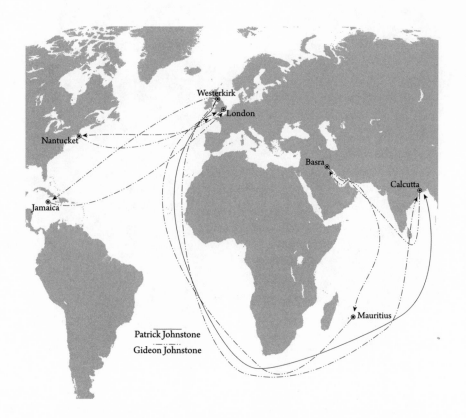

Patrick Johnstone
Gideon Johnstone

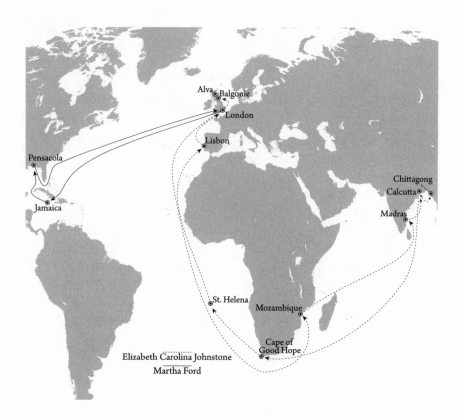

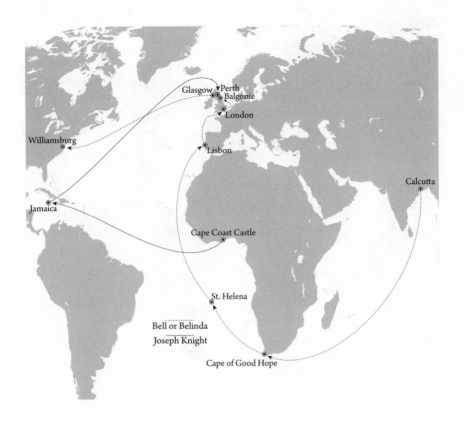

Glasgow　Perth
Balgonie
London

Williamsburg

Lisbon

Calcutta

Jamaica

Cape Coast Castle

St. Helena

Bell or Belinda
―――――――――
Joseph Knight

Cape of Good Hope

Index

abolition of the slave trade, 107,
111–12, 115, 145, 155, 160–62,
212, 378n38, 380n56; opposition
to, 115–16, 145, 160–61, 163,
168, 174, 266, 406n50
accounting, 27, 48, 55, 131, 135–36,
348n229
Adam, Robert and James, 77, 111
Admiral Stevens, 58, 59, 207,
353n1, 354n5
age of revolutions, 1, 14, 311n6
affection, arithmetic of, 286, 457n11
Allen, Henrietta, 108, 110, 208,
378n42
Alva, 77, 104, 111, 172, 272,
379n45
American Revolution, 70, 72, 122,
124, 143–44, 291, 298
American Indians. *See* Native Americans
Annandale, Marquess of, 23, 424nn18
and 19
Annandale peerage, 23, 79, 170–71,
233, 274, 416–17n163, 433n89
antiquity, 260, 266
anxiety, 2, 32, 53, 73, 98, 125, 195,
197, 239, 264, 271, 290–91,
389n21, 448n18
architecture, 77–78
archives, 23, 170–71, 277, 278
Armenians, 85–86, 140, 176, 257,
368n114
army, 26–27, 134–35, 361n62,
393–94n57, 394n58
Augustine, 83, 138, 165–66, 167,
366n101, 404n40
Austen, Jane, 51–52, 172–73,
346–47n218
Avedon, Richard, 279

bad infinity, 281, 385n92, 454n57
Bagehot, Walter, 149
Bailyn, Bernard, 124, 387n1,
448n15
Balgonie, 62, 87, 109, 110, 196,
207–8, 216, 238, 293, 296
Balmain, Charlotte (Johnstone),
201, 25, 27–28, 84, 97, 105, 156,
190, 192, 201, 207, 232, 286,
334n126, 438n125; and bundle
of muslins, 33–34, 61, 415n149;
illnesses of, 98, 371–72n2; marriage of, 27–28, 64–65, 425n21
Balmain, James, 21, 64–65, 105,
156, 198, 207, 221, 422n210;
and abolition of the slave trade,
111, 380n56; and excise, 21, 23,
64, 322n67, 357n26; letters to,
46, 50, 66, 98, 134, 171, 244,
264, 416–17n163, 438n122;
searches by, 79, 87, 236.
Balzac, Honoré de, 118, 385n92,
455n59
banishment, 90, 128, 227, 228. *See
also* transportation
Bath, 64, 77, 356–57n25
Bayly, C. A., 178
Bell or Belinda, 2, 5, 87–91, 202,
206, 208, 216, 227, 291–99; and
burial rites, 295–96; defense of,
297–98; descriptions of, 162,
203–4; importance of, 96, 155,
269, 292, 460n39; imprisonment
of, 188, 230, 297; information
about, 274, 275, 295, 298; and
the Johnstones, 296–98, 299;
journeys of, 188, 202–5, 207;
loneliness of, 290; moral sentiments of, 140, 260, 263, 294;